Bettina Koch
Patterns Legitimizing Political Violence in Transcultural Perspectives

Judaism, Christianity, and Islam – Tension, Transmission, Transformation

Edited by Patrice Brodeur, Carlos Fraenkel,
Assaad Elias Kattan, and Georges Tamer

Volume 1

Bettina Koch

Patterns Legitimizing Political Violence in Transcultural Perspectives

—

Islamic and Christian Traditions and Legacies

DE GRUYTER

ISBN 978-1-61451-577-7
e-ISBN (PDF) 978-1-61451-394-0
e-ISBN (EPUB) 978-1-61451-977-5
ISSN 2196-405X

Library of Congress Cataloging-in-Publication Data
A CIP catalog record for this book has been applied for at the Library of Congress.

Bibliographic information published by the Deutsche Nationalbibliothek
The Deutsche Nationalbibliothek lists this publication in the Deutsche Nationalbibliografie;
detailed bibliographic data are available on the Internet at http://dnb.dnb.de.

© 2015 Walter de Gruyter Inc., Boston/Berlin
Printing and binding: CPI books GmbH, Leck
♾ Printed on acid-free paper
Printed in Germany

www.degruyter.com

Acknowledgments

The basic idea for this book project emerged during a conversation with Hartmut Behr in 2009. Two problems we discussed helped to formulate the main ideas for this book: First, the growing disconnection between discourses in political theory, particularly in the history of ideas tradition, and other subdisciplines in Political Science and, second, the dominantly one-sided academic and public discourses on violence that focus primarily on what is usually called "Islamic terrorism."

Yet, moving from the initial idea to the book project did not happen in an afternoon. To make the project as sound as possible, I had to venture out to intellectual territories that were not necessarily at the heart of my previous research agenda. I could not have done it without the help of some of my colleagues. Ilja Luciak and Tony Spanakos shared some of their Latin American expertise with me, the novice, and commented on parts of my manuscript. I am similarly grateful, in alphabetical order, to Priya Dixit, Bob Goodin, Tom Izbicki, Tim Luke, Eva Nag, Cary Nederman, Ines Peper, Yannis Stivachtis, and Edward Weisband for their comments and continuous support. Dennis Moran read the entire manuscript. From the project's early stages on to its completion, particularly at times when the project was growing over my head, he remained a constant fountain of constructive thoughts and criticism. In addition, I would like to thank David Held, Pietro Maffettone, and Eva Nag warmly for their hospitality and inspirational conversations at Durham University—including the trips to the beach.

David Orden deserves special recognition for the generous financial support I have received through the *Global Issues Initiative* (GII) of the Institute for Society, Culture and Environment at Virginia Polytechnic Institute and State University. The GII funding freed me from some of my teaching obligations and provided some additional resources for research travel. I wish to thank Georges Tamer for his trust in the project and for his invitation to the book series; Alissa Jones Nelson made the publishing process as smooth as an author could wish. I am tremendously grateful to the anonymous reviewers' responses. Their comments and suggestions made it a far better book than the original manuscript. This book is dedicated to Peter Johanek, from whom I have learned the appreciation of the Middle Ages.

Contents

1 **Introduction: Legitimacy, Religion, and Violence** —— 1
1.1 Legitimacy, Rights, and Duties in the Liberal Constitutional State —— 9
1.2 Religion and Political Legitimacy —— 14
1.3 Overview of Chapters —— 19

2 **Medieval Foundations** —— 23
2.1 Legitimizing Violence in the Medieval Christian Tradition —— 27
2.1.1 Religious Justifications of the Crusades and Violence against Religious Dissenters —— 27
  Legitimizing the Crusades —— 30
  Legitimizing Violence against Religious Dissenters —— 35
  Legitimizing Violence against Dissenting Rule —— 42
2.1.2 Religious Justifications of Violence against the Church —— 49
2.1.3 Religious Justifications for Protesting against (Secular) Authorities —— 55
2.2 Legitimizing Violence in the Classic/Premodern Islamic Traditions —— 66
2.2.1 Concept(s) of Jihad —— 68
2.2.2 Sunni Perspective on Religious Dissent and (Foreign) Muslim Aggression —— 81
2.2.3 Sunni and Non-Sunni Perspectives on Disobedience and Revolt —— 94
2.3 Summary and Comparison —— 106

3 **Religion and Violence in Twentieth Century Islam and Christianity** —— 114
3.1 Latin American Christian Perspectives: Revolution and Counter-Revolution —— 116
3.1.1 Liberation Theology's Accounts on (Violent) Resistance —— 118
  Camilo Torres's Socio-Religious Argument for Violent Change —— 120
  Macro Politico-Religious Analysis and Revolution: José Comblin —— 125
  Ignacio Ellacuría's Theological-Philosophical Perspectives on Violence —— 134
3.1.2 Religious Justifications for Counter-Revolution —— 143
  Alfonso López Trujillo and Roger Vekemans —— 145
  The Societies for the Defense of Tradition, Family, and Property (TFP) —— 152

3.2   Islam and Violence in the Twentieth Century —— 158
3.2.1 Anti-State Violence in Contemporary Sunni Islam —— 160
       Al-Afghani's Pan-Islamism —— 161
       Hasan al-Banna and Muslim Liberation —— 166
       Sayyid Qutb: Jihad against Jahiliyya —— 173
       'Abd al-Salam Faraj: Theory put into Action —— 177
3.2.2 Shi'i Theory and the Iranian Revolution —— 180
       'Ali Shari'ati's Legacy —— 183
       Mutahhari's Jihad —— 188
       Khomeini: The Jurists' Guardianship —— 190
3.3   Summary and Comparison —— 199

4   Insights and Implications: Duties, Rights, and Legitimizing Violence —— 206
4.1   The West —— 206
4.2   Legitimacy, Rights, and Justice —— 210
4.3   Legitimacy and Religion —— 215
4.4   Patterns Legitimizing Political Violence —— 219
4.5   Implications for Conflict Prevention and Resolution —— 222

Bibliography —— 225

Index —— 248

1 Introduction: Legitimacy, Religion, and Violence

> Religions, by whatever names they are called, all resemble each other. No agreement and no reconciliation are possible between these religions and philosophy. Religion imposes on man its faith and its belief, whereas philosophy frees him in totally or in part.[1]

This book is about politics. It explores theoretical discourses in which religion is used to legitimize *political* violence. Its main concern is how Christianity and Islam are utilized for political ends, particularly those in which violence is used (or abused) as an expedient to justify political action. To clarify what is meant by "religious" and "political," this study follows H. A. Drake's definition of intolerance as a religious problem and coercion as a political one.[2] Consequently, violence as a means of coercion is primarily a political, not a religious, problem. For the purpose of this book, (violent) political action is understood as all (violent) actions that occur outside the private realm.

This book is also a response to the predominantly one-sided public and scholarly debate that focuses almost exclusively on fundamentalist or extremist movements in Islam or islams, which is overshadowed by the perception of Islam as a religion prone to violence. This judgment is closely related to the problem of international (Islamic?) terrorism and ignores the fact that national violence is much more prevalent than what is commonly labeled as "international terrorism" or other forms of transnational violence.[3] Neither of these problems is a prerogative of Islam. The religious legitimation of violence remains an integral part of the history of most if not all religions.

Although this study is not the first to utilize a comparative approach to politics in Christian and Islamic cultural settings, it nonetheless fills a gap. Most of

---

[1] Jamāl ad-Dīn al-Afghānī, "Answer of Jamāl ad-Dīn to Renan," *Journal des Débats*, May 18, 1883, in Nikki R. Keddie, *An Islamic Response to Imperialism: Political and Religious Writings of Sayyid Jamāl ad-Dīn "al-Afghānī"* (Berkley: University of California Press, 1983), 187.

[2] H.A. Drake, *Constantine and the Bishops: The Politics of Intolerance* (Baltimore: Johns Hopkins University Press, 2000), xvi.

[3] This study is explicitly *not* about "terrorism." As noted by Peter R. Neumann and M.L.R. Smith, *The Strategy of Terrorism: How it Works, and Why it Fails* (Oxon: Routledge, 2008), who consider terrorism primarily a tactic, 94, "[t]he term [terrorism] is both popular and its meaning is hotly contested amongst political actors, giving rise to sensationalism and political name-calling which rarely serves the cause of defining an intellectual concept." For terrorism as a tactic, see also Robert E. Goodin, *What's Wrong with Terrorism?* (Cambridge: Polity, 2006), 31–49.

the existing studies with a transcultural approach compare religious fundamentalism in the United States and the Islamic world, often indirectly (and accidentally) deepening the rift between the U.S. and the Islamic world.[4] This study follows a different path. First, it explores the premodern traditions in both religious cultures in predominantly Christian Europe and the Muslim world of the time. Second, it compares the modern theoretical discourses on legitimizing violence in the Islamic (primarily Middle Eastern[5]) world with those in Latin America, which shares a similar colonial past; in many respects, both regions are still not part of the industrialized world. Moreover, these regions remain of geopolitical concern for hegemonic powers. In both geographic regions and religious-cultural contexts, state power and its legitimacy are tied to religion, albeit in dissimilar ways. With the dominance of the Catholic Church in Latin America, a focus on the Catholic tradition can be also justified by means of a rather likely continuation from the premodern discourses. Consequently, the number of theoretical texts and treatises aiming to legitimize violence and counter-violence is significant. In addition, in these two geographic regions, premodern texts and authorities have been utilized to legitimize hegemonic and anti-hegemonic violence. Thus, contemporary discourse on violence can only be fully understood if their premodern precursors are not ignored. Essentially, what is framed as hegemonic and anti-hegemonic here relates to the problem of inclusion and exclusion.

At first glance, it might appear counter-intuitive to move from an investigation of religious foundations and premodern discourses on violence directly to the twentieth century. Because of the enormous impact of premodern authorities on the formulation of contemporary justifications of violence, this approach includes a large number of relevant cases. In the Islamic world, the impact of traditional Islamic schools on modern interpretations of Islamic law is considerable. A number of scholars from the premodern period still enjoy almost undisputed authority. In the Latin American context, movements such as the *Societies for the Defense of Tradition, Family, and Property* (TFP) consider medieval

---

4 See, for instance, Bruce B. Lawrence, *Defenders of God: The Fundamentalist Revolt Against the Modern Age* (Columbia: University of South Carolina Press, 1995). Jennifer L. Jefferis, *Religion and Political Violence: Sacred Protest in the Modern World* (London: Routledge, 2010).
5 Middle East, of course, is rather a modern Western concept. For a critical discussion see the contributions in *Is There a Middle East? The Evolution of a Geopolitical Concept*, ed. Michael E. Bonine, Abbas Amanat, and Michael Ezekiel Gasper (Stanford: Stanford University Press, 2012).

Christendom the ideal realization and fulfillment of Christian civilization.[6] In numerous instances, members of TFP have been linked with military regimes. Some of their opponents, closely connected with theologies of liberation, rely heavily on neo-Thomism. In addition, for both regions, it has been claimed and disputed that these hegemonic and anti-hegemonic movements are anti-modern in nature.[7] Consequently, without considering the medieval or premodern past, an analysis of twentieth and twenty-first century conflicts must remain fragmented.

Yet, this book is not particularly concerned with the question of whether religions in general, or monotheistic religions in particular, are prone to violence. These discourses (which are hotly debated among scholars of religious studies and related disciplines, particularly with respect to the question of monotheistic religions) inform this study as far as they enrich the epistemological interest of the political scientist, but they are not its main concern.[8]

As Hans G. Kippenberg notes, a "link between religion and violence is neither impossible nor necessary."[9] More importantly, Kippenberg highlights that even if a conflict is not caused by religion, this does not mean that religious interpretations of a conflict are avoided. A religious interpretation alters the conflict's nature.[10] This alteration of a conflict's nature has at least two implications. First, as suggested by numerous other scholars, it implies that conflicts in which

---

6 Plinio Corrêa de Oliveira, *Revolution and Counter-Revolution*, 3rd English ed. (Spring Grove: The American Society for the Defense of Tradition, Family and Property (TFP), 1993), 14–17, 20–23, 41.
7 Michaël Löwy, "Modernité et critique de la modernité dans la théologie de la liberation," *Archives de Sciences Sociales des Religions* 71 (1990): 7–23. John Gray, *Al Qaeda and What it Means to Be Modern* (New York: The New Press, 2003).
8 Hector Avalos, *Fighting Words: The Origins of Religious Violence* (Amherst: Prometheus Books, 2005), 19, even goes so far as to argue that all religions—not only monotheistic religions—are prone to violence. However, his discussion remains in the framework of religions that Jan Assmann, *Moses the Egyptian: The Memory of Egypt in Western Monotheism* (Cambridge: Harvard University Press, 1997), 170, has classified as "counter religions" or "secondary religions" that are based on canonical texts and institutionalized interpretation and that "reject all older and other religions as 'paganism' or 'idolatry'" (7). See also Jan Assmann, *The Price of Monotheism* (Stanford: Stanford University Press, 2010), 104. Among theologians, however, monotheism's inclination to violence is debated. For a good overview of the main arguments for and against the violence thesis, see, for instance, Dietmar Mieth, "Aggression durch den Glauben? Eine christliche Sicht zum Thema 'Religion und Gewalt' unter besonderer Berücksichtigung des Toleranzbegriffes," in *Im Zeichen der Religion: Gewalt und Friedfertigkeit in Islam und Christentum*, ed. Christine Abbt, Donata Schoeller (Frankfurt: Campus, 2008), 118–141.
9 Hans G. Kippenberg, *Violence as Worship: Religious Wars in the Age of Globalization* (Stanford: Stanford University Press, 2011), 199.
10 Ibid., 200.

religious interpretations appear to dominate the discourse have (in most, if not all, instances) roots in socio-economic or political injustices and inequalities.[11] Second, if the true nature of a conflict is concealed by religious rhetoric, prospects for resolving the conflict are at least hampered, if not made impossible. Although most conflicts in which religious interpretation plays a significant role have other causes, the interaction between religion and politics deserves serious consideration. Based on convincing empirical evidence, Brian J. Grim and Roger Finke have shown that any political restriction on religion, whether by supporting one religion over others and forming an alliance with the favored one or by actively restricting religious freedom, results in an increase of violence independently of the religions in question, although this occurs to a greater degree in predominantly Muslim countries.[12]

If we ignore religion for a moment and focus on other underlying reasons for conflict and violence, such as socio-economic and political injustices and inequalities, then we are faced with one of the *core* problems of politics: political legitimation and legitimacy. As Wilfried Hinsch notes, legitimacy belongs "primarily in the domain of the political and relates to the exercise of coercive state power. [L]egitimacy is taken to be a necessary condition of any justifiable use of state power."[13] Excessive use of violence, whether in resistance movements against the *legal* government or in excessive and violent government actions against the people, is usually an indicator that legal state power is no longer perceived as legitimate—or, in other words, that the acceptance of the existing power structure is jeopardized.

Despite some significant overlaps, discourses on legitimacy play out differently in the modern liberal constitutional state. Therefore, it is useful to outline, at least briefly and by no means exhaustively, some particular concerns within the modern Western predominantly liberal discourses on legitimacy. Although framing non-Western discourses within a Western theoretical context may provoke accusations of hegemonic Eurocentrism or Orientalism, for this study,

---

11 See, for instance, M. Amin Abdullah, "Introductory Elaboration on the Roots of Religious Violence: The Complexity of Islamic Radicalism," in *Innerer Friede und die Überwindung der Gewalt: Religiöse Traditionen auf dem Prüfstand. V. Internationales Rudolf-Otto Symposion, Marburg*, ed. Hans-Martin Barth and Christoph Elsas (Hamburg: EB-Verlag, 2007), 155–6. Mariella Ourghi, *Muslimische Positionen zur Berechtigung von Gewalt: Einzelstimmen, Revisionen, Kontroversen* (Würzburg: Ergon, 2010), 155. Brian J. Grim and Roger Finke, *The Price of Freedom Denied: Religious Persecution and Conflict in the Twenty-First Century* (Cambridge: Cambridge University Press, 2011), 2.
12 Grim and Finke, *The Price of Freedom Denied*, 51, 71, 167.
13 Wilfried Hinsch, "Legitimacy and Justice: A Conceptual and Functional Clarification," in *Political Legitimization without Morality?*, ed. Jörg Kühnelt (Dordrecht: Springer, 2008), 39.

this is a necessary approach. First, this study is a contribution to discourses within political science. Because most concepts within the discipline have been shaped in the Western tradition, in order to speak to the discipline, relating the discourse to the discipline's concepts is of utmost necessity. Second, a Eurocentric perspective is not automatically a devaluation of other cultures, at least not if it is used and understood primarily as a tool to assist transcultural translation and to relate discourses outside Western political science tradition to the discipline. This study does not engage in the currently popular concept of transcultural dialogue as promoted by Fred Dallmayr.[14] The aim of this study is much smaller and perhaps more realistic: it engages in "translation" into academic discourses without aimaing expliclicitly at a transcultural diologue. This study assumes, with Norbert Elias, that "[o]ne can translate knowledge from one language into another. This seems to indicate an existence of knowledge in separation from that of language. [...] Up to a point the same message can be conveyed by different sets of sound-symbols."[15]

However, we must emphasize "up to a point." Anyone who has been engaged in language translation or has read the same text in two different languages knows that some nuances may be lost in translation, and this untranslated five percent or so makes a difference. As long as not all people have fluency or near-native knowledge in all languages and cultures, translation cannot be avoided, and, thus, one must accept at least some ambiguity. This situation applies not only to languages, but also (and perhaps even more so) to the transcultural translation of concepts and ideas.

Concepts, ideas, and knowledge are subject to frequent cultural transitions and exchanges. For instance, the translation movement between the eighth and tenth centuries in which originally Greek texts in philosophy and sciences were translated into and adopted by the Arabic culture subsequently[16] affected science, philosophy, and political thinking in Western Europe in the Latin translations of these texts. Therefore, the rhetoric of "us" versus "them" becomes blurred. Although scholars in comparative political theory allege that thoughts and

---

[14] Fred Dallmayr, "Comparative Political Theory: What is it Good For?," in *Western Political Thought in Dialogue with Asia*, ed. Takashi Shogimen and Cary J. Nederman (Lanham: Lexington, 2008), 22. For a critique and the limits of the dialogical approach, see Hassan Bashir, *Europe and the Eastern Other: Comparative Perspectives on Politics, Religion, and Culture before the Enlightenment* (Lanham: Lexington, 2013).
[15] Norbert Elias, *The Symbol Theory*, ed. Richard Kilminster (London: Sage Publications, 1991), 132.
[16] Dimitri Gutas, *Greek Thought, Arabic Culture: The Graeco-Arabic Translation Movement in Baghdad and Early 'Abbāsid Society (2nd-4th/8th-10th Centuries)* (Abingdon: Routledge, 1998).

ideas from other cultures are frequently mistranslated and misunderstood in Western cultures,[17] this is not a prerogative of the so-called West. Whether these "mistranslations" are an expression of hegemonic imperialism that imply a devaluation of other cultures, as suggested in over-politicized colonial and postcolonial academic discourses, is more than doubtful, although it is a topic in itself. To emphasize that the cultural borrowing practice is by no means a one-way street, the example of Marx, who affected colonial and postcolonial discourses in both the Middle East and Latin America, may be sufficient. As is well known, Marx had some knowledge of Ibn Khaldun. Although this knowledge was second-hand or third-hand through William Mac Guckin de Sane and Friedrich Engels, the careful reader of Ibn Khaldun will find numerous ideas in the fourteenth-century thinker that are echoed in Marx.[18] Instead of reading Marxist ideas as alien to Middle Eastern or Islamic cultures, one can read Marx as an author who promoted ideas that were reconveyed to their cultural origin through the reception of Marx in the Middle East.

Another disputed question is whether the use of Western languages and related disciplinary terminology that does not have exact correspondences in different cultures signifies a hegemonic discourse. The problem, however, is far more complex; it is not simply a problem of more and less dominant language cultures. Similar problems apply in scholarly approaches to past cultures, although there these issues are less politicized. The politicization of scholarly approaches to non-Western political theory has led to some excesses. Following Martha Nussbaum, Alexander Weiß lists four "vices"—chauvinism, suspended normative skepticism, incommensurability, and perennialism—that are usually committed by (Western) readers of non-Western texts.[19] Unfortunately, the language of virtues and vices turns an epistemological problem into a moral judgment in the name of political correctness. The "vice" of chauvinism implies a stigmatization that the accused can hardly undermine on intellectually sound grounds and belongs in the realm of name-calling; it is anathema in any serious academic discourse.

---

17 Farah Godrej, *Cosmopolitan Political Thought: Method, Practice, Discipline* (Oxford: Oxford University Press, 2011), 91, who expresses concerns about whether "creative reinterpretation occurs *across* cultural borders rather than just *within* them."
18 Jean Paul Charnay, *Regards sur l'islam: Freud, Marx, Ibn Khaldun: Essais et philosophie* (Paris: L'Herne, 2003), 152; for Ibn Khaldun's "socialist" ideas, 81–115. See also Nicholas S. Hopkins, "Engels and Ibn Khaldun," *Alif: Journal of Comparative Poetics* 10 (1990): 12–13.
19 Alexander Weiß, "Vier Laster einer vergleichenden politischen Theorie und das Projekt einer globalen Demokratietheorie," in *Nichtwestliches politisches Denken: Zwischen kultureller Differenz und Hybridisierung*, ed. Holger Zapf (Wiesbaden: Springer, 2012), 65–73.

This study deliberately applies what is described as "descriptive chauvinism," defined by Weiß as the application of categories that originate in the scholar's academic context. As noted by Hans-Georg Gadamer, *"language is the universal medium in which understanding takes place. Carrying out understanding is interpretation."*[20] For Gadamer, a foreign language, which also implies a different or foreign culture, only implies increased hermeneutic difficulties in the intellectual process of acknowledging and overcoming its foreignness.[21] To overcome foreignness and to achieve understanding, it is necessary to transfer the previously unknown into a familiar language. Any demand to speak about the concepts and ideas of a different culture only in the other culture's terms, cloaked in the language of assumed "political correctness," denies itself the increased hermeneutic challenges of an intellectually sound transcultural translation. To use an example that is closer to home, one can only speak about the concept of the Greek *politeia* in a meaningful way if one either applies classic Greek or translates its meanings into familiar terms.[22]

The other "vice" that is willfully applied here is that of "perennialism," an "overestimation of the relevance of particular classic texts for texts of significantly later times."[23] Although it is ultimately up to the reader to judge whether the impact of classic texts has been overestimated, particularly when Islamic fundamentalist movements are addressed, the importance of interpretations of divine law from the ninth and tenth centuries, when the formation and establishment of the main legal schools occurred,[24] can hardly be overstated. The same applies to some "authoritative" texts (including Ibn Taymiyya's writings) that are frequently used by contemporary authors in support of their claims as well as to some texts with authoritative status in the Christian tradition.[25]

Using a different language, including different concepts, is beneficial in a way that can rarely be achieved if one remains within the original language traditions. Norbert Elias, who is by no means suspected of a hegemonic approach, emphasizes that "the range of knowledge [...], which covers all topics of commu-

---

20 Hans-Georg Gadamer, *Wahrheit und Methode: Grundzüge einer philosophischen Hermeneutik*, 7th ed. (Tübingen: Mohr Siebeck, 2010), 392, my translation; italics in the original.
21 Ibid., 391.
22 Here, I agree with Andrew F. March, "What Is Comparative Political Theory?," *The Review of Politics* 71, no. 4 (2009): 545–6, that we lack any convincing reasons why non-Western texts should be treated differently than texts originating in the Western tradition.
23 Weiß, "Vier Laster einer vergleichenden politischen Theorie," 69.
24 Wael B. Hallaq, *The Origins and Evolution of Islamic Law* (Cambridge: Cambridge University Press, 2005), 150–177.
25 Assmann, *Moses the Egyptian*, 170, emphasizes the importance of canonical texts for what he calls counter or secondary religions such as Christianity and Islam.

nication, is further limited by the structure of a given society and particularly by its power relations."[26] In addition, as Hayden White reminds us, "every use of language itself implies or entails a specific posture before the world which is ethical, ideological, or more generally political: not only all interpretation but also all language is politically contaminated."[27]

To highlight the problem in the context of the concept of political legitimacy, if one aims to speak about legitimacy in the Arabic language, one usually applies the term *shar'īya* (lawfulness, legitimacy, rightfulness). Although the corresponding meaning of the term's root does not imply any particular religious connotations, the dominant concept of *al-sharī'a*, the revealed law of Islam, makes it difficult to speak about legitimacy in the Arabic language without explicit (or at least implicit) religious-Islamic connotations, even though the term itself is much older than Islam. The religious connotation reflects power relations and is the expression of hegemony within the culture. Similar religious connotations are apparent in the Persian or Farsi *mashrou'iat* that covers both religious and political legitimacy.[28] In this sense, using a different language, including Western languages, can be employed as a tool to uncover these hegemonic power relations as well as to reveal political contaminations that are specific to one language culture. Because one must use language to communicate, political contaminations cannot be avoided, but they can and should be subject to critical reflection.

To underscore the differences between Western liberal discourses and discourses in which religion is considered *the* or *a* main source of legitimacy, I will briefly refer to Ronald Dworkin, Henry Shue, and Wilhelm Hennis. Dworkin and Shue are primarily concerned with rights and duties, namely the government's duty to acknowledge citizens' basic rights, which are usually recognized as constitutionally protected rights, to be in a position to expect citizens' obedience. Hennis's critical historical approach enables us to bridge the two discourses that are usually deemed incompatible, although this incompatibility is not undisputed.[29]

---

26 Elias, *The Symbol Theory*, 49.
27 Hayden White, *Tropics of Discourse: Essays in Cultural Criticism* (Baltimore: Johns Hopkins University Press, 1978), 129.
28 I wish to thank Djavad Salehi-Isfahani for clarifying the contemporary usage.
29 For the disputed incompatibility, see, for instance, P. R. Kumaraswamy, "Islam and Minorities: Need for a Liberal Framework," *Mediterranean Quarterly* 3 (2007): 94–109.

1.1 Legitimacy, Rights, and Duties in the Liberal Constitutional State

In *Taking Rights Seriously,* Ronald Dworkin suggests

> that we all accept the following postulate of political morality. Government must treat those whom it governs with concern, that is, as human beings who are capable of suffering and frustration, and with respect, that is, as human beings who are capable of forming and acting on intelligent conceptions of how their lives should be lived. Government must not only treat people with concern and respect, but with equal concern and respect. It must not distribute goods and opportunities unequally on the ground that some citizens are entitled to more because they are worthy of more concern. It must not constrain liberty on the ground that one citizen's conception of the good life of one group is nobler or superior to another's.[30]

Ronald Dworkin reaches his conclusion based on the initial question of whether citizens have the right to disobey the law and their government if a law infringes on their moral rights.[31] In essence, this is an argument about the distinction between a government's legitimate and illegitimate demands for citizens' obedience. The argument demarcates the limits of a state's monopoly on violence. To invoke Max Weber's famous definition of a state ("a human community within a certain territory that claims (successfully) the monopoly on the use of legitimate physical force [*Gewaltsamkeit*]"),[32] it explores (although without explicit or implicit recourse to Weber) the area in which Weber falls short: to distinguish between the state's legitimate and illegitimate use of force against its citizens.

Yet, Dworkin's normative argument is situated in the context of a modern democratic constitutional state—specifically, in the legal framework of the United States, in which at least some moral rights are constitutionally protected and in which the state's monopoly on violence is juridified (*verrechtlicht*) through the constitution. In most instances, citizens can rely on legal means to protect themselves against an abuse of the state's power. The right to (violent) resistance re-

---

[30] Ronald Dworkin, *Taking Rights Seriously* (Cambridge, MA: Harvard University Press, 1977), 272–3.
[31] Ibid., 190.
[32] Max Weber, *Wirtschaft und Gesellschaft: Grundriß der verstehenden Soziologie*, 5th rev. ed. (Tübingen: Mohr Siebeck, 1980), 822: "Staat ist diejenige menschliche Gemeinschaft, welche innerhalb eines bestimmten Gebietes das Monopol legitimer physischer Gewaltsamkeit für sich (mit Erfolg) beansprucht."

mains in place as a backup for the exceptional cases in which the legal means of defense fail.³³

However, if one leaves the framework of the modern democratic constitutional state for emerging nations—or, even more so, for premodern contexts, in which a hierarchically ordered society is the accepted norm—Dworkin's claim for equality may appear to be pure luxury (that it only appears so superficially has been implied and will be examined later in more depth). Notwithstanding the validity of Dworkin's argument for a person's right to a certain degree of equality, the fulfillment of other rights may be superordinated to equality, although not in the sense that one right should or could be traded for other rights or political ends.³⁴ In *Basic Rights*, Henry Shue makes a strong case for the acknowledgement of the priority of subsistence or basic economic rights. He develops the rights problematic as a normative claim toward U.S. foreign policy and argues for the triad of security, subsistence, and liberty because "[w]ithout security or subsistence one is helpless and consequently one may also be helpless to protect whatever can be protected on the risk of security and subsistence." In addition, Shue sees a "mutual dependence [...] between enjoyment of rights to some liberties and enjoyment of security and subsistence." The essential liberties in this context are the freedom to participate and the freedom to physical movement.³⁵

Shue, however, does not claim that these are the only basic rights. Rather, he aims to draw attention to those rights that are most frequently neglected.³⁶ Additionally, because he analyzes basic rights from the perspective of U.S. foreign policy, he does not concern himself with the interdependence of the recognition of (moral) rights and political legitimacy. Nonetheless, his emphasis on the right to subsistence spotlights a sensitive issue. It is not incorrect to assume that violations of the right to subsistence are among the core issues that have stimulated

---

33 Dieter Grimm, "Das staatliche Gewaltmonopol," in *Herausforderungen des staatlichen Gewaltmonopols: Recht und politisch motivierte Gewalt am Ende des 20. Jahrhunderts*, ed. Freia Anders and Ingrid Gilcher-Holtey (Frankfurt/M.: Campus, 2006), 25–6.
34 The classical post-9/11 example is the frequently repeated claim that it is necessary to sacrifice freedom for security based on a real or imaginary threat of terrorist attacks. The real threat, however, seems to lie in undermining democratic rights rather than in terrorism. Closer to our topic are frequent claims about the need to sacrifice (democratic) rights for economic development and growth. For a critique of such claims, see Robert E. Goodin, "The Development-Rights Trade-off: Some Unwarranted Economic and Political Assumptions," *Universal Human Rights* 1, no. 2 (1979): 31–42.
35 Henry Shue, *Basic Rights: Subsistence, Affluence, and U.S. Foreign Policy*, 2nd ed. (Princeton: Princeton University Press, 1996), 30, 70, 71, 91.
36 Ibid., 65.

civil unrest throughout history. Consequently, it is not surprising that one finds relatively early arguments that formulate the moral right to subsistence, as, for instance, in late medieval scholastic literature.[37]

Of greater political relevance are discourses that relate a ruler's disregard of his subjects' moral right to subsistence to the subjects' (moral) right to disobedience, although these arguments formulate this point only implicitly as an issue of rights and explicitly as an issue of the ruler's neglected duties, which essentially means stripping the ruler's legitimacy. Two relatively early examples can be found in the fourteenth-century political thinkers William of Pagula and Ibn Khaldun.[38]

Of course, neither William of Pagula nor Ibn Khaldun argues in the intellectual framework of normative political theory or philosophy in the liberal tradition of the modern constitutional state. The concept of *rights* leads a shadow existence. Consequently, it might be considered an unforgiveable anachronism to relate the discourses of these thinkers to a contemporary discourse on rights. However, if one considers a peasants' rebellion, whether in twelfth-century Egypt or in France, in which peasants protest against their unbearable living conditions, their actions imply an assumed subjective moral right to rebel to restore acceptable living conditions, even though the dominant discourse is duty bound. In this sense, the application of an anachronistic concept can be utilized to foster understanding instead of hindering it. Again, is it allowed? Yes, it is. As Georges Duby has noted, "[a]ll things considered, I believe the question can be answered in the affirmative. It was no more legitimate for historians to apply, say, the concept of class struggle to the feudal era, yet it has proved undeniably useful that they have done so."[39]

Nonetheless, to continue with our previous example, William of Pagula and Ibn Khaldun are bound to their religious-cultural experience and would be neither willing nor able to follow in the application of an anachronism as an analytical tool. Their normativity has different roots in religion and custom. They rely on a normativity that is prior to political rule and that is dismissed, at least in the

---

[37] Virpi Mäkinen, "Rights and Duties in Late Scholastic Discussion on Extreme Necessity," in *Transformations in Medieval and Early-modern Rights Discourse*, ed. Virpi Mäkinen and Petter Korkman (Dordrecht: Springer, 2006), 41.
[38] Bettina Koch, "A Medieval Muslim-Christian Lesson on Political and Economic Liberalization," *Journal of Chinese, Indian, and Islamic Cultural Relations* 1 (2008): 73–88. For William of Pagula's argument, see also Cary J. Nederman, "Property and Protest: Political Theory and Subjective Rights in Fourteenth-Century England," *The Review of Politics* 58 (1996): 323–344.
[39] Georges Duby, "Preface," in *A History of Private Life, Vol. II: Revelations of the Medieval World*, ed. Georges Duby (Cambridge: Harvard University Press, 1988), ix.

Benthamian utilitarian tradition, as an "ontological luxury" that relies on "ghostly entities."⁴⁰ Nonetheless, the underlying problem these thinkers address is similar to Dworkin's concern: what are the duties of a ruler/government to the people, and how are these duties related to the rights of the people? When does legitimate rule become illegitimate rule that makes obedience no longer mandatory? Even if one had the chance to present the normative argument of the liberal tradition to these thinkers, and even if they could follow the argument intellectually, it is doubtful that they would be willing to accept it. The liberal reasoning in the context of the modern constitutional state does not fit their historical and cultural experiences. One reason for this misunderstanding lies in a peculiarity of modern legitimacy, as identified by Wilhelm Hennis:

> The insignia of modern legitimate rule is that it is based upon 'penultimate foundations': legal procedures, specific forms of rule, 'rights'. Their ultimate orientation frees them, but also presupposes them: they are redirected to the ambience of the moral quality of social order. [...] The legal order presupposes the existence of moral law [Sittengesetz]; it sets a limit to the scope of legal action, but it is neither in the public nor in the private sphere its legal basis.⁴¹

By contrast, in a premodern European historical-cultural context (and in most other contexts outside the Western world), political legitimacy is tied to an ultimate foundation—in most instances, a divine one. However, regardless of whether legitimacy is tied to religious belief or to a liberal understanding of morality, government must operate with the recognition of the people's *Sittengesetz* and not outside of it. Consequently, Hennis's suggestion that a real "crisis of legitimation takes the form of a conflict of legitimacy, a moral doubt [*sittlicher Zweifel*] of the possibility of continuing obedience to the legal ruler,"⁴² points to the core of the problem and corresponds to his doubts about the possibility of "a *general* theory of legitimacy applying to all developed cultures, a concept of legitimacy that is of practical critical and normative utility and which could help us in telling right from wrong in our world."⁴³

---

40 Dworkin, *Taking Rights Seriously*, xi.
41 Wilhelm Hennis, "Legitimacy: On a Category of Civil Society," in Wilhelm Hennis, *Politics as Practical Science* (Basingstoke: Palgrave Macmillan, 2009), 101. For the original German, see Wilhelm Hennis, "Legitimität: Zu einer Kategorie der bürgerlichen Gesellschaft," in Wilhelm Hennis, *Politikwissenschaft und politisches Denken: Politikwissenschaftliche Abhandlungen II* (Tübingen: Mohr Siebeck, 2000), 250–296.
42 Ibid., 84.
43 Ibid., 102. The view proposed by Wilhelm Hennis complies with Alastair MacIntyre, *After Virtue: A Study in Moral Theory*, 3rd ed. (Notre Dame: University of Notre Dame Press, 2007), 67.

The core of Hennis's exploration on legitimacy is the transition from an order perceived as legitimate to illegitimate, which is also central for the eminent Latin American philosopher Enrique Dussel, who analyzes the problem of legitimacy in periphery countries and with respect to disadvantaged minorities in industrialized countries. Like Hennis, he discusses legitimacy by contrasting himself from Weber and Habermas. He grounds his argument in the distinction between coercion (legitimate) and violence (illegitimate). Contrary to Henry Shue, who acknowledges the existence of rights even if the people possessing them are not aware of them, Enrique Dussel concerns himself with the impact on legitimacy if formerly marginalized "new emerging social subjects" discover new rights.[44] At this moment,

> [a]ny use of force *against the new rights*, which revealing themselves historically and progressively in the very eyes of the victims, will no longer be for them "legitimate coercion" but strictly violence: use of force against the right of the Other, without any validity or objective quality (being the destructive force of the "exclusive reproduction" of the system in force, not the reproduction and development of human life).[45]

Here, an unavoidable conflict emerges between the victimized and the dominant system. "[T]he dominant system becomes intolerable [...] because of the existence of victims on a massive scale, its intrinsic impossibility [...] becomes a conscious reality in the critical consciousness of the community of victims."[46] At the same time, the dominant system insists on maintaining the existing order, although the previous foundation of legitimacy has vanished.

Dussel's underlying assumption that legitimacy depends on perspective as well as on historical and socio-economic circumstances is in keeping with Wilhelm Hennis's thesis that a general theory of legitimacy is an impossibility. For Hennis, who does not reflect explicitly on periphery states but primarily on premodern Europe, most real crises of legitimacy originate in conflicts about religion and skin color that "ultimately [rest] on faith and superstition."[47] This leads to the question: what is different if political legitimacy does not follow the logic of the modern liberal nation state but rather rests on religion. To put it differently by rephrasing Hennis, what has changed if the conflict of legitimacy takes the form of *religious* doubt about the possibility of continuous obedience to the legal ruler? This is certainly a problem in all states and political systems of

---

44 Enrique Dussel, *Ethics of Liberation: In the Age of Globalization and Exclusion* (Durham: Duke University Press, 2013), 407.
45 Ibid., 401–2. Emphasis in the original.
46 Ibid, 416.
47 Hennis, "Legitimacy," 91.

rule in which religion is used as at least one source (if not the only source) of legitimacy. On the surface, it does not seem to make a difference whether moral doubts are based on religious belief or on a post-enlightenment morality.

1.2 Religion and Political Legitimacy

If religion is the main source of political legitimacy in the way that one can speak of a theocratic state or a religious nomocracy, state-sponsored religious affiliation means (political) allegiance with the regime. As Larry Catá Backer puts it, "religious affiliation becomes the marker for full political citizenship."[48] In its extreme version, and in reverse perspective, this concept of political legitimacy implies unequal treatment of individuals or groups depending on their existent or nonexistent affiliation with the privileged religion. Whether portrayed in religious or secular terms, the unequal treatment of parts of the people boils down to a problem of minority rights. Although the recognition of minority rights, as Will Kymlicka notes, is "a legitimate component of the liberal tradition,"[49] disregard or suppression of religious or ethnic minorities is a source of violent conflict. The emphasis lies on the oppression of *minorities*, not on religion. Religion, hovever, can be and has been used throughout the centuries as a justification to oppress or even kill political opponents.[50]

Yet, the problem related to political legitimacy tied to religious belief is deeper and more complex than potential (violent) conflicts with minorities may imply. Religious legitimacy suffers under the inherent conflict between political necessity and religion's moral standards. In this conflict, governments "are ill-equipped to win" because if a government is "setting itself up as the guardian of the faith, the government invites itself to be judged by its fidelity to it."[51] In other words, if a government has to act on political necessity but in potential conflict with religious law or faith, it may jeopardize its legitimacy in

---

[48] Larry Catá Backer, "Theocratic Constitutionalism: An Introduction to a New Global Ordering," *Indiana Journal of Global Legal Studies* 16 (2009): 133.
[49] Will Kymlicka, *Multicultural Citizenship: A Liberal Theory of Minority Rights* (Oxford: Clarendon Press, 1995), 50.
[50] Mohamed Charfi, *Islam and Liberty: The Historical Misunderstanding* (London: Zed Books, 2005), 50 – 1. See also Bettina Koch, "Religious Dissent in Premodern Islam: Political Usage of Heresy and Apostasy in Nizam al-Mulk and Ibn Taymiyya," in *Religion, Power and Resistance from the Eleventh to the Sixteenth Centuries: Playing the Heresy Card*, ed. Karen Bollermann, Thomas M. Izbicki, and Cary J. Nederman (Houndmills: Palgrave Macmillan, 2014), 215 – 236.
[51] Tarek E. Masoud, "The Arabs and Islam: The Troubled Search for Legitimacy," *Daedalus* 128, no. 2 (1999): 128 – 129.

the eyes of the faithful. At the same time, the government's interpretation of the faith may be used to oppress more radical or unwanted versions of the faith, which may become a permanent source of conflict. Although this is a problem that applies to all political rule that is tied to religious faith, it is useful to clarify this dilemma with reference to what is usually referred to as Islamism.[52] An *ulama* that is supportive of government actions has the power to dismiss more militant interpretations of the faith or even to declare them heretical. In turn, militants may "reject the official ulema and their version of Islam as subservient to the state and not worthy of its name."[53] Consequently, if God is considered the absolute sovereign and no law or policy is acceptable that potentially contradicts divinely instituted law, a conflict that arises from different interpretations is pre-

---

[52] Islamism is a rather controversial and contested term. Throughout the book, the term has been used rather sparsely. Frequently, *Islamism* is used interchangeably with *political Islam* or *Islamic fundamentalism*. Richard C. Martin and Abbas Barzegar ("Introduction: The Debate About Islamism in the Public Sphere," in *Islamism: Contested Perspectives on Political Islam*, ed. Richard C. Martin and Abbas Barzegar [Stanford: Stanford University Press, 2010], 2) note that the neologism *Islamism* "usually refers to those Muslim social movements and attitudes that advocate the search for more purely Islamic solutions (however ambiguous this may be) to the political, economic, and cultural stresses of contemporary life." I follow this broader notion. Later in this book, the term *Islamism* reappears in the context of al-Afghani's *pan-Islamism* that, explicitly, does not aim at the introduction of an Islamic state. Yet, some scholars claim that *Islamism* or *Islamist* should be restricted to a movement or person that focusses strictly on the establishment of the Islamic state. For a critique see Henri Lauzière, "The Religious Dimension of Islamism: Sufism, Salafism, and Politics in Morocco," in *Islamist Politics in the Middle East: Movements and Change*, ed. Samer Shehata (Abingdon/New York: Routledge, 2012), 89. Often, these movements consider the Muslim society under the Prophet Muhammad in Medina as the ideal Muslim society that has to be restored. See Anders Strindberg and Mats Wärn, *Islamism: Religion, Radicalization, and Resistance* (Cambridge: Polity Press, 2011), 18–23. The controversy over the term *Islamism* may be illustrated by two scholarly views. While Syed Farid Alatas ("Rejecting Islamism and the Need for Concepts Within the Islamic Tradition," in *Islamism: Contested Perspectives on Political Islam*, ed. Richard C. Martin and Abbas Barzegar, [Stanford: Stanford University Press, 2010], 87–92) associates Islamism with Orientalist approaches and demands the establishment of a term that originates in Islamic culture, Angel Rabasa ("Ideology, Not Religion," in *Islamism: Contested Perspectives on Political Islam*, ed. Richard C. Martin and Abbas Barzegar [Stanford: Stanford University Press, 2010], 110) argues that "[i]f the term *Islamism* did not exist, it would have to be invented, for how else can we distinguish between Islam as a religion and the modern ideology that derives its ideational content from that religion?" Thus, essentially and epistemologically, although the debate over concepts and terminologies becomes frequently more politicized as soon as Islam is concerned, this relates back to Georges Duby's question above as to whether one is allowed to apply anachronistic concepts.
[53] Shahram Akbarzadeh and Abdullah Saeed, "Islam and Politics," in *Islam and Political Legitimacy*, ed. Shahram Akbarzadeh and Abdullah Saeed (London: Routledge Curzon, 2003), 10.

programmed and can only be resolved if it is agreed that *one* authority "can authoritatively decide what God's decrees are."⁵⁴

Although Reinhard Schulze traces puritan movements in Islam back to the 1740s,⁵⁵ the conflict between official interpretations and religious movements described above is primarily a modern phenomenon, although there are always exceptions to the general trend. Shahram Akbarzadeh and Abdullah Saeed highlight the fact that in earlier times, a ruler who protected his subjects' lives did not necessarily jeopardize his legitimacy, even if the ruler was not a devout Muslim. Rather, as these authors note, the factual separation of political and religious authority has been the norm at least since the early Abbasid period of the middle of the eighth century. They argue that the real turning point was not until "the dawn of secularism in the Muslim world in the twentieth century."⁵⁶ This understanding is supported by Hamit Enayat, who reminds us that the frequent claim of a unity of religion and politics in Islam based on a theological and normative perspective does not correspond with political reality. Indeed, he considers it a

> misconception about the fusion of religion and politics in Islamic culture [...] to think that in historical reality too all political attitudes and institutions among Muslims have had religious sanctions, or have conformed to religious norms. Often the reverse is true: the majority of Muslims, for the greatest part of history, lived under regimes which had only the most tenuous link with those norms, and observed the *Sharīʿah* only to the extent that it legitimised their power in the eyes of the faithful.⁵⁷

Furthermore, reformist writers such as Asghar Ali Engineer see no contradiction between Islam and "liberal secularism."⁵⁸ This understanding stands in sharp contrast to claims that are critical of the supposed separation of church and state in the Western world. For instance, ʿAbd Allāh Ṣāliḥ al-ʿUthaymīn states, "[t]he Western conception of the separation of church and state, of religion and politics, finds no counterpart in Islam, which views the political organization of human affairs as merely the means through which the ideals of religion

---

54 Muhammad Nazeer Ka Ka Khel, "Legitimacy of Authority in Islam," *Islamic Studies* 19, no. 3 (1980): 178.
55 Reinhard Schulze, "Islamischer Puritanismus und die religiöse Gewalt," in *Im Zeichen der Religion: Gewalt und Friedfertigkeit in Islam und Christentum*, ed. Christine Abbt and Donata Schoeller (Frankfurt: Campus, 2008) 48.
56 Akbarzadeh and Saeed, "Islam and Politics," 3.
57 Hamit Enayat, *Modern Islamic Political Thought: The Response of the Shīʿī and Sunni Muslims to the Twentieth Century* (London: I.B. Tauris, 1988), 1.
58 Asghar Ali Engineer, "Islam and Secularism," in *Islam in Transition: Muslim Perspectives*, ed. John J. Donohue and John L. Esposito, 2nd ed. (Oxford: Oxford University Press, 2007), 139.

can be best achieved."⁵⁹ Authors such as al-ʿUthaymīn (who is by no means the only one)⁶⁰ take for granted the modern "Western" nominal separation of church and state. They ignore the fact that this separation, at least in political reality, is by no means fulfilled and varies significantly between "Western" states. Interestingly, the assumed Western separation of church and state is not only considered to be fulfilled but is assumed to be something that has no past and that has always been true. As Rollin Armour reminds us, it ignores the fact that even though

> Muhammad's political and military activity might seem to be greatly different from Christianity, that is correct only in comparison with the beginning of the Christian movement, but not if compared to the Christianity of Muhammad's day. The Christendom of the Middle Ages was exactly like the society Muhammad had in mind, namely, a society in which religion, law, politics, economics, and all of society merged into one interlocking system.⁶¹

Moreover, if one overcomes simplistic views of distinguishing between the "West" and the "Other" and aims for a more complete view, one must recognize that the image of the West described by secularity and a clear distinction between church and state and between religion and politics is not accurate and fosters misunderstanding. It is true that a separation of church and state did not occur in Islamic culture, but not for the reasons usually stated. Whereas Shiʿi Islam involves hierarchy and something like an official clergy, a similar structure does not exist in Sunni Islam: there is no pope, no Church, no clergy. As Mohamed Charfi puts it, "[i]f secularism means the separation of church and state, it would not be possible for Sunnis to practice it, because for them it would be a separation between the state and nothing. A more suitable form must therefore be found for the separation of religion and politics."⁶²

If one moves away from the separation of church and state and focuses on the relationship of religion and politics, the Judeo-Christian and Islamic cultures have far more in common. This is the case not only because the religiosity of a

---

59 ʿAbd Allāh Ṣāliḥ al-ʿUthaymīn, *Muḥammad ibn ʿAbd al-Wahhāb: The Man and His Works* (London: I.B. Tauris, 2009), 148.
60 The stereotypical assumption of a clear separation between Church and State in the West is not limited to the West and Islam. Indeed, as indicated by Farah Godrej, *Cosmopolitan Political Thought*, 110, it seems to have become a marker for the distinction between the "West" and the "Other" regardless of the other's religious foundation.
61 Rollin Armour, *Islam, Christianity, and the West: A Troubled History* (Maryknoll: Orbis, 2002), 12.
62 Charfi, *Islam and Liberty*, 127.

society reflects on its government[63] but also because numerous "Westerners" are not necessarily in favor of a strict separation of religion and politics but rather appreciate a more active role for religion and religious authorities in politics. To use an example with reference to the United States, a majority of Americans favor the Bible as a source of legislation: "44 percent say the bible should be 'a' source, and 9 percent believe it should be the 'only' source of legislation. [...] Likewise, many Muslims want their democracy to incorporate Shariah, not a democracy that is solely dependent on Western values."[64]

In most Western countries, the interweaving of religion and politics is more subtle. Even without judging whether the interplay of religion and politics is favorable, the political observer or political scientist cannot simply ignore its existence. In addition to religion's influence on legislation, religion clearly informs the morality of a significant portion of the people and, in this sense, what Wilhelm Hennis has framed as "moral doubt" determines whether a formerly legitimate government is perceived as illegitimate. In liberal democracies, in most instances, illegitimacy is not an issue of considering the entire system of government illegitimate but rather of considering the legitimacy of individual government actions or laws.

However, our main concern is not the interweaving of religion and politics in liberal states. If one considers the past and current situations in numerous Latin American countries, the influence of institutionalized Christianity cannot be overlooked, particularly in terms of conservative forces that have had and continue to have an active alliance with the Roman Church. For instance, until 1994, Argentina had a law that required the president to be a Catholic.[65] It is not incorrect to consider most political struggles in Latin America religious struggles because "the violent response to liberation movements has been carried on with the explicit support of conservative Christian groups, both Catholic and Protestant."[66] To formulate it more carefully, the political struggles in Latin America have been fought with religious support and with religious arguments. As stated earlier, this situation changes the nature of conflict and affects what is

---

63 Abdolkarim Soroush, "The Sense and Essence of Secularism," in Abdolkarim Soroush, *Reason, Freedom, and Democracy in Islam: Essential Writings of Abdolkarim Soroush* (Oxford: Oxford University Press, 2000), 61.
64 John L. Esposito, *The Future of Islam* (Oxford: Oxford University Press, 2010), 41.
65 Paul E. Sigmund, "Introduction," in *Religious Freedom and Evangelization in Latin America: The Challenge of Religious Pluralism*, ed. Paul E. Sigmund (Maryknoll: Orbis, 1999), 4.
66 David Lochhead, "Monotheistic Violence," *Buddhist-Christian Studies* 21 (2001): 7. See also Elisabeth E. Brusco, "Colombia: Past Persecution, Present Tension," in *Religious Freedom and Evangelization in Latin America: The Challenge of Religious Pluralism*, ed. Paul E. Sigmund (Maryknoll: Orbis, 1999), 236.

considered legitimate or illegitimate government (actions). To summarize the Latin American relationship between religion and politics in the words of Daniel Levine,

> religion and politics have never been separate in Latin America. They have been closely joined ever since the Conquest, bound together in relations of mutual affirmation and accommodation. The historical legacy of these ties was a virtual identification of religion with society and culture and a close alliance of the church as an institution with dominant forces in state and civil society. It became commonplace to consider religion and the church as 'pillars' of the established order.[67]

Consequently, for the twentieth and twenty-first centuries, our comparison of religious justifications of political violence should focus on Christian Latin American discourses and Islamic discourses originating primarily in the Middle East. Given the authoritative nature of religious canonical texts and a number of earlier writers, this study would be incomplete if it did not consider premodern forerunners. The consideration of premodern discourses on violence is also necessary to understand whether and in what ways the utilization of religion for political purposes follows certain patterns that survive over time and that may be independent of particular religions.

1.3 Overview of Chapters

The book is organized in two major parts (*Medieval Foundations* and *Religion and Violence in Twentieth Century Christianity and Islam*) and a concluding chapter. The following part explores the theoretical foundations that legitimize violence in Latin Christendom and Islam from a historical perspective. It focuses on a historically informed examination of theoretical texts on the period corresponding with the Western Middle Ages. In addition, this section explores arguments justifying the Crusades and *jihad*. The theoretical analysis discusses justifications for the use of violence to maintain power (hegemonic discourses) as well as anti-hegemonic discourses legitimizing resistance to hegemonic power.

The sections that discuss the legitimation of violence in the medieval Christian tradition examine texts on the Crusades and treatises that fall broadly into the political theory genre, including political treatises and mirrors for princes as authored by William of Pagula, John of Salisbury, William of Ockham, Giles of

---

[67] Daniel H. Levine, "Conflict and Renewal," in *Religion and Political Conflict in Latin America*, ed. Daniel H. Levine (Chapel Hill: University of North Carolina Press, 1986), 238.

Rome, and James of Viterbo. It investigates theoretical discourses that legitimize the use of violence by spiritual and temporal authorities against subjects, religious dissenters, and "unbelievers" as well as counter-discourses that legitimize resistance and revolt.

Whereas the Western medieval Christian tradition is perceived as being rich in theoretical discourses legitimizing violence and counter-violence, the same is not true for the Islamic context. For decades, the scholarly discussion on medieval Islamic thought highlighted the absence of any theories of resistance in the medieval Islamic tradition.[68] This view, however, was based entirely on the study of orthodox texts in the Sunni tradition and has recently been challenged by Khaled Abou el-Fadl.[69] The chapter on legitimizing violence in the premodern Islamic traditions examines the writings of the dominant legal schools in the Sunni and Shi'i tradition, theological writings, and political treatises such as mirrors for princes and administrative handbooks. Most of these texts were written from a Sunni perspective. For instance, almost no Shi'i Isma'ili sources have come down to us. However, a number of these writings reveal the position against which they argue. Furthermore, a number of these theorems have been reconstructed in recent scholarship.[70] In addition, the section explores theories of *jihad*. The authors and movements to be discussed include movements like the Kharijites and the Nizari Isma'ilis and authors like Ibn Anas, Nizam al-Mulk, al-Mawardi, Ibn Rushd, Ibn Jama'a, Ibn Khaldun, and Ibn Taymiyya, but also non-Sunni schools like the Ibadi and Zaydi jurists.

The discussion of the medieval foundations is followed by an exploration of twentieth century Christian and Islamic discourses on violence. Both of these discourses are informed and influenced by nationalist, socialist, Marxist, or Marxist-inspired ideas. Similarly, radical versions of religion exist in both religious cultures. A significant number of the writings are inspired by the rejection of Western or capitalist economic dominance and Western (cultural) hegemony.[71]

---

[68] Erwin I. J. Rosenthal, *Political Thought in Medieval Islam: An Introductory Outline* (Cambridge: Cambridge University Press, 1962). Ann K. S. Lambton, *State and Government in Medieval Islam: An Introduction to the Study of Islamic Political Theory: The Jurists* (Oxford: Oxford University Press, 1981).

[69] Khaled Abou el Fadl, *Rebellion and Violence in Islamic Law* (Cambridge: Cambridge University Press, 2001).

[70] Michael Cook, *Commanding Right and Forbidding Wrong in Islamic Thought* (Cambridge: Cambridge University Press, 2000). Christian Lange, *Justice, Punishment, and the Medieval Muslim Imagination* (Cambridge: Cambridge University Press, 2008). Abou el Fadl, *Rebellion and Violence in Islamic Law*.

[71] For a valid criticism of the concept of "hegemony," see Jon Beasley-Murray, *Posthegemony: Political Theory and Latin America* (Minneapolis: University of Minnesota Press, 2010).

The section *Christian Perspectives: Revolution and Counter-Revolution* analyzes Christianity's impact on the legitimacy of violence and counter-violence in the Latin American context. As Daniel H. Levine emphasizes, "in Latin America, religion and politics have been closely intertwined since the Conquest, providing ideological, material, and institutional support and legitimation to one another."[72] In its struggle for independence, the region has a long history of revolutions and violence.[73] This chapter examines José Comblin, Gustavo Gutiérrez, Camilo Torres, and Ignacio Ellacuría and their intellectual counterparts, Roger Vekemans and Alfonso Lopez Trujillo. The latter argues for the Church's disengagement in politics and indirectly supports oppressive regimes. The quintessence of opposition to the theology of liberation movements can be located in the *Societies for the Defense of Tradition, Family, and Property* (TFP), originally founded by Brazilian Plinio Corrêa de Oliveira. The TFP has an explicit anti-communist orientation and is known for its extreme conservative views, including reactionary social and political positions. In addition, the TFP's ideology is tied to the concept of the "national security state." The TFP is known for its active collaboration with military regimes.[74]

Islam and Violence in the Twentieth Century addresses the theoretical Islamic discourses of the twentieth and twenty-first centuries and brings these discourses into dialogue with historic hegemonic and anti-hegemonic justifications of violence. In the context of Sunni Islam, the authors discussed are al-Afghani, al-Banna, and Sayyid Qutb as well as some of their students. Although al-Afghani is technically an author of the nineteenth century, he is certainly among the most influential thinkers in twentieth century Islam.[75] As Elie Kedourie notes, his prominence is rather a "posthumous affair" that may even mislead one to assume that he was as prominent during his lifetime as he later became.[76] In this sense, it is justified to treat him if not exactly as a twentieth-century thinker, then at least as a prelude to twentieth-century Islamic discourses.

For the Shi'i tradition, the writings of the Ayatollah Khomeini are essential, but also 'Ali Shari'ati and Murtaza Mutahhari deserve our attention. A question

---

[72] Daniel H. Levine, *Religion and Politics in Latin America: The Catholic Church in Venezuela and Columbia* (Princeton: Princeton University Press, 1981), 3.
[73] Stefan Rinke, *Revolutionen in Lateinamerika: Wege in die Unabhängigkeit 1760–1830* (München: Beck, 2010).
[74] See José Comblin, *The Church and the National Security State* (Mayknoll: Orbis, 1979), 81.
[75] Johannes J. G. Jansen, *The Dual Nature of Islamic Fundamentalism* (Ithaca: Cornell University Press, 1997), 26
[76] Elie Kedourie, *Afghani and 'Abduh: An Essay on Religious Unbelief and Political Activism in Modern Islam* (London: Cass, 1966), 5–6.

that arises is whether and to what extent the intellectual leaders of the Muslim Brotherhood and Iranian intellectuals influence each other. Because it is fair to say that almost no text in the Sunni tradition in support of anti-state violence has been published in the twentieth century that lacks references to the fourteenth-century theologian Ibn Taymiyya, the influence of medieval thinkers and doctrines on modern legitimation of the use of violence is given particular attention.

The concluding chapter's main concern is the identification of patterns for religiously legitimizing political violence that exist across religious cultures and across the centuries. Additionally, it reexamines the concepts of legitimacy as outlined in the introduction and reassesses the findings from the perspective of conflict resolution and conflict prevention. Religion remains one (in some instances, the only) source of state legitimacy and consequently remains a potential source of conflict and unrest. The concluding chapter also readdresses the relationship between religion and legitimacy by exploring who possesses the authority to define and to enforce orthodoxy. What are the consequences of an attempt to enforce the hegemonic interpretation coercively? Also, because perceptions of the *West* play a significant role in both Latin American and Middle Eastern discourses, conflicting usages of the *West* are briefly analyzed.

Finally, this book has been written by a political theorist in the history of ideas tradition. It has been written with a larger audience in mind than just specialists in either modern or premodern traditions of Middle-Eastern Islamic, Latin American, or European Christian thought. Consequently, whenever possible, references direct the reader to available translations, given that the translations are at least acceptable. In addition, diacritic symbols have been used sparingly and only when they were unavoidable. If they appear in quotations, however, they are represented as found. Because of the existence of competing transliteration systems, the consistent approach causes some unavoidable inconsistencies in the spelling of some key terms. The diplomatic approach has been given preference over an attempt to harmonize all spellings. In general, common terms appear without diacritic symbols, less common terms and titles of works are introduced with diacritic symbols.

I conclude with a note on the language used throughout the book: While there is a general demand, in some disciplines more than in others, to use an inclusive language, the inclusiveness approach occasionally conflicts with the topic and with historic realities related to the topic. None of the authors and movements discussed in this book is particularly inclusive. Discussing these authors and movements in an inclusive language would pretend an inclusiveness that does not exist. Confronted with two conflicting values, preference has been given to a language that is historically more accurate.

2 Medieval Foundations

In the period usually referred to as the Middle Ages or premodernity, the exercise of power was tied to a system of religious belief. Yet, the interdependence of religion and politics does not mean that rulers were always (or even most of the time) true believers or the most shining examples of sound faith. To the contrary, in Latin Christendom, rulers were frequently in conflict with religious authorities, particularly the papacy, and as outlined earlier, whereas religion legitimized the rule of Muslim rulers in the eyes of the faithful, for most of history, Muslim rulers have only exhibited loose adherence to religious norms. Nonetheless, rulership and other forms of dominance depended on religious belief systems as the main or only source of legitimizing power over others.

To phrase this observation in a different way, in a religious state or a state that uses religion as one of its foundations, expressions of heterodox belief create an "otherness," implying tacit or open dissent. As John B. Henderson notes, the "otherness" that originates within a culture is perceived as more dangerous than threats from the outside world, whether from foreign nations or different cultures.[1] In contrast, identifying and affiliating with the orthodox religion "serves also as a mark for political affiliation."[2]

However, a state's dependence on religious orthodoxy for legitimacy is a double-edged sword. This association not only demands that citizens or subjects are seen as affiliated with orthodox belief but also requires a similar affiliation with orthodoxy of those in leadership positions. If the orthodoxy of a leader is questioned, his political legitimacy may be jeopardized.[3] Generally speaking, the interaction between orthodoxy and power applies to all religions that are used to legitimize political power.

Depending on the religion that is used as the source of legitimacy, orthodoxy can be created and maintained in different ways. Religious orthodoxy has frequently been asserted to be specific to Christianity because of the existence of an institutionalized Church, whereas the lack of a similar institutional structure in Islam means that orthodoxy is not relevant in relation to Islam. For instance, Alexander Knysh suggests that Islam consists of "a rather fluid body of more or

---

[1] John B. Henderson, *The Construction of Orthodoxy and Heresy: Neo-Confucianism, Islamic, Jewish, and Early Christian Patterns* (Albany: State University of New York Press, 1998), 1.
[2] Backer, "Theocratic Constitutionalism," 133.
[3] The connection between religious orthodoxy and legitimacy in premodern times may seem evident. However, this connection remains of some relevance in the twentieth and twenty-first centuries. For some contemporary examples see P. R. Kumaraswamy, "Islam and Minorities: The Need for a Liberal Framework," *Mediterranean Quarterly* 18, no. 3 (2007): 108–9.

less 'generally accepted' beliefs" and proposes that the "binary opposition 'orthodoxy'/'heresy' should not be used indiscriminately with regard to Islamic history as a whole."[4]

Although there is some truth to this assumption, it is problematic. First, what is considered Christian orthodoxy is subject to change in a similar way. Second, Islam or better *islams*, has or have to create orthodoxies that are tied to power, although these orthodoxies may change according to time and power structures because all "[m]onotheistic religions structure the relationship between the old and the new in terms not of evolution but of revolution, and reject all older and other religions as 'paganism' or 'idolatry'."[5] Orthodoxies also emerge from the fact that "[a]ll counter-religions base themselves on large bodies of canonical texts."[6] Nonetheless, it is wise to be cautious with the labels "heretic" and "heresy" and their counterpart, "orthodoxy." These concepts reflect a hegemonic perspective. Uncritical application of these terms may lead to a perhaps unintentional alignment with the orthodox interpretation of a period in time.[7]

Despite all of the differences between Christianity and Islam, both have religiously legitimized violence directed against religious dissenters within the community and/or against external forces, usually forces associated with a different religious creed. As implied by Henderson, internal dissenters are usually considered a more dangerous threat, and thus have to be fought more forcefully. This aspect is also emphasized by Jan Assmann when he states that "[f]ar more worrying than the paganism of others is the falsehood to which one's own co-religionists are forever in danger of succumbing."[8]

In the Christian context, the best-known example of a perceived external threat from religious others is the Crusades. Despite the newly emerged interest in the Crusades from an Islamic perspective, the Crusades play a surprisingly insignificant role in the theoretical reflection of the time. The Mongol invasion and the fall of Baghdad were of greater significance in the collective memory of the time than the Crusades. Originally, the Crusaders were not even perceived as something new and different. In Muslim lands, Crusaders were usually identified

---

[4] Alexander Knysh, "'Orthodoxy' and 'Heresy' in Medieval Islam: An Essay in Reassessment," *The Muslim World* 83 (1993): 65–6.
[5] Assmann, *Moses the Egyptian*, 7.
[6] Ibid., 170.
[7] Herbert Grundmann, "Der Typus des Ketzers in mittelalterlicher Anschauung," in *Ausgewählte Aufsätze, Vol. 1: Religiöse Bewegungen*, ed. Herbert Grundmann (Stuttgart: Anton Hirsemann, 1976), 314.
[8] Assmann, *The Price of Monotheism*, 21.

as "Franks" (*Faranj* or *Ifranj*) based on their assumed ethnic origin. An Arabic term for Crusaders did not emerge until the midst of the nineteenth century, when it appeared among Syrian Christians.[9] Consequently, this study does not need to consider the Crusades.

The Crusades are also remarkably absent from the classic texts of Christian medieval theory. The primary focus of these works is internal affairs, the abuse of power, and the relationship between ecclesiastical and temporal power. Crusading, as implied by the invention of the new Arabic terminology in the nineteenth century, gained rhetorical significance in the nineteenth and twentieth centuries and remains virulent in the twenty-first century. As Jonathan Riley-Smith puts it,

> We are today subjected to religio-political hostility, erupting in acts of extreme violence, and a war of words in the course of which the Crusades feature prominently. We cannot hope to understand the circumstances in which we find ourselves unless we are prepared to face up to [the] fact that modern Western public opinion, Arab Nationalism, and Pan-Islamism all share perceptions of crusading that have more to do with nineteenth-century European imperialism than with actuality.[10]

This battle with and over words also affects one of the key concepts in Islam related to violence, the *jihad*. Scholarly discourses are not exempt from this battle. Some scholars criticize the frequent rendering of *jihad* into "Holy War" because "Holy War" "does not exist in Arabic, the translation into Arabic sounds alien, and in the Qur'an, *jihad* is always described as *fi sabil illah* [in the way of God]."[11] At the same time, objections against a synonymous and interchangeable use of "Holy War" and "Crusade" barely exist. The concept of "Holy War" is associated solely with Christianity, not with Islam.

Contrary to this apparently (politically) correct notion, note that the concept of a "Holy War" is as alien to medieval Christian sources as it is to Islamic writers of the time. In the Christian context, the concept of a "Holy War" is a modern scholarly invention. Some writers even contest whether the Crusades qualify as holy wars. In medieval Christianity, the Crusades were perceived as a partic-

---

9 Emmanuel Sivan, *Modern Arab Historiography of the Crusades* (Tel Aviv: Tel-Aviv University, Shiloah Center for Middle Eastern and African Studies, 1973), 9–10. Also published as chapter one of Emmanuel Sivan, *Interpretations of Islam: Past and Present* (Princeton: The Darwin Press, 1985), 4–43.
10 Jonathan Riley-Smith, *The Crusades, Christianity, and Islam* (New York: Columbia University Press, 2008), 79.
11 *The Crescent and the Cross: Muslim and Christian Approaches to War and Peace*, ed. Harfiyah Abdel Haleem, Oliver Ramsbotham, Saba Risaluddin, and Brian Wicker (Houndsmills: Macmillan, 1998), 67.

ular version of just warfare, not as a "Holy War." In this sense, the term "Holy War" is as anachronistic to medieval Christianity as it is to Islam.[12] Consequently, the analytical term "Holy War" can be used independently of its cultural-religious background, even if the terminology is not reflected in sources from the period.

Just war theory is the dominant concept in the Christian context. Although outlined in relation to Christianity, Arnold Angenendt's distinction between a secular just war and a holy war is useful for analytical purposes. For Angenendt, a secular just war aims at a rationally convincingly just end. In contrast, a war becomes sacred when weapons are raised explicitly for God, either against people of another religion or against those who have renounced the right or true religion.[13] In this sense, *jihad* can qualify as a holy war if fought *fi sabil illah* against people of other religions, heretics, or apostates. In a similar vein, Jean Flori emphasizes that although *jihad* does not mean "Holy War" *per se*, holy war is a significant component of *jihad*.[14] Independent of the contextually specific meaning of *jihad*, it involves the idea of divine sanctions and marks "[t]he transition from the mundane or materially driven fighting of pre-Islamic Arabia to the sacred, divinely sanctioned warring."[15]

Although in Islam, the concept of *jihad* can be and has been applied from early on to justify violence against religious dissenters, people of other creeds, or oppressive regimes,[16] the relatively late Christian invention of crusading is far more limited. Legitimizing violence against dissent and oppression requires further justification, in particular if that violence is directed against the chief representative of Christendom, the pope.

---

[12] Ernst-Dieter Hehl, "Heiliger Krieg – eine Schimäre? Überlegungen zur Kanonik und Politik des 12. und 13. Jahrhunderts," in *Krieg und Christentum: Religiöse Gewalttheorien in der Kriegserfahrung des Westens*, ed. Andreas Holzem (Paderborn: Schöningh, 2009), 325. For a *Begriffsgeschichte*-approach to "holy war" see the contributions in Klaus Schreiner (ed.), *Heilige Kriege: Religiöse Begründungen militärischer Gewaltanwendung: Judentum, Christentum und Islam im Vergleich* (München: Oldenbourg 2008).
[13] Arnold Angenendt, "Die Kreuzzüge: Aufruf zum 'gerechten' oder zum 'heiligen' Krieg?," in *Krieg und Christentum: Religiöse Gewalttheorien in der Kriegserfahrung des Westens*, ed. Andreas Holzem (Paderborn: Schöningh, 2009), 341.
[14] Jean Flori, "Jihad et guerre sainte," *Cités* 14 (2003): 58.
[15] Reuven Firestone, *Jihad: The Origin of Holy War in Islam* (Oxford: Oxford University Press, 1999), 127.
[16] An exception to the rule can be found in the Sufi tradition. See Manzar Zaidi, "A Taxonomy of Jihad," *Arab Studies Quarterly* 31, no. 3 (2009): 21–34.

2.1 Legitimizing Violence in the Medieval Christian Tradition

For the reasons previously outlined and despite the insignificant impact of the Crusades on medieval theoretical discourses in Christianity and Islam, this chapter examines some justifications for calling for and taking part in the Crusades. Given the relative insignificance of the Crusades in theoretical discourses in Medieval Latin Christendom, justifications for the Crusades will not be the sole focus of this chapter. This chapter also focuses on the dominant discourses and harvests the rich theoretical discussions on the legitimacy of power and violence as well as its limits. These discourses are not limited to temporal power. They also include discussions of papal and spiritual power. Most scholarly works on violence in the Christian Middle Ages, however, focus more on power than on violence.[17] Other studies address the topic primarily from the perspective of political history without displaying a specific interest in theoretical analysis.[18]

After a brief analysis of the justification for the Crusades, this section outlines the theoretical discourses that legitimize the use of violence by spiritual and temporal authorities against subjects, religious dissenters, and "unbelievers." Thereafter, it analyzes counter-discourses, that is, discourses legitimizing resistance and revolt. In addition to texts on the Crusades, this chapter examines primary sources that fall broadly into the genre of political theory, consisting of political treatises and mirrors for princes. The authors discussed here include Thomas Aquinas, William of Pagula, John of Salisbury, William of Ockham, and Giles of Rome.

2.1.1 Religious Justifications of the Crusades and Violence against Religious Dissenters

The early history of Islam is marked by fragmentation, with the emergence of different religious sects and violent conflict among dissenting groups. In the Christian context, violent suppression of religious dissenters or heretics is a relatively late phenomenon. In addition to theological reasons, the lack of violence in early Christendom results from the socio-political circumstances in which Christianity

---

[17] See, for instance, Günther Mensching (ed.), *Gewalt und ihre Legitimation im Mittelalter* (Würzburg: Königshausen und Neumann, 2003). Manuel Braun and Cornelia Herberichs (ed.), *Gewalt im Mittelalter: Realitäten – Imaginationen* (München: Fink, 2005).
[18] Warren Brown, *Violence in Medieval Europe* (New York: Longman, 2010). Claire Valente, *The Theory and Practice of Revolt in Medieval England* (Aldershot: Ashgate, 2003).

emerged.[19] For about the first 300 years of Christianity's existence, members of the religion were subject to persecution. With the exception of Armenian, Christianity was not linked to political power until the Roman Emperor Constantine's conversion to Christianity, motivated by the wish "to find a god who would protect him from magical arts but also give him a secure and successful reign."[20] Before Constantine's time, Roman authorities regarded Christianity as a "subversive sect."[21] Constantine, who ruled over a multi-religious empire, refused to persecute members of other creeds. The only exception to his non-persecution policy concerned Christian heretics. Constantine seized their meeting places and declared heterodox versions of Christianity and their promotion unlawful.[22] However, this does not mean that violent Christian militancy did not exist in early Christendom.[23]

Persecution of heretics is not necessarily restricted to their execution. Institutionalized executions of heretics did not take place until the beginning of the eleventh century or the second millennium.[24] From the perspective of Christian theology, the killing of heretics is an oddity. Killing heretics contradicts the Christian doctrine of non-aggression. It conflicts with the Christian foundation that rejects the violent elimination of heretics by leaving the (final) punishment to God. Indeed, Arnold Angenendt sees in the killing of heretics *den christlichen Sündenfall*, the Fall of Christianity (in analogy to the Fall of Man).[25]

In general, as Edward Peters notes, the Church has applied two strategies towards heretics: *caritas* and *potestas*. The means of *caritas* are "urged penitence, reform, preaching, exhortation, propaganda, and instruction in converting heretics and maintaining the faithful in their faith," whereas *potestas* refers to

---

19 For a more general outline of the origin of Christianity and the rival (Christian) sects that entered "the already crowded marketplace of competing religions," see Keith Hopkins, *A World Full of Gods: The Strange Triumph of Christianity* (New York: Free Press, 2000), 136–176, quote 136.
20 Drake, *Constantine and the Bishops*, 15.
21 Joan O'Grady, *Heresy: Heretical Truth or Orthodox Error? A Study of Early Christian Heresies* (Longmead: Element Books, 1985), 71.
22 Drake, *Constantine and the Bishops*, 315, 347.
23 For an exemplary study of early Christian militancy, see Thomas Sizgorich, *Violence and Belief in Late Antiquity: Militant Devotion in Christianity and Islam* (Philadelphia: University of Pennsylvania Press, 2009).
24 Malcolm Lambert, *The Cathars* (Malden: Blackwell, 1998), 4.
25 Arnold Angenendt, *Toleranz und Gewalt: Das Christentum zwischen Bibel und Schwert* (Münster: Aschendorff, 2009), 232, 239, 245.

the "use of legal coercion against heretics and their supporters." Key examples of the latter include the Albigensian Crusade and the Inquisition.[26]

The two concepts of *caritas* and *potestas* not only mark a transition in Christian theology, they also signify a transformation of religious social practices and socio-political realities. These transformations are significant both for the Crusades and for the changing approach towards religious dissent. The first substantial change concerns the monks and the general populace. In the tenth and eleventh centuries, the religiosity of the monks deepened, which occurred hand in hand with an increase in the foundations of new monasteries throughout Europe and a growth in popular piety. Both transitions occurred along with a new sensitivity to questions of orthodoxy and heterodoxy or heresy. Second, as Jill Claster notes,

> [t]he papal office had become a prize fought over by the noble families in Rome. When the opportunity arose—or was manufactured—the Holy Roman Emperors appointed their own nominees to the See of St. Peter. The power of the papacy had been so eroded over time that the popes had not been able to assert meaningful authority over Christendom for many centuries. In the atmosphere of spiritual revival in the eleventh century, the need for reform of the papal office and the spiritual quality of the men who held the office became acute.[27]

For Pope Urban II, calling for the First Crusade allowed him to achieve at least three goals in one strike: first, he could assist the Byzantine emperor Alexis I, who had called for military aid, and hope for more influence in and over the Eastern Church. Second, his contemporaries originally considered the Crusade primarily as a militarily protected pilgrimage to the Holy Land, enabling Urban to satisfy believers' increased spiritual needs. Finally, the Crusade gave him an opportunity to restore the power of the Church and the Holy See.

One key theological issue was the "obvious [one] that Peter, as a priest, could not perform a military action himself, but it was equally clear that he, and his heirs, had power to authorize violence."[28] In other words, the papacy had to depend on temporal powers to wield swords in the name of the Church. Therefore, the enterprise could only be successful with the support of temporal

---

[26] Edward Peters, "Introduction: Heresy and Authority," in *Heresy and Authority in Medieval Europe*, ed. Edward Peters (University Park: University of Pennsylvania Press, 1980), 7.
[27] Jill N. Claster, *Sacred Violence: The European Crusades to the Middle East, 1095–1396* (Toronto: University of Toronto Press, 2009), 32–3.
[28] Louise Riley-Smith and Jonathan Riley-Smith, "Introduction," in *The Crusades: Idea and Reality, 1095–1274*, ed. Louise Riley-Smith and Jonathan Riley-Smith (London: Edward Arnold, 1981), 5.

rulers. In this sense, the Crusades exemplify the exercise of coercion and (political) violence that could not have taken place without religious authorization.

Legitimizing the Crusades

The Crusades created a new prototype of the pilgrim, namely a pilgrim who militarily won passage to the Holy Land's sacred places of Christendom.[29] This military pilgrimage that turned into a salutary war blurred the distinction between the political and the religious because this type of warfare escapes from the political regulations of state power, formerly the exclusive domain of warfare. The warrior-pilgrim received his dignity from the ethos of the individual fighter. God gave him the opportunity to enter into His service as a "holy fighter."[30]

The changing concept of this particular version of warfare is also reflected in the crusaders' self-image: they assumed that God or Christ inspired and ordered the Crusade to regain his lost heritage. The crusaders perceived themselves as *milites Christi* or *pugnatores Dei*.[31] They also restored the image of the martyr. Interestingly, rather than the martyrs of early Christianity, they took the Maccabees as examples, who revolted against the "pagan" Seleucid Empire.[32] As Nicolas Morton notes, the Maccabee example had some attraction (despite the fact that it was a Jewish revolt) because monks and clerics were familiar with the Maccabean story in the Old Testament but "could not be expected to understand the conditions of the medieval Middle East."[33]

In this context, "hostility towards God" is the leading theological concept; it is a concept that is present in all premodern religions. Whoever makes himself hostile to God has to be eliminated. In keeping with the theological concept, the Muslims were diabolized and demonized as God's enemies.[34] In the Crusades' propaganda, the Muslims turned into the arch-enemies of ancient Christianity: they were perceived not simply as infidels or pagans, but as polytheists and idolaters.[35] This perception corresponds with Jan Assmann's observation

---

[29] Martin Völkl, *Muslime – Märtyrer – Militia Christi: Identität, Feindbild und Fremderfahrung während der ersten Kreuzzüge* (Stuttgart: Kohlhammer, 2011), 47.
[30] Hehl, "Heiliger Krieg – eine Schimäre?," 336.
[31] Völkl, *Muslime – Märtyrer – Militia Christi*, 88.
[32] Ibid., 76.
[33] Nicholas Morton, "The Defence of the Holy Land and the Memory of the Maccabee," *Journal of Medieval History* 26 (2010): 277.
[34] Angenendt, *Toleranz und Gewalt*, 232. Of course, the accusations of hostility to God was not limited to Muslims, but targeted also Jews and other Christian creeds like Greek Orthodox.
[35] Völkl, *Muslime – Märtyrer – Militia Christi*, 267.

that all "[m]onotheistic religions structure the relationship between the old and the new in terms not of evolution but of revolution, and reject all older and other religions as 'paganism' or 'idolatry'."³⁶ Although it sounds contradictory and inconsistent, Muslims and particularly Muhammad were generally seen as Christian heretics. This contradiction was partially eliminated by the Crusaders' discovery that Islam is indeed a different religion and not a Christian heresy, although the heresy claim remains a key feature of anti-Islamic propaganda. Notably, these images of Muslims as Christian heretics are observed in Thomas Aquinas or Peter the Venerable, who share similar views. Both regard Islam primarily as a Christian heresy.³⁷ Thomas portrays Muhammad as the founder of a sect of erroneous doctrines who "seduced the people by promises of carnal pleasure." Muhammad claimed to be "sent to power of his arms," which Thomas relates to robbers and tyrants. For Thomas, the Prophet Muhammad is "utterly ignorant of all divine teaching" and "perverted almost all the testimonies of the Old and New Testaments by making them into fabrications of his own."³⁸

Seeing Muhammad and his followers as Christian heretics is essential for Thomas because he does not support any compulsion or violent force against pagans who lack any knowledge of the Christian faith. In contrast, whenever heretics and apostates are concerned, compulsion is permitted. Similarly, warfare against heresies and blasphemies is permitted, although he would prefer to educate Christians against the temptations of erroneous beliefs.³⁹ Aquinas' views belong to the more moderate theological camp.

Like many medieval theologians, Aquinas's views of the Muslim creed are inconsistent. In one place, he describes Islam as a Christian heresy and not as a religion in its own right. Elsewhere, he acknowledges that the religious phenomenon in the East qualifies as a different religion, and accordingly, that Muslims had to be considered infidels. However, contrary to some of his contemporaries who argued from the perspective of the contested doctrine of a universal Christian empire that would not only allow but make it mandatory "to attack any *infideles*, including Muslims," Aquinas and other more moderate theologians "never accepted the idea that crusaders held *carte blanche* to attack and occupy Muslim lands."⁴⁰

---

36 Assmann, *Moses the Egyptian*, 7.
37 James Waltz, "Muḥammad and the Muslims in St. Thomas Aquinas," *The Muslim World* 66 (1976): 90.
38 Cited in Waltz, "Muḥammad and the Muslims in St. Thomas Aquinas," 83.
39 Waltz, "Muḥammad and the Muslims in St. Thomas Aquinas," 92.
40 Norman Housley, "The Crusades and Islam," *Medieval Encounters* 13 (2007): 199–200.

Thomas' account that regards heresy as worse than infidelity reflects the thesis introduced earlier: an internal threat, meaning deviation from the orthodox faith that promises eternal life, is perceived as far more serious than an external threat. The view that Muhammad and his followers were seen as Christian heretics rather than as representatives of a different faith is also reflected in Pope Urban II's statements and in related sources. These sources also indicate a relapse into earlier religious practices and beliefs that early Christianity had overcome: the concepts of "holy places" and of the "purification" of sacred places through "blood atonement." In particular, the ideas of blood atonement and impurity have no genuine origin in Christianity, although they are present in almost all earlier religions.

Even though it theologically represents a relapse into religious concepts that were previously overcome, the papal Crusades' rhetoric makes frequent and successful use of the language of impurification, purification, and blood atonement.[41] The purification of holy places implies purification from sins. Consequently, nobody should take the Cross "because they desire earthly profit but only for the salvation of their souls and the liberation of the Church." Furthermore, those who take the Cross are relieved "of all penance imposed for their sins, of which they have made genuine and full confessions, because they risked their belongings and lives for the love of God and their neighbours."[42] In the accounts of Urban II, the idea of "liberating Christianity" is omnipresent, but so is the problem that priests could not engage in military action, which leads to the repeated reminder that

> we [the pope] do not want those who have abandoned the world and have vowed themselves to spiritual warfare either to bear arms or to go out on the journey; we go so far as to forbid them to do so. [...] The discretion of your religious profession must prevent you in the business from running the risk of either insulting the apostolic see or endangering your own soul.[43]

Similar reservations apply to young married men, who are discouraged from taking the Cross without their wife's consent. Given that the First Crusade originally had two aims, the protection of pilgrims in the Holy Land and military aid for the Byzantine emperor, these reservations are reasonable, particularly considering

---

41 Angenendt, "Die Kreuzzüge," 350–5.
42 Urban II, "Urban to His Partisans in Bologna, 19 September 1096," in *The Crusades: Idea and Reality, 1095–1274*, ed. Louise Riley-Smith and Jonathan Riley-Smith (London: Edward Arnold, 1981), 39.
43 Urban II, "Urban to the Counts of Besalú, Empurias, Roussillon and Cerdaña and Their Knights, c. January 1096–29 July 1099," in *The Crusades*, ed. Riley-Smith, 40.

the socio-economic stability at home. Similar reservations are repeated by Robert of Rheims, whose history of the First Crusade was among the most popular accounts: "But we do not order or urge old men or the infirm or those least suited to arms to undertake the journey; nor should women go at all without their husbands or brothers or official permission. [...] Lay people, moreover, ought not to go on pilgrimage except with the blessing of their priest."[44] Consequently, Urban emphasizes the need for "the knights of other provinces [to] go to the aid of the Asian Church and to liberate their brothers from the tyranny of the Saracens [and] to help a church so near you to resist the invasion of the Saracens."[45]

After the first (more or less reliable) reports from the Holy Land reached the European continent, further justifications for the Crusades began to emerge. Primarily, these justifications were based on portraying the Muslims or Saracens as barbarian, brutal, and godless. For instance, Guibert of Nogent, who provides us with one of the most colorful histories of the First Crusade, emphasizes the cruelty of these "impious men" [Saracens] and describes "intolerable tortures" that pilgrims had to endure ("the hard skin of their heels being cut open and peeled back to investigate whether perhaps they have inserted something under it"). Moreover, he sees those who fight the Saracens as resisting "the perfidy of Antichrist and the Antichristians" and embeds his narrative in a just war discourse. For him, all wars previously fought qualify as unjust wars. The wars currently fought, however, are different because they "contain the glorious reward of martyrdom, in which [one] can gain the title of present glory." He even goes so far as to call all previous wars illegitimate; only wars fought for the protection of the Holy Church are absolutely legitimate.[46]

To some extent, the Crusades represent an almost perfect example of religiously legitimized political violence. At the same time, they imply the discursive transition from a political to a religious problem. First of all, crusading is warfare that only takes place through the initiative and legitimization of religious authority. The political goals of crusading are:
1. Securing people defined through a religious creed (Christians pilgrims),
2. Giving military aid to the Byzantine emperor,
3. Conquering land (Jerusalem and the Holy Land).

---

44 Robert of Rheims, *Historia Iherosolimitana* [Excerpt], in *The Crusades*, ed. Riley-Smith, 44–5.
45 Urban II, "Urban to His Partisans in Bologna, 19 September 1096," 39.
    Urban II, "Urban to the Counts of Besalú, Empurias, Roussiolin and Cernaña and their Knights, c. January 1096 – 26 July 1099," 40.
46 Guibert of Nogent, *Historia que dicitur Gesta Dei per Farnco* [Excerpt], in *The Crusades*, ed. Riley-Smith, 45–49.

In addition, the pope aims to secure his power base and (spiritual) authority. These are all political ends. Ideally, the crusaders' motivations relate to spiritual goals. Their motivations are religious, although their religiously motivated actions are not necessary solely religious but also political. The key theological terms here are martyrdom, atonement, and redemption. However, the actions taken to achieve these ends are political.

Over the centuries, the discourse changes, placing a stronger emphasis on religious issues. At the beginning of the thirteenth century, James of Vitry considers heresy and particularly the Saracens a threat to the survival of the Church as representative of the true faith:

> If we were not resisting the Church's enemies, the Saracens and heretics would have destroyed the whole Church. For this reason the poisonous limbs must be cut off and the decaying flesh must be cut out, so that the sound part is not corrupted; and the mad must be bound and the wicked destroyed so that the good may be left unharmed.[47]

James of Vitry's account also implies a clear transition from the emphasis on *caritas* to *potestas*. The difference between infidels and heretics is no longer relevant. This is also evident in Humbert of Romans's account (c. 1272–4). In his *Opus Tripartium*, he aims to refute arguments made by critics of the Crusades. To some extent, his refutation of the critics reads like a lesson in *realpolitik* covered under the cloak of just cause rhetoric. For Humbert, the just cause is proven by the claim (in his reading, "the fact") that the Christians are fighting for justice. Because it is a Christian cause, it is a just cause.

Translated into political science jargon, he defends the Crusades as preemptive wars. Humbert dismisses the objection that the Crusaders inflict harm by asserting that the campaign in the Holy Land was a success if more Saracens than Christians were killed. Attacking the Saracens in their own territory was of utmost necessity because it was important for Christians to weaken the Saracens' power and "aim to harm the Christians whenever they can. If the Christians had not done this, the Saracens would have already overwhelmed the whole of Christendom." Similarly, by putting forward the argument that if we did not kill them first, they would kill us, Humbert states that the Saracens "bear such malice towards Christians that they would have killed all Christians everywhere, [...] if they had not been prevented by the resistance of the Christians."[48] Humbert briefly mentions the conversion of Jews and suffering for sins, which would qual-

---

47 James of Vitry, "Sermones Vulgares [Excerpt]," in *The Crusades*, ed. Riley-Smith, 68.
48 Humbert of Romans, *Opera Tripartium* [Excerpt], in *The Crusades*, ed. Riley-Smith, 103–117; quotations: 110, 113.

ify as a truly religious justification. Beyond the claim that it is a Christian cause and therefore a just cause, no further justification is necessary.

Thus, to Humbert, the Crusaders' individual motivations are of no concern. Nonetheless, it is worth raising the question of whether the religious motivations of the individual Crusader are partial or full covers for more mundane interests. As Nicolas Paul has shown, crusading offered opportunities for social mobility and qualification for future ruling positions that could not be achieved without having taken the Cross.[49] Moreover, Pope Urban's warning that the Cross should not be taken for material means (the riches of the Holy Land) indicates the existence of substantial material interests. Chronicle accounts also list poverty, evasion of temporal punishment, and political liberation as motivations. These accounts have been frequently highlighted by scholars of the Crusades, suggesting other more dominant motivations than just religious motifs.[50] In this context, it is essential to recall that the Crusades were primarily perceived as a version of just war. For theologians who claimed the right to a universal Christian empire, the worldly motivations of crusaders are of minor interest. However, for moderate theologians, particularly Thomas Aquinas, worldly interests may jeopardize the just nature of the military enterprise because they imply that the war is not fought with the *recta intentio*. For Aquinas, "princes and other participants in war are to be held accountable for the inward state of emotion that accompanies their decisions and conduct on the battlefield."[51]

Legitimizing Violence against Religious Dissenters

Within medieval European societies, conflicts involving religious dissent appear primarily in two versions. Both are related to discourses on heresy. The most obvious version involves conflicts between "heretic"[52] movements and ecclesiastical and temporal authorities. Partly, these conflicts are fought in the language of the Crusades. The so-called "Albigensian Crusade" qualifies as one of the most prominent examples. As in early Christianity, "heretical" movements are

---

[49] Nicholas L. Paul, *To Follow in Their Footsteps: The Crusades and Family Memory in the High Middle Ages* (Ithaca: Cornell University Press, 2012), 46.
[50] Völkl, *Muslime – Märtyer – Militia Christi*, 119.
[51] Gregory M. Reichberg, "Aquinas' Moral Theology of Peace and War," *The Review of Metaphysics* 64 (2011): 470.
[52] It needs to be emphasized that inquisition registrar referred to the Cathars as "god men" and did not use the term "heretic." See, Mark Gregory Pegg, "On Cathars, Albigenses, and Good Men of Languedoc," *Journal of Medieval History* 27 (2001): 193.

social movements with religious character. Again, as already emphasized in the discussion of the Crusades to the Holy Land, the Church could only authorize military actions; she could not perform them herself but rather depended on the temporal power's military arm. Although this did not remain true later, the first executions of heretics after the year 1000 were carried out on the orders of temporal authorities.[53] This emphasizes two things: the Church's dependence on the temporal power and the temporal power's interest in taking actions against religious dissenters or heretics, whether for spiritual or profane reasons.

The second type of conflict that involves (accusations of) religious dissent concerns the conflict between temporal and ecclesiastical powers over supremacy, remains prominent throughout the late Middle Ages. Here, the previously mentioned idea of the universality of a Christian empire clashes with the temporal powers' claim to an independent political sphere that eventually culminates in Marsilius of Padua's theory challenging the Church's assertion of supreme power and subordinating her and her representatives to the secular realm.[54] Naturally, because the Church has only the power to authorize but not to commit violent actions herself, at least theoretically, the Holy See's accusations of heresy against temporal rulers had to be fought more with words than with the sword.

To exemplify these two patterns of conflict in which the Church utilizes accusations of heresy, either with the temporal sword or against it, this section first examines the Albigensian or Cathar movement and the tool of inquisition; thereafter, it explores the accusation of heresy directed against temporal rulers based on the papal plenitude of power (*plenitudo potestatis*) doctrine.

If the Albigensian Crusade (1209–1218) is primarily viewed from the perspective of the military actions that were taken, it was not fought in any way differently than mundane wars in the Middle Ages.[55] In this sense, the (military) actions taken to fight the Cathars are clearly political. It is also worth noting that Pope Innocent III, who launched the Albigensian Crusade, did not regard this "Crusade" similarly to the military expeditions to the Holy Land. As William Paden emphasizes, "[i]n launching the crusade Innocent III carefully distinguished the term for the earlier crusades, *negotium crucis* 'affair of the cross',

---

53 Angenendt, *Toleranz und Gewalt*, 252.
54 Bettina Koch, "Marsilius of Padua on Church and State," in *A Companion to Marsilius of Padua*, ed. Gerson Moreno-Riaño and Cary J. Nederman (Leiden: Brill, 2011), 139–179. Bettina Koch, "Priestly Despotism: The Problem of Unruly Clerics in Marsilius of Padua's *Defensor Pacis*," *Journal of Religious History* 36 (2012): 165–183.
55 Laurence W. Marvin, "War in the South: A First Look at Siege Warfare in the Albigensian Crusade, 1209–1218," *War in History* 8, no. 4 (2001): 373–395.

from *negotium pacis et fidei* 'affair of peace and faith', which he applied to the Albigensian operation."[56]

However, before elaborating on the religious justifications for the violent actions taken against the Cathars, it is necessary to briefly outline the movement's nature, which reveals some of the reasons why it was fought so forcefully. Indeed, Herbert Grundmann reminds us early on not to ignore the social origins of "heretic" movements.[57] First, the Cathar movement is a social, evangelical, and philosophical movement.[58] Second, the Cathars aimed for a life of simplicity. They did not accept the Church's authority because they believed that she had departed from the core principles of Christianity.[59]

The movement's core teachings were relatively similar to those of previous (and later) Christian reform movements, although not necessarily in their extremity. It is noteworthy that the Church perceived religious movements that took the belief to the extreme, which today we may refer to as religious fundamentalism, as a more serious threat than other (religious) movements that were *weltanschaulich*, more different. To use the anachronism, for their piety, "fundamentalist" movements enjoyed the people's respect and admiration.[60] In contrast, the established Church appeared as the representation of Christianity "light." This approach and the underlying problem of the relationship between religion and power, however, are not unique to Christianity. As Wael B. Hallaq has shown, in the formation process of the now established legal schools in Islam, only those schools that received political support were successful, and only those that reflected mainstream approaches rather than extreme interpretations received that support.[61]

---

56 William D. Paden, "Perspectives on the Albigensian Crusade," *Tenso* 10, no. 2 (1995): 93.
57 Herbert Grundmann, *Religious Movements in the Middle Ages: The Historical Links between Heresy, the Mendicant Orders, and Women's Religious Movement in the Twelfth and Thirteenth Century, with the Historical Foundations of German Mysticism*. trans. Steven Rowan, introduction Robert E. Lerner (Notre Dame: University of Notre Dame Press, 1995), 15. [First published as *Religiöse Bewegungen im Mittelalter: Untersuchungen über die geschichtlichen Zusammenhänge zwischen der Ketzerei, den Bettelorden und der religiösen Frauenbewegung im 12. und 13. Jahrhundert und über die geschichtlichen Grundlagen der deutschen Mystik* (Berlin: Ebering, 1935)].
58 Anne A. Davenport, "The Catholics, the Cathars, and the Concept of Infinity in the Thirteenth Century," *Isis*, 88, no. 2 (1997): 279.
59 Emily McCaffrey, "Memory and Collective Identity in Occitanie: The Cathars in History and Popular Culture," *History and Memory*, 13, no. 1 (2001): 114.
60 Grundmann, "Der Typus des Ketzers," 318.
61 Wael B. Hallaq, *The Origins and Evolution of Islamic Law*, 5th printing with corrections (Cambridge: Cambridge University Press, 2008), 169–170.

These observations are particularly true for the Cathars' movement: they appealed to people from wide ranging social groups. The Cathars attracted "[d]isillusioned clerics, nobles, patricians, the bourgeois upper and middle strata, artisans, traders, simple craftsmen, the lower social strata—all were present in early Catharism."[62] The fact that the movement had such wide support certainly indicated that it represented a serious threat to the established ecclesiastical and temporal authorities. The Cathars' attractiveness to local nobles had to be deemed as hazardous to royal power.

Other religious movements that were considered heretical share similar features. Malcom Lambert sees strong parallels between Eastern Bogomilism, other religious movements in the Manichean tradition, and Catharism. The Cathars "followed the gospels and the way of the apostles." Contrary to the Catholic Church, "they represented the good and their ascetic practices" they considered "the outward and visible sign of their goodness and the guarantee of their perfection."[63] However, one problem, typical of suppressed movements, is the fact that the sources that offer information on the Cathars are from their opponents rather than from the Cathars themselves. These sources include protocols from heresy processes. Usually, the protocols followed a standardized questionnaire. They are written in Latin, whereas most inquisitions were conducted in the vernacular, which means that most of the accused did not have the means to understand how their belief was actually recorded.[64] Consequently, some skepticism about these accounts is appropriate, and they should be read with caution. As Herbert Grundmann emphasizes, the accusations of heresy used topoi that have become literary; they created heresies that were never reality.[65] To illustrate this by example, Pierre des Vaux de Cernay's *Historia Albigensis*, contains the following description of the Cathars' belief:

> They said that almost all the Church of Rome was a den of thieves, and that it was a harlot of which we read in the Apocalypse. They so far annulled the sacraments of the Church, as publicly to teach that the holy baptism was just the same as river water, and that the host of the most holy body of Christ did not differ from common bread, instilling into the ear of the simple this blasphemy, that the body of Christ, even though it had been as great as the Alps, would have been long ago consumed and annihilated by those who had eaten of it. Confirmation and confession they consider as altogether vain and frivolous. They preach

---

[62] Lutz Kaelber, "Weavers into Heretics? The Social Organization of Early-Thirteenth-Century Catharism in Comparative Perspective," *Social Science History* 21, no. 1 (1997): 113–4.
[63] Lambert, *The Cathars*, 30.
[64] Herbert Grundmann, "Ketzerverhöre des Spätmittelalters als quellenkritisches Problem," *Deutsches Archiv für Erforschung des Mittelalters* 21 (1965): 550.
[65] Grundmann, "Der Typus des Ketzers," 325.

that holy matrimony was meretricious, and none could be saved in it if they should beget children.[66]

Scaling Pierre des Vaux de Cernay's argument down may lead us closer to the truth but also relatively close to what later became Lutheran and Calvinist "orthodoxies." The Church's prodigality is a general topic in church-critical accounts throughout the high and late Middle Ages. However, deeming confirmation and confession unnecessary may represent a breach with Catholic doctrine. Yet, these issues also concern sources of revenue. To avoid losing these mandatory "donations" as sources of income, the institutionalized Church even tried to withhold the right to hear confession from the mendicants, which they did free of charge.

Examining the heresy problem from a political science perspective, its meaning is obvious. Although the rhetoric applied involves numerous references to the Sacraments and deems heresy a religious problem, Catharism undermines the existing politico-religious order. In addition to the sacraments' theological content, they imply rules of social conduct and regulate significant aspects of social life from birth to death. As such, they are instruments of power, and came to be seen as instruments of oppression. Sectarian movements undermine and question the existing socio-political order and the necessity of the sacraments for salvation. Consequently, it is not surprising that the Church and the temporal authorities who receive part of their legitimacy from the Church respond fiercely to these movements, particularly if they are as popular as Cathars were, at least regionally in Italy and France.

As outlined earlier, when Innocent III launched the Albigensian Crusade, he saw it as an "affair of peace and faith." "Peace," here, can be translated as maintaining and securing the existing order. While legitimizing the violent overthrow of the Cathar communities, Innocent only refers indirectly to the movement's political implications. His main line of argument is similar to those already explored in the justifications of the Crusades to the Holy Land: the Cathars aim to destroy Christendom. Despite the Cathars' claim that they follow the examples of the gospels and the apostles, he accuses them of lying and ignorance: "they do not understand God's law but attack it, nourishing wanton doctrines of many different kinds of novelty and error."[67] Because the pope can only authorize but not exercise violent actions against religious dissenters, he appeals to the French

---

66 Pierre des Vaux de Cernay, *Historia Albigensis* [Excerpt], in *Heresy and Authority in Medieval Europe*, ed. Edward Peters (University Park: University of Pennsylvania Press, 1980), 124.
67 Innocent III, "Innocent to King Philip II of France, 17 November 1207," in *The Crusades*, ed. Riley-Smith, 79.

King, Philip II (and the secular powers more broadly), to take action. When addressing the king, he refers to him primarily as a son of the Church rather than as a representative of temporal power:

> And so, since wounds that do not respond to the healing of poultices must be lanced with the blade and those who have little regard for ecclesiastical correction must be suppressed by the arm of secular power, we have considered that we ought to call on your aid, most beloved son, to vindicate the injury to Jesus Christ and to seize *the little foxes* who, influencing the simple, are forever destroying the vineyard of the Lord of Hosts.[68]

His appeal to Philip also reflects the shift in Christian theology from *caritas* to *potestas*. Although he does not give up the idea that the dissenters have to be brought back to the Church, he only sees this possible through *potestas*, not through *caritas*. Only after the "degenerated shoots" have been rooted out does he consider it possible that "the perfidious heretical sectarians [...] may be brought back amid the suffering of war at least to a knowledge of truth."[69]

However, Innocent does not stop by appealing to the French king. Because one of the local nobles, the Count of Toulouse, has already joined the Cathar movement, he also aims to secure the military support of the nobles and the faithful in the region. In keeping with the general rhetoric against heresies in the high and late Middle Ages,[70] he appeals to the faithful in neighboring provinces to take up arms against the Count of Toulouse:

> But then the devil aroused against him his own servant, the count of Toulouse, who had often incurred ecclesiastical censure because of the many and great outrages he had committed against the Church and God and, like the changeable and crafty, slippery and inconstant man he was, had often been absolved for feigned repentance.[71]

In this appeal, however, he also emphasizes self-sacrifice or martyrdom because he believes "that it is expedient for it *that one man should die for* it, *so that the whole* should *perish not:* this generation infected by the contagion of heretical depravity that will be recalled from the error by the blood of a slain man, which will intercede for it better than any living man could."[72]

Here, however, he emphasizes that he has already used the sword the Church possesses by excommunicating the count of Toulouse. While he appeals

---

[68] Ibid.," 79–80.
[69] Ibid.," 80.
[70] Grundmann, "Der Typus des Ketzers," 322.
[71] Peter des Vaux de Cernay, *Historia Albigensis* [Excerpt], in *The Crusades*, ed. Riley-Smith, 81.
[72] Ibid., 82.

to martyrdom, a concept that is more prevalent in the context of the Crusades to the Holy Land, he maintains the distinction between the "affair of the cross" and the "affair of peace and faith." Those who fight the "pestiferous people, who simultaneously attack both peace and truth," he promises, God will release them of all of their sins. In urging them not to delay the cause, he stresses that it is "their business to bring peace to those people in the name of him who is *the God of peace and love*."[73]

The logic applied here is similar to the logic that Humbert of Romans later uses in his *realpolitical* approach to the Crusades to the Holy Land, although the assumed threat at home is more real than the one in the Holy Land. Nonetheless, both arguments hold that it would be better to kill the heretics before they destroy the sound Christian faith. Innocent, however, does not go as far as claiming that if we do not kill them first, they will kill us, which would have been rather dubious and implausible in the case of the Cathars because they were known for their peaceful and non-violent conduct.

The Cathar movement was successfully rooted out, although not from memory. As Luc Racout notes, the Albigensian Crusade played a significant role in the parties' polemics during the French War on Religion.[74] Moreover, in the 1960s and 1970s, "the Albigensian Crusade prompted a more widespread collective memory of political, cultural and economic oppression by the north and the south's continuing struggle for liberation."[75] During the Middle Ages, the crusade's rhetoric was frequently applied to maintain and strengthen subordination to the Church. As shown by the example of the count of Toulouse, the Holy See also considered crusading as an instrument to use against a nobility that wishes to evade papal supremacy. Pope Gregory IX used the ecclesiastical sword against the emperor Frederick II, and Urban IV launched a crusade against Frederick's son Manfred to subjugate temporal power. These attempts also reflect the contested doctrine of the universal Christian empire, which is better served by exploring theological treatises supporting that claim than by a further investigation of crusading rhetoric.

---

[73] Ibid., 83, 85.
[74] Luc Racaut, "The Polemical Use of the Albigensian Crusade During the French Wars of Religion," *French History* 13, no. 3 (1999): 261–279.
[75] McCaffrey, "Memory and Collective Identity in Occitanie," 123,

Legitimizing Violence against Dissenting Rule

As implied in the previous sections, the Holy See not only used accusations of dissenting belief to legitimize violence against ordinary believers and "heretic" movements but also against temporal powers. These accusations are tied to the concept of the universality of the Christian empire. In the thirteenth century, Pope Innocent IV "argued that the pope judges Christians by canon law, Jews by the Law of Moses, and all others by natural law."[76] The idea of papal universal jurisdiction remained virulent throughout the fourteenth century. At the dawn of the thirteenth and in the fourteenth century, crusading and crusading rhetoric had become a blunt sword. However, the Holy See had not given up the claim of universality. In contrast, the ecclesiastical and the temporal powers began to engage in an even more intense conflict over supremacy that is fought in religious terms.

As Joseph Canning puts it, this battle and the underlying theological doctrines are the "great paradox of medieval history that the church, originally instituted outside the governmental and legal structures of the Roman Empire, had itself over time become the prime developer of the language of power."[77] The Church's key theorem is the so-called two-swords-theory, originally developed by Pope Gelasius I but without much political impact until the theory reemerged in the late Middle Ages. This theorem is based on a reading of Luke 22, 38 "They said, 'Lord, look, here are two swords'. He replied, 'It is enough'." In this sequence from Luke, the two swords are read as representatives of the two powers, the temporal and the ecclesiastical. Both swords were in the possession of Jesus. The curial interpretation assumes that both swords were later in Peter's hands and all succeeding popes thereafter. This theorem has the following implications: originally, the papacy had authority over the ecclesiastical *and* the temporal spheres. Because the Church cannot yield the temporal sword, it has granted it to the temporal power to use, but not to own. Because the temporal power receives its sword from the papacy, all exercise of temporal power depends on the Church, and the Church has the rightful claim to *plenitudo potestatis*, a plenitude

---

[76] James Muldoon, "*Auctoritas, Potestas* and World Order," in *Plentitude of Power: The Doctrines and Exercise of Authority in the Middle Ages: Essays in Memory of Robert Louis Benson*, ed. Robert C. Figueira (Aldershot: Ashgate, 2006), 129.

[77] Joseph Canning, *Ideas of Power in the Late Middle Ages, 1296–1417* (Cambridge: Cambridge University Press, 2011), 11.

of power.[78] Politically, this power struggle was fought between Pope Boniface VIII and the French King Philip the Fair, and soon thereafter between Pope John XXII and emperor-elect Ludwig, Duke of Bavaria.[79] The clearest statement of the papacy's claim to absolute power was made by Pope Boniface VIII. In his famous bull *Unam sanctam* (1302), he states,

> Therefore there is one body and one head of this one and only church, not two heads as though it were a monster, namely Christ and Christ's vicar, Peter and Peter's successor, for the Lord said to this Peter, "Feed my sheep." [...] Whoever therefore resists this power so ordained by God resists the ordinance of God. [...] Therefore we declare, state, define and pronounce that it is altogether necessary to salvation for every human creature to be subjected to the Roman Pontiff.[80]

This short section draws explicitly on the relationship between disobedience and sin. Not following or objecting to the pope's command does not simply mean disobedience to the worldly representative of the Church, but is similar to disobeying God. This claim relates to the pope's claim of infallibility, which was disputed as much as the *plenitudo potestatis* theorem itself. Boniface's bull is a condensed and brilliant expression of medieval political theory. In *De ecclesiastica potestate* (1302), Giles of Rome, who is assumed to be at least the co-author of *Unam sanctam*,[81] provides us with a more elaborate version of the papal claim.

The following outline focuses primarily on Giles's theory but has to be supplemented with James of Viterbo's *De regimine Christiano* (c. 1303), written at about the same time and in a similar vein.[82] For Richard Scholz, Giles of Rome's *De ecclesiastica potestate* and James of Viterbo's *De regimine Christiano* represent the earliest and most substantial medieval treatises defending papal power. Both treatises also established papal arguments that were used in later conflicts between the temporal and the ecclesiastical powers, demonstrating

---

78 Bettina Koch, *Zur Dis-/Kontinuität mittelalterlichen politischen Denkens in der neuzeitlichen politischen Theorie: Marsilius von Padua, Johannes Althusius und Thomas Hobbes im Vergleich* (Berlin: Duncker & Humblot, 2005), 49–50.
79 For a more elaborate discussion of the historical context, see Bettina Koch, "Against Empire? John of Paris's Defence of Territorial Secular Power in the Context of Dante's and Marsilius of Padua's Political Theories," in *John of Paris: Beyond Royal & Papal Power*, ed. Chris Jones (Turnhout: Brepolt, forthcoming).
80 Bull *Unam Sanctam* (Nov. 1302), in Brian Tierney, *The Crisis of Church & State, 1050–1300* (Englewood Cliffs: Prentice-Hall, 1964), 188–9.
81 Bettina Koch, "Aegidius Romanus," in *Handbuch Staatsdenker*, ed. Rüdiger Voigt and Ulrich Weiß (Stuttgart: Franz Steiner, 2010), 13b-15b.
82 James of Viterbo, *De regimine Christiano: A Critical Edition and Translation*, ed. R.W. Dyson (Leiden: Brill, 2009).

an influence that was not restricted to their own time, but rather impacted the political discourse for centuries to come.[83] Although the topic of these treatises is not explicitly violence but rather power, they provide a theoretical foundation for the justification of violence. Moreover, despite the fact that these works are concerned with the papacy and Christendom, twentieth century Islamist thinking echoes many of the ideas that they put forward. However, we do not have any reason to assume any interdependence between fourteenth century curial and twentieth century Islamist thought.

Unam sanctam already reflects the key issue discussed by Giles of Rome and James of Viterbo: the pope not only rightfully claims but also possesses *plenitudo potestatis*, giving him supremacy over all temporal and ecclesiastical rulership. As Eckhard Homan notes, Giles of Rome's central concern is to demonstrate that legitimate temporal power depends on priestly inauguration because a truly just government can only exist within and in accordance with the Church.[84] For Giles, "there is no lordship with justice [...] except under the Church and as instituted through the Church."[85] Therefore, the only option for the ecclesiastical power is to appoint the temporal power.[86] Giles underscores his claim by noting that those who argue that temporal powers are only subjected to the ecclesiastical power in spiritual matters but not in temporal matters are mistaken because they do not understand the hierarchy of the swords:

> For if kings and princes were subject to the Church only spiritually, sword would not be under sword, temporal things would not be under spiritual, there would be no order among the powers, and the lowest would not be led back to the highest through the intermediate. If these things are ordained, then, the temporal sword must be under the spiritual, kingdoms must be under the Vicar of Christ, and *de iure*, even though some may act contrary to this *de facto*, the Vicar of Christ must have lordship even over temporal things.[87]

If the temporal power is not under the power of the supreme spiritual authority, then it is not any better than "thieves and robbers."[88] By spiritual power he means the Church as a whole and papal power specifically, as he equates the

---

[83] Richard Scholz, *Die Publizistik zur Zeit Philipps des Schönen und Bonifaz' VIII: Ein Beitrag zur Geschichte der politischen Anschauungen des Mittelalters* (Stuttgart: Enke, 1903), 46, 124, 131.
[84] Eckhard Homann, "*Posse absolutum versus iusticia*: Zur antinomischen Bestimmung der päpstichen Macht bei Aegidius Romanus," in *Gewalt und ihre Legitimation im Mittelalter*, ed. Günther Mensching (Würzburg: Königshausen und Neumann, 2003), 237.
[85] Giles of Rome, *Giles of Rome on Ecclesiastical Power: The De ecclesiastica potestate of Aegidius Romanus*, trans. with introduction by R.W. Dyson (Woodbridge: Boydell Press, 1986), 2.7.
[86] Giles of Rome, *On Ecclesiastical Power*, 2.5.
[87] Ibid., 1.4.
[88] Ibid., 1.5.

Church's power with the power of the pope or the papal office. Papal power and ecclesiastical power become interchangeable and even identical terms because the pope is no longer understood as the main or even sole representative and head of the Church; all ecclesiastical power and authority are merged in the person of the pope.[89] Although James of Viterbo makes generally the same argument, it differs in that he stresses the significance of the papal office more than Giles, whereas Giles does not explicitly distinguish between the person and the office. For James, however, the person who is pope does not even have to be holy; he is holy because of his status and position. The Roman Pontiff "acts on behalf, and holds the place, of the Holy of all Holies."[90]

Giles makes some statements that point in a similar direction, although this distinction is less developed. An underdeveloped version of a distinction between person and office shines through when he compares papal perfection to spiritual perfection. Giles is without any doubt that the pope possesses and personifies the highest level of perfection. Whereas others can have personal or spiritual perfection, the pope has *perfectio status* and combines *jurisdictio* and *plenitudo potestatis*. Because his *status* is beyond that of all others, nobody can judge him (besides God). Because he inaugurates temporal power, he also has the power and authority to judge the temporal power if it is not exercised to his satisfaction.[91]

In the typical scholastic manner, Giles comes to his conclusion by considering the roots of temporal and ecclesiastical power. For him, fullness of power resides in an agent who has no secondary cause. Papal power has its cause in God, without any secondary causes. Temporal power depends on papal authority, and therefore temporal power depends on a secondary (papal) cause, which excludes temporal power from possessing fullness of power. In contrast, "as there is power within the Church, the Supreme Pontiff has fullness of power, and he can do without a secondary cause whatever he can do with a secondary cause"[92] because he is "God's imitator."[93] In essence, Giles claims that the Roman Pontiff's competences are similar to God's because

> just as, in God, there is fullness of power absolutely, since God can do whatever any agent can do, and whatever He can do by means of any agents He can do without those agents, so

---

89 Heiner Bielefeldt, "Von der päpstlichen Universalherrschaft zur autonomem Bürgerrepublik: Aegidius Romanus, Johannes Quidort von Paris, Dante Alighieri und Marsilius von Padua im Vergleich," *Zeitschrift für Rechtsgeschichte, Kan. Abt.* 72 (1987): 72.
90 James of Viterbo, *De regimine Christiano*, 2.5.
91 Scholz, *Publizistik*, 47–8.
92 Giles of Rome, *On Ecclesiastical Power*, 3.9.
93 Ibid.

the Supreme Pontiff has fullness of power to such extent as there is power in the Church, since whatever any ecclesiastic can do the Supreme Pontiff can do. Hence, he is said to be the ordinary judge everywhere; and whatever the Supreme Pontiff can do by means of any ecclesiastics he can do without them.[94]

His argument on primary and secondary causes is meant to reject any claims that temporal and ecclesiastical power depend similarly and directly on God. Temporal power is only instituted through ecclesiastical negotiation, and all its means and organs must be subordinated to the will of the Church.[95] This argument also rests on the overall assumption of Christian universality in contrast to the diversity of temporal power and government: "Now the ecclesiastical power is more universal than the earthly because the Church herself is said to be Catholic, that is, universal."[96] However, the concept of universality is not limited to the claim of the one truthful religion, which means that whoever seeks salvation has to follow the Church's teaching. Giles's theory allows for diversity in the temporal world but unity and one supreme spiritual power that contains everything. He claims,

> in respect of magnitude and content, the heaven contains all things. So too every power, priestly and royal, heavenly and earthly, is contained in the power of the Supreme Pontiff, so that he can say, 'All power in heaven and on earth is given to me.' For even the material sword, by which earthly power is signified, is contained in the power of the Supreme Pontiff to command even if not to use.[97]

This leads to the question of what this fullness of power actually means if the pope can command the temporal sword but not use it. To phrase it differently, if the pope, rightly or wrongly, claims to possess *plenitudo potestatis* but lacks the temporal means to enforce it, how much power does he actually possess? Here, it is important to note that the Church actually possesses one means to enforce the power she claims, although soon after what Hilary Seton Offler calls "the last struggle,"[98] which is already emerging in this discourse, her means becomes an increasingly blunt sword: excommunication. Following the medieval tradition, Giles notes that the "excommunicated [...] deprived of the communion of the faithful, is deprived of all of the goods he possesses as a faithful man and

---

94 Ibid.
95 Scholz, *Publizistik*, 50.
96 Giles of Rome, *On Ecclesiastical Power*, 2.6.
97 Ibid., 3.10.
98 Hilary Seton Offler, "Empire and Papacy: The Last Struggle," *Transactions of the Royal Historical Society* 6 (1956): 21–47.

among faithful men."⁹⁹ At the first glance, being excluded from the Church and the sacraments does not sound that threatening. However, in medieval and early modern contexts excommunication implies not only spiritual sanctions that may affect one's afterlife but also has serious temporal consequences. Exclusion from the community of the faithful means the return to the pre-legal state of nature. The excommunicated individual is deprived of all his or her rights. For Giles, the deprivation of rights also excludes the excommunicated person from contesting the excommunication because the excommunicated has lost all legal tights and titles. In addition, the Church has extended its jurisdiction more and more to cases that were previously considered solely subject to temporal jurisdiction, which means the ecclesiastical sanctions are not restricted to ecclesiastical matters.¹⁰⁰

Giles's discourse focuses on power where the consequences of excommunication are severe. Technically, the excommunicated person is an outlaw. As such, he or she is not simply deprived of the right to property and other civil rights but also of the right to life. If the excommunicated individual is murdered, the murderer does not have to fear any legal consequences. This situation is somewhat similar to what Muhamed Charfi describes for a Muslim apostate in the modern age. If he "does not come under the jurisdiction of a fundamentalist state, the ulema of Al Azhar denounce him, and members of fundamental groups proceed to execute him on a street corner."¹⁰¹ Even if the violence is not religiously motivated but occurs based on profane reasons, it is nonetheless religiously sanctioned.

In basic terms, James of Viterbo's account agrees with Giles of Rome's. However, he takes a more moderate tone. Additionally, he adds a new perspective by integrating in his theory the hardships caused by tyranny. Contrary to Giles, James accepts legitimacy outside the Church, given that the temporal power is neither Christian nor rules over Christians because "it can be said that the institution of the temporal prince as a prince who is over men has its being from human law, but the institution of the temporal prince as a Christian prince who is over Christian men is from the spiritual power".¹⁰²

This reservation implies that the universality of ecclesiastical power is limited to Christian nations. He also concedes that God had permitted royal power to the people of Israel because they requested it. In this case, James sees royal power as punishment for the Israelites' distrust in God that led

---
99 Giles of Rome, *On Ecclesiastical Power*, 2.12.
100 Homann, "*Posse absolutum versus iusticia*," 239–40.
101 Charfi, *Islam and Liberty*, 52–3.
102 James of Viterbo, *De regimine Christiano*, 2.10 (305).

them to ask for a king.[103] However, the New Testament changes power relationships. As James notes, "in the New Testament the temporal power is placed under the spiritual not only in spiritual things but also in temporal, as being ordered to spiritual things. For this reason, the spiritual power can judge and punish it spiritually and temporally when it uses its power ill by acting against God and the Church."[104]

For James, the invention of Christianity and its union with the political sphere marks a turning point in the Church's attitude towards tyranny. First of all, he sees a direct correlation between tyranny and salvation because "tyranny occurs at the expense of salvation," both the ruler's and his subjects'. The ruler's tyrannical behavior works against salvation, as the subjects are led astray from a virtuous life into sin. Given the severe consequences of ill rule, James argues that the Church should correct and depose the tyrannical ruler because "if secular princes are to be converted from tyranny promptly, the salvation of the people will be better served." To act against tyranny and for salvation, James concludes that there must be an entity that judges temporal power: "By divine law, therefore, the temporal power must be judged by the spiritual." Hence, it is obvious that the temporal power must serve the spiritual power.[105]

James embeds his claim in the history of Christianity. Until the time of Constantine, when Christianity gained official status in the Roman Empire, the Church could not punish tyrants.[106] Even then, the Church was not sufficiently strong and had to be patient. Later, the Church's main concern was the spread of heresies within the Church. Only now "that she is established and strong, she must bring power to bear against rebels and adversaries of the Church, against whom the spiritual power can and must require the aid and service of the faithful power over which it has authority."[107]

Although James's argument is in tone more rational than Giles's, the doctrine that the Roman Pontiff has the right to power over the temporal powers, including the power to excommunicate them, was challenged by temporal rulers and theologians alike.

---

[103] Ibid., 2.10 (283).
[104] Ibid., 2.10 (289).
[105] Ibid., 2.7 (229).
[106] Ibid., 2.8 (247).
[107] Ibid., 2.10 (301).

2.1.2 Religious Justifications of Violence against the Church

The most prominent theological challenge to the papal doctrines of infallibility and *plenitudo potestatis* were written by William of Ockham, a medieval thinker described by Arthur Stephen McGrade as both "unavoidable" and "enigmatic."[108] Indeed, infallibility and *plenitudo potestatis* are central to Ockham's later writings, in which he explores, out of political and theological necessity, the larger theme of papal authority and the relationship between the Church and the Roman Empire. In his discourses, he emphasizes the freedom of the individual and certain natural rights, which he upholds at least for exceptional situations.[109] As noted earlier, the latter aspect is related to scholastic discourses. Originally, Ockham was more attuned to metaphysics, logic, and natural philosophy. However, his experience at Pope John XXII's Avignon court, where he was summoned together with other prominent members of the Franciscan order to defend the Franciscan doctrine of poverty against accusations of heresy, turned him into a political thinker. In Avignon, he found that Pope John was a heretic.[110] Later, Ockham and his fellow Franciscan Michael of Cesena were refugees at Ludwig's court, although they did not flee directly from the papal court to Ludwig's court, indicating that they may not have originally intended to seek Ludwig's protection.[111] Nonetheless, under Ludwig's protection, Ockham wrote fiercely against papal heresy. It is fair to say that his experiences at the papal court in Avignon politicized him. Indeed, his alienation from the *heretical* Church grew so strong that he withdrew himself "from obedience to the Avignonese church" because this church "professes many errors and heresies [and] never ceased from perpetrating the most serious and unspeakable injuries and injustices against the rights and liberties of the faithful."[112] For Ockham, the

---

[108] Arthur Stephen McGrade, *The Political Thought of William of Ockham: Personal and Institutional Principles* (Cambridge: Cambridge University Press, 1974), 1.
[109] Matthias Kaufmann, "Wilhelm von Ockham und Marsilius von Padua: Papstkritiker am Hofe Ludwigs des Bayern," in *Musis et Litteris: Festschrift für Bernhard Rupprecht zum 65. Geburtstag*, ed. Silvia Glaser and Andrea M. Kluxen (München: Fink, 1993), 570.
[110] Takashi Shogimen, "Defending Christian Fellowship: William of Ockham and the Crisis of the Medieval Church," *History of Political Thought* 26, 4 (2005): 608–9. Richard Scholz, *Wilhelm von Ockham als politischer Denker und sein Breviloquium de principatu tyrannico* (Stuttgart: Hirsemann, 1944), 18.
[111] Jürgen Miethke, *De potestate papae: Die päpstliche Amtskompetenz im Widerstreit der politischen Theorie von Thomas von Aquin bis Wilhelm von Ockham* (Tübingen: Mohr Siebeck, 2000), 250.
[112] William of Ockham, *The Power of Emperors and Popes*, trans. and ed. Annabel S. Brett (Bristol: Thoemmes Press, 1998), prologue.

Avignonese church turned things upside down "through unjust excommunications and illicit interdicts:

> [C]atholics are condemned and heretics approved; the innocent are slandered and the impious honoured; the worthy are barred from ecclesiastical honour, benefices and office while the unworthy are promoted; and the humble of the church are afflicted with intolerable burdens, nay reduced to servitude, contrary to the ecclesiastical liberty granted them by God and men.[113]

Like James of Viterbo, he sees heresy in relation to tyranny. In his account, the current Church rules over the faithful tyrannically.[114] In this sense, he reverses James's argument about the tyranny of temporal power that needs to be checked by ecclesiastical authority. For Ockham, the current pope is guilty of

> fornication, the oppression of good men, seizure or detainment of the possessions or rights of others, suppression of the truth, the teaching of heresies, slander of innocents, disturbance of the peace, unprovoked aggression against enemies, partiality, furthering the unworthy and demoting the worthy, simony, pride, avarice, sowing the seeds of discord, theft, lying, tyranny, homicide and things of this kind.[115]

This is Ockham's conclusion in his final work. Before he could come to this conclusion, he needed to answer the contested question of whether the pope can be a heretic. In addition, he needed to answer the question of whether disobeying authorities is disobedience to God. Furthermore, in the case that the pope can be and is a heretic, what actions against a heretical pope, including violent actions, are not simply justified but mandatory? These questions also mark the starting point for Ockham's political thinking.[116]

According to Takashi Shogimen, William's concept of heresy, which is the underlying problem of his theory of resistance to the heretical pope, is a "revolution in the medieval language of heresy." While it is a common medieval assumption that the ability to judge heresy is not only a question of knowledge but also a question of power, William rejects the power aspect of this formulation. For him, definitions of true faith and heresy are problems of a proper interpretation of theological texts, not of power.[117] In this sense, responsibility is re-

---

113 Ibid., chap. 7.
114 Ibid., chap. 15.
115 Ibid., chap. 16
116 McGrade, *The Political Thought of William of Ockham*, 47.
117 Takashi Shogimen, "William of Ockham and Conceptions of Heresy, c. 1250-c.1350," in *Heresy in Transition: Transforming Ideas of Heresy in Medieval and Early Modern Europe*, ed. Ian Hunter, John Christian Laursen, and Cary J. Nederman (Aldershot: Ashgate, 2005), 61, 65–6.

lated to knowledge, not to status.¹¹⁸ In this spirit, he justifies his investigation in his *Discourse of Tyrannical Government:* the pope needs to know how much power and authority he has, and the pope's subjects need to know how much power the pope can rightfully claim over them.¹¹⁹ In the same treatise, Ockham addresses whether obedience to power is mandatory at all times. First, he refers to examples from the Old Testament: "The children of Israel in the desert under Moses resisted many kings, and in the time of the judges they laudably resisted many kings who had permitted power over them, and threw off their yoke." Thus, obedience to power cannot be mandatory at all times, "for although sometimes permitted power is to be obeyed to avoid the power's wrath in case greater evil or danger results, it is nevertheless not to be obeyed for conscience sake. If there were no motive for obedience but its wrath alone, disobedience would be permissible."¹²⁰

The question of papal heresy and the measures that can and must be taken against papal heresy is the theme that runs through the greater part of Ockham's *Dialogus*. Ockham begins with an investigation of whether it is possible for a pope to be a heretic. Thereafter, he discusses whether there is an obligation to resist such a pope and what types of actions should be taken to resist him. Ockham's main target in the *Dialogus* is Pope John XXII, although John is not the only pope that he regards as a heretic.

Ockham argues that "every person not confirmed in grace can fall into sin and consequently can err against the faith."¹²¹ This rule, in a simple syllogism, also applies to the apostles and to the Roman pontiff. Humans can err, and the Roman pontiff is a human; therefore, he can err. Furthermore, every human being capable of using reason can err. Because a pope possesses the capability of reason, he can err in his belief. Thus, he can become a heretic, unless he loses his ability to use reason through illness or age because

> [w]hoever has not been confirmed in faith and has the use of reason can err against the faith; but the pope has not been confirmed in faith because if he were confirmed in

---

118 McGrade, *The Political Thought of William of Ockham*, 69.
119 William of Ockham, *A Short Discourse of Tyrannical Government: Over Things Divine and Human, but Especially Over the Empire and Those Subject to the Empire, Usurped by Some Who Are Called Highest Pontiffs*, ed. Arthur Stephen McGrade, trans. John Kilcullen (Cambridge: Cambridge University Press, 1992), 1.3–4.
120 Ibid., 3.3.
121 William of Ockham, *Dialogus*, I *Dialogus* 5.1, text and trans. John Scott (http://www.britac.ac.uk/pubs/dialogus/t1d51.html).

faith he would be confirmed in faith by some supernatural gift, but no supernatural gift by which he is confirmed in the faith appears to have been conferred on the pope.[122]

Humans can only achieve confirmation in faith through theological virtues (*fides spes et caritas et dona Spiritus Sancti*). According to Ockham, these virtues are occasionally found in a better degree of perfection in other men than in the pope. Consequently, and contrary to Giles of Rome, the pope is not necessarily the most virtuous man, and therefore he can err. Further, because he is no longer a true pope, he can be accused and judged by men.[123] Papal infallibility would only be possible if God had explicitly revealed to the Roman pontiff that he cannot err. However, God has only revealed infallibility to the congregation of the faithful (*congregacio fidelium*), not to the pope. As a pope can contradict himself in questions of faith, as Ockham demonstrates through the example of John XXII, he can also become a heretic.[124] From this, Ockham concludes that the congregation of believers only needs its Christian wisdom to decide what does and what does not correspond to Catholic truth. Therefore, besides God and Christ, the community of the faithful remains the only worldly body able to judge whether a pope is a heretic or not.

The community of the faithful has the capability to judge, but does this also mean that the community of the faithful has the responsibility to act? Ockham discusses this issue from the perspective of works of mercy (*opera misericordie*). Ockham argues that not all *opera misericordie* apply to everyone. For instance, restrictions apply to the commitment to defend someone with armed force.[125] Moreover, while a precept is always obligatory, this does not mean that it is obligatory in all instances. Furthermore, it is possible to defend a person not only with armed force but also in a number of different ways:

> Therefore while certain works of mercy must be afforded to heretics who oppose the catholic faith, nevertheless a defense which might in some fashion result in benefiting heretical wickedness or prejudicing the Christian faith must be completely denied to them and believers must provide the appropriate defense only to Catholics who oppose a heretic pope in support of orthodox belief.[126]

---

122 I *Dialogus*. 5.3.
123 Ockham, *The Power of Emperors and Popes*, chap. 28.
124 I *Dialogus*. 5.3.
125 William of Ockham, I *Dialogus* 6.39, text and trans. George Knysh, August 2002 (revised May 2004), (http://www.britac.ac.uk/pubs/dialogus/t1d6c.html).
126 I *Dialogus* 6.39.

Fighting a heretical pope does not necessarily mean killing the pope. At least, William does not explicitly mention a duty to kill a heretic pope. Nonetheless, whoever does not support those who fight the heretic pope commits a mortal sin; the only excuse not to fight is a person's impotence (*per solam impotentiam excusari*).[127]

For Ockham, however, all rules that should be applied (the exercise of the works of mercy) are logical consequences of the demands of Christian wisdom, accessible to all believers in Christ. For Ockham, not acting would be a disobedience to God and a mortal sin. In the Christian context, however, killing the oppressor, whether a heretic pope or a temporal ruler, does not bring a believer closer to God. Nonetheless, not acting and not supporting those who fight the heretic pope, might result in alienation from God. At the same time, Ockham expects that those who actively fight a heretic pope are sound and secure in their faith and absolute in their Catholic truth.[128] Killing, however, is not categorically excluded, although it is only a last resort if it is not possible to resist a force in other ways: "Again, it is permitted to anyone to resist force with force without the authority of the ruler or judge [...]. But sometimes force cannot be resisted unless the attacker is killed, therefore in that case it is permitted to wage at least a private war without the ruler's authority." [129]

The obligation to fight and resist a heretic pope and his supporters may differ depending on a person's status. However, whoever does not resist consents with the heretical pope (*ergo qui non resistit, consensit*). In essence, Ockham advocates "popular action to remove a heretical pope."[130] Ockham compares resistance to a heretic pope with resisting the devil; the heretic pope he calls "the devil's main general."[131] Because the pope's heresy can easily destroy the eternal lives of many, he must be fought with much more vigor than any ordinary heretic. Preachers and doctors of theology are supposed to resist a heretical pope by attacking the pope's heretical doctrines—despite or rather because of the intellectual climate of *angst* the heretical pope has produced.[132] Indeed, Ockham considers it the "official duty of preachers and doctors to resist the treachery

---

127 Ibid., 6.39.
128 McGrade, *The Political Thought of William of Ockham*, 65.
129 William of Ockham, *Dialogus*, Part 1, Book 7, chapters 42–51, ed. George Knysh (http://www.britac.ac.uk/pubs/dialogus/t1d742.html), I *Dialogus*, 7.45.
130 Takashi Shogimen, *Ockham and Political Discourse in the Late Middle Ages* (Cambridge: Cambridge University Press, 2007), 153.
131 William of Ockham, *Dialogus*, Part 1, Book 7, chapters 24–34, ed. George Knysh (http://www.britac.ac.uk/pubs/dialogus/RevRev1 %20Dial.%207.24–34.pdf), I *Dialogus* 7.30. I *Dialogus*, 7.43.
132 I *Dialogus*, 7.42. Ockham, *The Power of Emperors and Popes*, 15.

of a heretic pope attempting to corrupt the faith." If they fail in their duty despite having the power to resist the pope, then they are worthy of condemnation and guilty of tacitly agreeing with and supporting the heretical pope.[133]

The main responsibly for fighting and resisting the heretic pope lies with kings and princes, particularly the Roman emperor. If these individuals support a heretical pope despite being aware of his heresy, then their sin is graver than the sin of an ordinary man who supports a heretic pope, as they have the physical means and authority to resist such a pope. While Ockham compares the pope's heresy to a public crime and everybody has the responsibility to fight it, the main responsibility rests with kings and princes:

> Therefore everybody is obligated to resist a heretic pope as someone who is committing a public crime. And thus kings and princes have the function of opposing a heretic pope. [...] For it is the task of kings and princes to exercise temporal authority against a heretic pope, unless there be some among them who wish to submit voluntarily to martyrdom by divine inspiration.[134]

Unanimous resistance of heretical doctrines from the beginning, including from cardinals and preachers, would make it much more difficult for papal heresy to emerge, and after its emergence, would make it much easier to root out.[135] Nonetheless, Ockham places the main responsibility with the temporal powers, most prominently with the Roman emperor, because heretic popes have caused a great deal of harm to the Roman Empire. However, these popes also harm ordinary people, both with respect to their salvation as believers and in their temporal lives. A heretic pope's impact on people's temporal lives might be as severe as the consequences for their afterlives.

Ockham argues that the people have rights and liberties; they possess these rights and liberties through their human nature and have enjoyed them even before the incarnation of Christ (as infidels); no one has the right to take these rights and liberties away from them against their will. Ockham accuses the heretic pope of unjustly and illicitly taking these rights away from the people. In Ockham's view, the people are now worse off than they were as infidels.[136] Although Ockham is by no means the first medieval thinker to introduce moral-legal language, he turns a theological discourse into a discourse of legal

---

133 I *Dialogus*, 7.46.
134 William of Ockham, *Dialogus*, Part 1, Book 7, chapter 65–73, ed. George Knysh (http://www.britac.ac.uk/pubs/dialogus/t1d765.html), I *Dialogus* 7.69.
135 I *Dialogus*, 7.70.
136 Ockham, *The Power of Emperors and Popes*, chap. 9.

rights.¹³⁷ The people, whether they are ordinary people or representatives of temporal authority, do not simply have the religious duty to resist and fight a heretic pope, if necessary with violent force. They also have the right to defend the rights that the pope has taken away. In this sense, Ockham's religious justification for violent actions against a heretic pope moves into a secular argument about individual rights. This is not surprising because as Richard Scholz notes, the scholastic theology of Ockham's time is Weltanschauung. However, Ockham's Weltanschauung is not secularized in any modern sense, as he aims to discover God's will in the world.¹³⁸

2.1.3 Religious Justifications for Protesting against (Secular) Authorities

The correlation between rights and duties was not fully developed until the thirteenth or early fourteenth century. The twelfth century featured duty bound arguments that forcefully justify resisting and killing tyrannical rulers. Previous discourses primarily focused on the aspect of duty, although at a more philosophical level duties and rights are certainly interrelated, even if the language of rights is not used. However, these rights are not necessarily legal rights that can be enforced through legal institutions. This problem is apparent in premodern societies. Although the ruler's power is not absolute, legal measures against the abuse of power do not exist. The Christian Middle Ages' most common response to this dilemma is to consider tyranny as divine punishment or to appeal to patience and tolerance towards a (mild) tyrant. These approaches are based on the thinking that an excessively harsh response to the tyrant that leads to his death will likely result in a worse tyrant taking his place.¹³⁹ While divine punishment and patience are predominant in medieval Christian thought, some accounts allow for the violent overthrow of tyrannical rulers. The most prominent theorist of violent overthrow and tyrannicide is John of Salisbury, writing in the twelfth century.¹⁴⁰ The discussion of John's *Policraticus* will be fol-

---

137 Brian Tierney, *The Idea of Natural Rights: Studies on Natural Rights, Natural Law, 1150–1624* (Grand Rapits: Eerdmans, 2001), 36.
138 Scholz, *Wilhelm von Ockham als politischer Denker*, 1, 23.
139 Ptolemy of Lucca, *On the Government of Rulers De Regimine Principum: With Portions Attributed to Thomas Aquinas,* trans. James M. Blythe (Philadelphia: University of Pennsylvania Press, 1997), 3.7.3. Nico Patrick Swartz, "Thomas Aquinas: On Law, Tyranny and Resistance," *Acta Theologica* 30, no. 1 (2010): 153.
140 The discussion of John of Salisbury relies in part on Bettina Koch, "Johannes von Salisbury und die Nizari Ismailiten unter Terrorismusverdacht: Zur kritischen Bewertung eines Aspekts in

lowed by an analysis of William of Pagula's *Speculum Regis Edwardi*. However, the fourteenth century English canonist is less prominent than John of Salisbury's *Policraticus*, a work that was soon translated into vernacular and has inspired other works such as Christine de Pizan's *Book of the Body Politic*. Compared to John's *Policraticus*, William of Pagula's *Speculum Regis Edwardi* had and still has a rather shadowy existence in the history of political ideas. William's work is not disregarded because of its quality, but rather because of the unknown authorship of the *Speculum Regis Edwardi* and the absence of a modern edition and translation. Joseph Moisant, the editor of the 1891 Latin edition, assumed that Simon Islip was the speculum's author.[141] Since Leonard Boyle's research on the *Speculum Regis Edwardi*, the author of this mirror for princes has been identified as William of Pagula.[142] In their justifications of the use of violence against tyrannical rule, John's *Policraticus* and William's *Speculum Regis Edwardi* supplement each other.

While John of Salisbury's name is usually associated with the idea of tyrannicide, no concrete guidelines for tyrannicide are found in John's *Policraticus*. For quite some time, scholars have even disputed whether John's work even includes a conclusive theory of tyrannicide. Some argued that John only claims tyrants have frequently been slain throughout history. More recently, Cary J. Nederman, the leading expert on John of Salisbury, has dispelled all doubts on the existence of a conclusive theory of tyrannicide.[143] Therefore, the following analysis is deeply indebted to Cary Nederman's work on John of Salisbury.

Similar to James of Viterbo and William of Ockham, John of Salisbury's theory is embedded in a discourse on tyranny or unjust rule. However, John does not present his theory of tyrannicide in a single and conclusive chapter. Rather, as it is common for medieval treatises, the parts of the tyrannicide puzzle are scattered throughout numerous chapters. The quintessence of his thoughts is

---

der aktuellen Terrorismusdebatte," *Zeitschrift für Rechtsphilosophie* 11,2 (2013): 18–38. Bettina Koch, "Yesterday's Tyrannicide, Today's Terrorist? Historic Acts of 'Terror' in Islam and in the West in Light of the Contemporary Debates on Terrorism," in *International Relations, Culture and Global Finance*, ed. Akis Kalaitzidis (Athens: ATINER, 2011), 111–126.

141 *De speculo regis Edwardi III, seu tractatu quem de mala regni administratione conscripsit Simon Islip, cum utraque ejusdem recensione manuscripta nunc primum edita*, ed. Joseph Moisant (Paris: Alphonsum Picard, 1891).

142 Leonard E. Boyle, "The *Oculus Sacerdotis* and Some Other Works of William of Pagula," *Transactions of the Royal Historical Society*, 5th series, 5 (1955), 98–9; 107–8 and Leonard E. Boyle, "William of Pagula and the *Speculum Regis Edwardi III*," *Mediaeval Studies* 32 (1970), 329–36.

143 Cary J. Nederman, "A Duty to Kill: John of Salisbury's Theory of Tyrannicide," *The Review of Politics* 50 (1988): 365–389, esp. 366.

found in one of the shorter chapters: "whom it is permitted to flatter, it is permitted to slay."[144]

John distinguishes private, priestly, and public tyrants, and we are mostly concerned with the public tyrant because he is the object of tyrannicide. While John briefly refers to the existence of the other types of tyrants, his typology is by no means as elaborate as that of Bartolus of Sassoferrato, the prominent fourteenth century civilian, although Bartolus never develops a conclusive theory of tyrannical rule.[145] John does not discuss the priestly or private tyrants any further, but concentrates on the public tyrant. John defines the public tyrant as "one who oppresses the people by violent domination, just as the prince is one who rules by the laws."[146] He is the counterpart to the prince and dominates through violence, while the prince is responsible for the "punishment of violence."[147] John describes the prince as the "image on earth of the divine majesty" who "ought to imagine himself permitted to do nothing which is inconsistent with the equity of justice."[148] The prince rules according to law, which is "a gift of God, the likeness of equity, the norm of justice, the image of the divine will, [and] the custodian of security."[149] In contrast, the tyrant believes that he is absolved from God's law.[150] In keeping with the medieval tradition, John's prince is not the author or inventor of human law. Rather, because all law already exists through God and needs to be discovered through human wisdom, the prince is the "law-finder." The fact that the ruler installs and enforces the law, however, does not mean that he is released from the law. He is subject to God, from whom he receives his legitimacy; he is bound to divine law and equity.[151] Consequently, the prince's rule should mirror divine justice and equity. His duty is "the enforcement of the law and the protection of all sections of the com-

---

144 John of Salisbury, *Policraticus: Of the Frivolities of Courtiers and the Footprints of Philosophers*, ed. and trans. Cary J. Nederman (Cambridge: Cambridge University Press, 1990), 3.15.
145 Bartolo da Sassoferrato, *De tyranno*, in Diego Quaglioni, *Politica e diritto nel Trecento Italiano: Il "De Tyranno" di Bartolo da Sassoferrato (1314–1357), con L'edizione crittica dei trattati "De Guelphis et Gebellinis," "De regimine civitatis" e "De tyranno"* (Firenze: Olschki, 1983), 212. Maurice H. Keen, "The Political Thought of the Fourteenth-Century Civilians," in *Trends in Medieval Political Thought*, ed. Beryl Smalley (Oxford: Blackwell, 1965), 123.
146 John of Salisbury, *Policraticus*, 8.17.
147 Ibid.
148 Ibid., 4.1.
149 Ibid. 8.17.
150 Cary J. Nederman and Cathrine Campbell, "Priests, Kings, and Tyrants: Spiritual and Temporal Power in John of Salisbury's *Policraticus*." *Speculum* 66 (1991): 582.
151 John of Salisbury, *Policraticus*, 4.4; 4.6.

munity."¹⁵² In contrast, the public tyrant is destructive to all parts of society. John describes tyranny as more than a public crime because it disarms the law. It is usurpation that suppresses justice and "places the laws beneath [the tyrant's] will."¹⁵³ For John, tyranny is treason, not only against the common good but also against divine justice and even against God himself.

Considering all, or at least most, of John's references to tyrannicide, they sum up to a consistent theory of tyrannicide. The first time that John discusses the slaying of a tyrant, it appears in the context of flattery. As John neither knows nor introduces any institutional means for controlling, and if necessary, correcting a prince, the only way to correct him is through speech. In this context, John reveals himself as a very early advocate of freedom of speech, an idea that Ockham has pushed even further.¹⁵⁴ For John, it is the people's and particularly the honest man's duty to criticize the prince and correct him if signs of tyranny emerge. For John, the freedom to state one's opinion, especially in front of the prince, is an expression of liberty and respect for others.¹⁵⁵ In contrast, it is not possible to speak frankly or freely to a tyrant without putting one's life or one's fellows' well-being at risk. If the prince has become a tyrant, then the people's liberty is destroyed. Tyranny eliminates the possibility and advantages of speaking one's opinions freely. While a moral obligation exists to speak the truth to a friend and to the just prince because doing otherwise may jeopardize the friend's or the commonwealth's well-being, this obligation does not exist in the presence of tyrants. This distinction leads to John's famous statement: "[i]t is not permitted to flatter a friend, but it is permitted to delight the ears of a tyrant. For in fact him whom it is permitted to flatter, it is permitted to slay."¹⁵⁶ John's reasoning in this statement is first that if all attempts to correct the ruler have been unsuccessful, flattery becomes permissible to protect the people and the commonwealth from greater harm. Second, John supports his claim through numerous historic and biblical examples. For him, it is evident that all nations and all peoples consider tyranny harmful and consider its punishment as permitted.¹⁵⁷ Moreover, John considers the slaying of a tyrant to be in keeping with

---

152 Cary J. Nederman, *John of Salisbury* (Tempe: Arizona Center for Medieval and Renaissance Studies, 2005), 60.
153 John of Salisbury, *Policraticus*, 3.15.
154 Sharon Kaye, "There's No Such Thing as Heresy (And It's a Good Thing, Too): William of Ockham of Freedom of Speech," *The Journal of Political Philosophy* 6, no. 1 (1998): 41–52.
155 Cary J. Nederman, *Lineages of European Political Thought: Explorations Along the Medieval/Modern Divide from John of Salisbury to Hegel* (Washington, D.C.: The Catholic University Press, 2009), 67.
156 John of Salisbury, *Policraticus*, 3.15.
157 Ibid., 8.21.

both divine and human law.¹⁵⁸ While for John the slaying of the tyrant is covered by law, any "malice planned against the head [prince] and members of the corporate community is a crime of the utmost seriousness and approaches sacrilege."¹⁵⁹ Even though he also states that "[w]ickedness is always punished by the Lord; sometimes He uses His own sword, and sometimes He uses a sort of human sword,"¹⁶⁰ this does not mean that the tyrannicide is simply God's tool. Rather, for John, tyrannicide is a public duty because "whoever does not prosecute [the tyrant] transgresses against himself and against the whole body of the earthly republic."¹⁶¹ In other words, John assigns an obligation to every individual member of the community to protect the commonwealth against tyranny, if necessary through tyrannicide.¹⁶²

One of the interesting aspects of John's theory, although not uncommon for a medieval thinker, is his attempt to argue both philosophically and theologically, with the result that he provides a philosophical and theological justification for tyrannicide. Similarly typical for a medieval theorist, the philosophical and theological arguments are partially merged. The tyrannicide acts both to fulfil a public duty and to fulfil God's will. The duality of John's argument is also reflected in his statement that "it is just for public tyrants to be killed and the people to be liberated for obedience to God." He goes on to call slaying tyrants "an act of piety."¹⁶³ This passage fits into John's general concept that tyranny implies the corruption of the whole body politic. For John, corruption is an unavoidable consequence of tyranny. However, another implication of this line of thinking should be stressed. Because liberating the people from tyranny allows for obedience to God, John suggests that a people cannot live in obedience to God if they do not pursue tyrannicide. This assertion is in keeping with John's assumption that a tyrant can be sent as divine punishment. For John, tyrants can act as "ministers of God" and punish a people for its sins and hypocrisies. This idea leads him to the apparently paradoxical statement that "even the power of tyrants is in a certain way good, yet nothing is worse than tyranny."¹⁶⁴ John explains this statement by stating that "[a]ll power is good since it exists only from Him from whom everything good and only good exists. Yet occasionally power

---

158 Ibid., 8.17.
159 Ibid., 6.25.
160 Ibid., 8.21.
161 Ibid., 3.15.
162 Nederman, "A Duty to Kill," 369.
163 John of Salisbury, *Policraticus*, 8.20.
164 Ibid., 8.18.

is not good, but bad, for the person who uses it or suffers under it, although it is good in general, created by Him who uses our wickedness for goodness."[165]

Because all power is from God, it needs to be used in accordance with divine justice. If it is not used in accordance with the divine principles of justice, then tyrannicide is justified. The responsibility to liberate the people from tyranny rests with the just person in the commonwealth, and this responsibility is assumed to be independent of whether the tyrant is a minister of God or an ordinary tyrant who does not act according to God's will. The underlying logic is that if the tyrannicide leads to an opportunity to free the people, then the people have been sufficiently punished by God. Thus, while God might punish his people with tyranny, he also supports their liberation after they have accepted their punishment and have overcome their corruption.

Here, it is important to note that John of Salisbury assumes not only that each individual can act on behalf of the whole body politic but also that each individual has the potential for self-improvement and self-perfection to reach virtue and reason.[166]

Although John does not state this explicitly, he assumes that a just commonwealth in which the believer can live a life in obedience to God is only possible within a just commonwealth that is ordered in accordance with divine justice. A similar idea expressed in a more radical form is also a fundamental component of modern Islamist thought. However, as John is still a medieval thinker, he does not ignore the dominant approach of the time to tyranny, namely to wait patiently, pray to God, and await God's clemency to deliver freedom from oppression. For John, "the sins of transgressors are the strength of tyrants."[167] This statement implies that a pious life in obedience to God is the best protection against tyranny and that it would make the use of violence unnecessary.

In his discussion of tyranny and corruption, John primarily emphasizes the disturbance to the people's security and their subsistence. While these disturbances can be primarily read as concrete manifestations of violations of the overarching principle of divine justice, they also suggest the existence of fundamental rights that belong to all people, anticipating Henry Shue's concept of basic rights because "without security and subsistence one is helpless, and consequently one may also be helpless to protect whatever can be protected only on the risk of security and subsistence."[168] While these two rights are already foreshadowed in John of Salisbury's *Policraticus* and play a significant role in de-

---

165 Ibid.
166 Ibid., 6.29.
167 Ibid., 8.20.
168 Shue, *Basic Rights*, 30. Koch, "Johannes von Salisbury und die Nizari Ismailiten," 26.

scribing the manifestation of tyranny, they are even more prominent in William of Pagula's *Speculum Regis Edwardi*.[169]

William of Pagula's discourses, written in the 1330s, emphasized subjects' rights. Although he does not use a rights-based language, his language remains duty-bound. While John of Salisbury refers to the image of a totally corrupt regime, William of Pagula focusses on a more particular problem, namely the transgression of subjects' economic rights, which directly translates into a right to subsistence. Typical for a medieval *speculum regis*, he can only appeal to the king's good will by asking him to change his behavior.

One of William's main concerns is "the right of the king and his immediate family to provide for them when touring the realm by confiscating local goods or purchasing them at a fixed, non-negotiable price."[170] The English Parliament granted the crown the right to purchase goods for the king's household, and the Parliament renewed this right in 1331. William regards this practice as unjust.[171] The underlying problem is a common one in medieval society. If the king exercises his rule by traveling the country, then the people have to carry the burden of nourishing the king and his entourage. In other words, the king lives off his lands and his subjects. The king's entourage usually nourished itself by buying or taking from the people. Although this was common practice and was even sanctioned by the parliament, William opposes this practice and thought that it could even jeopardize the king's legitimacy. William's argument is rooted in Christian virtues, using language typical of a medieval Christian *speculum regis*. While the treatises are essentially about the king's and his en-

---

169 William of Pagula, *Mirror of King Edward III*, in *Political Thought in Early Fourteenth-Century England: Treatises by Walter of Milimete, William of Pagula, and William of Ockham*, ed. and trans. Cary J. Nederman (Tempe: Arizona Studies for Medieval and Renaissance Studies, 2002), 73–139. William's mirror for princes exists in two versions. I refer to the first version of William's *Mirror of King Edward III* as A and to the second one as B. Version A is referred to by numbered paragraphs; version B by chapters and numbered paragraphs. The discussion of William of Pagula is deeply indebted to Cary J. Nederman, "Property and Protest: Political Theory and Subjective Rights in Fourteenth-Century England," *The Review of Politics* 58 (1996), 323–433 and Cary J. Nederman, "The Monarch and the Market Place: Economic Policy and Royal Finance in William of Pagula's *Speculum Regis Edward III*," *History of Political Economy* 33 (2001): 51–69. I wish to thank Cary Nederman for his introduction to William of Pagula's work. The following outline is also based on Koch, "A Medieval Muslim-Christian Lesson on Political and Economic Liberalization," 73–88.
170 Cary J. Nederman, "Introduction to the *Mirror of King Edward III*," in *Political Thought in Early Fourteenth-Century England*, 64.
171 Ibid., 65.

tourage's transgression of subjects' rights, the language refers to the king's neglected duties towards his realm and towards his subjects.

However, to make a case about neglected duties, it is necessary to outline the purpose of governments and the king's duties. William primarily stresses three duties of the king, with all others derived from these three. First, the king should govern "to the honor of God," second to "the utility of the kingdom," and third "in order to acquire the love of the people." He continues by stating that

> the justice of the king is the peace of the people, the defense of the fatherland, the freedom of the masses, the defense of the race, the care of the sick, the joy of all, the solace of the pauper, the inheritance of sons, and the hope for one's own blessedness in the future, and the war with the vices.[172]

Like John of Salisbury, William regards justice as an imitation of God. The king has to cultivate justice and has to do what is right. However, in contrast to many other medieval writers, he comes to his point in a relatively straightforward manner. He does this in explicitly biblical language. This approach, although typical of the genre, limits William to the language of "you shall" and "you shall not," although he also at least occasionally invokes ancient philosophy, the *Magna Carta*, and common law. Interestingly, he does not fully exploit the power of the *Magna Carta*. Instead of referring explicitly to particular articles in the *Magna Carta* that would support his claim, he only refers to this legal document in general terms. The only exception is one reference to the *Magna Carta* that concerns the Church's liberties and property.[173] If the king or someone in the king's name takes property from the Church, he does injustice. Taking from the Church or the people by force is an act of injustice. If the king's servants and other members of his household commit such injustices and the king refuses to do anything about it, he is guilty of injustice himself.[174] A similar concept is also fundamental to John of Salisbury's thought. However, William adds that the king violates not only divine justice but also the oath he swore upon his coronation. William continues by asking, "[b]ut how is either justice or equity these days to buy something for a lesser price than the seller wishes to sell them for, and contrary to consent, when buying and selling are fixed by the law of peoples?"[175]

---

[172] William of Pagula, *Mirror of Kind Edward III*, A.1 (73). In B.2.2 (106), William emphasizes the king's need for "knowledge, understanding, and foresight."
[173] *Mirror of Kind Edward III*, A.4 (78).
[174] Ibid., A.3–4 (76–7).
[175] Ibid., A.1 (74).

For William, the king and his household rob the people not only by taking from them by force but also by taking from them by force at a lower than the appropriate price, if they want to sell at all. If the king confiscates goods or allows for their confiscation, he commits another injustice. William supports his claim by referencing Augustine, who equates this deed not only with injustice, but with an evil deed. As long as the king does not correct such misdeeds, the king approves this misbehavior.[176] In essence, William is concerned about the people's subsistence. Members of the king's household confiscate goods by force. If they pay for the goods they take, either they do not pay the appropriate price or their payment is delayed. For William, such behavior qualifies as robbery. As a consequence, the people are deprived of their livelihood.[177]

To illustrate the consequences of these misdeeds, William exemplifies them. He narrates the story of a poor man who had to sell an ox on a certain day for a particular price to pay his debts that were due on the same day. If he could not pay his debts, he was in jeopardy of losing his land. Members of the king's household confiscated the ox without pay. As a consequence, the man was deprived of his ox, his land, and the ability to support himself.[178] If the people's crops are taken away, they cannot cultivate their land.[179] Although both versions of William's *Speculum Regis Edwardi* are relatively short, William narrates numerous examples of the king's entourage's misdeeds. In another example, members of the king's household took a hen from an old woman. Although they paid for the hen, the woman did not want to sell, particularly not for a low price. Even if the transaction was against the woman's will, if she was paid the regular price then she could have bought a new hen. With the hen "she could have four or five eggs to maintain herself and her children."[180]

However, taking goods by force is not William's only issue. He also accuses the king and members of his household of depriving the people of their property and livelihood through forced labor. If members of the king's household "seize men and horses working around the fields, and animals that plough the earth and carry seed to the field, so that the men and the animals work two or three days in your [the king's] service, receiving nothing for the work."[181]

---

176 Ibid., A.3 (75–6.). Here, William refers not only to the habit of taking goods against the owner's will, but also to the habit of taking more than is needed.
177 Ibid., A.12 (84); B.5.11 (114).
178 Ibid., A.14 (86).
179 Ibid., A.9 (82).
180 Ibid., B.12.43 (131).
181 Ibid., B.3.5 (108).

Contrary to doing justice to the freedom of the masses, the peasants are forced to work without pay, they are robbed of their just wages, and they are deprived of their freedom because they are forced into temporary slavery. The freedom of the masses is jeopardized.[182] In essence, William addresses three of Henry Shue's main issues (security, subsistence, and freedom of movement), although not the fourth, the freedom to participate. Adjusting his argument to a hierarchical society that is not based on the concept of equal opportunity and individual freedom, William also accuses the king of violating Ronald Dworkin's main concerns. The king does not treat his people with "concern and respect" and he "constrain[s] liberty on the ground that one citizen's conception of the good life of one group is nobler and superior to another's."[183] The king is of course considered superior and more noble, but scaled down to fourteenth century realities, the king is supposed to treat the people with respect and concern rather than sacrificing the peasants' livelihood for his own well-being. However, through forced labor, the King deprives the peasants of their property and their ability to earn a profit. Whenever they are forced to cultivate the king's land, they cannot cultivate their own fields. In addition to being robbed of their wages, they may lose their crops because of being unable to bring in their harvest.

Through these and other examples, William illustrates how the king neglects his duties and violates the people's rights to their property, whether property is understood as material goods or labor, the only way for a peasant to gain property and earn a living. Although Parliament legitimized the habit of taking goods from the people by force, William views this practice as a violation of common law. However, William can do little more than beg the king to change this permanent practice of abusing the people's rights. Despite the fact that William has no power to force the king into changing his and his household's actions, he is explicit about the consequences: "If anybody does it, he will be hanged. It is better that someone should be hanged for crime than that he should be sunk into hell."[184]

William can only threaten the king with hellfire if he refuses to put an end to the misdeeds and injustices that occur in his realm. However, William goes some steps further. He threatens the king with other consequences. He writes that instead of acquiring the love of the people, he acquires their fear. Whenever they anticipate the king's arrival, they expect plunder and become distressed. They hide their goods or even prefer to consume them to avoid their seizure. The peo-

---

182 Ibid.
183 Dworkin, *Taking Rights Seriously*, 273.
184 *Mirror of Kind Edward III*, A.27 (93).

ple become distrustful and the king can no longer rely on them.[185] William even threatens the king by writing that continuing to disrespect and violate the people's rights and failing to correct the apparent disorder of his realm could jeopardize his kingdom.[186]

Combining worldly and religious arguments, William first refers to Edward's father's fate, who lost his realm, and then narrates other examples from history. He encourages Edward to follow the example of St. Edward who "conquer[ed] the Kingdom of Norway [...] with the sword of sanctity and with the arms of justice."[187] The conclusion of this argument is that if Edward does not correct his and his household's actions, then his kingdom is in jeopardy because the people have two interdependent options. The first option is the predominant pattern in medieval thought that also lingers in John of Salisbury's *Policraticus*. The people may cry to God for help. William predicts that God will hear the people's lament and bring help. Even if the people do no more than cry and pray to God, eventually they will be freed from their burden. However, the people can do more than just cry and hope for divine help. If the king's commands are against God's precepts, then they have the duty to resist them: "For in these things that are against the precept of God, one must not obey, but rather resist, the king, and he who does this obtains reward for himself."[188]

For William, the violation of the people's rights is a violation of God's commands. Thus, if the people resist the king, their resistance is justified through divine law. He supplements his divine law argument with some considerations based on common law, although his justifications for (violent) resistance of the king remain primarily religious. Based on common law, William vindicates the people's right to rise up and take another king. However, this is only a realistic option if an alternative leader is available who could replace the current king. William stresses that "[t]he people are not of one mind with you, although they seem to be of one body with you, and indeed, if they had another head, they would rise against you, just as they did against your father, and then, in truth, you will not have a multitude of people with you."[189]

If the people rebel against the king and accept another ruler, the people do not become free to participate. Their right to rebel is limited to the overthrow of the existing regime that abuses their rights. As soon as the new power is established, their right to participate ceases. Although William infuses his argument

---

185 Ibid., B.4.6 (109).
186 Ibid., B.11.37 (128).
187 Ibid., A.40 (99).
188 Ibid., A.32 (94).
189 Ibid., A.11 (83–4).

with some common law, his claim rests primarily on divine justice, which the king has disturbed. Note that William's discussion centers on the rather profane rights of subsistence, security, and the right to property. However, William renders the violation of these rights into a discourse on the violation of divine justice. As a result, Christianity affords the moral right to resist these injustices, turning a problem of socio-economic justice into a religious problem that is fought in religious language. Essentially, the problem that William of Pagula addresses displays some parallels to William of Ockham's claim. For Ockham, although the faithful's afterlife is at the center of his discourse, he is similarly disturbed about the abuse of the faithful's rights, prominently including the right to property. In Ockham's case the pope disturbs these rights, while in William of Pagula's *Speculum Regis Edwardi* these rights are disturbed by the English king.

2.2 Legitimizing Violence in the Classic/Premodern Islamic Traditions

The medieval Christian tradition is perceived as being rich in theoretical discourses legitimizing violence and counter-violence. However, we have seen that in accordance with the doctrine that whoever disobeys an authority is disobedient to God, the dominant discourse whenever counter-violence is concerned is one of obedience. For this reason, even crusading against Christian heretics could be justified because it could be seen as reactive warfare against rebels against Christ.[190] Nonetheless, the existence of a dominant discourse on obedience does not mean that counter-discourses do not exist. The same is true for the Islamic context, although with a different focus. For decades, the scholarly discussion on medieval Islamic thought highlighted the absence of any theories of resistance or counter-violence in the medieval Islamic tradition.[191] Yet, this view is based entirely on the study of orthodox texts in the Sunni tradition. More recently, Khaled Abou el Fadl has challenged this view. Abou el Fadl is critical of

---

190 Riley-Smith, *The Crusades, Christianity, and Islam*, 15.
191 Erwin I. J. Rosenthal, *Political Thought in Medieval Islam: An Introductory Outline* (Cambridge: Cambridge University Press, 1962). Ann K. S. Lambton, *State and Government in Medieval Islam: An Introduction to the Study of Islamic Political Theory: The Jurists* (Oxford: Oxford University Press, 1981).

scholars who have written on the topic of rebellion for their neglect of important texts.[192]

However, the emphasis on the orthodox "doctrine" of obedience (rather than on rebellion) is not without merit, as it reflects one of the chief differences between Christianity and Islam, at least as far as the historical development of the two religions is concerned. As discussed before, Christianity did not associate itself with power for approximately the first 300 years of its existence. During this period, Christians were subject to persecution. In contrast, while the first Muslim community under Muhammad cannot be called an Islamic state, at least from the perspective of political science, Islam and power have been associated from early on. Moreover, the history of early Islam is overshadowed by strife and rivalry between the different sects or branches of Islam that emerged soon after Muhammad's death. After the death of the third caliph, this conflict, known as *fitna* or the great discord, was fought, as Michael Bonner notes, "over leadership, morality, and the allocation of resources."[193] The experience of civil war-like strife has certainly affected the greater emphasis on obedience. At the same time, the (ongoing) conflicts between members of the different branches of Islam resulted in a desire for teachings legitimizing (violent) action against the other, independently of whether the conflict has a predominantly religious origin or whether it is fought over similar material and power related issues as associated with the *fitna*.

Thinking more generally about opposition in the Islamic context, it is usually associated with Shi'ism or versions of it. Although Hamid Dabashi calls Shi'ism "a revolutionary faith," he primarily associates the revolutionary impetus with Ali, Imam Hossein, and the *Kharijites* in the early history of Islam, and with the prerevolutionary Iran of the 1970s.[194] While the *Kharijites* are and remain related to a violent revolutionary approach, most accounts of the *Kharijites* were written by their opponents. One of the earliest refutations of *Kharijite* extremists was written by Salim Ibn Dhakwan, written in the late seventh century.[195] However, the main problem is the lack of accounts from the opposition groups themselves. Accounts from the hegemonic discourse are available, but

---

[192] Abou el Fadl, *Rebellion and Violence in Islamic Law*, 15–21. Abou el Fadl, however, argues mainly against Aziz al-Azmeh's *Muslim Kingship: Power and the Sacred in Muslim, Christian, and Pagan Politics* (London: I.B. Tauris, 1997).
[193] Michael David Bonner, *Jihad in Islamic History: Doctrines and Practices* (Princeton: Princeton University Press, 2006), 120.
[194] Hamid Dabashi, *Shi'ism: A Religion of Protest* (Cambridge: Belknap Press, 2011), 47–72.
[195] Patricia Crone and Fritz Zimmermann, *The Epistle of Sālim Ibn Dhakwān* (Oxford: Oxford University Press, 2001).

only very few if any counter-hegemonic texts are available that give us a clear idea of the rebellious groups from their own perspective. While it is possible to reconstruct some of the ideas and motivations of the counter-hegemonic group from the hegemonic discourse, the same reservations expressed by Herbert Grundmann for the study of Christian heresies apply here: uncritical assessment of the available "orthodox" texts could lead to an acceptance of the orthodox interpretations of the time.[196]

As far as counter discourses are concerned, the following outline relies primarily on scholarly reconstructions (here, Khaled Abou el Fadl's discussion of Shiʻi legal sources is extremely insightful). These scholarly reconstructions of ideas are supplemented by an against-the-grain reading of "orthodox" texts. Before approaching counter-hegemonic discourses, this chapter discusses hegemonic discourses from the Sunni tradition. The main emphasis of this discussion is on the writings of Nizam al-Mulk and Ibn Taymiyya. While the latter author was not necessarily mainstream in his own time, his relevance in modern Islamist discourses and, as noted by Georges Tamer, his current status as "perhaps the most influential author in Muslim conservative circles," justifies a fuller discussion of his ideas on the legitimization of violence.[197] Given the significance of the concept of *jihad* in Islam and its relevance for religiously sanctioned violence, this chapter begins with a brief and by no means comprehensive analysis of concepts of *jihad* in classic and premodern Islam.

2.2.1 Concept(s) of Jihad

As stated earlier, *jihad* is one of the key concepts in Islam related to the sanctioned use of violence and warfare, if not *the* key concept. As David Cook notes,

> [a]mong Muslims who acknowledge the association of jihad with warfare, most would define the term as warfare authorized by a legitimate representative of the Muslim community for the sake of an issue that is universally, or nearly universally, acknowledged to be of critical importance for the entire community against an admitted enemy of Islam.[198]

---

196 Grundmann, "Der Typus des Ketzers," 314.
197 Georges Tamer, "The Curse of Philosophy: Ibn Taymiyya as Philosopher in Contemporary Islamic Thought," in *Islamic Theology and Law: Debating Ibn Taymiyya and Ibn Qayyim al-Jawyiyya*, ed. Birgit Krawietz and Georges Tamer (Berlin: De Gruyter, 2013), 342.
198 David Cook, *Understanding Jihad* (Berkeley: University of California Press, 2005), 3.

However, this statement resembles some of the key features that were discussed in the context of justifying the Crusades. In this sense, *jihad* refers to warfare against the enemy of a community defined in religious terms and authorized by a legitimate (religious) authority within the community. Cook associates *jihad* with the "dogma of martyrdom" in the Qur'an. This reading has been criticized by Silvia Horsch-Al Saad, who emphasizes that martyrdom (*shahada*) as a witness of faith may be foreshadowed in the Qur'an, but the technical term *shahid* (martyr) originated later, although it remains unknown when the transition occurred that resulted in the link between *jihad* and *shahid*. In the end, the modification is related to the concept of martyrdom on the battlefield. Horsch-Al Saad finds a high esteem for warriors in pre-Islamic Arab culture.[199] While the relationship between martyrdom and *jihad* can be assumed by now as generally accepted, it is the outcome of centuries of interpretations and reinterpretations. What remains, however, is the ongoing conflict between a martyr and a traitor and between martyrdom and suicide.[200] In particular, the latter conflict is still prominent in the phenomenon of the suicide bomber. Most Muslims today consider suicide attacks to be un-Islamic, and in early readings suicide on the battlefield was believed to be punished in Hell.

In the original Muslim community in Mecca, prior to the Hijra, warfare and physical aggression were the exceptions and were used in moderation. This attitude towards violence changed significantly after the community of the faithful moved to Medina where the *umma* was created. As Reuven Firestone notes, in Medina a "growing sense of solidarity" emerged. Additionally, most likely as a response to the mistreatment and abuse by members of the community's non-Muslim kin, the traditional rules of revenge that excluded one's own tribe were significantly altered; it became acceptable to raid one's own or Meccan tribes.[201] In this way, mundane warfare is successively transformed into religiously sanctioned violence in the service of God (*fi sabil Allah*).

Although *jihad* (struggle or striving) is not semantically related to warfare in general or religiously sanctioned warfare in particular, *qital* and more specifically *qital fi sabil Allah* has become synonymous with *jihad*, while *harb* (war) remains reserved for warfare that is not religiously sanctioned.[202] However, various writers have asserted that *jihad* is at least not primarily related to violent actions and warfare, but rather refers first and foremost to a believer's internal struggle

---

199 Silvia Horsch-Al Saad, *Tod im Kampf: Figurationen des Märtyrers in frühen sunnitischen Schriften* (Würzburg: Ergon, 2011), 77–8, 88.
200 Ibid., 197.
201 Firestone, *Jihad*, 128–9, 131.
202 Ibid., 18.

for faith. This distinction is usually associated with the concepts of greater *jihad* (internal struggle) and lesser *jihad* (religiously sanctioned warfare). Contrary to this reading, David Cook argues convincingly that the emphasis on the "greater *jihad*" is primarily the result of apologetic reinterpretations in the nineteenth and twentieth century and have "virtually no validity in Islam" because "the armed struggle—aggressive conquest—came first, and then additional meanings became attached to the term."[203] Nonetheless, some philosophical works contain some notions that imply the highest regard for *jihad* as an internal struggle rather than as an act of fighting. Mariella Ourgui locates such an idea in al-Ghazali, although his legal works are rather different in this respect.[204]

Even for the earlier period, we cannot assume that one consistent concept of *jihad* existed. Simultaneously, no agreement exists about the precise conditions legitimizing *jihad*. As written by Michael Bonner, "jihad has never ceased changing, right down to our own day. If it ever had an original core, this has been experienced anew many times over."[205] These disagreements are not limited to the Sunni-Shi'i divide; they also depend on historical contexts and circumstances. However, the main differences between the Sunni and Shi'i concepts of *jihad* focus primarily on two issues. Sunni, Shi'i and Kharijites fundamentally agree that the imam has to sanction and authorize *jihad*. This rule has made it particularly difficult—if not impossible—for the Twelver Shi'is to authorize *jihad* after 873. With the disappearance of the last divinely appointed imam, they lack a recognized authority able to legitimize *jihad*. Second, as Michael Bonner notes, "while everyone agreed that jihad includes an aspect of fighting rebels (*ahl al-baghy*), the Shi'i jurists defined these rebels as the opponents of the Twelve Imams; which meant, basically, all Muslims other than the Shi'is themselves."[206]

Of course, the Shi'i jurists are not alone in declaring all others than the members of their own branch of Islam enemies of Islam, providing room for legitimizing inter-sectarian violence against others who are not recognized as Muslim. This is certainly true for the *Kharijites* who declared all non-*Kharijite* Muslims "to be not Muslims at all, but infidels (*kuffar*), and in this activity of *takfir* (declaring infidel), they were eager for violence and war."[207]

In this context it is worth noting that at a general level, violence became a matter and means that was considered unavoidable and approved by God. Violence is seen to be in the service of religion and the community of believers. In

---

203 Cook, *Understanding Jihad*, 42.
204 Ourghi, *Muslimische Positionen zur Berechtigung von Gewalt*, 19.
205 Bonner, *Jihad in Islamic History*, 4.
206 Ibid., 125.
207 Ibid., 126.

contrast to pre-Islamic times, the emphasis is at least theoretically no longer on warfare's material goals, but is justified both religiously and morally. The goal of this warfare is to defend the religion and to secure and strengthen the political and material foundations of the community.[208] However, examining the earliest more systematic accounts of *jihad* shows that rather than disappearing, the material aspect is now subject to substantial regulations. A similar observation can be made regarding means of conduct. One of the earliest discussions of *jihad* was recorded by Imam Malik Ibn Anas, the founder of the Sunni Maliki school. According to internal evidence, his famous *al-Muwatta* dates back before 767 but not later than 795, the year of Malik's death.[209]

In Malik's chapter on *jihad*, he compares someone who carries out *jihad* with a person who constantly and without any interruption prays and fasts until the jihadist has returned from his mission. For Malik, "a man who lives alone with a few sheep, performs the prayer, pays the *zakat*, and worships Allah without associating anything with Him" qualifies as the second best degree among the people, while the best degree belongs to the jihadist.[210] This comparison reemphasizes the stress on *jihad*'s primary meaning that is associated with warfare.

When Malik discusses the material aspects of *jihad*, he insists that *jihad* has to be well prepared and well-funded to ensure that the authorities are followed and obeyed during the military expedition and corruption is avoided. One who fights in a military expedition in which valuables are not spent "does not return with reward." For Malik, a well-funded military expedition stimulates the desire for *jihad*, while poorly-funded expeditions do not.[211] A well-funded expedition may include the payment of the individual fighters. The question that arises in relation to the payment of fighters is whether a fighter, even though he is a paid laborer, should have a share in the booty. For Malik, however, it is clear that each person who is present and free should have his share; the "man on horse-back has two shares, the man on foot has one."[212] The idea of shared booty also implies that the belongings of a slain enemy do not automatically belong to the person who has killed him. Ownership of the possessions of slain opponents depends on explicit permission from the imam. Malik's discussion of these issues implies that booty has been a frequent source of conflict. Otherwise,

---

208 Horsch-Al Saad, *Tod im Kampf*, 97, 101.
209 Wael B. Hallaq, "On Dating Malik's *Muwatta*," *UCLA Journal of Islamic and Near East Law* 1 (2002): 47.
210 Malik Ibn Anas, *Al-Muwatta of Imam Malik ibn Anas: The First Formulation of Islamic Law*, trans. Aisha Abdurrahman Bewley (London: Kegan Paul, 1989), 21.1.1, 21.1.4.
211 Ibid., 21.18.43.
212 Ibid., 21.6.16, 21.12.21.

there would be no need to discuss the matter. The same is true for stealing from the spoils and rape. If a free woman is raped then the bride-price has to be paid; if she is a slave then what has been "diminished of her worth" must be paid. However, note that the raped woman should not be punished.[213] Malik addresses the main types of misconduct that occur during military expeditions in a list providing advice for appropriate conduct: "Do not kill women or children or an aged, infirm person. Do not cut down fruit-bearing trees. Do not destroy an inhabited place. Do not slaughter sheep or camels except for food. Do not burn bees and do not scatter them. Do not steal from the booty, and do not be cowardly."[214]

While Malik is relatively explicit about who should not be killed (women, children, and the elderly), he is less explicit about who should be killed—with one exception: whoever turns away from Islam has to be killed without the opportunity to repent. The same applies to heretics. Those who have turned away from Islam but divulge should be given the chance to repent. If they do not repent, they should be killed.[215] Similarly to the less legalistic regulations on taking the Cross, the jihadist or mujahidin depends on his parents' agreement. If his parents prevent him from going on a military campaign, he should not contradict his parents.[216]

Most of these considerations are not in any way different from those surrounding mundane warfare. The religious impetus enters through particular expectations for the jihadist's conduct and by framing the military campaign in a religious context. Stealing and rape do not necessarily require religious rules, and they qualify as moral wrongdoings even outside religiously defined codes of conduct. Malik's discussion on achieving martyrdom introduces an issue that is specific to religion(s). He explains that

> [t]he nobility of the believer is his *taqwa*. His *deen* is his noble descent. His manliness is his good character. Boldness and cowardice are but instincts which Allah places wherever he wills. The coward shrinks from defending even his father and mother, and the bold one fights for the sake of the combat not for the spoils, and the martyr is the one who gives himself, expectant of rewards from Allah.[217]

Malik's description of a martyr clearly indicates that the proper motivation, including the proper conduct, is important for the jihadist as for the Crusader.

---

213 Ibid., 21.10.19, 21.13.22–26, 36.16–14.
214 Ibid., 21.3.10.
215 Ibid., 36.18.15.
216 Ibid., 21.5.14.
217 Ibid., 21.15.35.

2.2 Legitimizing Violence in the Classic/Premodern Islamic Traditions — 73

In another similarity to the Crusades, it is clear that jihadists' motivation is questioned because they are motivated by material gains rather than by a promised spiritual reward. Apart from the motivation of the individual jihadist, as Rudolph Peters reminds us, the fact that "jihad has been defined as warfare against the unbelievers does not necessarily mean [...] that such a war is founded exclusively on religious motives."[218]

In later treatises on *jihad*, the aspect of material gains for individual fighters is of significantly lesser interest. We illustrate later discourses of *jihad* by discussing Averroes's or Ibn Rushd's (1126–1198) chapter on *jihad* in his famous legal handbook *Bidāyat al-mudjtahid wa-nihāyat al-muqraṣid*[219] and Ibn Jamaʿa's (1241–1333) *Taḥrīr al-aḥkām fī tadbīr al-Islām*.[220] Hans Kofler compares Ibn Jamaʿa's work with al-Mawardi's (972–1058) *Al-aḥkām al-sulṭāniyya w'al-wilāyāt al-dīniyya*.[221] Although Kofler considers Ibn Jamaʿa's treatise as inferior to al-Mawardi's, he sees al-Mawardi's investigation of his topic in a purely theoretical fashion as an ideal that awaits fulfillment as a weakness, while Ibn Jamaʿa's work is written as a guideline for political practice and is therefore also a guideline for maintaining power.[222] Even though al-Mawardi may appear to be utopian to some degree, he nonetheless responds to a pressing issue: he aimed to restore the caliphate after the caliph became merely a puppet. While Ibn Jamaʿa focuses on maintaining power and al-Mawardi on restoring power, Ibn Khaldun (1332–1406) acts as a type of external observer without concrete ties to power, at least during his desert sabbatical when he wrote *Muqaddimah*. At first glance,

---

218 Rudolph Peters, "Introduction, in *Jihad in Medieval and Modern Islam: The Chapters on Jihad from Averroes' Legal Handbook 'Bidayat al-Mudjtahid and The Treatise 'Koran and Fighting' by the Late Shaykh al-Azar, Mahmud Shaltut*, ed. Rudolph Peters (Leiden: Brill, 1977), 4.
219 Averroes [Ibn Rushd], "The Chapter on Jihad from Averroes's Legal Handbook *Al-Bidāyah*," in *Jihad in Medieval and Modern Islam: The Chapters on Jihad from Averroes' Legal Handbook 'Bidayat al-Mudjtahid and The Treatise 'Koran and Fighting' by the Late Shaykh al-Azar, Mahmud Shaltut*, ed. Rudolph Peters (Leiden: Brill, 1977), 9–25. I refer to this work according to the counted parts, with the corresponding page numbers added in brackets.
220 Critical ed. in Hans Kofler, "Handbuch des islamischen Staats- und Verwaltungsrechtes von Badr-ad-din ibn Ğamāʿah," *Islamica* 6 (1934): 349–441, Hans Kofler, "Handbuch des islamischen Staats- und Verwaltungsrechtes von Badr-ad-din ibn Ğamāʿah," *Islamica* 7 (1935): 1–65, and Hans Kofler, "Handbuch des islamischen Staats- und Verwaltungsrechtes von Badr-ad-din ibn Ğamāʿah," *Abhandlungen für die Kunde des Morgenlandes*, 33, no. 6 (1938): 18–129. I refer to the work as Ibn Jamaʿa, *Taḥrīr al-aḥkām*.
221 Al-Mawardi, *The Ordinances of Government: Al-aḥkām al-sulṭāniyya w'al-wilāyāt al-dīniyya*. trans. Wafaa H. Wahba (Reading: Garnet, 1996). I refer to this book by chapter, with the corresponding page numbers added in brackets.
222 Kofler, "Handbuch des islamischen Staats- und Verwaltungsrechtes von Badr-ad-din ibn Ğamāʿah," *Islamica* 6 (1934): 349–50.

this selection of authors may appear to be arbitrary. However, these authors offer not only a broader perspective on premodern interpretations of *jihad*, they also address issues that become virulent in modern discourses. Moreover, they enable us to place Nizam al-Mulk's and Ibn Taymiyya's accounts in a broader context.

Averroes (Abu al-Walid Muhammad Ibn Muhammad Ibn Rushd) is the grandson of a famous legal scholar of the same name. While he is a legal scholar (and physician) in his own right, in the West he is primarily known as a philosopher and commentator on Plato and Aristotle.[223] His relatively short treatment of *jihad* is of particular interest because he does not hide scholarly disagreements. He does not see any disagreement over the assumption that "jihad is a collective not a personal duty." Contrary to Malik, who clearly stated that a jihadist needs his parents' approval before he can take part in a military expedition, Averroes argues that although almost all scholars agree on the issue, the parents' permission is not required in cases where nobody else could fulfill the obligation. In this particular case, the collective obligation becomes a personal one.[224] Although Averroes opens the door only slightly to the interpretation of *jihad* as an individual duty, he remains silent about concrete contexts, leaving the understanding that *jihad* may be an individual duty open to a wide range of interpretations and applications. One of these interpretations is found in Ibn Jamaʿa's *Taḥrīr al-aḥkām*. Here, he distinguishes between two types of *jihad*, *jihad* as a collective duty and *jihad* as an individual duty. Although most jurists hold the view that *jihad* was even a collective duty under the Prophet, some are of the opinion that it was an individual obligation.[225] For Ibn Jamaʿa, *jihad* remains a collective duty if (1) the unbelievers remain in their territories and do not attack Muslim lands and (2) if the Muslims are superior to their enemies and outnumber them. Without an explicit external threat, it is sufficient for the ruler to initiate a military expedition once a year. This collective duty obliges all adult male Muslims who are free and not handicapped in body or mind. In contrast to Malik, Ibn Jamaʿa rejects the idea of pay for individual fighters. *Jihad* is a duty, and one cannot expect pay for the fulfillment of a duty. Although an individual does not sin through inaction when someone else is fulfilling the collective duty, the individual fighter who has taken up the commitment acquires an individual duty. Ibn Jamaʿa distinguishes this individual duty from a second version of *jihad* as individual obligation. *Jihad* be-

---

223 Peters, "Introduction," 5–6.
224 Averroes, "The Chapter on Jihad from Averroes's Legal Handbook *Al-Bidāyah*," part 1 (9–10),
225 Ibn Jamaʿa, *Taḥrīr al-aḥkām* 11.2.

comes an individual duty in a defensive situation. This is the case when Muslims or Muslim lands are attacked by infidels.[226]

This general distinction of *jihad* as a collective or an individual duty is also reflected in the writings of al-Mawardi. For him, offensive or preemptive *jihad* is a collective duty, while defensive *jihad* is an individual duty. The goal of the collective obligations is "to expand the Islamic political and moral order." Enemies are to be prevented from seizing Muslim lands so that Muslims can travel freely and securely without any threat to their person or property. However, al-Mawardi does not agree with Ibn Jama'a that the collective duty for the individual fighter turns into an individual duty on the battlefield. For him, "offensive jihad is never an individual obligation, it is only a collective obligation."[227]

For Averroes, the targets of *jihad* are unbelievers, including the People of the Book. Averroes makes an exception for those who belong to the Quraysh tribe and Arab Christians; they have to either convert to Islam or pay the poll tax.[228] Al-Mawardi's argument is similar to Ibn Jama'a's: the enemy has to be fought until conversion, or, if the enemy refuses to convert, until it submits to Muslim political authority and pays the poll tax.[229] Averroes emphasizes that there is no difference between the People of the Book and the polytheists. They have to be fought "until they have been converted or until they are willing to pay poll-tax."[230] Ibn Jama'a adds that the ruler or caliph should first fight the nearest unbelievers, followed by the second nearest unbelievers.[231] While Ibn Jama'a generally allows for the killing of a defeated enemy, he makes exceptions for unbelievers who are the fighter's father or another next of kin. Additionally, women and children should not be killed, even if they may escape and rejoin the unbelievers.[232] In general, Averroes agrees with Ibn Jama'a on this point. He notes that there is "no disagreement about the rule that it is forbidden to slay women and children, provided that they are not fighting, for then women, in any case, may be slain."[233] However, he does not object to the use of mangonels to assail fortresses, even if women and children are likely to be among the vic-

---

226 Ibid., 11.3–4.
227 Mairay Syed, "Jihad in Classical Islam Legal and Moral Thought," in *Just War in Religion and Politics*, ed. Jacob Neusner, Bruce D. Chilton, and R.E. Tully (Lanham: University Press of America, 2013), 142, 145.
228 Averroes, "The Chapter on Jihad from Averroes's Legal Handbook *Al-Bidāyah*," part 7 (23).
229 Syed, "Jihad in Classical Islam Legal and Moral Thought," 145.
230 Averroes, "The Chapter on Jihad from Averroes's Legal Handbook *Al-Bidāyah*," part 6 (23).
231 Ibn Jama'a, *Taḥrīr al-aḥkām* 2.2, 12.1.
232 Ibid., 12.13–14.
233 Averroes, "The Chapter on Jihad from Averroes's Legal Handbook *Al-Bidāyah*," part 3 (15).

tims.²³⁴ If women and children are used to shield fighters, then necessity allows for the killing of these women and children.²³⁵

Muslim fighters cannot simply attack unbelievers. Before fighting them, it is required to summon them to Islam. They can only be attacked if they have been summoned to Islam and they do not follow the call.²³⁶ Ibn Jama'a suggests that although it is not mandatory, if the first call is not successful then the enemy should be summoned to Islam a second time. After the second call, the enemy may even be attacked at night. If the enemy worships idols or angels, their women and children may be captured and their properties plundered. If the enemy belongs to those who are obliged to pay the poll tax including Jews, Christians, and Parsees, then they should be fought until they convert or pay the poll tax.²³⁷

When sectarians are concerned, Ibn Jama'a recommends a slightly different approach. To qualify as a sectarian, two conditions must be fulfilled: first, the sectarianism must be proclaimed. Second, the sectarians must have the means to succeed in their sectarian goals.²³⁸ If they rise against the ruler and demand his removal from office, refuse to obey, or fail to fulfill their duties, and the ruler can only return them to obedience by fighting them, then they are undoubtedly sectarians. However, if they revolt because they have suffered injustice, then the ruler is advised to remove the injustice and fight them only if they continue to revolt, even after the injustice has been removed. If they repent, he should accept their repentance. If they persist, he has to fight them. However, they should not be treated as unbelievers, but as sinners and rebels.²³⁹

The main goal is for these individuals to return to obedience. Violence (fighting them) should thus be the last resort. Only after all other methods (warning, encouraging, and intimidating them) have failed can they be fought and killed.²⁴⁰ Ibn Jama'a's approach to religious dissenters is relatively moderate. The goal is the restoration of and submission to the ruler's authority, which corresponds with the ruler's second duty of maintaining the foundations of faith, preventing heretical belief, presenting proof of Islam, and supporting the theological-juridical science.²⁴¹ However, Ibn Jama'a does not distinguish between

---

234 Ibid., part 3 (18).
235 Ibn Jama'a, *Taḥrīr al-aḥkām* 12.12.
236 Averroes, "The Chapter on Jihad from Averroes's Legal Handbook *Al-Bidāyah*," part 4 (19).
237 Ibn Jama'a, *Taḥrīr al-aḥkām* 12.2.
238 Ibid., 16.2.
239 Ibid., 16.1.
240 Ibid., 16.4.
241 Ibid., 2.4.

different types of dissenters, at least not explicitly. The main focus of his writing is on the political necessity of maintaining order, which includes obedience from all parts of the populace. In this context, it becomes almost irrelevant whether the subjects have converted to Islam and obey or whether they refuse to convert but pay the poll tax and obey. This observation corresponds with Ibn Jamaʿa's suggestion that it would be desirable for the ruler, after conquering Muslim territory, to request that the caliph vest him with the administrative power over the lands to avoid disorder and division. In this way, usurpation becomes legalized governorship.[242]

Although al-Mawardi's approach to religious dissenters follows basically the same logic as Ibn Jamaʿa's, his discussion is more elaborate. In addition to the *jihad* against the People of the Book and polytheists, he discusses *jihad* against believers by dividing them into three categories: "first, the jihad against apostasy (al-ridda); second, the jihad against dissension (al-baghī); and third, the jihad against secession (al-muḥāribūn)."[243] However, contrary to Ibn Jamaʿa, who attributes certain duties to a (secular) ruler who governs with the blessing of the caliph, al-Mawardi, in his attempt to restore the caliphate's power, ascribes the following duties to the caliph: "First, he must guard the faith, upholding its establishment and the consensus of the nation's ancestors, arguing with emerging heretics or suspicious dissenters, demonstrating the truth to them, and administrating the legal penalties, so that the faith should remain pristine and the nation free from error."[244]

Although al-Mawardi emphasizes religious fidelity to a greater degree than Ibn Jamaʿa, the key issue in both works is maintaining power and the elimination of all dissent. As far as apostates are concerned (al-Mawardi does not distinguish between those who were born Muslims and converts), al-Mawardi treats apostates who are scattered through Muslim lands differently than those who establish their own community. Individual apostates who are no real threat to the *umma* should be treated similarly to excommunicated Christians. They lose their right to property, and it is forbidden to inherit from them, regardless of whether the heir is a Muslim or an infidel. The apostate is excluded from marriage and from the community of others. Nobody should eat from an animal he has slaughtered. In addition, idolaters and apostates may be killed.

The case is rather different for groups of apostates who assemble "in a place away from Muslims where they become a power to reckon with." In this case,

---

242 Ibid., 2.3.
243 Majid Khadduri, *War and Peace in the Law of Islam* (Baltimore: Johns Hopkins Press, 1955), 74.
244 Al-Mawardi, *The Ordinances of Government*, chap. 1 (16).

"after holding a discussion with them and presenting them the proof of Islam," fighting them is mandatory. They should be treated like the regular enemy and fought in open battle. Surprise attacks are explicitly allowed. Unless they repent, captives may be killed.[245] The rules are slightly harsher when they are fought outside Muslim lands. However, if they refuse to pay their taxes to a just ruler because they believe they are not obligated, then they qualify as apostates and should be fought accordingly. If they refuse to pay taxes but admit the obligation, then they should be treated as law-breakers.[246]

If they are not apostates but rather innovators who rebel and break away from the community of the faithful, al-Mawardi only recommends fighting them if they fall into disobedience and do not recognize the ruler's authority. As long as they do not live in isolated places, remain under the control of the regular power, are small in number, and pay their taxes, they should not be fought. If they refuse to recognize the ruler and do not fulfill their obligations, "they must be fought until they cease to oppose and become obedient again."[247] Although the payment of dues is considered a religious obligation, and thus the refusal to pay the dues becomes religiously colored and may be even associated with apostasy, the conflict nonetheless remains a conflict over material goods. The material aspect is also reflected in al-Mawardi's recommendation that the rebels should neither be "attacked with catapults nor have their homes burned down or their date palms and other trees felled, because theirs is still Muslim territory which protects its residents even though they may rebel."[248]

Here, sparing property and the land's resources becomes a prerogative that is related to the rebels living in Muslim territory, whereas Malik suggests that trees and homes should never be destroyed. This explicitly includes the trees and homes of an infidel enemy. The reason for this shift becomes obvious when one considers where the two authors lie along the timeline of Islamic expansion.[249] Whereas Malik writes during an excessive period of expansion during which the destruction of resources that may occur under Muslim power is counter-productive, al-Mawardi writes in the context of the vast Seljuq Empire.

Related to this problem is the question of why fighting rebels is discussed under the concept of *jihad*. Here, Ibn Khaldun's distinction between just and un-

---

245 Ibid., chap. 5 (61).
246 Ibid., chap. 5 (63).
247 Ibid., chap. 5 (65).
248 Ibid., chap. 5 (66).
249 For Islam's expansion and conversion from the seventh to the ninth century, see Ira M. Lapidus, *Islamic Societies to the Nineteenth Century: A Global History* (Cambridge: Cambridge University Press, 2012), 343–68.

just wars is insightful. Generally, Ibn Khaldun distinguishes between four different types of war. Two of them he labels unjust. These are wars between "neighboring tribes and competing families" and wars "caused by hostility [...] among savage nations."[250] The other two types of war are just and holy and consequently divinely sanctioned. These wars are the *jihad* against the enemy and the "dynastic war against seceders and those who refuse obedience."[251] Applying Arnold Angenendt's definition of holy wars introduced earlier, only the first of Ibn Khaldun's just wars may qualify as holy, despite the fact that he labels both as just and *jihad* and therefore sanctioned by divine authority. The first two do not qualify as just and divinely sanctioned because they are motivated by revenge, jealousy, and envy, and the latter two are fought on "behalf of God and His religion" or on "behalf of royal authority and the effort to found a kingdom."[252] Both are wars of *jihad* and justice. For Ibn Khaldun, *jihad* and royal authority are securely linked because of the (ideal) unity of caliphate and royal authority:

> In the Muslim community, the holy war is a religious duty, because of the universalism of the (Muslim) mission and (the obligation to) convert everyone to Islam either by persuasion or by force. Therefore, caliphate and royal authority are united in (Islam), so that the person in charge can devote the available strength to both of them at the same time.[253]

Because Islamic order can only be secured successfully if it is related to power, Ibn Khaldun considers not only the regular *jihad* as just but also imperial warfare, whether defensive or offensive.[254] In this sense, all wars that are fought to extend Muslim territory and to secure power are divinely sanctioned. The basis for this interaction is similar to the Christian context. In *Tahir's Letter to His Son*, Tahir reminds his son and rulers in general that "royal authority belongs to God. He gives it to whomever He wants to give it and takes it away from whomever He wants to take it away."[255] Another key issue in this context is the importance that Ibn Khaldun ascribes to religion for political stability. More than that, Ibn Khaldun holds that without God and religion (meaning Islam), a realm will not be able to exist. He exemplifies this claim by arguing that prior to their conversion to Islam, Arabs were the antithesis of civilization. In addition to the fact

---

250 Ibn Khaldun, *Muqaddimah*, 2.65.
251 Ibid., 2.66.
252 Ibid., 2.65.
253 Ibid., 1.415.
254 Malik Mufti, "Jihad as Statecraft: Ibn Khaldun on the Conduct of War and Empire," *History of Political Thought*, 30, no. 3 (2009): 388.
255 Ibn Khaldun, *Muqaddimah* 2.133.

that the polytheist Arabs have fought unjust wars, Ibn Khaldun describes them as having a strong tendency to plunder. "They show no respect for other people's property, live in anarchy, and without (respecting) laws."[256] Because the well-being of the realm depends on God's will, without God and religion, the community will not be able to exist because he considers the Arabs "a savage nation [...]. Savagery has become their character and nation."[257] Although the Arabs are successful conquerors, their savagery causes the almost immediate ruin of the conquered regions.[258] In short, Ibn Khaldun describes Arabs as "rude, proud, ambitious, and eager to be the leader."[259] According to Ibn Khaldun, Arabs are conditioned to prefer freedom from all kinds of authority. This affection for liberty is also accompanied by every single Arab's demand for leadership.

In contrast, Muslim rule means order, hierarchy, and justice. The Muslim ruler looks "after the affairs of the poor and indigent," takes "regard for people who have suffered accidents and for their widows and orphans," and provides stipends for them from the treasury. He gives shelter to the ill, and he takes care of the appointment of "physicians who will treat their diseases."[260] To maintain the (just) order, fighting rebels is therefore just and qualifies as a religiously sanctioned form of violence. However, reality does not always conform to expectations. Even under Muslim rule, some rulers use force and oppress their subjects. As a consequence, the people become fearful and depressed. To protect themselves, they lie, use tricks, and become deceitful. The subjects cease to be trustworthy on the battlefield and may refuse to support the ruler's enterprises. The military order and border protection decays and the subjects tend to conspire to kill the ruler. In the end, the realm will be destroyed.[261] This idea of counter-violence that is also present in Ibn Jama'a's writings will be discussed again later.

However, it is worth noting that both defensive and offensive (including imperial) warfare are religiously sanctioned, similarly to the oppression of religious dissenters and rebels. The basic goals of premodern *jihad* are not particularly religious and do not differ from those of mundane warfare: gaining and maintaining power and resources. The conversion of the conquered was not required. Indeed, as Ira Lapidus notes, at least during the first two centuries the conversion

---

256 Ibid., 1.270–272, 1.274.
257 Ibid., 1.270.
258 Ibid., 1.276.
259 Ibid., 1.273.
260 Ibid., 2.139
261 Ibid., 1.340.

of non-Arabs was not even desired because "Arab-Muslim conquerors attempted to maintain themselves as an exclusive Muslim elite."²⁶²

2.2.2 Sunni Perspective on Religious Dissent and (Foreign) Muslim Aggression

Nizam al-Mulk (1020–1092) and Ibn Taymiyya (1263–1328) represent two paradigmatic examples of legitimizing the use of violence against political threats that they associate with religious dissent and apostasy. Ibn Taymiyya is concerned with the purity of "orthodox" Sunni belief. Georges Tamer describes Ibn Taymiyya as

> an extremely committed Muslim who endeavored with the utmost effort to defend Sunni Islam with both sword and pen: having courageously fought with the Mamluk army against the Crusaders, the Tatars [Mongols], the Shiites and the Armenians, he enthusiastically wrote against every idea and practice in which he saw a threat against orthodox Islam, For him, writing was just as much a form of holy jihad as military service.²⁶³

Although Ibn Taymiyya is a significant figure considering the immense volume of his writings and is certainly an interesting scholar-activist and thinker to study, it is also important to remember that in his own times, he was perceived as a troublemaker rather than as a mainstream thinker. Although he was heavily criticized and ridiculed during his lifetime, from his death to the late eighteenth or nineteenth century his legacy barely existed because "he was often overlooked" and "very rarely read or studied."²⁶⁴ In contrast, Nizam al-Mulk's *speculum regis* and administrative handbook *Siyar al-Muluk* was in use until the end of the Ottoman Empire. Whereas Ibn Taymiyya battled against the Mongol invasion among other things, Nizam al Mulk, the grand vizier and "architect" of the Seljuq Empire, battled against the Nizari Isma'ilis. For this reason, he not only legitimized the use of violence against political dissenters in religious terms, he also engaged in an intellectual propaganda battle. To fight the enemy intellectually and construct his "orthodoxy," he founded madrassas and hired the most prominent scholars of the time.²⁶⁵ The most prominent among them was al-Gha-

---

262 Lapidus, *Islamic Societies to the Nineteenth Century*, 346.
263 Tamer, "The Curse of Philosophy," 370.
264 Yossef Rapoport and Shahab Ahmed, "Ibn Taymiyya and his Times," in *Ibn Taymiyya and His Times*, ed. Yossef Rapoport and Shahab Ahmed (Oxford: Oxford University Press, 2010), 16.
265 Omid Safi, *The Politics of Knowledge in Premodern Islam: Negotiating Ideology and Religious Inquiry* (Chapel Hill: The University of North Carolina Press, 2006), 47. Tilman Nagel, *Staat und*

zali (1059–1111), perhaps the most influential scholar of the time. Al-Ghazali is also seen as a key figure in developing the doctrine of the mandatory death penalty for charges of apostasy. He regards an apostate "automatically [...] to be a dangerous enemy of the Islamic state."[266] Simultaneously, scholars start merging and discussing other versions of religious dissent such as heresy (*zandaqah*), blasphemy (*sabb Allah*), unbelief (*kufr*) or (*nifiq*) primarily as manifestations of apostasy (*riddah*).[267] As seen in the previous section, the distinction between different concepts of religious dissent does not disappear completely. Nonetheless, the dominant legal discourse is increasingly focused on apostasy. This tendency is clearly apparent in Ibn Taymiyya's writings.

While al-Ghazali and Ibn Taymiyya are also very well known for their polemics against the philosophers, this section does not discuss the two thinkers' hostility towards Muslim philosophers. Contrary to Leo Strauss's assumption that Muslim philosophers were writing in a hostile environment and were subject to frequent persecution, Dimitri Gutas reminds us that as far as Muslim Arabic philosophers are concerned, Strauss's position is unsound because "it is contradicted by historical facts—there is not a single philosopher who was ever persecuted, let alone executed, for his *philosophical* views."[268]

Although Ibn Taymiyya was rediscovered in the eighteenth and nineteenth centuries, it is not true that all of his writings became instantly popular. Different groups were attracted by different parts of his oeuvre. Muhammad Ibn Abd al-Wahhab, who aimed for a purified Islam and joined forces with Muhammad Ibn Saud, which led to the formation of the first Saudi state, relied on different writings of Ibn Taymiyya[269] than contemporary Islamist extremists. For the latter group, Ibn Taymiyya's Mardin fatwa and three anti-Mongol fatwas have become the "obligatory references."[270] More recently, Yahya Michot has presented us with

---

Glaubensgemeinschaft im Islam: Geschichte der politischen Ordnungsvorstellungen der Muslime, Vol. 2: *Vom Spätmittelalter bis zur Neuzeit* (Zürich: Artemis, 1981), 74.
266 Rudolph Peters and Gert J. J. De Vries, "Apostasy in Islam," *Die Welt des Islams* 17 (1976/77): 17.
267 Frank Griffel, "Toleration and Exclusion: Al-Shāfi'ī and al-Ghazālī on the Treatment of Apostates," *Bulletin of the School of Oriental and African Studies* 64, no. 3 (2001): 352.
268 Dimitri Gutas, "The Study of Arabic Philosophy in the Twentieth Century: An Essay on the Historiography of Arabic Philosophy," *British Journal of Middle Eastern Studies* 29 (2002): 20.
269 Al-'Uthaymīn, *Muḥammad ibn 'Abd al-Wahhāb*, 72, 87. Natana J. Delong-Bas, *Wahhabi Islam: From Revival and Reform to Global Jihad* (Oxford: Oxford University Press, 2004), 34.
270 Yahya Michot, *Muslims under Non-Muslim Rule: Ibn Taymiyya on Fleeing from Sin; Kinds of Emigration; the Status of Mardin: Domain of War and Peace; the Conditions of Challenging Power: Texts Translated, Annotated, and Presented in Relation to Six Modern Readings of the Mardin Fatwa* (Oxford: Interface Publications, 2006), 10.

a rather anti-extremist Ibn Taymiyya.[271] Therefore, these two versions of Ibn Taymiyya need to be considered briefly with a focus on *jihad* and religious dissent.

Although Ibn Taymiyya also argues against non-Sunni (heretical) sects, his teaching that allows for *jihad* against the Mongols is primarily an argument of *jihad* as a tool in foreign affairs. Both arguments follow a similar logic and are interdependent. In contrast, Nizam al-Mulk's main concern is an internal threat, as he perceives a Muslim sect that has, in his view, abandoned Islam. As noted earlier, both premodern and modern justifications for the use of violence focus primarily on the concept of *jihad*. As Sherman Jackson notes, "the Muslim valuation and articulation of jihad were just as much, if not more, a product of *history* than of religion." While war between rivaling tribes was more the norm than the exception in Islam's early history, war was perhaps the only means by which a young religious community could survive and guarantee its freedom. At first, warfare was a historical necessity. However, this does not mean that "Islam can only accept a world that is entirely populated by Muslims and, as such, Muslims must, as a religious duty, wage perpetual jihad against non-Muslims. Islam can peacefully coexist with non-Muslims."[272] This view is also shared by Ibn Taymiyya, who does not "categorically divide the world into the Domains 'of Islam' and 'of war.'"[273] According to Rudolph Peters, writings about the modern doctrine of *jihad* primarily stress two issues, "the mobilization of Muslims for a specific occasion such as revolt or war, or the instruction of Muslims as the 'real' or 'true' doctrine of jihad."[274] For instance, the example of Afghanistan's history shows that proclaiming *jihad* has been a common and successful means of mobilizing otherwise rivaling tribes and factions against non-Muslim invasion.[275] Ibn Taymiyya's defense of *jihad* follows a similar line of reasoning. In the context of medieval Islamic political and religious thought, however, his view is unique.

As already emphasized, the right to revolt against authority is not commonly accepted in the medieval Sunni tradition to which Ibn Taymiyya belongs, although this idea is more established within the Shi'i tradition because the Shi'i, as a continuously persecuted minority, considered all Sunni authority to be illegitimate. Ironically, when the Shi'i Fatamids actually gained significant ter-

---

[271] Ibn Taymiyya, *Against Exremisms*, ed. Yahya M. Michot, foreword Bruce L. Lawrence (Beirut: Dar Albouraq, 2012).
[272] Jackson, "Jihad in the Modern World," 395, 400–1.
[273] Yahya M. Michot, "Introduction," in Ibn Taymiyya, *Against Exremisms*, xxi.
[274] Rudolph Peters, *Jihad in Classical and Modern Islam: Updated Edition with a Section on Jihad in the 21st Century* (Princeton: Wiener, 2005), 103.
[275] Thomas Barfield, *Afghanistan: A Cultural and Political History* (Princeton: Princeton University Press, 2010), 122–3.

ritorial power (the Cairo caliphate), they primarily ruled over a Sunni majority population. However, in most instances they were ruled by Sunni authorities. In most of these circumstances the Shi'ites chose not to revolt simply because a successful revolt against Sunni domination would have been an unlikely outcome.[276] Similarly, Ibn Taymiyya suggests revolt only against non-Muslim rule. Muslim rule is preferable to disorder wherever it exists, even if the ruler is tyrannical and *kafir* because the social order of Islam cannot exist without political rule.[277]

In his scholarly theological writings—compared to his more political fatwas that attracted modern and contemporary extremists—Ibn Taymiyya remains within the traditional Sunni doctrine that does not allow for any active resistance or revolt against a governmental authority unless it repudiates Islam. Moreover, Ibn Taymiyya never "challenges the legitimacy of any particular sultan, or a fortiori that of the Mamluk regime."[278] Even in the case of sinful orders, a Sunni Muslim is encouraged not to rebel, though he should not follow the sinful command either. At most, the traditional Sunni position is to practice passive resistance simply by not following sinful orders. This precise position can be found in the writings of Ibn Taymiyya:

> To obey the authorities and to wish them well is a duty incumbent upon all Muslims unless they are asked to do something sinful. They are not to rise up against them so long as they establish salah among them.[279]

Elsewhere, Ibn Taymiyya goes so far as to suggest that even passive resistance is not permissible. The believer is supposed to disdain the ruler's sin but should obey his orders nonetheless because "[t]he Prophet has asked us to obey every man of authority (*amir*), even if he is a black slave."[280] This perspective, however, does not mean that Ibn Taymiyya is calling for unqualified obedience. Due to human fallibility, unqualified obedience is owed only to the Prophet and to God, not to other human rulers whether spiritual or temporal because "[n]o one should follow any person other than the Messenger in things in which he

---

[276] Sivan, *Radical Islam*, 90–92.
[277] Qamaruddin Khan, *The Political Thought of Ibn Taymīyah* (Islamabad: Islamic Research Institute, 1973), 37–8.
[278] Sivan, *Radical Islam*, 95–6.
[279] Ibn Taymiyyah, *Ibn Taymiyyah Expounds on Islam: Selected Writings of Shaykh al-Islam Taqi ad-Din Ibn Taymiyya on Islamic Faith, Life, and Society*, compiled and trans. Muhammad 'Abdul-Haqq Ansari (Riyadh: General Administration of Culture and Publication, 2000), 510 [Fatwa 28].
[280] Ibid., 514 [Fatwa 35].

differs from the Messenger."²⁸¹ Indeed, Ibn Taymiyya reclaims and reemphasizes his position when he states,

> [e]veryone whom God asked us to obey, whether scholar, ruler, father, or husband, is because obedience to him is obedience to God. That is why if his commands conflict with the commands of God he must not be obeyed. [...] But if one knows that the order of a ruler or the counsel of the scholar is against God's command, compliance with such order or counsel is definitely a sin against God.²⁸²

Ibn Taymiyya nonetheless suggests that the believer should show patience with a sinning or otherwise imperfect or unjust ruler. Moreover, "the Prophet has advised the believers to bear patiently the injustices which their rulers commit, and refrain from fighting them so long as they establish *salah*." For Ibn Taymiyya, it is only "heretical sects" such as the Muʿtazilah who wrongly believe that one should fight unjust or sinful rulers.²⁸³

However, the teaching of the Muʿtazilah was the official doctrine for several decades until al-Mutawakkil abandoned their doctrine for Sunni orthodoxy between 842 and 846. Thereafter, the Muʿtazilah were fought as heretics.²⁸⁴ The case of the Muʿtazilah highlights one fact that applies to all systems using religion to legitimize the exercise of power: the orthodox belief is the one approved by the religious or political regime in power, and regime change may cause yesterday's orthodoxy to become today's heresy (and vice versa). However, the interesting aspect of Ibn Taymiyya's argument is not his exploration of Muʿtazilah heresies, which is primarily directed against their understanding of humans' free will,²⁸⁵ but rather his statement that one should obey and not rebel against any ruler who performs the ritual prayer (*salah*). In Ibn Taymiyya's theological writings, performing *salah* is the key qualifier for a ruler (or any other person) to be considered a Muslim because "of those who offer *salah* no one would be *kafir* [unbeliever] unless he is a hypocrite."²⁸⁶ Moreover, "[a]mong the heretical sects we may have people who have faith in their heart but are guilty of ignorance, wrongdoing, and mistakes with regard to the Sunnah. Such people are

---

281 Ibid., 519 [Fatwa 19].
282 Ibid., 520 [Fatwa 19].
283 Ibid., 536 [Fatwa 28]. Although the Muʿtazilah were originally an Islamic school, they were also a religious movement. However, they were persecuted as a heretical sect, and Ibn Taymiyya understood the Muʿtazilah as such.
284 Sabine Schmidtke, "Neuere Forschungen zur Muʿtazila unter besonderer Berücksichtigung der späteren Muʿtazila ab dem 4./10. Jahrhundert," *Arabica* 45 (1998): 380.
285 Jon Hoover, "The Justice of God and the Best of All Possible Worlds: The Theodicy of Ibn Taymiyya," *Theological Review* 27 (2006): 58–63.
286 Ibn Taymiyyah, *Ibn Taymiyyah Expounds on Islam*, 554 [Fatwa 3].

neither *kafir* nor hypocrites."[287] Indeed, Ibn Taymiyya claims that "[t]hose who excommunicate the exponents of heresy and fancy [...], like the Shi'ah, the Mu'-tazilah and others, go against the Qur'an and the Sunna, the Consensus of the Companions and the Successors."[288]

Yet, this tolerant and moderate sounding Ibn Taymiyya encountered in his usually overlooked works[289] is not the Ibn Taymiyya who has drawn the attention of twentieth and twenty-first century Islamists. The polemic Ibn Taymiyya writes against the Mongol occupation attracts modern Islamist thinkers. Ironically, in his contentious writings, Ibn Taymiyya responds to the political needs of the Mamluk authorities. The Mamluks had a political interest in calling for *jihad* against the Mongols. The question they had to answer was whether the Mongols were still to be considered Muslims (Sunni, although they adopted Islam under Shi'i influence) or whether they could be considered infidels. If they could reasonably be considered non-Muslim or even apostates, then one could proclaim *jihad* against them; otherwise, any aggression against them could not be justified that easily through religious means.[290] Ibn Taymiyya, however, willingly complied, not simply out of political motives but also and perhaps primarily on the grounds of his own religious orthodoxy and his personal experiences. In this context, Ibn Taymiyya argued that the Mongol ruler could not be considered a legitimate (Sunni) Muslim ruler because "a Sunni ruler becomes illegitimate if he does not apply a substantial part of the Shari'a. [T]he ruler who neglects or transgresses Islamic law is ipso facto an infidel, or rather an apostate, and hence the object of jihad."[291] Ibn Taymiyya does not understand this statement as an encouragement or even a legitimization for protests by the people. For him, *jihad* remains primarily a collective duty, and his teachings are not meant to imply that individuals can rise against the authority as concluded by later readers.

One of Ibn Taymiyya's key issues is the fact that the Mongols, while they formally converted to Islam, see no contradiction between Islamic law and traditional Mongol law; they did not abandon their traditional law for the Shari'a. Moreover, Ibn Taymiyya raises doubts as to whether the Mongol ruler Ghazan

---

287 Ibid., 555 [Fatwa 3].
288 Ibid., 556 [Minhaj as-Sunnah 3:62].
289 A detailed analysis of Ibn Taymiyya's theology can be found in Jon Hoover's excellent study *Ibn Taymiyya's Theodicy of Perpetual Optimism: Islamic Philosophy, Theology and Science: Texts and Studies* (Leiden: Brill 2007).
290 Emmanuel Sivan, *Radical Islam: Medieval Theology and Modern Politics*, enlarged ed. (New Haven: Yale University Press, 1990), 96–7.
291 Ibid., 99.

truly converted to Islam. He accuses him and his court of not following the pillars of Islam such as pilgrimage, prayer, and fasting. Instead of Shari'a, they preferred the Law of Chinggis Khan, whom the Mongols considered as important as Muhammad.[292] As outlined earlier, even for the more scholarly Ibn Taymiyya, the watershed question used to distinguish between a Muslim and an infidel is the question of whether the ritual prayer *salah* is performed. Whoever does not perform *salah* has to be considered *kafir*, an unbeliever, against whom *jihad* is not only justifiable but mandatory. In this context, he considers a legitimate government to be a government that fulfills its main function, namely by maintaining "order through coercion, but coercion exercised in a correct way, i.e., by enforcing God's law."[293] In Ibn Taymiyya's words, "[t]he purpose of political authority is to subject the whole of human life to God and to make His word supreme." With reference to the Qur'an (8:39), he states "[f]ight them until there is no more tumult or oppression, and there prevails justice and faith in God altogether and everywhere."[294] Ibn Taymiyya understands government offices to be "religious obligations" of which the noblest merit is "seeking only the pleasure of God." Consequently, political authority is primarily a "religious matter and sought as a means to secure God's pleasure and favor."[295] This commitment is precisely what he accuses the Mongols of neglecting. Consequently, his argument focuses on "the legitimacy of waging jihad against Muslims who revolt against the established political authorities or refuse to abide by the rules of the *shari'a*, and therefore compromise the pure religion."[296] For this purpose, Ibn Taymiyya first established the doctrine that *jihad* is the greatest pillar of Islam. He states,

> [t]he command to participate in jihad and the mention of its merits occur innumerable times in the Qur'an and the Sunna. Therefore it is the best voluntary [religious] act that man can perform. All scholars agree that it is better than the *hajj* (greater pilgrimage) and the *'umra* (lesser pilgrimage), than voluntary *salāh* and voluntary fasting, as the Koran and Sunna indicate.[297]

Ibn Taymiyya considers the religious and temporal merits of *jihad* both for those who participate and for those who do not actively participate. *Jihad* itself "im-

---

[292] Reuven Amitai-Preiss, "Ghazan, Islam and Mongol Tradition: A View from the Mamlūk Sultanate," *Bulletin of the School of Oriental and African Studies* 59 (1996): 9–10.
[293] Peters, *Jihad in Classical and Modern Islam*, 43.
[294] Ibn Taymiyyah, *Ibn Taymiyyah Expounds on Islam*, 500–1 [Fatwa 28].
[295] Ibid., 502; 504.
[296] Peters, *Jihad in Classical and Modern Islam*, 44.
[297] Ibn Taymiyya, "Jihad," in Peters, *Jihad in Classical and Modern Islam*, 47.

plies all kinds of worship" and "[m]ore than any other act it implies love and devotion for God."²⁹⁸ However, contrary to modern Islamists' views and contrary to some premodern doctrines that have already been discussed, for Ibn Taymiyya, *jihad* remains a collective duty (*fard kifaya*) and not an individual duty.²⁹⁹ His list of occasions that call for fighting is extensive; all of the reasons he offers are related to neglecting established rules of Islam such as not offering the five daily prayers, not performing any of the pilgrimages, or refusing to pay *zakah* or to carry out the obligatory fast (Ramadan). In addition, one "should also fight those who do not recognize that adultery, gambling, drinking wine, and other shameful acts are forbidden, or who refuse to judge cases against life, property, honor, and sex, according to the rules of the Shariʿa laid down in the Qurʾan and Sunna." ³⁰⁰ In other words, sinning or erring in faith is no longer subject to correction or punishment, but is rather an indication of an abandonment of the faith, legitimizing fighting the sinner who is now considered an unbeliever.

This long list, together with his accusation that the Mongols did not truly convert to Islam, allows Ibn Taymiyya to argue that *jihad* against the Mongols is not only justifiable, it is a (collective) religious obligation. Although he never defied the legitimacy of any particular sultan and wrote his polemical justification of *jihad* against the Mongols in support of the Mamluk regime, his arguments against the Mongols' soundness of faith can be applied to a wide range of contexts that Ibn Taymiyya did not have in mind, namely that his reason could be used to challenge the legitimacy of a Muslim state's ruler if his faith and the performance of his religious duties are questioned. Ibn Taymiyya's argument allowing for *jihad* against other Muslim states has been considered innovative. With respect to the historical context, Ibn Taymiyya legitimizes *jihad* by one regime over another regime that is perceived, whether for religious or political reasons or a mixture of both, as un-Islamic. However, the characterization of the Mongols as non-Muslim, including the underlying pattern that associates the political enemy with apostasy, is not new.

On the contrary, a similar strategy or version of it seems to run through the entire history of Islam, or at least a significant part of it, though these arguments are not always used to justify *jihad* against external authorities or other modern states, but rather to fight political or religious opposition within a given territory.³⁰¹ A paradigmatic example of such a case is the Seljuq Empire's response to

---

298 Ibid., 48.
299 Ibn Taymiyyah, *Ibn Taymiyyah Expounds on Islam*, 531 [Fatwa 15].
300 Ibid., 565 [Fatwa 28].
301 This tactic of labeling political or religious opposition or opponents as unbelievers is of course not unique to Islam. For example, similar reasoning was applied during the Christian Ref-

the Nizari Isma'ili thread. The Seljuq Turks had conquered the area encompassing modern day Iran, Syria, and Iraq. To stabilize their power base, they "rapidly added Islamicate legislation to that of the step" and "adopted Islamic symbols of sovereignty," utilizing "Sunni Islam and Persianate literacy culture." They replaced and eliminated their Shi'i predecessors with a new Sunni elite.[302] However, it is not correct to view the conflict between the Seljuqs and the Isma'ilis simply along a Sunni-Shi'i line. Richard Bulliet emphasizes the factors played by "local autonomy and patriotic identification" and a divide between leading families. Some of these families joined the service of the new regime in power, whereas others remained in often violent opposition.[303] The situation is comparable to that of today's Bahrain, where a Sunni minority rules over the Shi'i majority and excludes the vast majority from power and influence.

One of the more successful (violent) opposition groups were the Nizari Isma'ili. During the so-called Alamut period, they established an independent territorial power within the Seljuq Empire in the mountainous regions of today's Iran and Syria. Their rule lasted from around 1090 to 1256, until both the Seljuq Empire and the Nizari Isma'ili state were conquered and destroyed by the Mongols.[304] Consequently, although it has not been perceived as such, the Seljuq's fight against the Nizari Isma'ili can be regarded as similar to Ibn Taymiyya's justification of declaring *jihad* on the Mongols. In both cases, *jihad* would have been declared upon a territorial power. However, it is more reasonable, at least from the Seljuqs' perspective, to consider the Nizari Isma'ilis together with al-Mawardi rebels or apostates who assemble "in a place away from Muslims where they become a power to reckon with."[305] This view is more in keeping with the Seljuqs', who regarded the Nizaris as internal rebels who had abandoned faith rather than as a territorial power of their own right.

Ironically, Nizam al-Mulk, in his famous *Siyar al-Muluk* that echoes "an official anti-Isma'ili attitude,"[306] revealed positions on drinking or gambling that could be read as justifications for fighting based on Ibn Taymiyya's harsh critique of the Mongols as opposed to Islam. *Siyar al-Muluk* is a classic example

---

ormation, with Catholics accusing Lutherans of atheism, Lutherans accusing Calvinists of atheism, and other conflicts.
302 Linda T. Darling, *History of Social Justice and Political Power in the Middle East: The Circle of Justice From Mesopotamia to Globalization* (Florence: Routledge, 2012), 89.
303 Richard W. Bulliet, "Local Politics in Eastern Iran under the Ghaznavids and Seljuks," *Iranian Studies*, 11 (1978): 41.
304 Farhad Daftary, *The Ismā'īlīs: Their History and Doctrines* (Cambridge: Cambridge University Press, 1990), 324.
305 Al-Mawardi, *The Ordinances of Government*, chap. 5 (61).
306 Farhad Daftary, *The Assassin Legends: Myths of the Isma'ilis* (London: I. B. Tauris, 1995), 24.

of hypocrisy by the governmental authority, which considers it necessary to uphold Islamic laws of conduct in public but not in the private settings at court, which are invisible to the general public. The book includes a chapter on drinking parties in which the ruler is encouraged to provide a sufficient quantity of decent wine for his guests. The book also provides advice for couriers on how to respond to orders given by the ruler in a state of intoxication. Although giving orders while drunk should be avoided, *Siyar al-Muluk* is sufficiently realistic to assume that this might occasionally occur. Consequently, it advises courtiers and other servants to return when the ruler is sober and request confirmation (or revision) of the order.[307]

Although this misconduct is a sin according to Islamic law, it seems to be essentially acceptable and partly even encouraged. "[F]easting, drinking, hunting, polo and wrestling" are recommended activities for the ruler to keep his spirit up as long as they are done in moderation. If a ruler is "occupied day and night with entertainments, hunting and drinking," he neglects his duties and may lose his realm.[308] Nonetheless, displays of drunkenness have to be avoided in public so that they remain invisible to the subjects.

As stated earlier, Ibn Taymiyya labeled the Nizari Isma'ilis as Shi'i extremists. Contrary to the Seljuq courtiers, the Nizari Isma'ilis, particularly under their first leader Hasan-i Sabbah, were known for the strict enforcement of Islamic law and for their piety. Despite their Shi'i "heresies," their conception of a purified Islam is much closer to Ibn Taymiyya's realm of thought than the Seljuq Empire's conception, which Ibn Taymiyya perceives as a legitimate authority. To some extent, it is even possible to draw some parallels between the Cathars and other medieval Christian reform movements and the Nizari Isma'ilis. However, addressing Nizam al-Mulk and the Nizari Isma'ili movement under Hasan-i Sabbah is not without difficulties. The Isma'ili were "perhaps the most severely persecuted community within the Muslim world, subjected to massacres in many localities."[309] The Nizaris, who established their own territorial power, are primarily known for their guerilla tactics of assassinating officials of the Seljuq Empire and crusaders. Because of these tactics, the Nizari Isma'ilis are better known by the name "Assassins." Nizam al-Mulk, "who nurtured a deep hatred for the Isma'ilis,"[310] is usually assumed to be the first and most

---

307 Nizam al-Mulk, *The Book of Government*, 1.29; 1.15.
308 Ibid., 1.17.3; 1.4.5.
309 Daftary, *The Assassin Legends*, 6.
310 Farhad Daftary, "Ḥasan-i Ṣabbāḥ and the Origins of the Nizārī Isma'ili Movement," in *Medieval Isma'ili History and Thought*, ed. Farhad Daftary (Cambridge: Cambridge University Press, 1996), 187.

prominent victim of these assassinations, although recently, Neguin Yavari doubted that the Nizaris were actually behind his assassination and suggested that he "was most probably murdered with the foreknowledge of the Sultan, and his death blamed on the Isma'ili."[311] The Nizaris' infiltration of the sultan's court might have contributed to Nizam al-Mulk's downfall and assassination.[312] However, as a consequence of their well-known assassination tactics, the Nizaris were blamed for almost all assassinations that occurred during the so-called Alamut period.

According to Farhad Daftary, the Nizaris used their assassination tactics for the humane purpose of avoiding unnecessary bloodshed. "The assassinations were performed in as public a setting as possible, since part of the purpose was to intimidate other actual or potential enemies."[313] The Nizaris did not rely on assassinations alone; they also engaged in conversion, open rebellion, and infiltration. Through these combined tactics, the Nizaris were able to conquer strategically important fortresses, primarily in mountainous areas. Unfortunately, all original Nizari Isma'ili documents of the Alamut period are lost; the writings of the Seljuq Empire in which the Nizaris appear are full of polemics against the Nizari Isma'ilis. These polemics reveal the justification for their persecution.

Under Nizam al-Mulk, the Seljuqs not only fought a military battle against the Nizari Isma'ili, but they also fought an intellectual battle in response to the Isma'ilis' reputation for respecting learning. For example, the Isma'ilis hosted prominent scholars in their headquarters such as the prominent (at least for a short time) Isma'ili Nasir al-Din Tutsi, who switched religious affiliations a number of times. As mentioned above, to undermine the Isma'ilis' reputation, Nizam al-Mulk appointed al-Ghazali. Frank Griffel reads al-Ghazali's appointment as primarily political because al-Ghazali considered both the philosophers and the Isma'ilis as unbelievers. For al-Ghazali, they "undermine the moral and legal authority of revelation." Therefore, he regarded killing them as obligatory.[314] The attempt to undermine the Isma'ilis' intellectual reputation is also reflected in Nizam al-Mulk's famous *Siyar al-Muluk*. Nizam al-Mulk wrote this book in his last years of service as grand vizier of the Seljuq Empire, which is

---

311 Neguin Yavari, "Mirrors for Princes or a Hall of Mirrors? Nizam al Mulk's *Siyar al-muluk* Reconsidered," *al-Masāq: Islam and the Medieval Mediterranean*, 20 (2008): 55. For a similar claim see also Safi, *The Politics of Knowledge*, 74–77.
312 Nagel, *Staat und Glaubensgemeinschaft im Islam*, 91.
313 Daftary, *The Ismāʿīlis*, 353.
314 Frank Griffel, *Al-Ghazali's Philosophical Theology* (New York: Oxford University Press, 2009), 102–3.

also the year in which he appointed al-Ghazali. The first and main part of the book was completed in 1091, and about one year later he added another eleven chapters. These additional chapters deal primarily with heresies and revolts and reflect on the territorial power established by the Nizari Isma'ili's in 1090 under Hasan-i Sabbah, although not on the assassinations. The Nizaris had not yet turned to this tactic when Nizam al-Mulk was completing *Siyar al-Mulūk*.

Some sections in *Siyar al-Muluk* attempt to undermine the Isma'ilis' intellectual reputation. For instance, he describes members of the *da'wa*, the Isma'ili missionaries, as being imperfect in speech, i.e., they were portrayed as being imperfect in the language of Islam. Furthermore, according to Frank Griffel, Nizam al-Mulk laid out a middle ground by politically defining who should be considered a Muslim and who should not. This middle ground does not mean that he attempted to balance the disagreements between rivaling sects. On the contrary, his policy includes and supports the suppression of a number of Muslim sects.[315] Moreover, Nizam al-Mulk feared the influence of the Isma'ilis after Isma'ili agents had gained access to Sultan Malik Shah.[316] For Nizam al-Mulk, all opposition to the caliph, who was by then more of a puppet than a serious authority, ruling more as a titular head of Sunni Islam than anything else,[317] is considered disobedience to the Prophet, similar to disobedience to God, replacing the Sunna with heresy.[318] While the caliph's status as a puppet and the consideration of disobedience to the caliph as disobedience to the Prophet might sound contradictory, Nizam al-Mulk aimed to maintain the caliph's office as an authority that provides legitimacy. The sultan intended to abolish the caliphate. To undermine the Nizari's infiltration tactics, he disapproves of the employment of all non-Muslims, meaning non-Sunnis, although he had and maintained "cordial relations with several Jewish bankers;" even Nizam al-Mulk's steward was a non-Muslim.[319]

With respect to the Isma'ilis, the general approach has already been foreshadowed: the Isma'ilis are portrayed as unbelievers who speak improperly, i.e., they have no proper command of the language of the Qur'an. Moreover, *Siyar al-Muluk* accuses the Isma'ilis of imposing heavy taxes, making the drink-

---

[315] Frank Griffel, *Apostasie und Toleranz: Die Entwicklung zu al-Ghazālīs Urteil gegen die Philosophie und die Reaktion der Philosophen* (Leiden: Brill, 2000), 243, 253.
[316] Ibid., 225.
[317] Shafique N. Virani, *The Ismailis in the Middle Ages: A History of Survival, a Search for Salvation* (Oxford: Oxford University Press, 2007), 7.
[318] Nizam al-Mulk, *The Book of Government*, 1.3.9.
[319] Aptin Khanbaghi, *The Fire, the Star and the Cross: Minority Religions in Medieval and Early Modern Iran* (London: I. B. Tauris, 2006), 43.

ing of wine lawful, and permitting commerce with mothers, sisters, and daughters.[320] Given the rather lax attitude on the consumption of alcohol in *Siyar al-Muluk* and the heavy taxes that the local population had to endure under Seljuq domination, these accusations can be easily regarded as political polemics and propaganda. In general, the examples and stories narrated in *Siyar al-Muluk* on heresies that have to be fought refer to the Isma'ilis. The one exception are the Zoroastrians, who appear throughout the book under different medieval names and are occasionally referred to by the regions in which the Isma'ili movement were strong.[321] In essence, Nizam al-Mulk aims to create a genealogy of heresy, starting with the pre-Islamic Mazdak, relating the Isma'ili threat directly back to Mazdak and his followers.

In his attempt to display the Nizari Isma'ilis as just a new manifestation of an old heresy, he attributes to them a feature that is associated with pre-Islamic Mazdikis who, as Kathryn Babayan notes, "advocated the sharing of land and women, for they saw them as the main reason men became greedy, envious, and deceitful. They were causes of social disorder."[322] For Nizam al-Mulk, the abolition of private property and marriage is simply scandalous because "[r]eligion exists for the protection of wealth and wives; if these two become free, then what be the difference between beasts and men, for it is of animals to be equal in feeding and coupling, not intelligent human beings."[323]

Nizam al-Mulk's judgment of the Isma'ilis is unmistakably harsh. He states that there has never been "a more vile, more perverted or more irreligious crowd than these people, who behind walls are plotting harm to this country and seeking to destroy the religion." He goes on to assert that "these dogs will emerge from their hiding places, and will revolt against this empire and support the claims of the Shi'a."[324] They are nothing more than rabble-rousers who should be fought and killed wherever one finds them. The harsh response to the Isma'ilis is justified through the assessment that these rebels betray Islam and are therefore even worse than unbelievers (who do not know better). The Sunnis, and in particular, the Turks, are portrayed as the opposite of this heretic threat. For Nizam al-Mulk, it is certain that "God [...] has favored the Turks because they are orthodox Muslims and do not tolerate vanity and heresy."[325]

---

320 Nizam al-Mulk, *The Book of Government*, 2.45.35.
321 Ibid., 2.46.39.
322 Kathryn Babayan, *Mystics, Monarchs, and Messiahs: Cultural Landscapes of Early Modern Iran* (Cambridge: Harvard University Press, 2002), 170.
323 Nizam al-Mulk, *The Book of Government*, 2.44.8.
324 Ibid., 2.43.2.
325 Ibid., 2.41.4.

The strategy of polemicizing against the Isma'ilis, however, is all too visible. They are portrayed as rebels, unbelievers, and heretics without any morals. The labels "heretic" and "unbeliever" have been used in some medieval Islamic texts and treatises almost interchangeably and often in the same sentence, referring to the same religious group. Usually, accusations of heresy and unbelief appear together with the charge of unjustified rebellions. As outlined earlier, traditional Sunni thought does not justify rebellion and resistance against rulers because their authority is supposed to be God's will and disobedience is associated with disobeying the Prophet. Consequently, all rebellion against ruling authorities has to be considered as disobedience to God. Therefore, the Seljuq, particularly according to Nizam al-Mulk's rhetoric against the Isma'ilis, can be read as falling into the generally accepted politico-religious language of the time. Nonetheless, a rebellion *per se* is a political act, even if it is justified by religious means. The difference between Sunni and Shi'i is not essentially about religious doctrines, at least not about the core doctrines related to Islam's five pillars, but about leadership and its legitimacy: who is/was rightfully the successor of the Prophet? This question about religious-political leadership lies in the area between the political and religious realms.

However, taking Nizam al-Mulk's *Siyar al-Muluk* as a whole and taking his justifications of sins into account, one can argue that the religious aspect of power is a means to an end rather than an end in itself. Moreover, the example of the Nizari Isma'ilis demonstrates how religious and political goals are interwoven. The interrelationship between religious, socio-economic, and political aspects becomes even more visible by looking at the conflict from the Isma'ilis' perspective.

2.2.3 Sunni and Non-Sunni Perspectives on Disobedience and Revolt

Looking at the conflict between the Seljuqs and the Nizari Isma'ilis from an Isma'ili perspective, it seems that the Nizari Isma'ili actually have a legitimate case, at least viewed from a contemporary perspective, which would view the Nizari Isma'ili as a liberation movement against a colonial power sanctioned by international law.[326] According to Farhad Daftary, the leading expert on the Isma'ilis, the Nizari movement has been regarded either "as a mere schismatic Isma'ilis movement" or "as an Iranian revolutionary movement with 'nationalistic'

---

[326] Koch, "Johannes von Salisbury und die Nizari Ismailiten unter Terrorismusverdacht," 31.

ideals."³²⁷ The Nizaris are, without a doubt, a religious movement that is usually associated with messianic thinking. Because of their messianic expectations, they had little reason to write about their thoughts.³²⁸ However, sources strongly indicate that they are also a political and socio-economic movement. For instance, the Nizaris were known for their communal projects and communities based on the principle of equality. To express equality among each other, they addressed each other as *rafiq* (comrade).³²⁹ W.B. Bartlett considers them as "an openly Persian movement, which appealed to proud nationalistic emotions in the region." To comply with nationalistic feelings, the Nizaris used Persian, rather than Arabic, as the primary language for religious services and intellectual writings. Because the Persian population was heavily taxed by the Seljuqs, who were considered an oppressive foreign force, the Nizaris also had supporters among non-Shi'i segments of the population. The local populace was also "angered by oppression of alien and loosely-disciplined overlords."³³⁰ Apparently, the Nizari Isma'ilis had a valid point. Their influence and popularity was not limited to their strongholds. They succeeded in infiltrating parts of the urban and rural population in large regions of what is now Iran. In addition, they successfully infiltrated the Seljuq army and court.³³¹

Remembering that the Nizari Isma'ili's popularity resulted not simply from cultural-religious differences between the new regime and the majority population but also and perhaps even more so from socio-economic (high tax burdens) and political reasons (the replacement of one elite with a new one), it is worth exploring how another Sunni author responds to issues of socio-economic injustice. Ibn Khaldun, whom we have already discussed in a different context, speaks explicitly to these concerns. He addresses the deprivation of property through forced labor and exceedingly high taxes, a problem similar to the one identified by William of Pagula.

However, note that although Ibn Khaldun was a well-known figure during his lifetime, he was known as a diplomat and politician rather than as a political

---

327 Daftary, "Ḥasan-i Ṣabbāḥ and the Origins of the Nizārī Isma'ili Movement," 181.
328 Patricia Crone, *God's Rule: Government and Islam* (New York: Columbia University Press, 2004), 205.
329 Daftary, "Ḥasan-i Ṣabbāḥ," 189.
330 W.B. Bartlett, *The Assassins: The Story of Medieval Islam's Secret Sect* (Stroud: Sutton, 2001), 46.
331 Carole Hillenbrand, "The Power Struggle between the Seljuqs and the Isma'ilis of Alamūt, 487–518/1094–1124: The Seljuq Perspective," in *Medieval Isma'ili History and Thought*, ed. Farhad Daftary (Cambridge: Cambridge University Press, 1996), 218.

thinker.[332] In this sense, his faith is similar to that of Ibn Taymiyya. Although some ideas that seem to echo Ibn Khaldun's are found in sixteenth century Ottoman writings,[333] his work was not broadly received until the eighteenth century in the Ottoman Empire, and then in the West he was rediscovered in the nineteenth century.[334] After his rediscovery, he attracted the interest of numerous intellectual circles, and his work was hijacked for various ideological causes that presented a "more mythical icon than a realistic portrait" of Ibn Khaldun.[335] Additionally, in *Muqaddima* Ibn Khaldun is more of an observer who is interested in how people act. Consequently, his pronouncements regarding the legitimacy of certain actions are referred to rather indirectly. Moreover, his key concepts are *'umrān* (civilization or culture) and *daula* (state), which implies that his focus is not necessary on the people, but on the representatives of power.[336] With these reservations in mind, it is nonetheless worth examining the writings of Ibn Khaldun. Before discussing how people act according to Ibn Khaldun, it is important to address their motivations for action.

Like most premodern authors, Ibn Khaldun emphasizes the importance of justice. Although scholars disagree whether Ibn Khaldun should be read primarily as a Muslim or a secular author, the previous discussion of Ibn Khaldun's ideas on *jihad* implies that we can assume at least a religiously colored conception of justice. However, his main concern is not justice, but rather the absence of it because injustice not only "ruins civilization," it also means "the complete destruction of the dynasty."[337] As noted earlier, Ibn Khaldun emphasizes the unity of royal authority and the caliphate. A weakness of one means a weakening of Islam. This emphasis can also be seen when he defines injustice:

---

332 Táhir Hamami, "Ibn Khaldun: Life and Political Activity or the *'allama* on Board," in *Ibn Khaldun: The Mediterranean in the 14th Century, Rise and Fall of Empires: Exhibition in the Real Alcázar of Seville, May-September 2006*, ed. Jesús Viguera Molins (Seville: Fundatión El legado andalusí, 2006), 304–315.
333 Cornell Fleischer, "Royal Authority: Dynastic Cyclism, and "Ibn Khaldûnism" in Sixteenth-Century Ottoman Letters," in *Ibn Khaldun and Islamic Ideology*, ed. Bruce B. Lawrence (Leiden: Brill, 1984), 47–8, 51. Cornell H. Fleischer, *Bureaucrat and Intellectual in the Ottoman Empire. The Historian Mustafa Âli (1541–1600)* (Princeton: Princeton University Press, 1986), 303–4.
334 Westerners owe the renewed interest in Ibn Khaldun's thought to Arnold Joseph Toynbee in particular. See, Robert Irwin, "Toynbee and Ibn Khaldūn," *Middle Eastern Studies* 33 (1997): 461–480.
335 Cengiz Tomar, "Between Myth and Reality: Approaches to Ibn Khaldun in the Arab World," *Asian Journal of Social Science* 36, no. 3–4 (2008): 610.
336 Aziz Al-Azmeh, *Ibn Khaldun in Modern Scholarship: A Study in Orientalism* (London: Third World Centre for Research and Publishing, 1981), 18.
337 Ibn Khaldun, *Muqaddimah*, 2.95.

> Whoever takes someone's property, or uses him for forced labor, or presses an unjustified claim against him, or imposes upon him a duty not required by the religious law, does an injustice to the particular person. People who collect unjustified taxes commit an injustice. Those who infringe upon property (rights) commit an injustice. Those who take away property commit an injustice. Those who deny people their rights commit an injustice. Those who, in general, take property by force, commit an injustice.[338]

The relationship between injustice and property (rights), already discussed for William of Pagula, partly for William of Ockham, and for Nizam al-Mulk from a different perspective, is again central here. Similarly to William of Pagula, Ibn Khaldun describes forced labor as "one of the greatest injustices" because it deprives the people of their ability to accumulate the basic necessities for maintaining their life and capital. Violations of property rights more generally, he sees as "even greater and more destructive to civilization."[339] The latter occurs in a more sophisticated way than described by William of Pagula. It is not simply that members of the dynasty's household take a sheep or a camel here and there. Instead, Ibn Khaldun has in mind a large scale manipulation of the market which is caused "by buying their possessions as cheaply as possible and reselling the merchandise to them at the highest possible price by means of forced sales and purchases."[340]

A second deprivation of property occurs due to exceedingly high taxes that are considered a violation of Islamic law.[341] Despite the prohibition, trade taxes, excise taxes, and luxury taxes are relatively common. These taxes rise slowly over time so that "no one knows specifically who increased them or levied them. They lie upon the subjects like an obligation and tradition" until they exhaust the subjects and accumulate to a burden beyond equity.[342] Eventually, the people become desperate and are forced out of their businesses. In their desperation, because they cannot make a living in a natural way through commerce, agriculture, or the crafts, they aim for unnatural ways like digging for treasure.[343] For Ibn Khaldun, forced labor, the manipulation of the market, and excessively high taxes are all manifestations of the ruler's neglect of the duties set upon him by God.

---

338 Ibid., 2.96.
339 Ibid., 2.98.
340 Ibid., 2.99.
341 Dieter Weiss, "Arabische Wirtschaftspolitik im Lichte der Systemtheorie von Ibn Khaldun," *Die Welt des Islams* 28 (1988): 590.
342 Ibn Khaldun, *Muqaddimah*, 2.81.
343 Ibid., 2.281.

These oppressive actions have consequences for the ruler. As indicated earlier, the subjects become fearful and depressed; they lie, use tricks, and become deceitful. The military order and the border protection become unreliable because the subjects are no longer trustworthy on the battlefield. Eventually, the subjects conspire against the ruler to kill him, although it is more likely that the ruler will be killed by a member of his household than by an ordinary subject. Ibn Khaldun refers to rebels "who are members of the ruling family and other (types of rebels)" without making it explicit who the other rebels might be.[344] Because the realm is already in moral decay, it is also likely that God interferes and destroys the dynasty or allows it to be destroyed.[345] The idea of divine intervention, without the typical notion that the people may cry and pray to God for help as typical in Christian writings of the time, is mentioned throughout *Muqaddimah*, either to indicate God's support or God's refusal or punishment.[346]

However, Ibn Khaldun does not state that the people have a *right* to rebel, although he emphasizes that the ruler neglects his duties. Instead, Ibn Khaldun stresses that they will rebel anyway; the consequences are the dynasty's decay and perhaps the ruler's death. While Ibn Jamaʿa also indicates that the people might rebel in a case of a *fāsiq* imam or ruler who then has the right to fight the people until they return to obedience,[347] in Ibn Khaldun's scenario, that ruler simply lacks the means to secure his power and to force the people, including the military, to obey and support him.

Although the main reasons for rebellions are socio-economic in nature, Ibn Khaldun's argument is infused with religious language. Although he does not provide us with a religious justification for violence, he nonetheless presents us with a socio-economic explanation couched in religious language that can be applied to the situation of the Nizari Ismaʿilis and the Persian population under Seljuq rule. Despite the explicit political and socio-economic nature of the conflict, the Seljuqs succeeded in presenting this conflict as a truly religious problem. Indeed, they were so successful that even some contemporary scholarly writings deny that the Nizaris were Islamic, comparing the Nizari Ismaʿilis with al-Qaeda. For instance, Hamit Bozarslan suggests that both groups have left Islam.[348] The Nizari Ismaʿilis share the fate of frequent comparisons with con-

---

344 Ibid., 1.340, 2.109–10.
345 Ibid., 2. 257.
346 Briton Cooper Busch, "Divine Intervention in the 'Muqaddimah' of Ibn Khaldun," *History of Religions* 3 (1968): 325–7.
347 Ibn Jamaʿa, *Taḥrīr al-aḥkām*, 2.7.
348 Hamit Bozarslan, "Le Jihâd: Réceptions et usages d'une injonction Coranique d'hier à aujourd'hui," *Vingtième Siècle: Revue d'histoire* 82 (2004): 28.

temporary jihadist and terrorist groups with the Kharijites, whose ideas are still linked, at least polemically, to the Muslim Brotherhood and jihadist groups in Egypt.[349]

Given that we know so little about both the Nizari Isma'ilis and the Kharijites, they are perfect projection foils for idealization and condemnation. In the same way as the Nizaris, the Kharijites are frequently associated with terrorist techniques.[350] Originally, together with the Shi'i, they revolted against the Umayyad dynasty because the Umayyads "continued to exacerbate the emerging class difference between the small patriarchal network of the tribal elite and the masses of the Muslims."[351] Similar to contested authors such as Sayyid Qutb, the Kharijites are either portrayed as an early democratic movement or as terrorists. The terrorism label in itself is misleading and not very helpful as an analytical term. The label is not attached to the Kharijites in any analytical manner, but is used rather poetically, in a way that projects a modern or contemporary concept back to a time and age that did not have any concept of terrorism, but one of violent conflict resolution. Nonetheless, the Kharijites were the only group of rebels against 'Uthman who "retained a clear conviction that [it] had been right to kill him."[352] Ann Lambton distinguishes between moderate and extremist branches of the Kharijites. According to her, the extreme Kharijites thought that "all of their adversaries should be put to death with their women and children. [They] excluded from Islam all quietists [and] permitted assassination for religious reasons and also considered it lawful to kill the wives and children of the heterodox." The moderates agreed that all non-Kharijite Muslims were infidels but believed "that they might be killed or despoiled only in war. An unjust *imam* was to be resisted in any and every way."[353] Patricia Crone adds to this account that the general assumption that the Kharijites refuse any form of government in favor of rule by God's law alone only applies to the Najdiyya.[354]

During the rebellion against 'Uthman, which marks the beginning of the *fitna*, 'Ali was supported by Shi'ites, Kharijites, and others, although these groups desired different outcomes. William Montgomery Watt notes that "the Kharijites wanted an impersonal law to control the state, whereas the Shi'ites

---

349 Jeffrey T. Kenney, *Muslim Rebels: Kharijites and the Politics of Extremism in Egypt* (Oxford: Oxford University Press, 2006), 19.
350 Hamid Dabashi, *Authority in Islam: From the Rise of Mohammad to the Establishment of the Umayyads* (Edison: Transaction Publishers, 1989), 129.
351 Dabashi, *Shi'ism*, 109.
352 Crone, *God's Rule*, 55.
353 Lambton, *State and Government in Medieval Islam*, 24–5.
354 Crone, *God's Rule*, 54.

wanted the supreme control to be given to a charismatic leader."³⁵⁵ However, they were united by their socio-economic situation.³⁵⁶ Thus, it is useful to narrate the situation that they were responding to. Although Salim Ibn Dhakwan's account differs only slightly from the narrative that is known through Sunni accounts, it is nonetheless useful to refer to him and not to Sunni sources simply because he offers an alternative account. From the textual evidence, Patricia Crone and Fritz Zimmermann gather that he was an Ibadi, meaning a moderate Kharijite. They suggest that he was "possibly an Omani, and apparently an acquaintance of Jābir, which is to say that he was a sectarian, possibly a provincial, and apparently a very early figure."³⁵⁷

In *Sīrat Sālim* he outlines the later years of ʿUthman's reign, which can be described as a corrupt and nepotistic regime. Salim Ibn Dhakwan pictures ʿUthman as a ruler or leader who gives to his family what belongs to the Muslim community as a whole. "He bought lands and built housing with God's money, and squandered it on his children and (other) family." He refuses to punish transgressors of the law if they were members of his family, thus denying justice to others.³⁵⁸ Bedouins were excluded from *jihad* because he did not want them to have their share of the booty; instead of qualified people, he appointed (unqualified) family members.³⁵⁹ To silence opposition,

> [h]e sent out spies to listen to people's criticism of him. When they heard a man say something, they reported it to him, and he would then deprive him of his rightful share in God's *fayʾ* on account of it. Others he punished by confiscating the property they owned, by having them flogged, or by subjecting them to discretionary punishment.³⁶⁰

The only aspect that did not appear in Sunni accounts is the accusation that ʿUthman confiscated property, although he omits other details known to Sunni sources.³⁶¹ Although Ibn Jamāʿa writes centuries later, in the story that follows ʿUthman did not follow Ibn Jamāʿa's advice of listening to any accusations of injustice caused by him and to correct them, although the "believers talked to him about his sins he was committing against God." For Salim, the people fulfilled

---

355 William Montgomery Watt, *Islam and the Integration of Society* (London: Kegan Paul, 1961), 104.
356 Ibid., 112.
357 Crone and Zimmermann, *The Epistle of Sālim Ibn Dhakwān*, 186.
358 Sālim Ibn Dhakwān, *Sīrat Sālim*, in Crone and Zimmermann, *The Epistle of Sālim Ibn Dhakwān*, 2.44–5.
359 Ibid., 2.47–8.
360 Ibid., 2.50.
361 Crone and Zimmermann, *The Epistle of Sālim Ibn Dhakwān*, 187–8.

their duty towards ʿUthman who then "declared their opinion foolish, poured abuse on them, hurt them, and expelled them from their homes without justification."[362]

In short, ʿUthman maintained his oppressive and nepotistic practices; in addition, he accused his opponents of making war on God and ordered them to be killed.[363] Eventually, "[w]hen the Muslims had made every effort to persuade ʿUthman to do what was right and he was still denying them satisfaction and obstructing (justice), they took to fighting him. And so the Muslims killed him for going astray without repenting."[364]

Salim Ibn Dhakwan describes a conflict primarily about mundane socio-economic and political issues. ʿUthman is accused of disregarding people's property rights, of gathering resources that belong to the community as a whole for his own kin, and promoting (unqualified) family members. Criticism is answered with severe punishment. In short, he describes the disadvantaged population as rebelling against a corrupt and oppressive regime. Although justice and people's rights are framed in religious language, the conflict is not about religion, at least not primarily. Because the Muslim rebels paid allegiance to ʿAli, the conflict seemed to have been settled. However, Salim outlines how soon thereafter some Kharijites became radicalized, although Crone and Zimmermann indicate that right from the beginning, the Kharijites were divided into more moderate and more extreme groups.[365] As one of the moderates, Salim accused the Kharijites of being wrong in their later criticism of ʿAli whom they blame for having abandoned the path of God. Instead, Salim suggests that they have distorted the Qurʾan and suspended God's judgment.[366] What followed was a conflict over exegesis. The Kharijites declared that all who did not follow a particular interpretation of what had been settled already as God's judgment to be infidels, meaning that they "forfeited their covenant of protection."[367] Moreover, they considered all of those infidels who did not actively engage in fighting. Additionally, all of those who hid their religion and were labeled quietists were declared to be infidels, although Salim accused them of hypocrisy.[368]

Salim concludes his epistle with an appeal to the Kharijites in which he expresses his disapproval of extremist religious views. He asks the Kharijites "to

---
362 Sālim Ibn Dhakwān, *Sīrat Sālim*, 2.49.
363 Ibid., 2.52–3.
364 Ibid., 2.57.
365 Crone and Zimmermann, *The Epistle of Sālim Ibn Dhakwān*, 212.
366 Sālim Ibn Dhakwān, *Sīrat Sālim*, 2.61.
367 Ibid., 2.63.
368 Ibid., 3.72–4.

fear God, not to make wrongful violence part of their religion, not to shun the path of those whom God guided before them, not to affiliate to people and (at the same time) act contrary to their practice, and not to separate from those who follow the conduct of the people to whom they affiliate."[369]

Viewed from a different perspective, he asks the Kharijites to stop transforming socio-economic issues into religious issues, which remain political because they are about inclusion and exclusion, and thus about group identity. Inclusion means belonging to the Kharijites; all other Muslims are branded as infidels. The exclusiveness of the identity also demands that members of the group can only live among people who are alike but not among infidels, narrowly defined. Belonging to the group means possessing rights, duties, and responsibilities. Not belonging (with the exception of the People of the Book) means not possessing any legal existence. Thus, the "infidels" can be killed or enslaved, and their property can be taken. Finally, "the existence of pagans is an affront against God because they do not recognize His existence, and they must therefore be either converted or exterminated."[370]

Patricia Crone and Fritz Zimmermann translate the Kharijites' belief that they were the only believers into modern language: "they are the only human beings. Only they had rights, duties, and responsibilities; all others were [perceived as] wild animals." They relate this kind of thinking to archaic societies who aimed to maintain their homogeneous tribal identity. If their homogeneity was under threat, they aimed to relocate their community and defended it violently. In this sense, they contradicted the Arabs' imperialist ambitions that used an inclusive religion for the foundation of a new imperial identity.[371] One identity uses Islam as an inclusive group identity, whereas the other fuses Islam with tribal identity and turns it into an exclusive group identity. Both add distinctive claims of truth to their causes. The chicken and egg question is whether the Kharijites would have become violently radicalized without the experience of socio-economic and political injustice. Originally, the Kharijite movement accepted the institutionalized violence of Mohammad and the first caliphs. They were perceived as enforcers of divine law and justice. The Kharijites' turn to violence was not a necessary consequence as can be shown through a later development involving the Najdiyya, usually regarded as a militant and violent-prone branch of the Kharijites.

---

369 Ibid., 3.133.
370 Crone and Zimmermann, *The Epistle of Sālim Ibn Dhakwān*, 212.
371 Ibid., 216–7.

Contrary to the mainstream Arab assumption that rulership is necessary for the administration of justice, in the ninth century some Najdiyya developed an alternative model of community based on the idea that if the believers would follow God's law, then God would not depend on human rulership to enforce that law. However, leadership cannot be completely abolished. At minimum, the spiritual guidance of a wise man is needed.[372] At the same time, imams have the tendency to turn into kings, meaning oppressive rulers or tyrants. This model culminates in the concept of the sultan as the all-powerful king in the Seljuq Empire, envisioning the sultan as "the shadow of God on earth."[373]

If the spiritual leader turns into a king/tyrant, refuses to fulfill his duties, and falls into sin, the Kharijites view violent rebellion as the appropriate response. The tyrannical leader has to be fought and deposed. If imams turn into kings and violent rebellion is eventually necessary, it seems to be reasonable not to have an imam in the first place because the imamate leads to violence and harm. Moreover, no legal obligation to institute the imamate exists.[374] This view was shared by Muʿtazili ascetics and the Najidiyya alike. The latter group aimed to shed the obligation to rebel. They were obligated to oppose illegitimate rule, but their experience of violent suppression led them to conceive of alternative concepts of community. This alternative was based on self-rule, which allowed them to abstain from rebelling against their imam. Instead, they established, to use an anachronistic term, an "anarchist" community in which all "believers were entitled to their own opinions on law and doctrine on the basis of *ijtihād*." Moreover, each believer was responsible for her own salvation. While they continued to regard themselves as the only Muslims, they "seem to have lived in perfect amity with their so-called infidel neighbours."[375]

The idea of no rulership to avoid oppression and injustice, however, is an extreme, although non-violent, move in itself and can be regarded as the utmost exception. The norm is the existence of a ruling authority that has the tendency to turn, at least occasionally, into an ill and oppressive regime. With the help of Khaled Abou el Fadl, the following section outlines non-Sunni legal positions on the abuse of power. Certain pre-modern legal arguments are later used by Khomeini to justify the Iranian Revolution.

According to the Imami School, disobedience to a just ruler damages the opponent's well-being in the hereafter. Like the mainstream Sunni position, the same school is not in favor of resisting an unjust ruler because of the harm

---

372 Patricia Crone, "Ninth-Century Muslim Anarchists," *Past & Present* 167 (2000): 10.
373 Al-Azmeh, *Muslim Kingship*, 183.
374 Crone, "Ninth-Century Muslim Anarchists," 13–5.
375 Ibid., 25–6.

that is potentially causes and because of its ineffectiveness. However, assisting the unjust ruler is similarly discouraged. At best, opponents are left with passive resistance.[376] The Imami jurists also held that any use of violence against an unjust ruler, including killing him and his supporters, is dependent on an imam's approval. Yet, as outlined above, following the disappearance of the last divinely appointed imam and, thus, the absence of a recognized authority, rebelling against an unjust ruler was practically impossible. The Imami jurists worked around it by arguing that his deputy may authorize rebellion if harm and *fitna* can be avoided. In most circumstances, by rebelling, more harm is done and may cause the rebels' ruin. If the rebellion could be performed without causing harm to others or jeopardizing their safety, rebellion may be permitted. The rule that no harm should be caused, however, is a serious and not easily overcome obstacle, which renders rebellion very unlikely, if not impossible. While the Imami jurists discourage any engagement in open rebellion, they argue that the rebels against an unjust ruler are not committing infractions. This would only be the case if the rebel acts against a just ruler. This opinion also implies that, independently of the jurists' position, rebellions took place, which leads to the question of how those who are not actively involved in the rebellion should act or not act. Here, the Imami jurists argue that Muslims "should not support or aid unjust rulers in any material way. Working with unjust rulers might be a pragmatic necessity, but one should not engage in such conduct unless one knows, to a degree of certainty, that doing so will not entail committing an injustice."[377]

The Muslim's loyalty thus does not rest with the unjust ruler, nor may a Muslim engage in any action from which the ruler may benefit. Yet, similar to scholastic thinkers in the twelfth century, to circumvent the "trap" that the appropriate authority that can legitimize a rebellion is missing, the jurists invoke the legal concept of *ḍarūra* (necessity). Depending on circumstances, something that is usually forbidden can be justified out of necessity.[378] Similarly, the *ḍarūra* principle can be invoked to legitimize rebellion.

The general approach, however, that encourages passive resistance and disobedience to orders that violate God's command is not too different from Ibn Taymiyya's account as outlined above. However, the Zaydi School, which also belongs to the Shi'i tradition, favors a different approach. Zaydi argues that an "unjust ruler is placed in the category of the iniquitous by defiance, while a *bāghī* is

---

376 Abou el Fadl, *Religion and Violence in Islamic Law*, 296.
377 Ibid., 299.
378 Mawil Izzi Dien, *Islamic Law: From Historical Foundations to Contemporary Practice* (Notre Dame: Notre Dame University Press, 2004), 82–92.

placed in the category of the iniquitous by interpretation."³⁷⁹ A *bāghī* rebels against a just ruler; his rebellion qualifies as a sin. One can only commit a sin against a just ruler (and against God), however. Whether somebody meets the criteria of *bāghī* is an interpretation the Zaydi jurists argue they are qualified to make, independent of the existence of a rightfully guided imam. Similarly, they take up the responsibility of judging whether a ruler is just or unjust. If they conclude that the ruler qualifies as an unjust ruler, rebelling against him might be obligatory. Moreover, the Zaydi jurist Ibn al-Murtada argues that "oppressors who usurp villages, towns, and provinces may be treated as bandits. [This is because] they cause corruption on the earth, and usurp money when no one can assist [the victim]. Therefore, they deserve to be treated as bandits if the *imam* prevails over them."³⁸⁰

If applied to the Nizari case, this argument would make the Nizari Ismaʿilis' rebellion justified because they and the Persian majority perceived the Seljuqs as foreign usurpers who robed the land and the people. Contrary to the Nizaris, the Zaydi jurists do not approve of assassinations as a means of fighting an unjust ruler.³⁸¹ Yet, like the Imami jurists, the Zaydi jurists suggest that one should only engage in a rebellion if success is likely. A similar position is known from Ibn Taymiyya when Muslim life under non-Muslim rule is concerned. Similarly, he argues that Muslims are forbidden from supporting an infidel ruler.³⁸²

The only exception for the Zaydi jurists for allowing assistance to an unjust ruler is in the case of *jihad* against unbelievers. In this case, the ruler's injustice is not diminished but is less grave than the enemies' unbelief. In that case, Muslims are discouraged from promoting or supporting any of the ruler's injustices. If he fights rebels, they should not assist him.³⁸³

Because we have already encountered the Ibadi Salim Ibn Dhakwan, who was extremely critical of the Kharijites' approach to violence, it is worth briefly addressing the Ibadi jurists' position on violence. As it is already obvious from their support of the rebellion against ʿAli and ʿUthman, they are not opposed to violent opposition. However, like the Imami and the Zaydi schools, they suggest not only open and armed rebellion, but, depending on circumstances, non-cooperation and other means of active and passive resistance. For the Ibadi, the ruler forfeits his legitimacy as soon as he murders or approves of the murder of an innocent person. Similarly, if the ruler becomes gravely sinful, armed rebel-

---

379 Abou el Fadl, *Religion and Violence in Islamic Law*, 302.
380 Cited in Abou el Fadl, *Religion and Violence in Islamic Law*, 305.
381 Ibid., 306.
382 Cited in Michot, *Muslims Under Non-Muslim Rule*, 63–4.
383 Abou el Fadl, *Religion and Violence in Islamic Law*, 306.

lion becomes legitimized.[384] The guiding idea is the same that is already familiar from John of Salisbury. If the ruler allows injustice to be done in his name, the ruler is responsible for the injustice committed in his name. Again, in agreement with John of Salisbury (and the Nizari Isma'ilis), the Ibadi jurists do not oppose the assassination of an unjust ruler—given that he has to be warned first.[385]

In short, the Ibadi jurists legitimize violent actions against a ruler based on religious (grave sins) and socio-economic reasons (oppression and injustice). While the Imami jurists are more reluctant, they nonetheless find a way around justifying rebellion against an unjust ruler. Here, the emphasis lies on oppression. Declaring the ruler *kafir* is not a prominent means in their argument. For the Zaydi jurists, the religious argument rests more with the rebel than with the unjust ruler. The key question is not whether the ruler has committed sins to forfeit his legitimacy but, rather, whether the rebel commits a sin by rebelling, which renders the rebellion against socio-economic and political injustices into a religiously sanctioned act.

2.3 Summary and Comparison

All authors and movements discussed in the previous sections operate against the backdrop of divinely inspired and created cosmic orders. Whether Muslims or Christians, they share the idea that ultimately all power comes from God. Thus, all politically relevant terms (like justice, power, authority, legitimacy, or warfare) are defined and used in religiously contextualized language. The religious framing of the discourses, however, does not come as a surprise. Both political identity and legitimacy are linked to religious affiliation. In addition to nation (*natio*) or tribe, the main source for community building is religion.

The historic circumstances in which both religious cultures emerge suggest some significant differences in the religions' approach to violent conflict resolution. Both social movements surface in a hostile environment. Christianity emerges within the socio-political circumstances of the Roman Empire. Initially, the social movement was exempt from the need for an established approach to violence. By contrast, Islam emerges in a tribal society that, although similarly hostile, gave reason to the possibility of an independent community, which could only be established through violent means. The different contexts in which the two religious cultures emerge imply, at least initially, the need for dif-

---

384 Ibid., 311–2.
385 Ibid., 317.

ferent answers, depending on the particular socio-economic and political circumstances. They also influence the perception of (potential) threats to the community; similarly, the perception influences the (violent) responses to the perceived threats.

Yet, the examples discussed so far also illustrate the transformability of the discourse in relation to the underlying motifs and problems. An attempt to categorize the different ideas and movements needs to take the transformation of the discourses into account. At least in most cases, there is little if any difficulty in identifying hegemonic and anti-hegemonic discourses, although a previously anti-hegemonic discourse may change into a hegemonic discourse or vice versa. Identifying whether a discourse is primarily motivated by religious or by socio-economic and political factors is a far more challenging enterprise. The task becomes more manageable if we introduce a third category in which religion and power are perceived as identical. For the political scientist, the identification of religion with power renders the argument into a political one; a scholar in religious studies may come to the opposite conclusion. Yet, similar to associating violence with the political sphere, this study associates power with politics, not with religion—even if power is understood as originating in God. However, we nonetheless have to accept that the distinction between the religious and political may be blurred.

Is jihad primarily hegemonic or anti-hegemonic? Does jihad describe primarily a religious activity or is it, despite its religious connotation, primarily a mundane enterprise that is stimulated primarily by socio-economic and political reasons? How and where do the Crusades fit into the narrative?

When reassessing the origins of the *jihad* doctrine in the early Muslim community, acts of violence or, more generally, physical force, may be best described as anti-hegemonic violence aiming for the survival of the newly founded community in a hostile environment. The main causes of violence are a) survival and b) access to resources that allow for the survival of the community. These two aspects never disappear completely. During the *fitna*, as outlined earlier, the main conflict is not over exegesis, but over leadership and resources. Simultaneously, *jihad* transforms from a solely anti-hegemonic means of conflict resolution to a hegemonic and an anti-hegemonic enterprise. Religious coloring comes into otherwise mundane warfare through (1) the requirement for a religious authority's sanction, (2) the community's religious identity, and (3) the tendency to label the enemy or opponent as *kafir*, which is, essentially, a marker for inclusion and exclusion. Thus, it is not surprising that Malik's first systematic discussion of *jihad* emphasizes primarily profane aspects of *jihad* like the distribution of booty and appropriate conduct towards the fellow jihadist, the enemy, and women. The only truly religious aspect in Malik's treatise relates to the jihadist's motivation: rewards in the world to come rather than material gains.

Later authors put less emphasis on the material aspect of *jihad*. Except for the defensive *jihad*, the motif of the Muslim community's survival is no longer in the center of the reflection. This shift, however, does not come by surprise. Muslim power is established. Thus, the emphasis lies on expansion and obedience to power. Despite the fact that the enemy is displayed either as an unbeliever or as somebody who has left the straight path of faith, the main issue is subjection to power. In this context, it is worth noting that conversion is not in the center of the argument. The enemy either has to convert or pay the poll-tax. In both instances the goal and outcome is obedience to Muslim authority and is therefore primarily political and hegemonic. The mundane aspect of power and domination is religiously colored only insofar as the power is associated with Islam and therefore religious identity. The rather mundane aspect remains visible in the suggested responses to internal dissent. The more a dissenting group becomes a threat to the existing authority and its legitimacy, the fiercer the dissenters have to be fought. If the dissenters refuse to recognize the ruler's authority, as al-Mawardi puts it, "they must be fought until they cease to oppose and become obedient again." Among the authors discussed in the section *Concept(s) of Jihad* only Ibn Khaldun emphasizes the goal of converting "everyone to Islam either by persecution or by force." Yet, his, also common, distinction between just and unjust wars displays a *realpolitical* approach. Warfare is just if it is directed against an enemy, whether it is external, dynastic, or separatist. Thus, the primary ends are political and hegemonic. While Ibn Khaldun stresses the need for religion as a means for stability and order itself, it is a rather different question whether religion is a means to an end or a means in itself. A religious emphasis comes into play by associating Islam with justice and by stressing the religious duty aspect of *jihad*. Yet, at least for the first authors, religious dissent is only a problem if it is associated with disobedience and the refusal to recognize the established authority.

Thus, viewed from this perspective, the differences between the concepts of *jihad* and the Crusades are clearly visible, although both involve religiously sanctioned warfare. Yet *jihad* is a concept that was in the Islamic toolkit early on, while crusading is a relatively late invention with a distinct historic relevance between the late eleventh century and the end of the fourteenth century, although rhetorically the concept lives on. The invention of the concept itself signifies a shift in Christian theology—from *caritas* to *potestas*. The initial justification is military assistance to an ally, the Byzantine emperor Alexis I. Enrique Dussel reads the Crusades as an attempt to reconnect continental Europe with the Mediterranean and with it to one of the regional cultural and political centers; this connection was lost through the Arab expansion, which pushed the European continent to the periphery of the interregional system of political and cultural centers.[386] If one ignores the general assumption that is shared by Christianity and Islam that all power comes from God and that all exercise of power therefore has at least some religious coloring, the original motifs for initiating the Crusades can be described as primarily political. If one follows Enrique Dussel's interpretation, then the Crusades are also an attempt to become an interregional hegemonic power.

Yet, motifs and rhetoric are not always the same. Here, we must distinguish between the self-perception of the (ideal) crusader and the rhetoric of popes and theologians. The crusader's motivation is as much a problem as the jihadist's motivation. Both Malik and Aquinas emphasize the need of the right intention (*recta intentio*) that appears to be absent in most of the fighters; material goals are at the forefront. However, the rhetoric and the self-image transform the political and socio-economic motifs into a religious motif; it idealizes sacrifice and martyrdom. Papal rhetoric contributed to this self-image. Papal propaganda turns the "enemy" into God's enemy who is a heretic, an idolater, or a polytheist. Dying in battle against God's enemy is linked to promised rewards in the fighter's afterlife. The official end of the Crusades becomes the liberation of Christianity. To achieve this end, preemptive warfare becomes justified (if we do not kill them, they will kill us). Similar to *jihad*, the Crusades become justified because they are a religious cause. Because they are Christian, they are just. Yet, to a certain degree, the concept of the Crusade is much narrower than the concept of *jihad*. While dynastic warfare and other wars that are fought in order to maintain and expand power fall under the broader pre-modern concept of *jihad*, eventually, the Crusades' rhetoric considers *only* wars that are fought in the name of God as just warfare, which discredits dynastic wars and renders them illegitimate. Thus, it needs to be emphasized that, although the primary motifs for the Crusades are predominantly political and socio-economic, the primary legitimation is religious in nature and delegitimizes previous forms of violent warfare. Yet, the struggle over the authority to legitimize (just) warfare is in itself political. It reflects papal politics aiming to regain and stabilize power over temporal political action at a time when the power to sanction *jihad* still legally belongs to the *imam* or caliph in the Muslim world, however diminished the caliph's power base may be.

The concept of Crusade proved sufficiently successful as a tool to motivate. It could be applied to other contexts. Here, the so-called Albigensian Crusade is a

---

386 Dussel, *Ethics of Liberation*, 24.

paradigmatic example. At the heart of the matter is a social movement that threatens both the Church's and the temporal authority's legitimacy. Thus, the Albigensian crusades exemplify hegemonic warfare. Nonetheless, the military expeditions against "heretic" Christians have been perceived as something different from the military expeditions to the Holy Land. The perceived difference is visible in Innocent's III wording. They are not "affairs of the cross," but "affairs of peace and faith." Yet, peace is a political goal; faith is a religious one. To legitimize the expeditions against the Cathars, it appeared to be necessary to display the members of the Cathars as religious renegades. They need to be fought not because they undermine the legitimacy of both the established Church and the temporal authorities, but because they have betrayed the Christian faith and are about to "destroy the vineyard of the Lord." Contrary to the Middle Eastern contexts, the option of submission through tax-paying does not exist; consequently, the only available option is resubmission to "orthodoxy" or complete destruction.

The strategy of displaying the political enemy as the enemy in faith is not a prerogative of Christian crusading rhetoric. A similar strategy is visible in Nizam al-Mulk's battle against the Nizari Isma'ilis and in Ibn Taymiyya's polemics against the Mongols. However, in Ibn Taymiyya's case, we have to assume that he was driven by honest faith and religious concerns and not just by politics. For Nizam al-Mulk, the option discussed in legal treatises on *jihad* that allows for tolerating religious dissent as long as the authority in power remains accepted and taxes are paid does not appear to be an option. For him the situation requires, similar to the Church's response to the Cathars, either a return to the "orthodox" faith or complete destruction.

In essence, Nizam al-Mulk aims to legitimize warfare against a dissenting group in a conquered territory. Without the internal problems of the Seljuq Empire, the response to the Nizari Isma'ilis might have been more tolerant. Yet, without the internal turmoil of the Seljuq Empire, the Nizari Isma'ili movement might have proven less successful. Given that the caliph's authority was reduced to a puppet, the Seljuqs had the power to define who qualifies and does not qualify as a Muslim. Because of and contrary to Christianity, Islam does not allow easily for the killing of members of one's own creed, the authority and power to declare somebody a non-Muslim is essential. Yet, in the case of the Seljuqs, the political motifs of fighting the internal threat are obvious, although legitimation is cloaked entirely in religious language. By contrast, the case of the Nizari Isma'ilis is less obvious and depends on the interpretation of the movement itself. Is it primarily a Persian nationalist movement or is it primarily a schismatic movement? It is reasonable to assume both, although the main motivation for their support seems to rest in socio-economic and political oppression. Their anti-hegemonic strategy plays to both resentments and appears to be broad enough to generate support even from outsiders.

Ironically, Ibn Taymiyya could be placed right in the middle between Nizam al-Mulk's and the Nizari Isma'ilis' strategies. Despite the fact that his polemics against the Mongols were politically appreciated, he represents nonetheless a special case because it is reasonable to assume true religious motivation behind his actions. Yet, essentially, he combines both Nizam al-Mulk's and the Nizari Isma'ilis' strategies. He aims to demonstrate that the Mongols do not qualify as Muslim (Nizam al-Mulk) while trying to purify Islam at the same time (Nizari Isma'ilis). To legitimize military actions against the Mongols, he redefines the criteria that have to be fulfilled to qualify as Muslim, which turns a sinner or a heretic instantly into a non-Muslim or even an apostate. Although religiously motivated, he serves a political cause that aims to prevent Mongol hegemony.

Given the significance of the struggle between temporal and ecclesiastical authority in the Christian context, it is worth noting that a similar conflict between caliph and sultan does not exist in Islam. Yet, under different historical circumstances, such a conflict, as implied by the terms sultan and caliph, would not have been completely outside the realm of possibility. However, history took a different cause, which renders the conflict between ecclesiastical and temporal authority a particularly Christian problem. The Christian discourse operates within the cosmological belief that all power comes from God. The papal perspective, as discussed previously, assumes that all temporal power needs ecclesiastical power as a mediator between God and temporal rule. Without ecclesiastical mediation and oversight, just rule is impossible. Indeed, for the sake of salvation all human beings must be subjected to the ecclesiastical power, meaning the papacy. Similar to the argument in the context of the Crusades that likens justice to Christianity, the papal argument maintains that rule outside Christianity and without the recognition of papal authority equals injustice and oppression. This is a universal claim.

James of Viterbo emphasizes this aspect by associating rulership in a Christian commonwealth that does not recognize the superiority of the papal office with tyranny. He considers tyranny a hindrance to salvation. Yet, the key issue is not so much the link between tyranny and prevention of salvation, but the understanding of tyranny itself. A commonwealth that is not completely ordered in accordance with the papal authority's will is tyrannical. The refusal to accept the pope's claim that he can judge all temporal rule and, if the pope considers it necessary, that he can depose a ruler as he pleases turns temporal rule into tyranny that jeopardizes the salvation of each individual who lives under such a ruler. The means to enforce this policy is excommunication, which makes the excommunicated an outlaw who can be subjected to violent actions without any consequences—except for the outlawed, of course.

This claim for absolute authority over all Christendom, indeed, mankind, could not stand without opposition. To illustrate the rejection of the papal claim, we could have discussed theorists like Marsilius of Padua or John of Paris who are less outspoken about violent resistance against the papacy than Ockham. Ockham, however, turns the papal claim upside down by associating it with heresy, sin, and oppression. Contrary to James of Viterbo, Ockham argues that it is the Church that rules tyrannically over the faithful and leads away from salvation to condemnation. Ockham's argument is anti-hegemonic insofar as it opposes the Church; at the same time, his argument is hegemonic because it sides with the Roman emperor. His main argument is theological with particular emphasis on salvation. Yet, simultaneously, he emphasizes the violation of people's rights. Property and liberty are in the center of his discourse on rights violation. Ockham turns resisting the (heretic) pope, whether through violent or non-violent means, into a religious duty, which renders his justification of violence primarily into a religious cause, despite the violation of other rights that are associated with the political and the economic sphere.

In this sense Ockham's argument is closer to the legal discourses in the non-Sunni tradition than to John of Salisbury's or William of Pagula's legitimation of violent action against unjust rule. With the non-Sunni jurist Ockham shares the focus on the actor against violent oppression. Although the Imami jurists are rather reluctant in legitimizing violent resistance because of the potential harm done, i.e., they do not legitimize collateral damage, the Zaydi jurists' main concern is whether the person who takes violent action against the ruling authority commits a sin. For Ockham, he would commit a sin if he does not act against tyrannical papal heresy. The Zaydi jurists associate (violent) opposition against a just ruler with sin. John of Salisbury associates it with treason. Yet, anti-hegemonic violent action against an oppressive and sinful ruler is legitimized. The Zaydi jurists, however, do not go so far as the Ibadi jurists, who, similar to the Nizari Isma'ilis and John of Salisbury, legitimize assassinations. Given the nature of the legal argument, it does not come as any surprise that their argument is primarily religious. They operate on the basis of Islamic law. Yet, it needs to be emphasized that the jurists respond to a predominantly political problem, not a religious one: oppression and injustice.

Although John of Salisbury presents us in *Policraticus* with a consistent theory of tyrannicide, it is noteworthy that his argument oscillates between a primarily theological and a primarily philosophical argument. While there is no doubt that his argument is anti-hegemonic, the question whether his argument is primarily religious or socio-economic and political escapes an unambiguous answer. Yet, the link between just rule and salvation is essential to his reasoning. Indeed, his argument suggests only in a commonwealth that is ordered in accordance with the principles of divine justice a truly Christian life is possible. Simultaneously he considers tyranny a public crime, which identifies tyranny primarily as a political problem. While one may see some parallels to Giles of Rome or James of Viterbo, John does not demand Church authorities' absolute power over temporal rulers.

Although William of Pagula argues from the perspective of divine justice the king is supposed to embody, the primary reasons for legitimizing the people's rebellion and their right to take another king are socio-economic injustices, such as forced labor, confiscation of goods, and the violation of the subjects' property rights. This argument is almost similar to Ibn Khaldun's, although the latter is more sophisticated. Although Ibn Khaldun mentions violations of Islamic law and divine punishment, his primary account is socio-economic and political. Moreover, he does not see the need to legitimize the people's rebellion. If the ruler oversteps his boundaries to an extent the people cannot endure any longer, they will rebel anyway.

Finally, Salim Ibn Dhakwan's assessment of the Kharijites exemplifies the transformation of a conflict that was originally caused by socio-economic and political injustice but later on turned into a conflict over exegesis, the proper interpretation and application of religious doctrines. Here, we have a clear example (in accordance with Hans Kippenberg's notion) of a conflict that changes its nature through a religious interpretation of the conflict. Whether the religious radicalization of the Kharijites would have occurred without the experience of socio-economic injustice cannot be answered, although it is worth asking because political conflicts are less difficult to solve than conflicts that have been transformed into conflicts over contested truth claims.

3 Religion and Violence in Twentieth Century Islam and Christianity

In the modern world, perceived legitimate use of violence is not necessarily simply a question of moral and legal rights in a domestic setting. Both Latin America and the Middle East have been and remain of geopolitical interest for other political and economic players. The regions' geopolitical relevance was particularly evident during the Cold War. In a *realpolitical* sense but not necessarily in a *moral* sense, political legitimacy is not always dependent on the interplay between the ruler and the ruled but also on the interests and interference of foreign (hegemonic) forces. This is particularly true for Latin America and the Middle East. For Latin America, José Comblin has framed the issue in the concept of the "national security system." With changing hegemonic players involved, his analysis applies to most if not all developing regions of geopolitical interest. Comblin writes,

> after World War II, a next but similar political system and ideology came out of the United States and spread all over the continent, chiefly under the armed forces. This is the national security system, proselytized primarily by the Pentagon, the Central Intelligence Agency (CIA), and other American organizations. The principles are: integration of the whole nation into the national security system and the policy of the United States; total war against communism; collaboration with American or American-controlled business corporations; establishment of dictatorship; and placing absolute power in the hands of the military.[1]

With changing dominant powers, examples of foreign support for authoritarian regimes are numerous, whether it is the Persian Shah's rule with the backing of England and Russia in the nineteenth and early twentieth centuries or,[2] more prominently, the Iran-Contra Affair of the 1980s.[3] For Iran, Ali M. Ansari argues that the fear of regime change through international intervention has resulted in

---

1 Comblin, *The Church and the National Security State*, 54.
2 See Sayyid Jamal ad-Din al-Afghani, "The Reign of Terror in Persia," *The Contemporary Review* 61 (1892): 238–248. In his address at Queen's House, London, he heavily criticizes England's approval of the Shah and demands the Shah's deposal. Al-Afghani refers explicitly to the Shah's concession to the British Imperial Tobacco Corporation, which negatively impacted the economic situation of many Iranians and led to protest movements in 1891 and 1892.
3 See Cheryl A. Rubenberg, "US Policy toward Nicaragua and Iran and the Iran-Contra Affair: Reflections on the Continuity of American Foreign Policy," *Third World Quarterly* 10, no. 4 (1988): 1467–1504 for a convincing analysis.

a paranoia that has turned into "a tool for the suppression of dissent."[4] Viewed from an international relations' perspective, a dependent regime's "legitimacy" is established and maintained through foreign acceptance and support, not through the will of the people. Regular means of regime change through protest, election, or revolution are jeopardized. Therefore, foreign interventions for other than humanitarian reasons undermine the principle of a people's right to self-determination. Moreover, the radicalization and escalation of an existing conflict is more than likely. Indeed, a regime's exterritorial dependency *per se* jeopardizes its legitimacy potentially.

As indicated by the controversy surrounding the newly elected Pope Francis' role under the military junta in Argentina, national religious authorities played and continue to play a role in actively or passively supporting or opposing the regimes in place.[5] As outlined in the introduction, this is similarly true for Middle Eastern countries. Thus, with religious authorities involved, the question of a regime's legitimacy or illegitimacy becomes religiously colored, at least in the domestic context. Focusing on the dominantly Islamic Middle East and Christian Latin America, however, is justified not only by the involvement of religious authorities in (violent) conflict. Modern Islamic Middle Eastern and Christian Latin American discourses reveal a considerable overlap. Both discourses are informed and influenced by socialist, nationalist, Marxist, or Marxist-inspired ideas. Similarly, radical versions of religion exist in both religious cultures. Moreover, these two regions share colonial experiences. A significant amount of literature is inspired by the rejection of Western or capitalist economic dominance and Western (cultural) hegemony. Hamid Dabashi highlights some significant parallels between Latin American liberation theology and contemporary movements in the Islamic world.[6]

As previously implied, the larger historical-political context is relevant. Yet, the following analysis reduces to the utmost minimum references to these contexts. These contexts are significant and worth bearing in mind. An over-emphasis of the international perspective, however, distracts from domestic problems. A geopolitical perception does not singlehandedly explain *why* and *how* domestic conflicts are fought and supported by religion or religious rhetoric. Rather, the international perspective adds an additional layer of concealment to the underlying causes of a violent conflict.

---

[4] Ali M. Ansari, "*L'état, c'est moi:* The Paradox of Sultanism and the Question of 'Regime Change' in Modern Iran," *International Affairs* 89, no. 2 (2013): 283.
[5] Matthias Drobinski, "Vorwürfe gegen Papst Franziskus: Die Wahrheit wird euch frei machen," *Süddeutsche Zeitung* 65 (18.03.2013): 4.
[6] Hamid Dabashi, *Islamic Liberation Theology: Resisting the Empire* (London: Routledge, 2008).

3.1 Latin American Christian Perspectives: Revolution and Counter-Revolution

In the Latin American context, revolutionary and counter-revolutionary violence is not a matter of violence that could be directed against members of a different creed. Rather, as Cecelia Lynch notes, "[t]he problem for the activists in the liberation tradition in Latin America was not how to act in a secular world, but how to act in a world in which the official structures of violence were controlled by those professing the same belief in the same denomination, namely Roman Catholicism."[7] The watershed between the revolutionary and the counter-revolutionary camps is marked by the divide between the official Church and the "revolutionary" church. The official Church mandates that the Church should withdraw from temporal matters, while in effect she usually sides with the established regimes and associates struggles for (individual) rights with Lucifer. By contrast, the "revolutionary" camp, in various increments, supports violent armed struggle.[8]

Of course, this dualistic view of the Latin American church, although in tendency true, is an over-simplification. Numerous cardinals and bishops, and as such representatives of the institutional Church, opted for opposition to the military juntas that dominated Latin America's political landscape during the second half of the twentieth century.[9] Moreover, in its struggle for independence, the Latin American region has a long history of revolution and violence. Here, again, the hierarchical Church tended to side with the colonial regime, whereas some priests supported the struggle for independence.[10] Yet, during and after the struggle for independence, the Church "progressively lost its legal and political power and influence," even though some clergy played an important role in the revolution and some priests were among their most significant supporters.[11]

---

7 Cecelia Lynch, "Acting on Belief: Christian Perspectives on Suffering and Violence," *Ethics & International Affair* 14 (2000): 90.
8 John Gerassi, "Introduction: Camilo Torres and the Revolutionary Church," in Camilo Torres, *Revolutionary Priest: The Complete Writings & Messages of Camilo Torres*, ed. John Gerassi (New York: Random House, 1971), 4.
9 Although the examples are numerous, see Rodolfo Cardenal, "The Martyrdom of the Salvadorean Church," in *Church and Politics in Latin America*, ed. Dermot Keogh (Basingstoke: Macmillan, 1990), 225–246 or Mario I. Aguilar, "Cardinal Raúl Silva Henríquez, the Catholic Church, and the Pinochet Regime, 1973–1980: Public Responses to a National Security State," *The Catholic Historical Review* 89, no. 4 (2003): 712–731.
10 Rinke, *Revolutionen in Lateinamerika*, 117–120.
11 Enrique Dussel, *A History of the Church in Latin America: Colonialism to Liberation (1492–1979)*, trans. Alan Neely (Grand Rapids: Eerdmans, 1981), 81, 87, 90.

Over the decades following the revolutions, the official Church lost ground with liberal governments but regained influence through the support of conservative regimes. Particularly neocolonial military regimes could often rely on the support of the official Church. Their mutual reliance was embedded in their joint opposition to Communism and Marxist ideologies more generally. Thus, they provided "ideological, material, and institutional support and legitimation to one another."[12]

This section is concerned with liberation theologians' and their opponents' role in the struggle for liberation of the 1960s and 1970s and beyond. Here, two aspects are significant: the assumed possibility of cultural independence from the industrialized world and the increasing militarization of a region that, as Enrique Dussel notes, was aimed against its own people because the military failed to understand the real problem: "domination and economic, political, and cultural imperialism, and the suppression of all human potential of the Latin American that impede development."[13]

Religious justifications of counter-violence gained semi-official recognition at the Medellín Conference of 1968 that played a significant role in shaping what is commonly known as theology of liberation.[14] The following Conference of the Latin American Bishops 1979 in Puebla, under the new secretary general Alfonso López Trujillo, marked a turn back to more conservative positions.[15] The Puebla conference that was held under the surveillance of the CIA did not completely succeed in its conservative counter-agenda. As Paul Sigmund puts it, the conference's final document "included something for everyone."[16] Yet, López Trujillo, backed by Cardinal Sebastiano Baggio in Rome, was actively involved in attempts to delegitimize liberation theology. For this purpose, he employed the Belgian Jesuit Roger Vekemans, who also campaigned against the Allende regime in Chile. Simultaneously, the Vatican aimed at silencing Jon Sobrino, Gustavo Gutiérrez, and Leonardo Boff, leading figures of the liberation theology movement.[17]

---

12 Daniel H. Levine, *Religion and Politics in Latin America: The Catholic Church in Venezuela and Columbia* (Princeton: Princeton University Press, 1981), 3.
13 Dussel, *A History of the Church in Latin America*, 131.
14 David Abalos, "The Medellin Conference," *Cross Currents* 19 (1969): 113–132.
15 Emile Poulat, "The Path of Latin American Catholicism," in *Church and Politics in Latin America*, ed. Dermot Keogh (Basingstoke: Macmillan, 1990), 19.
16 Paul E. Sigmund, *Liberation Theology at the Crossroads: Democracy or Revolution?* (New York: Oxford University Press, 1990), 102.
17 Peter Hebblethwaite, "The Vatican's Latin America Policy," in *Church and Politics in Latin America*, ed. Dermot Keogh (Basingstoke: Macmillan, 1990), 55, 59–60.

To unfold the intellectual panorama of revolution and counter-revolution, this chapter first examines theological voices that legitimized (violent) revolution. For this purpose, we discuss José Comblin, Camilo Torres, and Ignacio Ellacuría. This discussion is followed by an analysis of their intellectual counterparts Roger Vekemans and Alfonso Lopez Trujillo. In addition, the positions of the *Societies for the Defense of Tradition, Family, and Property* (TFP) are analyzed. TFP can be considered as quintessential opposition to the theology of liberation movements. TFP was originally founded by the Brazilian Plinio Corrêa de Oliveira. Soon after Corrêa de Oliveira had founded the first TFP, other Societies emerged in approximately 20 other countries, mainly in Latin America. Corrêa de Oliveira's writings were almost instantly translated into Spanish, English, and Italian. The TFP has an explicit anti-communist orientation and is known for its extreme conservative views, including reactionary social and political positions. Moreover, the TFP's ideology is tied to the concept of the "national security state" and is known for its active collaboration with military regimes.[18]

3.1.1 Liberation Theology's Accounts on (Violent) Resistance

A document that was issued by more than 900 priests from Latin America at the Medellín Conference, the second conference of Latin American bishops that was summoned to address "immediate social problems from a religious perspective,"[19] denounces violence and legitimizes counter-violence. The priests who signed the document condemn

> the violence that a minority of privileged people has waged against the vast majority of deprived people. It is the violence of hunger, helplessness, and the underdeveloped. It is the violence of persecution, oppression, and neglect. It is the violence of organized prostitution, of illegal but flourishing slavery, and of social, economic, and intellectual discrimination.[20]

In their statement, the priests criticize religious leaders who identify with political authorities and who are "tied up with the dominant class." Simultaneously,

---

18 Comblin, *The Church and the National Security State*, 81.
19 John R. Pottenger, *The Political Theory of Liberation Theology: Towards a Reconvergence of Social Values and Social Science* (Albany: State University of New York Press, 1989), 12.
20 Peruvian Bishops' Commission for Social Action, "Latin America: A Continent of Violence," in *Between Honesty and Hope: Documents from and About the Church in Latin America*, ed. Peruvian Bishops' Commission for Social Action, trans. John Drury (Maryknoll Publications: Maryknoll, 1970), 81.

it is a statement of self-criticism of a Church that "has often remained silent in the face of abuse perpetrated by the civil and military authorities."[21] To end this violence, "a fundamental change in the socioeconomic structures" is required. The priests are not univocally in favor of violent actions. Yet, "[m]ore than a few feel that the time is already past for accomplishing [socio-economic change] by purely nonviolent means." Thus, the condemnation of violent actions against oppression results in just another injustice. Condemnation of violence also means that the Church serves again as the opium of the people in favor of those who practice "the violence of exploitation and oppression."[22]

The document eventually aims to recognize "the right of any unjustly oppressed community to react, even violently, against its unjust oppressor" and for denouncing "oppressive structures" that hinder development and transformation, even though they do not favor indiscriminate violence and do not want to "draw an idyllic picture of violence."[23]

The document was issued more than two years after Camilo Torres's body was found. Soon after Torres had joined the Colombian guerrilla fighters, his "subversive violence was crushed by coercive military violence."[24] With the Medellín document, the majority of priests seem to have legitimized Camilo Torres's turn to violent resistance post mortem. This is even true for clergy who personally reject any use of violence and insist on nonviolent counter-movements instead. For instance, Hélder Câmara, the archbishop of Olinda and Refice in Brazil, who is known for his struggle for social justice through nonviolent means as an alternative to revolutionary change and who,[25] especially after he denounced torture publicly, suffered violent persecution and was eventually silenced by the Brazilian military regime,[26] had the deepest respect for Torres's decision to take actively part in combat. Indeed, he believes that the "memory of Camilo Torres and Che Guevara deserves as much respect as that of Dr. Martin Luther King."[27] Yet, Câmara, although he rejects violence primarily out of personal conviction,

---

21 Ibid., 82.
22 Ibid., 83.
23 Ibid., 84.
24 Dussel, *A History of the Church in Latin American*, 166.
25 Judex, "Una alternativa a la révolution: La accion no violenta organizada de Hélder Câmara," *Estudios Centro Americanos* 24, no. 246 (1969): 87–94.
26 Kenneth P. Serbin, "Dom Hélder Câmara: The Father of the Church of the Poor," in *The Human Tradition in Modern Brazil*, ed. Peter M. Beattie (Scholarly Resources: Wilmington, 2004), 250–1, 261.
27 Helder Camara, "Violence in the Modern World," in *Between Honesty and Hope: Documents from and About the Church in Latin America*, ed. Peruvian Bishops' Commission for Social Action, trans. John Drury (Maryknoll Publications: Maryknoll, 1970), 52.

also rejects it for pragmatic reasons. Particularly for Brazil, where the military regime was supported by the U.S. government, he fears that popular violent uprising may provoke a military intervention by the "great power."[28]

Camilo Torres's Socio-Religious Argument for Violent Change

In the *Message to the Colombians from the Mountain*, published about a month prior to Camilo Torres's violent death, he announced that he has joined the armed struggles. His turn towards armed struggle is the outcome of a decade's long personal struggle. Eventually, he found that all legal means had been exhausted; the only remaining alternative he saw was in combat. In this statement, he summarizes his frustration:

> When the people demanded a leader, and found him in Jorge Eliécer Gaitán, the oligarchy murdered him. When the people demanded peace, the oligarchy sowed violence throughout the country. When the people could no longer withstand violence and organized the guerrillas to seize power, the oligarchy pulled a military coup out of its hat so that the guerrillas, who were tricked, would surrender [...].[29]

Yet, Camilo Torres did not come to this conclusion straight away. Indeed, he could have taken a completely different path. As a member of one of the traditional families in Colombia, he was part of the elite and could have had a solid academic career. Although he was an ordained priest who favored "an enlightened concept of the role of the pastor,"[30] he was also a sociologist. As such, he is the founder of the first academic program in sociology at a Latin American university and is usually considered as the pioneer of sociology in Colombia. For his engagement in combat, Torres applies his academic analysis.[31] In a purely technical sense, Camilo Torres cannot be called a liberation theologian, although he heavily influenced the Peruvian theologian Gustavo Gutiérrez who is considered the author of the first systematic articulation of liberation theology.[32]

---

[28] Ibid., 53.
[29] Camilo Torres, "Message to the Colombians from the Mountains," in *Revolutionary Priest: The Complete Writings & Messages of Camilo Torres*, ed. John Gerassi (New York: Random House, 1971), 425.
[30] Torres, "Is the Priest a Witch Doctor?," in *Revolutionary Priest*, 100.
[31] Alejandro Sánchez Lopera, "Ciencia, revolución y creencia en Camilo Torres: ¿Una Colombia secular?," *Nómadas* 25 (2006): 244, 248.
[32] Christian Smith, *The Emergence of Liberation Theology: Radical Religion and Social Movement Theory* (Chicago: University of Chicago Press, 1991), 135.

If one examines Camilo Torres's writings for religious reasons to call for revolutionary change and for his personal engagement in combat, the key and recurring concepts are charity and love. One of the two concepts we have already discussed is the shift from *caritas* to *potestas* in the context of Christian approaches to heretics at the dawn of the Crusades. The second aspect, love of one's neighbor, in the reading of liberation theologians "becomes reality when we love the impoverished on the earth."[33]

Torres's theological reflection on action goes hand in hand with his sociological analysis. Part of his sociological analysis refers to the period that is usually referred to as *la violencia*, a civil war between Colombia's liberal and conservative parties that started with the assassination of Jorge Eliécer Gaitán in 1948.[34] *La violencia* is particularly known for its brutality and for the extreme forms of violence applied.[35] *La violencia* involves also a religious dimension. The violence targeted particularly non-Catholics. Suzanne Dailey calls it the "Conservative Party-Roman Catholic alliance" that was "engaged in secret machinations to eliminate enemies."[36]

Interestingly, Camilo Torres does not consider the religious dimension of *la violencia*, but focuses primarily on the peasants' socio-economic and cultural situations. Elsewhere he criticizes the Concordat of 1887 that forms the legal foundation for inter-religious violence because it affects "freedom of conscience [and] freedom of religion" negatively.[37] Yet, when he discusses *la violencia* his main concern is the blockage of normal channels for economic, cultural, political, military, and ecclesiastical advancement. Although the ecclesiastical channel is not completely blocked, advancing comes for the "price of absolute conformity to the values of the dominant minority" and "conformity to the state."[38] Moreover, he considers it primarily a feature of underdeveloped countries that the military's main purpose is to "maintain the established order." Simultaneously,

---

[33] Roberto Oliveros, "History of the Theology of Liberation," in *Mysterium Liberationis: Fundamental Concepts of Liberation Theology*, ed. Ignacio Ellacuría and Jon Sobrino (Maryknoll: Orbis, 1993), 8.
[34] Carlos Mario Gómez, "Economía y violencia en Colombia," *Quórum: Revista de Pensamiento Iberoamericano* 2 (2001): 159.
[35] Norman A. Bailey, "*La Violencia* in Colombia," *Journal of Inter-American Studies* 9, no. 4 (1967): 561–575.
[36] Suzanne Dailey, "Religious Aspects of Colombia's *La Violencia*: Explanations and Implications," *Journal of Church and State* 15 (1973): 400.
[37] Torres, "Crossroads of the Church in Latin America," in *Revolutionary Priest*, 332.
[38] Torres, "Social Change and Rural Violence in Colombia," in *Revolutionary Priest*, 232, 233.

"the minority elite has the greatest interest in maintaining this order on which their privileges depend."[39]

Yet, *la violencia* creates "abnormal" social advancements (through the confiscation of goods or land) and class consciousness. The peasants' "frustration" has turned into "aggressiveness."[40] Although in *Social Change and Rural Violence in Colombia* he associates the peasants with the formation of a majority pressure group, they do not have the means to act in an organized fashion. Elsewhere, Camilo Torres criticizes the unity of the ecclesiastical, financial, and political powers that are united by a common interest. In contrast, the popular class as a whole does "not possess an awareness of their common needs or a unity of action."[41]

For Torres, the existence of two subcultures contributes to the peasants' situation. One subculture comprises the minority of the elite; the other resembles the popular class. Each subculture has its own means of self-expression, reflected in language. The existence of these two versions of class-related expression blocks inter-class communication completely. For instance, if the upper class refers to "violence," it understands it as "banditry," whereas the lower class understands "violence" as "nonconformity." For Torres, such polarization jeopardizes the resolution of social and political problems through common sense.[42] He partly blames the politician's ignorance for this problem; the politician should not be "allowed to discuss any subject with total intellectual irresponsibility. At the very least, he ought to be required to consult an expert, a book, or at any rate a dictionary!"[43] In addition to the communication gap between the classes, Torres believes that the ruling class will never be willing to act against its own interests or what they perceive as such. Neither will they ever be willing to give up any of their privileges or invest in development.[44]

For Torres it is a fact that necessary structural change requires the popular class's pressure. Furthermore, peaceful revolution "is directly determined by the foresight of the ruling class, although the desire on the part of this class is difficult to arouse." Finally, because the ruling class, as implied above, lacks foresight, violent revolution is a likely and valid alternative.[45] Likewise, it is an expression of injustice that the ruling class is the only profiteer of the order

---

39 Ibid., 225–6.
40 Ibid., 235–6.
41 Torres, "How Pressure Groups Influence the Government," in *Revolutionary Priest*, 251.
42 Torres, "Two Subculture," in *Revolutionary Priest*, 258–9.
43 Ibid., 256.
44 Torres, "The Integrated Man," in *Revolutionary Priest*, 276.
45 Torres, "Revolution: Christian Imperative," in *Revolutionary Priest*, 284.

maintained by the military. The members of the ruling class have the means to retaining the existing order through their access to all economic, political, and military power.[46] Torres concludes that an authority that acts against its own people is illegitimate and tyrannical. Moreover, he describes the "present government" as "tyrannical because it receives the support of only twenty percent of the voters and because its decisions emanate from the privileged minorities. The temporal defects of the church must not shock us. The church is human."[47]

Thus, preaching the seizure of power by the majority is mandatory. Torres considers the seizure of the government by the majority not simply required. It is the only way to achieve "economic, social, and political reform that favors the majority." It is the only action that deserves to be called a revolution. "If it is necessary in order for men to love each other, the Christian must be revolutionary."[48]

He continues by contrasting the current situation with the desired one that can only be realized if Christians engage in the necessary actions. The current conditions neither allow for feeding and clothing the needy, nor for housing the needy (the vast majority).[49] Thus, he calls for revolution to

> obtain a government that will feed the hungry, clothe the naked, and teach the unschooled. Revolution will produce a government that carries out works of charity, of love for one's fellows—not for only a few but for the majority of our fellow men. This is why the revolution is not only permissible but obligatory for these Christians.[50]

Here, the two Christian concepts he employs to legitimize (violent) revolution are already foreshadowed. He calls for "active charity" because it is a Christian's obligation to "fully understand the problem of material poverty; to solve this problem, the assistance of all men is needed." A person who does not understand these problems and does not act upon them does not qualify as a Christian.[51] For Torres, going to church and receiving the sacraments is not enough. He does not see any grace in such passive activities. Salvation requires good faith, not the following of rituals. Thus, he does not exclude the possibility of salvation outside the official Church. Formal membership in a Christian congregation is also not a prerequisite for salvation. Grace lies in the good faith of a

---

46 Ibid., 273–4.
47 Torres, "Message to the Christian," in *Revolutionary Priest*, 368.
48 Torres, "Crossroads," 330.
49 Ibid.
50 Torres, "Message to the Christian," 368.
51 Torres, "Revolution," 265.

person's actions.⁵² Supernatural life relates to and depends on works of charity. "Charity is essentially supernatural life."⁵³ Likewise, a Christian is defined by love, by Christian love. Love is what "distinguishes and defines" a Christian because "[e]xternal practices serve as a means of attaining love, and they should in turn be motivated by love. [...] Consequently, the temporal commitment of the Christian is a mandate of love."⁵⁴

Because a Christian *must* engage himself or herself in structural change, the Christian may be required to join a nominally non-Christian movement. Yet, for Torres it is impossible to carry out revolutionary change if the movement is not embedded in "a complete and integrated *Weltanschauung.*" In his eyes, an ideologically uncommitted person can never become a revolutionary leader. Because Torres considers Christianity and Marxism the only available integral *Weltanschauungen*, it may be necessary to commit oneself to a struggle of structural change that is not necessarily Christian in nature. While he sees the undogmatic approach of an uncommitted person as a hindrance to successful engagement, a Christian should not be so dogmatic to refuse collaboration with other groups, although becoming the "useful idiot" for a non-Christian movement has to be avoided. As far as Marxism is concerned, he maintains, "practice has been shown that religion is not 'the opium of the people'."⁵⁵ Although he was said to be "stoutly non-Communist," he was nonetheless determined to work with whatever alternative movement had a similar end, namely, changing the "archaic" system of the oligarchs.⁵⁶ Even though Camilo Torres's approach was not very popular in Colombia, liberation theology's influences eventually radicalized Catholic base communities in Nicaragua. Increasingly, people saw their situation less as an outcome of their personal shortcomings, but in the structural deficiencies of hegemony; a significant number of Christian activists joined the Sandinista National Liberation Front (FSLN).⁵⁷

One of the key issues in Camilo Torres's thinking is his emphasis of class differences at a range that exclude the vast majority of the people from participating in social, economic, and political life, a condition that can only be changed

---

52 Ibid., 263.
53 Ibid.
54 Torres, "The Integrated Man," 248.
55 Torres, "Revolution," 287–9.
56 Cornelia and Irving Sussman, "The Case of Camilo Torres: The Problem of Obedience," *Catholic World* 204, no. 1224 (1969): 356.
57 Ryne Clos, "In the Name of the God Who Will Be: The Mobilization of Radical Christians in the Sandinista Revolution," *Journal for the Study of Radicalism* 6, no. 2 (2012): 2, 34. While FSLN was predominatly supported by Catholics, some Protestants also supported FSLN. See ibid., 12.

through (revolutionary) structural change. Torres's aspirations, consequently, clash with the system of the *National Security State*, a system that is based on *National Security Doctrine* that is commonly described as "ideological, strategic, and tactical guidance for officers trained in the United States and at war colleges within Latin America [that] provided [...] justification to stop progressive social and political change movements and to enforce their vision of the national security state."[58] Additionally, the *National Security State* is associated with a "strong pro-American and anti-communist view," the self-perception of being the sole defender of "Western values," and "realist theories of the state and the role of power politics" that are related to "concerns for internal national security."[59] Yet, the concept of the *National Security State*, although with changing values emphasized, is not restricted to Latin America. With numerous examples from the Middle East, Charles Tripp illustrates that concepts of the national security state have their dispersal in other regions than Latin America.[60] Thus, it is fair to say that the national security state is particular to a certain type of authoritarian regime but not necessarily bound to one particular cultural or religious setting.

Macro Politico-Religious Analysis and Revolution: José Comblin

For numerous years, the first generation liberation theologian José Comblin (1923–2011) worked closely with Hélder Câmara in Brazil. Before accepting an invitation from Câmara, Comblin taught at the Universidad Católica de Chile. While he was working with Câmara, Comblin became a target of the military regime in Brazil and was expelled in 1971. Thereafter, he lived in Chilean exile. His book on the national security state brought him into conflict with Augusto Pinochet's military junta and resulted in his expulsion from Chile in 1978. After the military putsch in Chile, the Chilean Catholic Church's reaction to the regime can be described as complex. Liberal tendencies that were critical of the regime "coexisted" with the suppression of liberal tendencies and support of the milita-

---

58 David Pion-Berlin, "Latin American National Security Doctrines: Hard and Softline Themes," *Armed Forces & Society* 15 (1989): 411.
59 Leslie W. Hepple, "Geopolitics, Generals and the State in Brazil," *Political Geography Quarterly* 5, no. 4 (1986): 581.
60 Charles Tripp, *The Power and the People: Paths of Resistance in the Middle East* (Cambridge: Cambridge University Press, 2013), 51–68.

ry junta.⁶¹ Although José Comblin's *The Church and the National Security State* reflects on the situation in Chile, he addresses a problem that is not specific to one Latin American state. Although in the 1970s and beyond one finds different shades of national security systems in Latin America, including Central America, Brazil may serve as yet another paradigmatic example of this system. The role of the Catholic Church during the military dictatorship was at least as complex as in Chile. In Brazil, cardinals, bishops, and intellectuals involve such antithetical figures as Hélder Câmara and Plinio Corrêa de Oliveira, the founder of the *Society for the Defense of Tradition, Family, and Property* that sided with the military regime. The conflict between the military junta and critical voices within the Church were fueled by the military's response to criticism. As David Pion-Berlin notes, although the "radical opposition to the 1964 Brazilian military coup could have dissolved once economic growth provided its rewards, [...] the Brazilian military let its exaggerated fears of leftist activity get the better of it, provoking a long period of unrestrained, disproportionate, and unnecessary state terror."⁶²

Contrary to Camilo Torres, unless violent actions cannot be avoided, José Comblin is by no means a strong supporter of violent actions. Indeed, for him, "[o]nly as a last resort do the poor have recourse to violence."⁶³ Yet, his analysis in *The Church and the National Security State* concludes with legitimizing revolutionary change and the need for a "theology of revolution."⁶⁴ For Comblin, the "strongest support of dictatorship and tyranny is fear." Thus, "liberty necessarily includes some prospect of martyrdom. The struggle for freedom, therefore, includes some risk, even the risk of death."⁶⁵

Before exploring Comblin's analysis of the national security state and the Church's relation to it, it is useful to discuss his concept of theology first. José Comblin is one of the "major architects" of the Medellín conference; his theology breathes the spirit of Medellín.⁶⁶ For Comblin, theology is a human science that,

---

61 Steven R. Browers, "Pinochet's Plebiscite and the Catholics: The Dual Role of the Chilean Church," *World Affairs* 155, no. 2 (1988): 51–58. For the complexity of the Church's role, see also Paul E. Sigmund, "Revolution, Counterrevolution, and the Catholic Church in Chile," *Annals of the American Academy of Political and Social Science* 483 (1986): 25–35.
62 David Pion-Berlin, "The National Security Doctrine, Military Threat Perception, and the 'Dirty War' in Argentina," *Comparative Political Studies* 21 (1988): 384–5.
63 José Comblin, "The Holy Spirit," in *Mysterium Liberationis: Fundamental Concepts of Liberation Theology*, ed. Ignacio Ellacuría and Jon Sobrino (Maryknoll: Orbis, 1993), 474.
64 Comblin, *The Church and the National Security State*, 224.
65 Ibid., 193.
66 Jan Hoffman French, "A Tale of Two Priests and Two Struggles: Liberation Theology from Dictatorship to Democracy in the Brazilian Northeast," *The Americas* 63 (2007): 421.

for the most part, lacks methodology. Theology is eclectic in nature. For him, the key issue concerns "right" and "wrong" theologies. Whether a theology qualifies as right or wrong depends on its situated-ness. He explains this distinction by stating that "in any human situation, in any debate, there is a right statement and a wrong statement, a right attitude and a wrong attitude."[67] Similarly, he distinguishes between a "true theology" and an "established theology." A false theology is a complete system of "truth" the believers are expected to listen to and to obey. It is a "theology of silence" that is an "expression of power" and an "ideology of privileges." He equates this false or established theology with the orthodoxy of the institutionalized Church. This theology conflicts with the "true theology" that "does not want to ignore the problems of the world at a given time. [...] Rather, it wants to restore in the world the hope of the poor so that their voice can be heard." For Comblin, a theology that is not situated in history, in time, is empty and meaningless.[68] This distinction also relates to his concept of two churches: the Church that represents the institutional Church's upper hierarchy that helps and always helped legitimizing power of kings and emperors, and the church of the lower echelon that follows a democratic and spiritualistic tradition and is bound to the principles of social justice and charity. The latter, as we have seen, resembles one of the key theological concepts in Camilo Torres.[69]

This understanding of a theology in the *hic et nunc* is paradigmatic for liberation theology and finds one of his earliest and clearest expression in Gustavo Gutiérrez's exploration of liberation theology as *political*. For Gutiérrez, liberation theology is "political theology" in the sense that it deals "with the classic question of the relation between faith and human existence, between faith and social reality, between faith and political action."[70] This concept of political theology, however, has nothing in common with Carl Schmitt's notion of political theology.[71] Gutiérrez's political theology is not concerned with questions of political legitimacy, at least not directly. Thus, it is not meant as mixing the political and the religious sphere. Rather, it relates the current struggle for liberation that requires

---

67 Comblin, *The Church and the National Security State*, 12, 14.
68 Ibid., 16, 19, 22.
69 Ibid., 43. However, Michael A. Gismondi, "Transformations in the Holy: Religious Resistance and Hegemonic Struggles in the Nicaraguan Revolution," *Latin American Perspectives* 13, no. 3 (1986): 20, implies that Comblin overdraws the distinction between the two churches, particularly in historic perspective.
70 Gustavo Gutiérrez, *A Theology of Liberation: History, Politics and Salvation*, 15th anniversary ed. (Maryknoll: Orbis, 1988), 29.
71 Carl Schmitt, *Politische Theologie: Vier Kapitel zur Lehre von der Souveränität*, 9th ed. (Berlin: Duncker & Humblot, 2009).

social revolution to change the existing order and involves "counterviolence [that opposes] the violence which the existing order produces" back to the historicity of Jesus' mission. This being in the world and responding to the injustice that exist in the world has a political dimension.[72] Accordingly, Gutiérrez's understanding of political theology is, by its nature, counter-Schmittian.

Yet, Comblin does not see this opposition to the existing violence as opposition to all that is not "Christian." "[A]ccording to the Bible the atheists are fools, but not enemies." More importantly, "the theological problem today does not consist of the struggle against atheism, but against the false gods of our times."[73] These false gods relate to two myths. Comblin identifies one myth as the myth of "unity of action in Western civilization" based on "Western scientific and technical culture." According to this myth revolution cannot take place because all actions have to take place within the system and its laws; each person has to find his or her place within the existing system, in accordance with the hierarchy that is immanent to the existing order.[74] This myth relates to a second myth, the "myth of total war against communism [that] hides the awareness of an opposition between developed and underdeveloped countries."[75] Comblin confronts this two components myth with a counter-myth, a myth of "total action that is able to destroy the whole system and to build another, radically different society." Comblin sees this myth "unavoidable in today's Third World."[76] Corresponding to the counter-myth, he associates revolution with the promotion of liberation. He regards the theology of liberation as a particular version of liberation.[77]

For Comblin, these two opposing views are also reflected in the history of the Church and in the history of Christianity. The first one is related to a "privatized Christianity" that "also legitimizes and supports the establishment," and the Church regards the second one as heresy and false Christianity. Comblin considers this judgment the outcome of the established Church's denial of social change accompanied with her tendency to sacralize the status quo of the established religious and political powers.[78]

Comblin regards it particularly true in Latin America where the Church has usually acted in two alternative fashions. Either she submits herself to the state.

---

72 Gutiérrez, *A Theology of Liberation*, 130, 135.
73 Comblin, *The Church and the National Security State*, 26.
74 Ibid., 24.
75 Ibid., 57. Pottenger, *Political Theory of Liberation Theology*, 118.
76 Comblin, *The Church and the National Security State*, 24.
77 Ibid., 30.
78 Ibid., 39, 44.

In this case, the state uses the Church for its "'realistic' objectives." Alternatively, the state submits itself to the Church, which means that the Church uses "the instruments and power of the state" to achieve her "'mystical' aims." More recently, by following either of these alternatives, the Church has adopted a particularly anticommunist attitude.[79] Moreover, the Church has ignored the tremendous social changes that came with decolonization and neo-colonization and the economic, cultural, and political shifts Comblin associates with the beginning of industrialization, a process through which Latin America searched and gained a new identity that is different from Europe's and North America's "Western" identity.[80]

The model of state the Church submits herself to the model of the national security state. The national security model is based on geopolitical consideration. Comblin regards the United States as the main architect of the national security system (although Leslie W. Hepple claims that Comblin's interpretation that U.S. influences are "behind the entire development" is "somewhat inaccurate," Hepple does not reveal any of Comblin's flaws).[81] Yet, Comblin reinforces his interpretation and sees U.S. influence as one of the major obstacles that hinders Latin American nations in their maturity.[82] His analysis is supported by other liberation theologians. For instance, José Ignacio González Faus associates with North America the export of violence that is "always masked as the defense of justice or freedom, even the defense of God (and sometimes simply boldfaced defense of one's own interests)."[83] For Comblin, this national security ideology that relates itself to "Western civilization" is based on three tenets, "science, democracy, and Christianity."[84] In contrast to the national security ideology, in Latin America, democratic arrangements are utterly absent. At best, there is democracy for the elite because the vast majority of the people remain excluded from real citizenship and political participation. As Comblin notes in one of his later works, "[o]nly a minority follows the life of the nation; the vast majority of the popular masses in the countryside or the city are not informed and have

---

[79] Ibid., 53–4.
[80] Ibid., 170–1.
[81] Hepple, "Geopolitics, Generals and the State in Brazil," 585.
[82] José Comblin, *Called for Freedom: The Changing Context of Liberation Theology*, trans. Phillip Berryman (Maryknoll: Orbis, 1998), 122.
[83] José Ignacio González Faus, "Sin," in *Mysterium Liberationis: Fundamental Concepts of Liberation Theology*, ed. Jon Sobrino and Ignacio Ellacuría (Maryknoll: Orbis, 1993), 539.
[84] Comblin, *The Church and the National Security State*, 77.

no idea what is going on."⁸⁵ Although this observation reflects on post-military dictatorship experiences, it refers back to the concept of the state he regards as a foundation of the national security system. In this understanding, the "state is the nation and the nation is the people. The state is its own power, and that political power is entirely in the hands of its most representative bearer, the armed forces."⁸⁶

Essentially, this concept of the state excludes the people from the state and is aiming for its own citizens' submission.⁸⁷ Thus, the concept of the state is based on the elites, particularly the military elites; it aims for the ability "to create force and violence" and identifies its national security objectives with that of the West.⁸⁸ Because Christianity is associated with "Western values" and because the authors of the national security ideology "think a general agreement between the church and the armed forces would [generate] a firm support for the whole society," the coalition between the military and the Church is seen as the best solution for both "powers" involved.⁸⁹ Comblin heavily criticizes this applied concept of Christianity. For him, the military has learned perfectly well how to use clerical language and how to integrate papal encyclicals in its speeches. Yet, its Christianity is a dead Christianity, a fixed Christianity that is nothing more than a "collection of symbols" used as a means in accordance with the military's needs for creating national identity. It only borrows the rhetoric of Christian nation-building and uses it to create and to mobilize national feelings. Because "[d]ead religious symbols are highly antisubversive [...] the national security system seeks a fixed, passive, archaic Christianity."⁹⁰

Comblin's second criticism targets the national security systems's "anticommunist crusade" that utilizes the Church-military regime coalition. In this scenario the Church is obliged to enter into an anticommunist crusade; her main targets are "the atheistic tenets of Marxism."⁹¹ Thus, any opposition to this system is instantly seen as an attack on Western values and as a heresy. Comblin, however, does not stop with criticizing the institutionalized Church for her coalition with the military regimes. Explicitly, he targets the *Society for Tradition,*

---

85 Comblin, *Called for Freedom*, 122. See also Rudolf von Sinner, "Brazil: From Liberation Theology to a Theology of Citizenship as Public Theology," *International Journal of Public Theology* 1 (2007): 350.
86 Comblin, *The Church and the National Security State*, 96.
87 Pottenger, *The Political Theory of Liberation Theology*, 113.
88 Comblin, *The Church and the National Security State*, 74–6.
89 Ibid., 79.
90 Ibid., 80, 84, 107.
91 Ibid., 85–6, 170.

Family, and Property (TFP). This counterrevolutionary movement that concerns us later in greater detail Comblin criticizes heavily because it

> is based on the military system's purpose and means. It is a pathological phenomenon, its members are almost neurotics, and many of them directly help the secret services. For them the secret service is a kind of evangelization, a new inquisition in which they can worship God by delivering the church from heresy and corruption. Ideologically, they are living in the Middle Ages.[92]

For TFP, of course, this coalition with the military juntas comes with privileges. They have access to mass media and can control official Catholic teachings. In return for their support of the regime, the regime enforces some of its religious doctrines by law.

In addition to his criticism of the national security ideology's anti-communist crusade and the Church's involvement in it, Comblin attacks the anthropology that is fundamental to the national security ideology. Comblin emphasizes that the national security ideology's anthropology is based on a friend versus enemy antagonism and on an obstructed concept of freedom. The national security ideology's anthropology and the ideology's concept of the state clash with Christianity.[93] Comblin contrasts the national security state system that is based on force, violence, oppression of the majority, and an explicit anti-communist outlook with another concept of the state he considers in conformity with true Christianity. His alternative concept of the state places the people as a whole in the center of the state, not the (military) elite:

> The makers of a political society are the people. The security and the survival of the state may not be the main purpose of the people. [...] They may remain in proportion to the social services they fulfil; they may be replaced by other political systems more suitable to new circumstances. The states pass; the peoples remain. The purpose of the state has to be useful to the political society.[94]

Similarly, the state cannot be the sole author of law and justice; the state needs to be justice's servant. To avoid totalitarianism, the state cannot be above law and justice, but needs to be underneath it. Comblin's concept of the state puts the people in the center. He also assumes that people have rights, human rights. The concept of human rights has to be an integral part of the pastoral approach. This new pastoral approach he contrasts with Mussolini for whom human rights

---

92 Ibid., 81.
93 Ibid., 89, 95.
94 Ibid., 96.

are non-existent. In Mussolini's concept, which is similar to the national security ideology, humans are born with duties rather than with rights. Humans have only rights if the state grants them. Because the people's rights depend on the state, the state can deprive the people of these rights as needed.[95]

In addition to the national security ideology itself, Comblin criticizes the ideology of development that has been adopted by military regimes. It aims for some economic growth to increase the nation's power. While it increases the power of the state, it increasingly marginalizes the masses politically and socio-economically.[96] As already criticized by Camilo Torres, eventually the national security state deprives the people of their right (following the national security logic that the people do not have any rights, only states have rights) to organize themselves in "public organizations through which citizens could demand their rights. The national security state wants only isolated individuals, unarmed, submissive, and dedicated."[97]

At a first glance, beyond Comblin's critique of the military regimes' abuse of a false and dead version of Christianity for political means and sections of the institutionalized Church's willingness to comply, his analysis does not seem to have much of a Christian outlook. Except for his distinction between true and false Christianity, Comblin might have come to a similar conclusion by applying a Marxist critique. Yet, although Marxist ideas are definitely not absent in his analysis, contrary to Camilo Torres, he rejects Marxism as an alternative ideology because in his reading, "the Marxist system has shifted from the idea of class struggle for liberty to the idea of national security, closely resembling the national security systems of the rightist military dictatorships."[98] In short, he sees Marxist ideas in relation to the Soviet Union. Comblin's approach, however, can be considered as mainstream within liberation theology. As Enrique Dussel notes, "liberation theologians unanimously reject dialectical materialism. No liberation theologian accepts the materialism expounded by Frederick Engels in his *Dialectic of Nature*, or of Lenin, Bukharin, or Stalin. Marx is accepted, and adopted, as a social critic."[99]

In compliance with the general liberation theologians' approach, Comblin rejects Marxism as a state ideology, but not as an analytical tool. At the same

---

95 Ibid., 103.
96 Pottinger, *Political Theory of Liberation Theology*, 113.
97 Comblin, *The Church and the National Security State*, 117.
98 Ibid., 132.
99 Enrique Dussel, "Theology of Liberation and Marxism," in *Mysterium Liberationis: Fundamental Concepts of Liberation Theology*, ed. Jon Sobrino and Ignacio Ellacuría (Maryknoll: Orbis, 1993), 87.

time, he stresses the incompatibility of communism and Christianity. Communism has to be "rejected by the church as heresy or error like liberalism or fascism."[100] His goal, however, is to overcome the structural violence of the national security system, which requires liberation and liberation theology as theology of revolution.[101] Yet, he does not reject the existing status quo solely for theological reasons but also for reasons resting in social ethics. Eventually, he merges the ethical and the theological aspects of his argument. The Latin American Church has to oppose the status quo because the people have the right to its survival "as a people, as God's people." The liberation of the people is the Church's true mission.[102]

Comblin's theological argument is based on the unity of *libertas ecclesia* and *libertas populi:* "The freedom of the church is not only the freedom to proclaim God's promise; it is also freedom for the people born in virtue of this proclamation." Thus, it means the "real application of the eternal gospel [that gives] this eternal gospel a true meaning for today's world."[103] Comblin's argument is based on the idea that Christianity was for most of its historic existence a counter-revolutionary ideology. Only in the aftermath of the French Revolution had the counter-revolutionary impetus been suppressed by the institutionalized Church and replaced by other political philosophies. The sociological outcome of liberation is a society that is based on the "relationship of person with person." A society that fulfills true liberation is not concerned with material causes, but is "based on liberty and free agreement."[104]

Whereas only the people can free themselves, true liberation outside of God is impossible. "Only God is able to create a movement towards liberty without manipulation. So liberty relates unavoidable to God." Liberation is "an ongoing struggle against new shapes of law and power." It is also on "ongoing debate and struggle between church and Christianity," which relates back to Comblin's narrative of true and false theologies.[105]

Similarly to pre-modern Christian social movements (as discussed with the Cathars), Comblin argues that revolutionary movements have always been con-

---

100 Comblin, *The Church and the National Security State*, 200.
101 It is worth noting that the concept of "structural violence" that has been introduced by Johan Galtung, "Violence, Peace, and Peace Research". *Journal of Peace Research* 6, no. 3 (1969): 167–191, into social science discourses emerged from Latin American experiences; yet, liberation theologians do not speak of "structural violence," but demand "structural change."
102 Comblin, *The Church and the National Security State*, 117.
103 Ibid., 119–20.
104 Ibid., 160.
105 Ibid., 162, 164, 165.

sidered a threat to political and ecclesiastical security. Consequently, liberation is not free of the risk of physical harm. Indeed, Comblin stresses that "the strongest support of dictatorship is fear. The idea of liberty necessarily includes some prospect of martyrdom. The struggle for freedom, therefore, includes some risk, even a risk of death. It also has to overcome all the lesser irrational factors—aggressiveness, rivalry, envy, desire for tranquility and amusement, and so on—which separate human beings from their vocation."[106]

Yet, Comblin rejects any ideas that require the people (the masses) to give up their popular religion and replace it with an elitist religion. Liberation has to rely on the lower classes, not on the upper classes or the state. Rather, the church has to support the lower classes. Instead of changing "popular religion according to the criteria of an elitist sociology, [the church has to foster liberation] according to authentic theological criteria."[107] The need for revolution and, therefore, a theology of revolution grows out of the historic reality of social dynamics and changes. Comblin concludes by reuniting social ethics and theology: "In this condition, one cannot define a social ethics without a theology of revolution—without an analysis of the pastoral approach and strategy for the change and the particular events of change that make up history and the actual fate of humankind."[108]

In one of his later works, José Comblin reassesses the need for social change and the outcome of democratization in Latin America. In his analysis, in the 1990s democracy in Latin America still suffers under the experience of military dictatorship. Instead of democracy based on true liberation, the main foundation of democracy is the fear of the military, which he does not consider "a sufficient basis for establishing a true democracy." Moreover, the educated elites still aim for the imitation of the West—instead of generating an independent national identity. With the crisis of democracy in the West in mind, following the Western model only implies adding further weakness to already weak democracies.[109]

Ignacio Ellacuría's Theological-Philosophical Perspectives on Violence

José Comblin suffered exile; naturalized Salvadorian Ignacio Ellacuría (1930 – 1989) also experienced exile. But he was also a victim of violence, not just threats of violence. In 1989, together with five other Jesuit priests, he was assas-

---

106 Ibid., 193 – 4.
107 Ibid., 215.
108 Ibid., 224.
109 Comblin, *Called for Freedom*, 131.

sinated.[110] The contexts in which Ignacio Ellacuría has to be placed are liberation theology generally and the socio-economic and political conditions in El Salvador during the 1960s to 1980s specifically. Before entering into Ellacuría's thought, the Salvadorian church-state relations deserve some consideration. Indeed, the violence in El Salvador that ended the civil war (1980–1992) with a peace treaty in 1992 cannot be fully understood without considering the Church's role. That the peace treaty was eventually possible was also the outcome of Ignacio Ellacuría's contributions that make dialogue between the conflicting parties possible.[111] The general pattern that conservative elites were in league with the Church (or vice versa) because the Church was seen as defenders of conservative privileges who could generate the support of the masses, whereas the liberal elites were in opposition to the Church, applies to the situation in El Salvador as well. However, the church-state relationship in El Salvador is more complex. First, in the aftermath of the formation of El Salvador, priests, primarily Jesuits, were expelled from the country. Neither the constitution of 1880 nor the constitution of 1886 recognizes Catholicism as the official state religion. As Andrew Stein notes, the period from the 1870s to 1980, the outbreak of the civil war, was marked by violence, coups, and fixed elections. The Church played along and, at least in general, recognized the government in power as legitimate.[112] Indeed, the Church did more than just recognize the governments. Usually, the Church responded to peasant rebellions with the threat of hell.[113]

This general church-state agreement eroded in the late 1960s and early 1970s. This period is marked by the "expulsion of foreign clergy, murder of human rights workers, and church denunciations of government actions." The Universidad Centoamericana José Simeón Cañas (UCA) emerged as one of the opposition centers. Death threats against Ignacio Ellacuría, who served as the university's rector from 1979 until his death, and fellow Jesuits at UCA were rather common; the university was bombed repeatedly. Simultaneously, Archbishop Óscar Romero, although originally recognized as a bishop of the traditional Church, openly denounced state excesses and "emerged as a defender of

---

110 Jon Sobrino, "Ignacio Ellacuría, the Human Being and the Christian: 'Taking the Crucified People Down from the Cross'," in *Love that Produces Hope: The Thought of Ignacio Ellacuría*, ed. Kevin F. Burke and Robert Lassalle-Klein (Collegeville: Liturgical Press, 2006), 54–5, draws some parallels between Jesus' death and Ellacuría's because both were killed bases on false accusations.
111 Phillip Berryman, *Subborn Hope: Religion, Politics, and Revolution in Central America* (Maryknoll: Orbis Books, 1994), 82.
112 Andrew J. Stein, "El Salvador," in *Religious Freedom and Evangelization in Latin America: The Challenges of Religious Pluralism*, ed. Paul E. Sigmund (Maryknoll: Orbis, 1999), 114–5.
113 Cardenal, "The Martyrdom of the Salvadorean Church," 228.

human rights, a 'voice of the voiceless',"¹¹⁴ which brought him not only in conflict with Rome but also led to his assassination in 1980.¹¹⁵ The outcome of the Church's transformation from a coalition-church to an opposition-church was responded by

> physical violence against the ecclesiastical institution, the Catholic colleges; the Catholic radio was victim of various bomb attacks and systematic interferences; priests and religious houses were searched and attacked with bombs and machine guns: the same happened to churches and houses of lay collaborators. Likewise there was military occupation of churches, violations of the Eucharist and sacred vessels.¹¹⁶

During the civil war, Ignacio Ellacuría, one of the leading public intellectuals in El Salvador, emerges as negotiator for the war's peaceful resolution. Yet, prior to the civil war, El Salvador was certainly not free from violence. The military coup of 1972 was instantly followed by a wave of violence. People were killed or disappeared.¹¹⁷ Supported and partly motivated through pastoral work, peasant organizations emerged. Stimulated by the frequent experience of electoral fraud, peasant organizations became increasingly frustrated because a peaceful solution to political change was more and more out of reach. As expressed in the slogan "Better to die of a bullet than of hunger," peasant organizations considered more militant forms of action. Phillip Berryman describes the 1970s as a decade in "which the major protagonists, the oligarchy and the military on the one side and the popular organizations—and by implication, people of the Catholic church—on the other, acted out the conflict."¹¹⁸

The pre-civil war conflict is the context for Ellacuría's discourse on violence that concerns us in this section. This discourse is particularly influenced by the document issued at the Medellín conference as discussed at the beginning of this chapter.¹¹⁹ Other intellectual influences are the Austrian theologian Karl Rahner under whom Ellacuría studied in Innsbruck and the philosopher Xavier Zubiri under whom Ellacuría completed his doctoral dissertation in philosophy and

---

114 Phillip Berryman, "El Salvador: From Evangelization to Insurrection," in *Religion and Political Conflict in Latin America*, ed. Daniel H. Levine (Chapel Hill: The University of North Carolina Press, 1986), 71.
115 Stein, "El Salvador," 116–7. Cardenal, "The Martyrdom of the Salvadorean Church," 237, 240.
116 Cardenal, "The Martyrdom of the Salvadorean Church," 242.
117 Berryman, *Subborn Hope*, 63–4.
118 Berryman, "El Salvador," 65–8 (quote 68).
119 José Sols Lucia, *La teología histórica de Ignacio Ellacuría* (Madrid: Editorial Trotta, 1999), 143–6.

with whom he later collaborated.[120] It needs to be noted that more recent scholarly interest in Ellacuría's work focuses primarily on his philosophy and Zubiri's influence on Ellacuría and on his theology more generally.[121] These influences are clearly visible in Ellacuría's discourse on violence, although recent scholarship on Ellacuría appears to be almost apologetic on this part of his work, which was controversial when it was first published because he "did not unconditionally condemn the use of revolutionary violence as an option for victims of oppression."[122] Ellacuría goes further than not unconditionally condemning violence, however. In the writing that concerns us most, he concludes, "in case of established violence, whatever form it may take, we may be not only permitted but even required to use the force that is necessary to redeem the established violence."[123] It is fair to say, although it is not the central topic here, that Ellacuría's discussion of violence does not stand in contradiction to his theology and philosophy more generally, although some scholars consider this work the "more abstruse" among his works.[124]

Most prominently, Ellacuría's discourse of violence appears in the third part of his *Teologá política*, first published in 1973. *Teologá política* appeared in English in 1976 under the title *Freedom Made Flesh*. In his discussion of violence, Ellacuría integrated theological, philosophical, biological, and psychoanalytical approaches. Yet, the entire discourse is framed theologically and rests in his understanding of salvation that he shares with José Comblin and other liberation theologians. He rejects the "continuing prejudice that salvation is ahistorical. Although people may deny it with their works, it continues to be one of the most serious obstacles to truly living and reflecting on the faith."[125] Salvation being

---

[120] Martin Maier, "Karl Rahner: The Teacher of Ignacio Ellacuría," in *Love that Produces Hope: The Thought of Ignacio Ellacuría*, ed. Kevin F. Burke and Robert Lassalle-Klein (Collegeville: Liturgical Press, 2006), 128–143. Robert Lassalle-Klein, "Ignacio Ellacuría's Debt to Xavier Zubiri: Critical Principles for a Latin American Philosophy and Theology of Liberation," in *Love that Produces Hope*, 88–127.
[121] See, for instance, Michael E. Lee, "Liberation Theology's Transcendent Moment: The Work of Xavier Zubiri and Ignacio Ellacuría as Nonconstructive Discourse," *Journal of Religion* 83 (2003): 226–243. Robert Lassalle-Klein, "Jesus of Galilee and the Crucified People: The Contextual Christology of Jon Sobrino and Ignacio Ellacuría," *Theological Studies* 70 (1990): 347–376.
[122] Michael E. Lee, *Bearing the Weight of Salvation: The Soterology of Ignacio Ellacuría*, Foreword Gustavo Gutiérrez (New York: Crossroad, 2009), 27, 76 (quote).
[123] Ignacio Ellacuría, *Freedom Made Flesh: The Mission of Christ and His Church* (Maryknoll: Orbis, 1976), 229.
[124] Teresa Whitfield, *Paying the Price: Ignacio Ellacuría and the Murdered Jesuits of El Salvador* (Philadelphia: Temple University Press, 1994), 224.
[125] Ellacuría, *Freedom Made Flesh*, 11.

historical also means that salvation is political or has at least a political dimension, which related back to the "definite political import in Jesus' messianic mission."[126] While the political dimension is emphasized by liberation theologians generally, the idea that "faith and politics are united in the Christian" is also essential to Romero's defense of priests' work with popular organizations.[127]

Ellacuría emphasizes the political conditions under which Jesus and his followers lived. He describes the moment of Judea's incorporation into the Roman Empire as "an atmosphere of maximum politization" that was marked by spontaneous uprisings that were instantly crushed by the Roman governor of Syria. Similar to the situation in many Latin American countries, the "lower levels of the priesthood were in closer contact with the popular movements, but the upper levels were acting in convenience with the political and economic powers." The political dimension is reinforced by the perception of the Romans who considered Jesus a rebel against their rule. Thus, Jesus' crucifixion is a political crucifixion, although Ellacuría sees Jesus' activity as primarily religious, it appeared to be political; "his closest followers saw him as a political figure." Ellacuría concludes from his analysis of the historical Jesus that Christianity, right from the beginning, stands in a "politico-religious tradition."[128]

While Ellacuría admits some parallels to the Zealots, he emphasizes that he agrees with historians of religion that Jesus was not part of the Zealot movement. To reemphasize the political dimension, Jesus represents an alternative to the Zealots. The historical-political aspect has implications for Ellacuría's understanding of the Church's mission:

> If we do not take note of the essential historicity of the Church's mission in proclaiming the gospel message, then it is presumptuous or useless for us to examine the question of the Church's mission at all today. The slightest reflection will bring us to the realization that the Church's mission is historical, that this is an essential dimension of the whole question. Many misunderstandings in theory and practice arise from a denial of this dimension or and important evaluation of it.[129]

This historicity also means that Christianity in Latin America must be different from the Christianity practiced in Europe; it needs to be de-Westernized and can-

---

126 Ibid., 41.
127 Berryman, "El Salvador," 71.
128 Ellacuría, *Freedom Made Flesh*, 41–2, 46, 49, 54. See Sols Lucia, *La teología histórica de Ignacio Ellacuría*, 92–96.
129 Ellacuría, *Freedom Made Flesh*, 81.

not be understood as essential to Western civilization.[130] For Ellacuría, historicity comes in three forms, "1) historicity as real-life authenticity; 2) historicity as effectiveness in history; 3) historicity as hope in an eschatological future."[131] Salvation in history leads to liberation. Ellacuría rejects all Marxist or other ideologically determined concepts of liberation. Liberation is not even an alternative to other forms of liberation; rather, "[o]nly in name it is similar to the secular and political liberation [...]. It is not to be equated with socio-political liberation."[132] In this sense, Ellacuría contradicts Michael E. Lee's interpretation, which emphasized that liberation does not mean simply socio-economic liberation by stressing three different dimensions of liberation that are central to liberation theology. Only Lee's third level corresponds with Ellacuría's theological concept of liberation, although he is in agreement with Ellacuría when he emphasizes that the outcome of liberation means justice and peace and the absence of violence.[133]

Ellacuría reemphasizes the theological meaning of liberation by noting that "liberation is not confined to socio-political liberation." It relates to all forms of oppression as the Psalms "talk about liberation from sin, sickness, and death; from enemies and persecutors; from the violent, the unjust, and the oppressor. In the Psalms we find a cry for liberation which seems to suggest that man in history is being oppressed by all sorts of unjust domination and the God is the supreme liberator."[134] Eventually, he defines liberation as struggle against injustice in all its manifestations.[135] As Comblin, he admits and criticizes the Church for her contribution to injustice and oppression. Thus, the Church must engage in fighting injustice because injustice, theologically, means sin. Moreover, "injustice is a negation of man and [...] causes man to negate God."[136] For the Church being in the world means that she has to be with the poor and confront the injustice of poverty.[137] "But if there are poor people

---

[130] Ignacio Ellacuría, "The Christian Challenge of Liberation Theology," in *Essays on History, Liberation, and Salvation*, ed. Michael E. Lee, Commentary Kevin F. Burke (Maryknoll: Orbis, 2013), 132–5.
[131] Ellacuría, *Freedom Made Flesh*, 93.
[132] Ibid., 98.
[133] Lee, *Bearing the Weight of Salvation*, 13, 18.
[134] Ellacuría, *Freedom Made Flesh*, 100.
[135] Ibid., 110.
[136] Ibid., 113–5.
[137] Ignacio Ellacuría, "The Historicity of Christian Salvation," in *Essays on History, Liberation, and Salvation*, ed. Michael E. Lee, Commentary Kevin F. Burke (Maryknoll: Orbis, 2013), 154–6.

around, then the Church cannot be holy or salvific unless it lives in, with, and for the poor."[138]

The discourse on salvation and liberation leads Ellacuría to the often raised question about the relationship between violence (an injustice) and the cross. The question about the relationship between violence and the cross is also the starting point for Ellacuría's analysis of violence. It is worth noting that Ellacuría's discourse on violence is relatively free of Marxist influences. Yet, he follows the inner logic of historicity as laid out in his theology of salvation or soteriology by locating violence in the world and, more specifically, in the Third World and Latin American context:

> It is not that violence is exclusive to the Third World, but that violence shows its true scope and outlines only in the context of the Third World. Hence it is in that context that violence reveals its true nature. It is in the Third World that violence fully displays what in only hinted at in other areas of the world.[139]

The situation in the Third World is particularly grave and serious because of the particular version of violence that is present: institutionalized violence. Institutionalized violence "reveals the terrible ambiguity of violence" because it leads to two distinct manifestations of violence. "The first one is the root kid of violence." "It is present as injustice, and it is immersed in the mystery of iniquity." The second "is present as resistance to situations which in themselves are violent because they violate human dignity and oppress man's liberty."[140]

It is worth noting that Ellacuría considers both violence and counter-violence to be violence, whereas other authors, like Enrique Dussel, speak of violence only if it is illegitimate (note that difference to illegal) violence, whereas legitimate "violence" is perceived as coercion, not violence. When legal coercion collapses morally, it loses its legitimacy and turns into violence and is usually caused by unjust structure.[141] Dussel's philosophical-ethical problem is a theological problem for Ellacuría. Dussel's "unjust structures" are "sinful structures" for Ellacuría. Ellacuría objects particularly to three versions of unjust violence that are abuses of power, "1) legislation that tries to perpetuate an unjust situation in the political and socio-economic order; 2) political torture in all its forms; 3) falsehood propagated deliberately to misguide the conscious awareness of the

---

138 Ellacuría, *Freedom Made Flesh*, 146.
139 Ibid., 167.
140 Ibid., 170.
141 Dussel, *Ethics of Liberation*, 401, 403.

people. This would be covert, legalized violence, but it remains the worst violence of all. It is unjust violence, or, the violence of injustice."[142]

With reference to Visser 't Hooft, Ellacuría notes, if the Church does not fulfil her obligation "to liberate human beings from the terrible injustice in which they live" and "refuses in practice to assume any responsibility towards the disintegrated of the earth" she "is as guilty of heresy as someone who rejects a particular article of faith."[143] To change the existing unjust and oppressive structures, violent revolutionary change may become necessary:

> There is no reason why revolution must be equated with violence, but the process of revolutionary change may be forced to take a violent form in countries where the oppressor groups are indifferent to the aspirations of the people and, on the context of maintaining law and order, use coercion to resist necessary change.[144]

He equates violence with injustice because it "deprives man of his personal rights by force and prevents him from giving shape to his own personal life on the basis of his own personal judgment."[145] Contrary to Dussel, who draws the distinction between coercion (legitimate) and violence (illegitimate), Ellacuría invokes the distinction between violence and aggression or aggressiveness. Both from a psychological (Freud) and a biological (Lorenz) perspective he considers aggressiveness natural and even necessary for survival. It is paired with love and freedom. Aggressiveness is original to human beings and "intrinsic to man's nature." By contrast, violence is "rationalized aggressiveness." If it is based on "cold calculation of reason" it becomes a "daemonic force" and is related to evil.[146]

Simultaneously and corresponding to Camilo Torres, he regards violence as a "symptom."[147] It is a symptom "that something is not all right. When signs of violence present themselves, they may well be signs of the fact that aggressiveness and struggle are at work in a positive sense; but they are also signs that something is wrong, that something is faulty."[148] Yet, Ellacuría relates violence also to evil. Whereas the first form of violence, the violence of oppression and injustice, is always evil, the second form of violence, the counter-violence, "may be absolutely necessary even though it undoubtedly entails evils." Thus,

---

[142] Ellacuría, *Freedom Made Flesh*, 198.
[143] Ibid., 171.
[144] Ibid.
[145] Ibid., 199.
[146] Ibid., 181–190.
[147] Torres, "Two Subcultures," 257.
[148] Ellacuría, *Freedom Made Flesh*, 192.

at times, the second form of violence is required. Eventually, Ellacuría renders the first violence "evil violence" and the second violence "good violence" and relates the second violence to the punishment of sin.[149] In his theological turn, he integrates an argument that resembles an idea that is omnipresent in medieval treatises, namely the concept of divine punishment: "An all-powerful and enraged God must stand for the oppressed and inflict punishment on the unjust oppressor. The punishment is not left to God because the oppressed should not do the job; it is left to God because the oppressed cannot in fact do the job in the concrete, so God is asked to do it for them."[150]

Simultaneously, people realize that they have rights and that these rights have been violated; this gives rise to revolutionary violence that confronts institutionalized violence, which is the "highest magnification of violence" and a "very grave sin" of social injustice. This process of realization is precisely that moment Enrique Dussel describes as a legitimacy crisis of the existing (oppressive) order.[151] For Ellacuría, there is no "Christian authenticity" in those who defend the existing order. Violence is needed to overcome the existing injustice and oppression because the extreme injustice "calls for extreme remedies." The goal is the redemption of sin through violent means, as well as the reduction and elimination of evil.[152] Eventually, Ellacuría reminds the combatant that "1) Not everything in the existing structure is evil, neither as structure nor as personal achievement; 2) the Christian message demands that we move out of the whole schema of violence versus resistance to violence by the use of force as quickly as possible."[153] Thus, Ellacuría hopes for true liberation that ends violence, although Comblin reminds us that liberation is a permanent process because of the "ongoing struggle against new shapes of law and power."[154]

---

149 Ibid., 193, 196. In a later essay, published shortly before his violent death, Ignacio Ellacuría, "Latin American Quincentenary? Discovery or Cover-up?," in *Essays on History, Liberation, and Salvation*, 35, Ellacuría stresses that he "always maintained that violence is wrong, but sometimes it may be unavoidable."
150 Ellacuría, *Freedom Made Flesh*, 196.
151 Ibid., 199. Dussel, *Ethics of Liberation*, 407.
152 Ellacuría, *Freedom Made Flesh*, 209, 229.
153 Ibid., 229.
154 Comblin, *The Church and the National Security State*, 165.

3.1.2 Religious Justifications for Counter-Revolution

When addressing justifications for counter-revolution, one needs to bear in mind that these justifications come primarily in two forms, an active and a passive form of legitimizing counter-revolution. Intellectually, actively legitimizing violence is the least problematic of these forms. In the discourses that passively or indirectly legitimize counter-revolution, the reader is confronted with the paradox of legitimizing violence by condemning violence. The paradox relates to the problem of "complicity" as explored by Robert E. Goodin and Chiara Lepora. Although they analyze the complicity problematic in the context of humanitarian work, the underlying problem discussed here is basically the same.

As outlined by Goodin and Lepora, complicity may take more active forms such as "full joint wrongdoing," "conspiracy," and "co-operation" as well as passive forms such as "connivance," "condoning," "consorting," and "contiguity."[155] All involve some sort of consenting to actions, whether actively or passively. Supplementary to the cases Goodin and Lepora invoke, we are concerned with complicity that uses the means of theologically discrediting the opponent (liberation theology). By delegitimizing the liberation theologians' understanding of Christianity, actions that received legitimacy through liberation theology's exegesis are discredited through the Church's counter-exegesis. Simultaneously, the existing structural violence gains implicit legitimacy because (violent) actions against it are delegitimized. Essentially, the Church follows the same logic as applied during medieval times in cases of religious dissent: She demands obedience to the Church and the existing socio-economic and political structure. To illuminate the paradox of supporting violence while condemning violence, it is worth considering the Catholic Church's responses to liberation theology more generally and do discuss particular examples of the counter movement in more detail thereafter.

With the beginning of Pope John Paul II's tenure, the Curia engaged in an intensive intellectual and polemic battle against the teachings of liberation theologians. The pope accuses liberation theologians of their "preferential options for the poor" because in his eyes, it endorses violent class conflict. Thus, "he regularly condemns violence, stresses the 'non-political' character of the Church's mission, and underscores the need for unity and discipline in the ranks."[156] This approach goes hand in hand with an increasingly anti-communist agenda

---

[155] Chiara Lepora and Robert E. Goodin, *On Complicity and Compromise* (Oxford: Oxford University Press, 2013), 31–58.
[156] Daniel H. Levine, "From Church and State to Religion and Politics and Back Again," *Social Compass* 37, no. 2 (1990): 340.

that was set into motion after the Cuban Revolution but was reinforced under John Paul II's tenure. Eventually, the Latin American church is paralyzed and turns, generally, to more government friendly attitudes towards the military juntas.[157] Although the rhetoric that is used is emphatically apolitical, the goal and the implications are political nonetheless. They are aimed at the reaffirmation of the Church's institutional power. Simultaneously and in keeping with the thesis introduced earlier that the internal enemy is considered the more dangerous threat than the external enemy, Pope John Paul II labels liberation theologians and the "Church of the Poor" an "internal enemy;" they are portrayed as antagonistic and dangerous to the Church. Their teachings are seen as "acts of aggressions against orthodoxy and ecclesiastical unity." Thus, the pope's approach undermines any possibility for dialogue.[158] This attitude is also reflected in the pope's personnel politics. In 1984, he promoted Alfonso Lopez Trujillo, the long-time President of the Latin American Bishops' Conference, to Cardinal and praised his contributions to the Church by emphasizing that "[h]is contribution to the study and clarification of theology, particularly of the so-called theology of liberation, has been and remains an eminent service to the Church."[159]

If one reassesses the Church's reaction to liberation theology in light of the discussion in previous chapters, one is confronted with a dispute over orthodoxy versus heterodoxy or even heresy. Thus, at the surface the response to liberation theology's teachings is primarily a theological debate about proper exegesis that gears itself apolitical. Yet, the implications of the theological debate have at least two political dimensions. First, they refer to the (political) power of the Church as an institution and the Roman Curia particularly. Second, attempts to delegitimize liberation theology theologically undermine their ability to oppose what they see as structural violence and social injustice of the military juntas. As such, delegitimizing liberation theology's social cause opens the gate to various forms of implicit or explicit collaboration and complicities between the institutional Church and the regimes in power. At least indirectly, the Church's attempt to remain politically neutral implicitly gives legitimacy to political violence against dissenting parts of the populace, which leads to the paradox of supporting violence by condemning violence.

---

157 Enrique Dussel, "La politique vaticane en Amérique Latine: Essai d'interprétation historico-sociologique," *Social Compass* 37, no. 2 (1990): 220, 223.
158 Guillermo Melendez, "The Catholic Church in Central America: Into the 1990s," *Social Compass* 39, no. 4 (1992): 556–8.
159 Cited in Gerald S. Twomey, "Pope John Paul II and the 'Preferential Option for the Poor'," *Journal of Catholic Legal Studies* 45 (2006): 340.

Alfonso López Trujillo and Roger Vekemans

The response to liberation theology is a concerted action of both the Vatican and conservative bishops and cardinals in Latin America. The two most prominent exponents in Latin America, Alfonso López Trujillo and Roger Vekemans, certainly used their ties to the Vatican and to other conservative bishops in the region to orchestrate their counter-movement.[160] To unify opposition, soon after López Trujillo was elected President of the Latin American Bishops' Conference, he organized a conference on liberation theology in Toledo, Spain, which attracted predominantly critics of liberation theology.[161] López Trujillo also teamed up with the Belgian Jesuit Roger Vekemans. Together, they founded *Tierra Nueva*, a journal that aimed at attacking liberation theology intellectually and theologically. Compared to López Trujillo, Roger Vekemans is a rather complex figure. Like Camilo Torres, he started out with Christian democratic concepts. In Chile, he worked with "popular organizations closely linked to the Christian Democratic Party."[162] Vekemans actively took part in making the Christian Democratic Party attractive to the masses. Originally, the party was supported exclusively by the middle class.[163] In short, Roger Vekemans started out as a reformist activist but he eventually moved "to the right end of the ranges of available alternatives."[164]

Both López Trujillo and Vekemans main criticism is liberation theologians' reading of Christ's political role. It is worth noting that López Trujillo and Vekemans consistently refer to Christ, whereas the liberation theologians refer to Jesus, the human being, stressing the human nature of the Son of God. Although it seems essentially a theological or exegetical question, it is a question with fundamentally political implications. Exegesis concerns the priest's role in the world. Although López Trujillo and Vekemans approaches use slightly different perspectives and strategies, they are complementary and aim for a similar end,

---

160 Milogras Peña, "The Sadalitium Vitae Movement in Peru: A Rewriting of Liberation Theology," in *Religion and Democracy in Latin America*, ed. William H. Swatos (New Brunswick: Transaction Publishers, 1995), 108. Also published under the same title in *Sociological Analysis* 53, no. 2 (1992): 159–173.
161 Smith, *The Emergence of Liberation Theology*, 262, n. 2.
162 Levine, "From Church and State to Religion and Politics and Back Again," 339.
163 Emanuel de Kadt, "Paternalism and Populism: Catholicism in Latin America," *Journal of Contemporary History* 2, no. 5 (1967): 95.
164 Levine, "From Church and State to Religion and Politics and Back Again," 340.

namely maintaining what they consider the Church's political neutrality.[165] Despite the fact that their approach gears toward an essentially apolitical Church, their language involves a political notion that is political in itself, although their concept of the political differs fundamentally from the concept of the political invoked by their liberation theologian counterparts. López Trujillo's and Vekemans's main target is the "political priest." To unfold what they mean by the political priest and why they reject the concept, we need to explore what Alfonso López Trujillo and Roger Vekemans regard as the core function of the Church in the world. Neither López Trujillo nor Vekemans deny the political and socio-economic problems in Latin America. They affect primarily the poor. As López Trujillo notes,

> [n]ational problems usually have their immediate victims: the poor—villages and *barrios* without physicians, without money to buy medicines, without opportunities for education, with problems of malnutrition, with a lack of decent homes, with large groups of unemployed or underpayed workers standing in long lines to buy fuel to prepare their meager meals, with no light, no water; with exploitation at every level, even in the same social class; and people being used by politicians so that they can gain more votes at the cheap cost of false promise.[166]

He does not completely deny the need for liberation, as emphasized by liberation theologians. Yet, he claims that they differ fundamentally on the means of how to bring about liberation. He also disagrees with liberation's concrete meaning. He associates liberation with redemption and salvation—as stressed by Ignacio Ellacuría and others.[167] Nonetheless, he accuses liberation theologians of understanding freedom entirely as the outcome of revolution in a "messianistic Marxist framework."[168]

Whereas López Trujillo addresses the existing problems directly, Vekemans speaks more generally of the "pressing demands of the world in the process of being born."[169] Although they admit to the existence of social and political problems, they differ fundamentally with liberation theologians on how to react and act upon them. As for the liberation theologians, their reasoning is grounded in a theological understanding of Jesus' role in the world and the role of the Church

---

165 Roger Vekemans, *Caesar and God: The Priesthood and Politics* (Maryknoll: Orbis, 1972), 21. Alfonso Lopez Trujillo, *Liberation or Revolution? An Examination of the Priest's Role in the Socioeconomic Class Struggle in Latin America* (Huntington: Our Sunday Visitor, 1977), 69.
166 López Trujillo, *Liberation or Revolution?*, 10.
167 Ibid., 15.
168 Ibid., 36.
169 Vekemans, *Ceasar and God*, 98.

and the individual priest that derives from it. To answer the question of the Church's role in the world, López Trujillo raises the question of whether Christ was a Zealot, although no liberation theologian regards Jesus a Zealot, who aimed for violent political change or whether he was a pacifist. He concludes that he was "neither a guerrilla nor a pacifist." Again, the distinction between Jesus and Christ is significant.

For López Trujillo, Christ "exposes injustice, but He is not oriented towards the destruction of 'order' or towards a reform of institutions or structures; neither is He caught in immobility."[170] By contrast, the revolutionary structural change Marxism is aiming for "does not only mean the violent overthrow of a government to put up a new one, but only to change the system, the structures."[171] Neither is compatible with López Trujillo's reading of the Gospel and Christ's role in the world. His key point refers to the distinction between the politically necessary and the theologically appropriate. What is politically necessary does not and cannot derive directly from the Gospel. More importantly, he considers it theologically unsound to equate "the poor" in the Gospel with a particular "class," although he admits that the prophets have improved the rights of the "social powerless." They have the "right to work and the certainty of not being exploited."[172] Yet, he rejects the very idea of "class" and particularly the idea of the "proletarian class" because it mixes Christian and Marxist viewpoints and turns the Gospel into a text to which the "dialectics of class struggle" are applied.[173]

Without invoking Marx or Marxism explicitly, Roger Vekemans seconds López Trujillo's concern by emphasizing that apostolic movements have the tendency of turning into secular movements, which eventually renders them into "a loveless, lifeless spirituality."[174] Simultaneously, he does not see Pope Boniface VIII's Bull *Unam Sanctam* that aimed for the subordination of the temporal under the spiritual sphere of any acute value. Despite all of the dangers that came with the emancipation of the political sphere, Vekemans sees some positive effects in this development. It "gave maturity to temporal values and human freedom, and essentially to the civilization process, understood as the *sui juris* structurization of the temporal."[175] Because the medieval or post-Reformation dichotomy of the temporal and the spiritual or ecclesiastical spheres does not exist

---

170 López Trujillo, *Liberation or Revolution?*, 17.
171 Ibid., 36.
172 Ibid., 19, 21–2.
173 Ibid., 23.
174 Vekemans, *Caesar and God*, 10,
175 Ibid., 14.

anymore, the Church's role in the world has changed. She has accepted the autonomy of the political.

Whereas Vekemans and López Trujillo argue from different perspectives, they arrive at similar conclusions. For López Trujillo the outcome of an inappropriate mixing of the two spheres by invoking Marxist ideas and analysis is simple and manifest: it leads to hostility among classes and to "a condition of sin." Vekemans describes the outcome as mankind distancing itself from the Church resulting in "a world weakened by sin and in rebellion against the Creator."[176] Additionally, Vekemans accuses the liberation theologians of turning theology and the Gospel into a social ideology, despite the fact that the "gospel does not dictate any precise position."[177] In both instances they accuse liberation theologians, whether directly or indirectly, of applying an inappropriate historicity to the Gospel and to the history of salvation by drawing false conclusions from their exegesis. This false or inappropriate exegesis has implications for the acceptability of violence and revolutionary change.

In rejecting any notions of violence, López Trujillo assumes that revolution necessarily involves violence. More importantly, he condemns any attempts aiming at baptizing revolution and revolutionary violence with "theology." Mixing socialist revolution with matters of faith is for him simply undebatable.[178] If theology is used "to support revolution in an unconditional manner" the outcome is "imperative imperialism." If theology becomes political in a revolutionary fashion, López Trujillo fears for the autonomy of the religious sphere:

> Too close bonds between religion and political activities result in that the former becomes ancillary and a satellite of the latter. Critical judgment is weakened or pulverized. Scientific requirements disappear as if by magic. If a person does not conform he is seen as an "enemy" in a typical Maoist way of classifying people.[179]

The irony of this statement, however, is that the Church denounces liberation theologians as enemies of the Church, accusing liberation theologians of falling into a Marxist trap that makes them consider whoever does not consent with them, including the Church, to be enemies themselves. Simultaneously, López Trujillo admits that most liberation theologians do not intend to be Marxists. They distance themselves from Marxism assuming that by distancing themselves from Marxist philosophy they are not endangered of "Marxist penetration." Yet,

---

176 López Trujillo, *Liberation or Revolution?*, 26. Vekemans, *Caesar and God*, 4.
177 Vekemans, *Caesar and God*, 35, 47.
178 Ibid., 37, 40–1.
179 Ibid., 46.

López Trujillo considers entering into a dialogue with Marxists based on Marxist analysis and Marxist methodology to be an unintended betrayal of their intentions. More importantly, he regards the Marxist framework of class struggle as "dialectics of hate" that impedes the Christian value of love: "people would go to war because of their love for the proletarians and to liberate the oppressor by fighting him."[180] Although López Trujillo admits that violence might be sometimes necessary, it is certainly not the domain of the priest. Violence belongs exclusively to the political sphere, not to the religious sphere. The priest's domain is justice and conversion. Without any reference to Marxist revolutionary violence, Roger Vekemans seconds López Trujillo's distinction between the religious and the political. Vekemans particularly fears that a politicized religion would render Christ's mission (salvation) meaningless:

> If we accept, as Weber asserts, that the means proper to politics is violence, we should also have to accept that what in this case would unite Christians would be violence itself, even though this violence would be 'legitimized': through recourse to theology. The priest' political concern—ever urgent and absolutizing—would become so important that Christ "would become a meaningless formality in the face of the 'real problems'."[181]

Both Vekemans and López Trujillo emphasize the need for the Church's neutrality in political conflict, independently whether these systems are capitalist, Marxist, or socialist. Yet, López Trujillo warns his reader of confusing neutrality with indifference, although his own wording is not entirely free from confusion. He stresses that the Church has a legacy of fighting for justice and highlights her contributions to such struggles. In this sense she "cannot be neutral."[182]

However, how does a Church that is neither political nor indifferent look like? And what is the proper relation between the priest and politics? Roger Vekemans describes their relationship as another dialectics, a dialectics of commitments:

> It is clear that we cannot ignore the negative factors underlying the dialectical tension between Church and mankind, evangelization and civilization, and consequently between priesthood and politics. This dialectical tension, however, must be eased not by "fluidity of the boundaries," nor still less by the absence of commitment, but rather by the specifically priestly modality commitment in politics. It is not a question of choosing between a commitment to politics or a non-commitment, but between two kinds of commitment.[183]

---

[180] Ibid., 88, 95.
[181] Vekemans, *Caesar and God*, 101. In the quotation, Vekemans cites Roger Heckel, "Le Prêtre et la Politique."
[182] López Trujillo, *Liberation or Revolution?*, 69, 71.
[183] Vekemans, *Caesar and God*, 96.

Whereas Vekemans admits that politics and political engagement may not be only a right but also a duty, priesthood must restrict itself to a special type of political involvement. He distinguishes between a "political involvement with the political" and a "priestly involvement with the political."[184] Political involvement with the political he associates with the tensions of pluralism that lead to differing political positions that are incompatible and clashing, sometimes even without the possibility of reconciliation. In contrast, he equates priestly involvement in the political with "effectively bringing the humanity of Christ and the presence of God to the concrete present through the mystery of the Eucharist uniting a plurality of men around the table of sacrifice."[185] In short, the priest's political role is to unify mankind in Christ and in the Eucharist. He has to guide and enlighten mankind in order to find a just social order. His "political" engagement ends precisely here because it is the responsibility of the laity to turn the priest's constructive criticism into political action.[186] Although Roger Vekemans associates politics with violence, López Trujillo emphasizes that even if a Christian is subject to slavery, he only "may shout for freedom without violence; but it is in reality an aspect of his basic cry for charity,"[187] which resembles the dominant medieval approach to resistance and disobedience. Similar, López Trujillo sees the Church as a "mansion of dialogue" and a "center of encounter and reconciliation." It is the place everyone attends "when times are bitter and tragic." At the same time he warns that the Church is not the place "to load the believers with new and unbearable burdens that do not call for an answer of faith."[188]

Vekemans and López Trujillo agree that the political priest who is politically engaged in politics has to be avoided because the political priest undermines the Church's mission of proclaiming salvation and the priest's commitment to unifying mankind. If a priest turns to militancy, understood as any type of political engagement beyond the narrowly defined priestly function, he betrays his commitment to solidarity to all man and commits himself to "solidarity of coterie." In contrast, priestly engagement in the political means "placing him right in the center of human activity, at the central point of an essential commitment, in which solidarity regains its full significance in an eschatological perspective of the kingdom of God."[189]

---

184 Ibid., 89–9.
185 Ibid., 100.
186 Ibid., 112, 114.
187 López Trujillo, *Liberation or Revolution?*, 44.
188 Ibid., 71.
189 Vekemans, *Caesar and God*, 102.

In a similar vein, the priest has to remind man to be nourished by the Eucharist because the kingdom of God cannot be gained by worldly activities alone. This is to say that priest's proper place is with the sacraments; if he engages politically in the political sphere, he is in danger of neglecting his priestly duties. This is particularly true for "militant" political commitments. Only if the Church and her priests respect and honor the genuine role and commitment, the Church can "show her efficacy in the face of the problems of the modern world."[190] Following the same train of thought, López Trujillo warns that the people will not "respond to his call of conversation" if a priest identifies himself or is identified with a particular political system or ideology. Likewise, only if priests maintain their neutrality they have reason to hope that "even nonbelievers are listening to their words of peace in the most difficult moment." Only if the Church and the priests maintain their independence they are enabled for an "effective evangelical denunciation whenever basic human rights are violated."[191]

Whereas their argument for a neutral stance in a conflict to reunite the people in the name of Christ has some merits and does not lack consistency, the political theorist is instantly reminded of Machiavelli's warning against neutrality. Staying neutral in a conflict between two parties involves the danger of falling prey to the succeeding party. Moreover, "always he who is not your friend asks for neutrality and he who is your friend asks you to come out openly with your weapons. Yet irresolute princes, attempting to escape present danger, most of the time follow the neutral road and most of the time fall."[192] If one applies Machiavelli's teaching in combination with the complicity argument as outlined at the beginning of this section, then the call for priestly neutrality implies connivance and condoning with the military juntas and with the structural violence that unquestionably exists. Despite the fact that neither Roger Vekemans nor Alfonso López Trujillo deny the existence of socio-economic and political problems, their emphasis on political neutrality undercuts the movements' aspirations that aim for structural change. Following Machiavelli's logic, this political stand implies consorting with the existing socio-economic and political conditions, including their corresponding power structure.

---

190 Ibid., 112.
191 López Trujillo, *Liberation or Revolution?*, 106.
192 Niccolò Machiavelli, *The Prince*, in *Machiavelli: The Chief Works and Others*, Vol. 1, trans. Allan Gilbert (Durham: Duke University Press, 1958), 21.

The Societies for the Defense of Tradition, Family, and Property (TFP)

It is worth noting that Roger Vekemans and López Trujillo, while rejecting all active political engagement by members of the clergy, direct their criticism entirely at liberation theology and not at conservative movements such as the Societies for the Defense of Tradition, Family, and Property (TFP). The first TFP, the Sociedade Brasileira de Defesa da Tradição, Família e Propiedade, was founded in 1960 by Plinio Correâ de Oliveira.[193] Initially the society was founded in response and opposition to land reforms in Brazil. The societies are also known for their conservative and anti-communist and anti-Marxist agenda.[194] Intellectually and ideologically Correâ de Oliveira is the Brazilian counterpart to Hélder Câmara and José Comblin. As Daniel Levine notes, TFP combines "an extreme traditional religious stance with reactionary social and political positions that are closely tied to the ideologies of national security being elaborated by military regimes."[195] This tie between TFP and the military regime is nourished through mutual suspicion against parts of the institutional Church after Vatican II and particularly after Medellín. Yet, the bond between TFP and the military has also some sentimental foundations. TFP presents a version of traditional Catholic practices most of the military was grown up with. It reflected the traditional and conservative concepts of society they associated with. They agreed fundamentally on key features of what a good political order looks like. Indeed, TFP's influence was even reinforced through the emergence of military regimes. In addition to the reactionary social, political, and economic stances, the most salient aspect of TFP's doctrine is "a belief in the absolute sanctity of the healthy virtues of social inequality."[196] Again, the main source of conflict is associated with the appropriateness or inappropriateness of religion's interpretation (Catholicism) and its political implications. What is the most appropriate political and socioeconomic order that reflects and corresponds with the understanding of religion (Catholicism)?

For Correâ de Oliveira, there is only one true religion, namely Roman Catholicism. Yet, when he refers to the Church and Catholicism, he does not mean the Catholicism represented by the Catholic Church of his times, particularly not after Vatican II. The Second Vatican Council represents for him "one of the greatest calamities, if not the greatest, in the history of the Church: From the Council

---

[193] Roberto De Mattei, *The Crusader of the 20th Century: Plinio Correâ de Oliveira* (Gracewing: Leominster, 1998), 140.
[194] Jean-Marie Abgral, *Soul Snatchers: The Mechanics of Cults* (New York: Algora, 1996), 47.
[195] Levine, *Religion and Politics in Latin America*, 28.
[196] Ibid., 49, 53.

on, the 'smoke of Satan' penetrated the Church in unbelievable proportions."[197] This "ultratraditional" view is also shared by Roberto de Mattei, the biographer of Corrêa de Oliveira. Both "see the triumph of Modernism and the result of the infiltration of Communism and free masonry in Catholic theology at work at Vatican II."[198]

The rejection of Vatican II already indicates that Corrêa de Oliveira and TFP have a conception of Catholicism that does not correspond with the actual doctrines of the Vatican as representative of the Catholic Church. The opposition to the outcome of the Second Vatican Council, however, does not mean that Corrêa de Oliveira were without any support among bishops. Two of the conservative Brazilian bishops that were in league with TFP represented the Brazilian Church at the Vatican Council, which implies that TFP had significant support from a spectrum of the institutionalized Church.[199]

TFP's understanding of Catholicism resembles that of an idealized medieval Christendom, prior to the fourteenth century. The counter-revolution, TFP anticipates, aims for the restoration of this fictional concept of Christendom that is perceived as the authentic order of Christian civilization and man.[200] According to TFP, this concept of medieval Christendom is based on three principles:

- A profound respect for the rights of the Church and the Papacy, and the sacralization, to the utmost possible extent, of the values of temporal life, all of this out of opposition to secularism, interconfessionalism, atheism, and pantheism, as well as their respective consequences.
- A spirit of hierarchy marking all aspects of society and state, of culture and life, out of opposition to the egalitarian metaphysics of the Revolution.
- A diligence in detecting and combating evil in its embryonic or veiled form, in fulminating it with execration and a note of infancy, and in punishing it with unbreakable firmness in all its manifestations, particularly those that offend against orthodoxy and purity of customs, in opposition to the liberal metaphysics of the Revolution and its tendency to give free rein and protection to evil.[201]

In addition, the version of medieval Christendom favors papal infallibility and the doctrine of Immaculate Conception. Although Corrêa de Oliveira does not

---

197 Corrêa de Oliveira, *Revolution and Counter-Revolution*, 145.
198 Massimo Faggioli, "Vatican II: The History and the Narratives." *Theological Studies* 73, no. 4 (2012): 755.
199 Rodrigo Coppe Caldeira, "Bispos conservadores brasileiros no Concílio Vaticano II (1962–1965): D. Geraldo de Proença Sigaud e D. Antônio de Castro Mayer," *Horizonte* 9, no. 24 (2011): 1011.
200 Corrêa de Oliveira, *Revolution and Counter-Revolution*, 41.
201 Ibid., 76.

refer to Giles of Rome, Boniface VIII, or James of Viterbo, his Christian ideology reflects their idea of the relationship between temporal and ecclesiastical power. The pope has power over all spiritual things and has the moral oversight and indirect power over the temporal sphere. To restore organic medieval monarchy, legitimacy of "royalties and earthly powers" roots entirely in Christ. The political has to be ordered according to the Church's doctrines.[202] Thus, the anticipated "medieval" order is anti-liberal, anti-egalitarian, and anti-secular, but monarchic and aristocratic, based on inequality and hierarchy. With Thomas Aquinas, Corrêa de Oliveira asserts that "Providence institutes inequity among the angels as well as among men."[203]

According to Corrêa de Oliveira, the restoration of the desired order requires a counter-revolution, which implies that the existing order or rather disorder is the outcome of revolution. Corrêa de Oliveira's understanding of revolution reflects on a distinct understanding of history and Church history. He associates revolution with illegitimacy and "disordered passions" that are "impulses towards sin."[204] Whereas he refers to one revolution that is responsible for disorder, he regards the revolution as the outcome of three revolutionary waves. These three revolutions are the Reformation, in Corrêa de Oliveira's terminology, the Pseudo-Reformation, the French Revolution, and Communism. The first revolution introduces religious doubt to the world; it is also associated with liberalism and ecclesiastical egalitarianism. The French Revolution contributed to disorder through atheism and secularism; communism, eventually, introduced the disorderly egalitarian elements to the economic field. The contemporary world is dominated by "Bolshevization."[205]

The revolution symbolizes the "crisis of Western and Christian man, i.e., Europeans and their descendants, Canadians, Americans, Latin Americans, and Australians."[206] The crisis of Western Christendom has caused Christendom to cease existing. The revolution that resulted in the ceasing of Christendom is marked by revolts against fundamental principles of order: a revolt against

---

202 Ibid., 92, 43–5.
203 Ibid., 50. The focus on inequality and elitist nobility is reemphasized in Plinio Corrêa Oliveira, *Nobility and the Analogous Traditional Elites in the Allocutions of Pius XII: A Theme Illustrating American Social History* (York: The American Society for the Defense of Tradition, Family and Property (TFP), 1993).
204 Corrêa de Oliveira, *Revolution and Counter-Revolution*, 46.
205 Ibid., 3–4, 31.
206 Ibid., 10.

kings and the pope, a revolt against ecclesiastical and temporal nobility and aristocracy, and the introduction of the idea of popular sovereignty.[207]

Although Corrêa de Oliveira draws a direct line from Luther to Lenin, he asserts that the revolution has precursors. Intellectually, the precursors are humanism, Roman Law, and the introduction of pagan morality that undermine Scholasticism. In addition, the revolution has prefigures. "Arius and Mohammed were prefigures to Luther."[208] The outcome of these revolutionary waves is an illegitimate socio-political order that is associated with atheism, secularism, egalitarianism, and amorality. Egalitarianism in particular undermines the divinely order because

> a universe of equal creatures would be a world in which the resemblance between creatures and the Creator would have been eliminated as much as possible. To hate in principle all inequality is, then, to place oneself metaphysically against the best elements of resemblance between the Creator and creation. It is to hate God.[209]

Whereas revolution is associated with disorder or anti-order, egalitarian principles, and atheism, Corrêa de Oliveira sees a natural relationship between the counter-revolution and the military. The military, by its nature, is counter-revolutionary. It represents order and follows "values that are greater than life itself and for which one should be willing to die." Moreover, military morality is based "entirely upon the idea of honor, of force placed at the service of good and turned against evil." Moreover, they fight and die for the common good."[210] Thus, to restore order, the alliance between the military and TFP is natural and organic. The counter-revolutionary military hierarchy and honor code invites to engage with the military in the complicity of cooperation. Moreover, because a military order reflects inequality as implied in divine creation, military order can be regarded as divinely sanctioned, whereas the hierarchy of the existing Church has jeopardized the divinely inspired order. Particularly the Second Vatican Council symbolizes a communist infiltration of the Church. Corrêa de Oliveira sees it as "the greatest success attained by the smiling post-Stalinist communism" that resulted in "the Second Vatican Council's enigmatic, discon-

---

[207] Ibid., 17. See also Cyril Le Tallec, *Les sectes politiques: 1965–1995* (Paris: L'Harmattan, 2006), 53.
[208] Corrêa de Oliveira, *Revolution and Counter-Revolution*, 14–5, 42.
[209] Ibid., 50.
[210] Ibid., 70, 113.

certing, incredible, and apocalyptically tragic silence about communism" that turned the Council into an "*a*pastoral Council."[211]

It is worth noting that Corrêa de Oliveira associates the military with force, not with violence. Violence he links exclusively with communism. In reverse application, the underlying logic is similar to Enrique Dussel's who associates coercion with legitimate use of power and violence with illegitimacy.[212] As outlined in the discussion of José Comblin's analysis of the national security state, military juntas are interested in an agreement between Church and state to give their rule additional legitimacy and a Christian outlook through rhetoric and religious symbols.[213] The military, however, is not interested in the restoration of a religious state that subordinates the political realm to religious law and the authority of the papacy. Nonetheless, sufficient overlap between TFP and the military exists.

Yet, it needs to be noted that the overlap is primarily ideological, not religious, although Corrêa de Oliveira and TFP interprets their shared ideology religiously and, thus, adds another layer of religious legitimacy to their shared ideas of socio-political order. As the current Peruvian TFP-secretary reminds us, the foundation of the first TFP was a reaction to the left-wing government of President João Goulart and its land reform. Corrêa di Oliveira and his fellow campaigners saw the land reform as an attack of their private property rights. In 1964, the Goulart-government was overthrown by a military coup.[214] Private property is first and foremost a political or socio-economic issue. For Corrêa de Oliveira and TFP, "property is sacred."[215] Similar, the notion of hierarchy and elitism, favored both by the military and TFP, has no genuine roots in Christianity, but rather reflects medieval feudalism. Yet, Corrêa de Oliveira gives these political principles a particular religious coloring by attaching them to a version of Christendom he perceives as authentic.

Yet, by framing the discourse over the establishment of a new order in the language of restoration and counter-revolution, the "counter-revolutionary" movement attains a defensive outlook. Although in reverse, the underlying logic resembles features of Ignacio Ellacuría's concepts of violence and counter-violence. This defensive narrative is reinforced by statements like, "if the Rev-

---

211 Ibid., 144.
212 Dussel, *Ethics of Liberation*, 409.
213 Comblin, *The Church and the National Security State*, 79–80.
214 Luis Alberto Chávez Hartley, "El perfil de un Batallador católico: Centenario de Plinio Correa de Oliveira," *La Razón Histórica: Revista hispanoamericana de Historia de las Ideas* 16 (2011): 87.
215 Corrêa de Oliveira, *Revolution and Counter-Revolution*, 112.

olution is killing us, nothing is more indispensable than a reaction that aims to crush it." Combating Revolution becomes a necessity of survival that has to be fought "by all just and legal means." Moreover, combat is not only "licit," but "even indispensable."[216] Without defining explicitly what is meant by just and unjust war, the Counter-Revolution associates itself with just warfare. The general narrative, however, implies that just warfare is associated with a Christian course, which resembles justifications for the Crusades as discussed earlier. Indeed, in addition to the establishment of a socio-political order that is based on the principles narrated above, Corrêa de Oliveira aims for the "defense of the Church against the infidels and the protection of the freedom of missionaries in pagan lands or those dominated by communism."[217] In other words, it aims for the conversion of mankind as a whole to a concept of Christendom that resembles anti-modern and particularly medieval features of society.

Similar to Camilo Torres, Corrêa de Oliveira asks whether the counter-revolutionary may cooperate with non-Catholics, whether they are "Protestants, Moslems, [or] others." While Corrêa de Oliveira assumes that there is "no authentic Counter-Revolution outside the Church," he asserts that it is

> conceivable that certain Protestants or Moslems, for instance, are in a state of soul in which they begin to perceive all the wickedness of the Revolution and to take a stand against it. Such a person can be expected to form obstacles, at times even great ones, against the Revolution. If they respond to grace, they can become excellent Catholics and, therefore, efficient counter-revolutionaries.[218]

Thus, and contrary to Torres, collaboration with non-Catholics is only in the range of possibility if the non-Catholics are already some sort of unrealized Catholics. The goal, then, is conversion because Corrêa de Oliveira rejects all notions of equality and of equal rights for different religions.

It is important to note that TFP merges socio-political and religious motivations and cloaks the socio-political ends (a hierarchic anti-egalitarian order) in religious language that is associated with an "authentic" interpretation of Christianity. The final goal is the establishment of a Christian state that is ruled according to the principles of divine law that gives the Roman Pontiff (in his medieval manifestation) moral and theological oversight. Ideally, this version of the Christian state is introduced throughout the world. If the state would be ordered according to the hierarchical principles but without the orientation towards re-

---

216 Ibid., 72, 109.
217 Ibid., 112–3.
218 Ibid., 120–1.

ligious law, it would be insufficient because the absence of Christian values is associated with immorality and hatred; it would result in an unstable order.

In addition to violent means, the Counter-Revolution aims for the means of "television, radio, major press, and a rational, efficient, and brilliant publicity." The possibility of a successful Counter-Revolution is proven historically through "the conversion of the Roman Empire; the formation of the Middle Ages; the reconquest of Spain."[219]

3.2 Islam and Violence in the Twentieth Century

As discussed in the chapter on pre-modern discourses on violence in Islam, Sunni and Shi'i justifications for the use of violence reveal significant differences. Because Sunni authors generally argue from the perspective of power, while Shi'i thinkers primarily reason from a perspective of no or lesser political power, often linked to minority status within modern Nation-state boundaries, except for Iran and technically Iraq, this outcome is not surprising. In the twentieth century, however, Sunni and Shi'i discourses show significant overlaps. The similarities between Sunni and Shi'i radical thought are somewhat remarkable, particularly because Sunni theorists tend not to read the texts of their Shi'i counterparts and vice versa. Rather than a specific lack of interest, this situation often results from the language barrier between Arabic and Persian or Farsi, which might be illustrated by one of al-Afghani's writings. Originally written in Persian, his famous *Refutation of the Materialists* responded explicitly to a religious movement in India. Although the *Refutation of the Materialists* gained significant interest among Sunni intellectuals, the text is only accessible in Arabic translation. Yet, the translation into Arabic was completed by Muhammad 'Abduh, who did not know any Persian; consequently, "the discrepancy between the original and the Arabic is not surprising."[220] Al-Afghani, however, is an exceptional case because he disguised himself as a Sunni Muslim despite his definite Persian and Shi'i origin. Moreover, al-Afghani used ideas from Muslim philosophy and the

---

[219] Ibid., 88, 104.
[220] Nikki R. Keddie, *An Islamic Response to Imperialism: Political and Religious Writings of Sayyid Jamāl ad-Dīn "al-Afghānī,"* 2nd ed. (Berkeley: University of California Press, 1983), ix-x. An English translation of the Refutation of the Materialists can be found in the same volume, 130–180. For a translation of the Arabic "translation," see Sayyid Jamal ad-Din al-Afghani, *Réfutation des Matérialistes*, treduction sur la 3e édition Arabe avec introduction et notes par A.-M. Goichon (Paris: Paul Geuthner, 1942), 59–171.

Mu'tazilites, which were preserved in Shi'i theology, and introduced these concepts into Sunni discourses.²²¹

Despite the lack of active interaction between Sunni and Shi'i political activists and theorists, both Sunni and Shi'i assume that in the "Muslim world a state of apostasy [is] a condition that is especially dangerous because it is unconscious." More radical forces perceive the cure to this problem to be violent rebellion and the introduction of the Shari'a state.²²² *Jihad* is the rhetoric that has been employed and continues to be in use.²²³

Sunni and Shi'i activists do not suddenly engage in a mutual ecumenical movement. On the contrary, resentments between Sunni and Shi'i activists persist despite some ecumenical attempts by moderate intellectuals. Ecumenism has been rejected due to its perception as "Christian," and notable continuing anti-Shi'i sentiments relate Shi'ism to the Mongol invasion and apostasy, which is particularly true for those who based their revolutionary thought on fourteenth century Ibn Taymiyya.²²⁴ The appreciation of Ibn Taymiyya has caused some oddities in the literature on Islamic "terrorism." For instance, Walter Laqueur discusses Ibn Taymiyya in the context of contemporary Islamic terrorism without acknowledging the creative reinterpretations that were necessary to make him an authoritative source for violent actions. Instead, Laqueur brands him as a terrorist thinker, although Ibn Taymiyya did not even have a concept of terrorism.²²⁵

Contemporary radical thinkers in various Islamic traditions identify *jahiliyya* (pre-Islamic) and *jihad* as the leading concepts that justify political violence. Sherman Jackson notes that *jihad* in pre-modern times was perceived "not only as a means of guaranteeing the security and freedom of the Muslims but

---

221 Kedourie, *Afghani and 'Abduh*, 6–5. Nikki R. Keddie, *Sayyid Jamāl ad-Dīn "al-Afghānī:" A Political Biography* (Berkeley: University of California Press, 1972), 10–11.
222 Emmanuel Sivan, "Sunni Radicalism in the Middle East and the Iranian Revolution," *International Journal of Middle East Studies* 21 (1989): 2.
223 Devin R. Springer, James L. Regens and David N. Edger, *Islamic Radicalism and Global Jihad* (Washington, D.C.: Georgetown University Press, 2009), 18–19.
224 Sivan, "Sunni Radicalism," 13–16. The rediscovery of Ibn Taymiyya partly resulted from Rashid Rida's edition of Ibn Taymiyya's works. See Jansen, *The Dual Nature of Islamic Fundamentalism*, 32.
225 Walter Laqueur (ed.), *Voices of Terror: Manifestos, Writings and Manuals of Al Qaeda, Hamas, and Other Terrorists from Around the World and Throughout the Ages* (Naperville: Sourcebook, 2005), 391–3. Laqueur applies logic that would additionally deem Ernst Hartwig Kantorowicz a Nazi simply due to Joseph Goebbels's admiration for Kantorowicz's book on Frederick II (Ernst H. Kantorowicz, *Friedrich der Zweite*, 15th ed. (Stuttgart: Klett-Cotta, 1995).).

as virtually the *only* means of doing so."[226] Although interpretations of *jihad* have changed from the pre-modern to the modern or contemporary times, *jihad* apologists perceive their situation to be similar to pre-modern times: the Muslim world is threatened by non-Muslim forces, and Islam has become corrupted by Western influences. Consequently, *jahiliyya* and *jihad* resemble two sides of one coin. Contemporary Christian discourses that denounce the political enemy as apostate or unbeliever as a means to justify violence have widely disappeared, but Islamic discourses still prominently present the opponent as non-Muslim, similar to pre-modern treatises.[227] The use of violence is clearly not legitimized for the sake of violence itself but as a response to perceived political illegitimacy. Secularists generally consider the "religious state as an absolutist repressive institution," which lacks legitimacy due to its repressive nature. In contrast, Islamist camps claim that only a religious state can be legitimate because "the divinity of government [flows] from the divinity of the law (the *sharīʿa*)." Ideologically, the distinction can be made between "legal legitimacy" (sovereignty rests in the people, and *sharīʿa* and the political realm are distinct) and "religious legitimacy" (God's governance).[228] The extent of the influence of socio-economic injustice on violent radicalization is disputed,[229] although references to socio-economic disadvantages and injustices are frequent in Islamist writings.

3.2.1 Anti-State Violence in Contemporary Sunni Islam

This chapter covers al-Afghani, Hasan al-Banna, Sayyid Qutb, and ʿAbd al-Salam Faraj for Sunni perspectives. The first three individuals set the theoretical foundation; Faraj is one example illustrating how these ideas were transferred into violent action by later generations. The following chapter consults Khomeini, Murtuza Mutahhari, and Ali Shariʿati in the context of the Iranian Revolution for the Shiʿi perspective. The literature on these thinkers has great ideological

---

226 Sherman Jackson, "Jihad in the Modern World," in *Islam in Transition: Muslim Perspectives*, ed. John J. Donohue and John L. Esposito (Oxford: Oxford University Press, 2007), 400.
227 One of the few exceptions can be found in Pablo Richard, "Theology in the Theology of the Liberation," in *Mysterium Liberationis: Fundamental Concepts of Liberation Theology*, ed. Ignacio Ellacuría and Jon Sobrino (Maryknoll: Orbis, 1993), 150–168, who describes both the Conquistadors and the military dictators of his time as "idolatrous oppressors" (155).
228 Salwa Ismail, "Democracy in Contemporary Arab Discourse," in *Political Liberalization and Democratization in the Arab World: Vol. 1: Theoretical Perspectives*, ed. Rex Brynen, Bahgat Korany, and Paul Noble (Boulder: Lynne Rienner, 1995), 101–2.
229 Muhammad Qasim Zaman, *Modern Islamic Thought in a Radical Age: Religious Authority and Internal Criticism* (Cambridge: Cambridge University Press, 2012), 222.

bias. Depending on the ideological point of view, the same authors can be portrayed as truly democratic thinkers or active supporters of terrorism. The truth most often lies somewhere in between these two extremes.[230]

As Johannes J. G. Jansen notes, Ibn Taymiyya (1263–1328) and al-Afghani (1838–1897) are the two most influential figures in twentieth century Islam.[231] Ibn Taymiyya was already discussed at length in an earlier chapter. Although al-Afghani died before the dawn of the twentieth century, he concerns us now. As Elie Kedourie puts it, his "eminence [...] was very much a posthumous affair"[232] through his students, and some of them, particularly Muhammad ʿAbduh particularly, idolized him. His main influence is found in twentieth century rather than nineteenth century Islam.

Al-Afghani's Pan-Islamism

According to Jansen, al-Afghani identifies two main sources for Islam's decline: fanaticism, referring to the "misuse and misinterpretation of religion with the intention of legitimising the existing religious and social order," and tyranny.[233] Al-Afghani's criticism of the misuse of religion as a stabilizing tool to maintain the existing order, which he perceives as unjust, is related to a main controversy surrounding al-Afghani: is he motivated by true religious belief or is he using religion as a tool for political purposes? Does he even qualify as an unbeliever? Al-Afghani's personal belief cannot be conclusively established. We can only access his writings and actions. Yet, it is fair to say that al-Afghani's Islamic orthodoxy was disputed both during his life and after his death. Nikki R. Keddie, Elie Kedourie and other scholars have raised doubts about al-Afghani's beliefs.[234] Their interpretation was almost instantly criticized.[235] There is a political reason

---

230 While Sayyid Qutb and Khomeini have been labeled terrorists, the same label has been applied to al-Banna and the Muslim Brotherhood since the inception of the Brotherhood.
231 Jansen, *The Dual Nature of Islamic Fundamentalism*, 26.
232 Kedourie, Afghani and ʿAbduh, 5.
233 Jansen, *The Dual Nature of Islamic Fundamentalism*, 27.
234 Kedourie, Afghani and ʿAbduh, 3, 16. 20, 43–4; Keddie, *An Islamic Response to Imperialism*, 45, 85.
235 Menahem Milson, "The Elusive Jamāl al-Dīn al-Afghānī," *The Muslim World* 58 (1968): 304–307. In the response, Elie Kedourie, "'The Elusive Jamāl al-Dīn al-Afghānī': A Comment," *The Muslim World* 59 (1969): 312–314, Kedourie undermines most criticism. In line with the defense of al-Afghani's belief is Anwar Moazzam, *Jamāl al-Dīn al-Afghānī: A Muslim Intellectual* (New Delhi: Naurang Rai, 1984), 11–13 (defense of Afghani's religiosity), 100–103 (acknowledgment of his unorthodoxy while dismissing any accusations of holding heretical views).

to portray al-Afghani as a sound and orthodox Muslim because he was frequently accused of heretical views throughout his political career. Thus, doubting his religious soundness is associated with his enemies' claims.[236] Although more scholars provided supporting evidence that al-Afghani merely used religion "as an instrument for the achievement of pre-eminently political goals,"[237] this understanding does not remain unchallenged. Zaki Badawi argues that religion for al-Afghani instills "in the human soul the basis for human society and civilization" and states that "the ideal state cannot be realized in the world except through Islam."[238] More recently, Josep Puig Montada unconvincingly disputed Keddie's and Kedourie's claim.[239]

Although the debate about al-Afghani's religiosity might sound like shadowboxing of mere intellectual relevance, this conversation centers on the key question of whether religion is a tool to be used like any other (secular) ideology for the purpose of achieving a political goal. It is certainly not wrong to claim that al-Afghani politicized Islam as an ideology and more broadly as a civilization and understood Islam not primarily as a religion.[240] The confusion over al-Afghani results from a number of different factors. First, al-Afghani follows medieval Islamic philosophy and advocates for the message to be adjusted to the audience. Thus, he used "one argument for the elite and another for the general public."[241] Second, he was suspected of heretical ideas and took special care with his Muslim audience to appear as an orthodox Muslim of the Sunni creed. Third, his

---

236 Hunt Janin, *The Pursuit of Learning in the Islamic World, 610–2003* (Jefferson, McFarland: 2005), 138–9.
237 L. M. Kenny, "Al-Afghānī on Types of Despotic Government," *Journal of the American Oriental Society* 86, no. 1 (1966): 20a.
238 Zaki Badawi, *The Reformers of Egypt – A Critique of Al-Afghani, 'Abduh and Ridha* (Slough Berks: The Muslim Institute/The Poen Press, 1396/1976), 7b-8a. See also Abdul-Hādī Hā'irī, "Afghānī on the Decline of Islam," *Die Welt des Islams* 13, no. 1/2 (1971): 121–125.
239 Josep Puig Montada, "Al-Afghânî, a Case of Religious Unbelief?," *Studia Islamica* 100/101 (2005): 203–220. Montada emphasizes the relevance of "The universe proves the superiority of the Muslims by the fact that they did achieve what they achieved thanks to religion" (207) in the Arabic and French translations of the *Refutation of the Materialists*. He admits that this sentence in missing in the original and in Keddie's translation. He ascribes the sentence to al-Afghani even though Muhammad ʿAbduh was responsible for the questionable Arabic translation on which the French is based. Al-Afghani's response to Renan, on which most of Keddie's and Kedourie's argument is based, is dismissed as flattery (220).
240 Hani Srour, *Die Staats- und Gesellschaftstheorie bei Sayyid Ğamāladdīn "Al Afghānī" als Beitrag zur Reform der islamischen Gesellschaften in der zweiten Hälfte des 19. Jahrhunderts*, (Freiburg: Klaus Schwarz, 1977), 176. Cf. Margaret Kohn, "Afghānī on Empire, Islam, and Civilization," *Political Theory* 37, no. 3 (2009): 416.
241 Keddie, *An Islamic Response to Imperialism*, 19.

publications in Arabic generally speak to Sunni orthodoxy. The same is not the case for his publications in other, including Western, languages. It is primarily obvious that his translations into Arabic were Islamized by Muhammad 'Abduh. His response to Renan and other texts have not been made available in Arabic because 'Abduh regards them as potentially jeopardizing al-Afghani's Muslim reputation.[242] The two aforementioned texts particularly illustrate how al-Afghani aimed to appeal to different and contradictory elitist debates.[243]

The chameleonic nature of al-Afghani's writings certainly contributed to his appeal to later generations. Almost everyone could find something appealing in his writings. He failed, however, in his major appeal for unity. Albert Hourani identifies unity as "the theme which runs all through al-Afghani's work. Both the common danger, and the values which all Muslims share, should outweigh differences of doctrine and traditions of enmity. Differences of sects need not be a political barrier [...]."[244]

Additionally, Hourani reminds us that obedience was more or less an absolute duty in traditional Sunni thought, and "only a minority of later thinkers taught that revolt could be legitimate."[245] Although al-Afghani did not invent the idea of legitimizing revolt and violent resistance, he definitely popularized it and aimed for the "liberation from the yoke of colonial rule. He [Afghani] maintained that Islam provided the common, most fundamental bond and basis for Muslim solidarity."[246] Nikki R. Keddie localizes the breaking point in his Indian experience. Thereafter, he became a forceful advocate of *jihad*. She argues that his Indian experiences "helped convince him that traditional religious sentiments were the most powerful weapons available to a Muslim who wishes to raise a movement strong enough to sweep the foreigners from Muslim lands."[247]

Al-Afghani advocates political assassination, coup d'état and revolution to achieve regime change.[248] The traditional Sunni doctrine of obedience, which does not uphold these actions, needed to be defamed as misuse and misinterpretation of religion. Thus, al-Afghani does not use religion or Islam *per se* as a tool

---

242 Ibid., 37–8. Kedourie, Afghani and 'Abduh, 45.
243 Larbi Sadiki, *The Search for Arab Democracy: Discourses and Counter-Discourses* (New York: Columbia University Press, 2004), 101.
244 Albert Hourani, *Arabic Thought in the Liberal Age, 1798–1939* (Oxford: Oxford University Press, 1970), 115. If this message would be heard, the world would be a much more peaceful place.
245 Ibid., 6.
246 John L. Esposito, *Islam and Politics* (Syracuse: Syracuse University Press, 1984), 50.
247 Keddie, Sayyid Jamāl ad-Dīn "al-Afghānī," 28.
248 Srour, *Die Staats- und Gesellschaftstheorie bei Sayyid Ğamāladdīn "Al Afghāni,"* 126–7.

for political purposes. He uses a particular untraditional or unorthodox interpretation that allows for violent resistance. This critical view of traditional religion aligns with his elaboration on religion and philosophy in his response to Renan, where he broadly speaks of Islam and accuses traditional Islam of preventing (scientific) progress and being at least partly responsible for the inferiority of the Muslim world during his lifetime.[249]

Al-Afghani's admiration for modern sciences and reason (philosophy) is found in a number of his writings.[250] A similar admiration for modern science is present in his essay *Despotic Government*, in which he reveals his approval of "enlightened government" (*al-ḥukūmah al-mutanaṭṭisah*). The essay attempts "to incite his readers to resist and overthrow tyranny."[251] For al-Afghani, despotic government means that subjects are robbed of their rights. Al-Afghani particularly objects to two types of despotic rule: "cruel government" (*al-ḥukūmah al-qāsiyah*) and "oppressive government" (*al-ḥukūmah al-ẓālimah*). He equates cruel government with highway robbery. The despot treats his subjects like enemies and illegally takes his subjects' property (even though there is no rule of law).[252] An oppressive government "unjustly and unlawfully enslave[s] people born free" and impose forced labor on its subjects. An oppressive government treats subjects like mere livestock, and the "oppressors constantly try to seize their [subjects'] possessions by force and to extort the fruit of their labors and the product of their toil by compulsion."[253] Al-Afghani associates the latter situation with most Eastern governments and British rule in India. Most of his accusations and characterizations of these versions of tyranny resemble the previous discussion of Ibn Khaldun (forced labor, disrespect of the subjects' property, and lawlessness), whom al-Afghani admires greatly. Moreover, al-Afghani's analysis corresponds with Henry Shue's triad of security, subsistence, and liberty as the most essential basic rights, which was outlined in the introductory chapter. This similarity between the rights that Shue describes as utmost essential and their absence under despotic government is most obvious in al-Afghani's com-

---

249 Al-Afghānī, "Answer of Jamāl ad-Dīn to Renan," in Nikki R. Keddie, *An Islamic Response to Imperialism*, 183, 187.
250 Most explicitly, his "Lecture on Teaching and Learning" in Keddie, *An Islamic Response to Imperialism*, 101–108 mocks the treatment of Aristotle as if he were a pillar of Islam while condemning Galileo, Newton, and Kepler as infidels because the "truth is where there is proof, and those who forbid science and knowledge in the belief that they are safeguarding the Islamic religion are really the enemies of that religion" (107).
251 Kenny, "Al-Afghani on Types of Despotic Government," 27b, n. 43.
252 Al-Afghani, "Despotic Government," in Kenny, "Al-Afghani on Types of Despotic Government," 22a-b.
253 Ibid., 22a-23a.

parison of a despot with a highway robber, who "holds up travelers and steals their money, their provisions, their clothes which protect them from the heat and cold, and the other necessities of life, leaving them in the wilderness or desert bare-foot, naked and hungry, with all resources cut off."[254] Similar accusations are found in al-Afghani's essay "The Reign of Terror in Persia," where he speaks of "neither law nor government, only cruel, rapacious, unscrupulous and sleepless tyranny."[255] Al-Afghani outlines a system that is completely corrupt on all levels of government. Officials are not paid and randomly take from the people. Thus,

> [t]he only way they can live is by robbing the people and shifting for themselves. These burdens, with their attendant horror of false imprisonment and torture, fall heavily upon the shoulders of the Persians when they submit, but worse is their fate now if they venture to remonstrate."[256] For al-Afghani, it is obvious that the Shah has to be deposed. He sees only two ways out for the Persian people: "European protection or Persian revolution.[257]

Bearing in mind that the Shah had granted privileges to the British Imperial Tobacco Corporation and the British monopoly in Persia negatively impacted the economic situation of many Iranians and caused protest movements in 1891 and 1892, European protection was the most unlikely option for which the people (and al-Afghani) could realistically hope. Indeed, he particularly opposed British imperialism and colonial rule throughout his life, and he sought to use this context to strengthen a pan-Islamic movement. His devotion to pan-Islamism is linked to his Indian experience.[258] To achieve this goal, he needed to portray himself as truly orthodox Muslim. The *Refutation of the Materialists* needs to be read in this context. It has been noted that "there seems to be little real difference between Afghani's doctrine and those of Sayyid Ahmad whom he savagely attacked in his *Refutation of the Materialists* and that Afghani objected more to Sayyid Ahmad's anglophilia than to his heterodoxy."[259]

Although his cause is closer to Nizari Isma'ilis, to discredit Sayyid Ahmad's movement by relating the Neicheri Sect to Mazdak and the *bāṭinīs* he uses strategies similar to Nizam al-Mulk.[260] Contrary to Nizam al-Mulk, he does not de-

---

254 Ibid.,"22a.
255 Al-Afghani, "The Reign of Terror in Persia," 240.
256 Ibid., 244.
257 Ibid., 240.
258 Keddie, *An Islamic Response to Imperialism*, 23, 59.
259 Kedourie, *Afghani and 'Abduh*, 36.
260 Al-Afghani, "The Truth about the Neicheiri Sect and an Explanation of the Neicherie" [Refutation of the Materialists], in Keddie, *An Islamic Response to Imperialism*, 155 – 7.

mand them to be killed, which supports the suggestion that he was more opposed to their anglophilia than to their teachings. The genuine Muslim Indian discourses questioned the justification of *jihad* against the British; this topic was later abandoned because the British colonial power granted religious freedom that made *jihad* less justifiable.[261] The question of religious freedom was of minor to no particular interest to al-Afghani. The argument that non-Muslim rule, which was prominently introduced through Ibn Taymiyya's Mardin fatwa, is a justification for violent resistance was more or less neglected by al-Afghani, yet the issue becomes significant later.

Al-Afghani presents, however, the legitimization of violence in response to a political problem: foreign oppression and socio-economic injustice. His interpretation fits the larger context given that Zaki Badawi claimed that al-Afghani thought the ideal state could only be realized through Islam in a cultural rather than a religious sense, coupled with the Islamic identification as native and non-Islamic as foreign. By dressing his ideas in the language of Islam and using Muslim identity and religion as a tool, he represents an almost classic case of Kippenberg's suggestion that a conflict, even one that is not caused by religion, alters its nature if religiously interpreted.[262] Later thinkers blurred the distinctions between political and religious motivations. This increasing blurredness is partially a consequence of al-Afghani's amalgamation of religion and politics for a foremost political goal and less obvious in Hasan al-Banna, the founder of the Muslim Brotherhood.

Hasan al-Banna and Muslim Liberation

Hasan al-Banna is usually described as "the father of contemporary Islamism." Roxanne Euben and Muhammad Qasim Zaman argue that "many of the positions and arguments associated with Islamists such as Qutb, Mawdudi, and Khomeini are a systematic articulation of a worldview already evident in the model of leadership and sociomoral reform Banna left behind."[263] However, Ahmad S. Moussalli maintains that "Quṭb, al-Mawdūdī, and Khumaynī are more radical:

---

[261] M. A. Khan, *Islamic Jihad: A Legacy of Forced Conversion, Imperialism, and Slavery* (Bloomington: iUniverse, 2009), 217–220. Yohanan Friedman, "Jihād in Aḥmadī Thought," in *Studies in Islamic History and Civilization in Honour of Professor David Ayalon*, ed. Moshe Sharon (Jerusalem: Cana, 1986), 230.
[262] Kippenberg, *Violence as Worship*, 200.
[263] Roxanne L. Euben and Muhammad Qasim Zaman, *Princeton Readings in Islamist Thought: Texts and Contexts from al-Banna to Bin Laden* (Princeton: Princeton University Press, 2009), 49.

they call for a total overthrow of secular governments and forbid any compromise even on questions of means and methods. They uphold the concepts of the *ḥākimiyya* (governance) of God and the *jāhiliyya* (paganism) of the world."²⁶⁴ Although all of these authors, including al-Banna, call for the establishment of Islamic government, Moussali considers al-Banna to be less radical because the others have "no notion of gradual change or possible compromise and emphasize the need to overthrow secular government as a nonnegotiable religious duty."²⁶⁵

Similar to al-Afghani, Hasan al-Banna develops his thoughts and establishes his movement in opposition to Western material culture and in response to colonial rule, leading to the call for *jihad* against Great Britain. When Hasan al-Banna founded the Muslim Brotherhood in 1928,²⁶⁶ Egypt had been semi-independent for six years. Yet, considerable British influence in Egypt and the region remained, and the problems of social and economic injustice, as well as oppression and exploitation, continued.²⁶⁷ Religious movements such as the Brotherhood "claimed that national independence could only be achieved through moral reform and strict adherence to Islam."²⁶⁸ This claim insinuates that a lack of or a corrupted religiosity contributes to the socio-economic and political problems of the time.

Hasan al-Banna's status as an active supporter of violent overthrow in Egypt, however, is controversial. Indeed, the question of Hasan al-Banna's support for revolution or less radical means of change usually determines whether he qualifies as a more moderate or a more radical thinker. These classifications are partly political in themselves. For instance, Moussalli associates al-Banna's ideas with the "Muslim Brotherhood in Egypt, Jordan, Syria, and elsewhere and with other mainstream movements in the Muslim world such as the Islamic Front in Sudan,

---

264 Ahmad S. Moussalli, "Ḥasan al-Bannā's Islamist Discourse on Constitutional Rule and Islamic State," *Journal of Islamic Studies* 4, no. 2 (1993): 163.
265 Ahmad S. Moussalli, *Moderate and Radical Islamic Fundamentalism: The Quest for Modernity, Legitimacy, and the Islamic State* (Gainesville: University Press of Florida, 1999), 107.
266 Ḥasan Bannā, *Memoirs of Hasan al Banna Shaheed*, trans. M.N. Shaikh (Karachi: International Islamic Publishers, 1981), 142: "We determined on solemn oath that we shall live as brethren; work for the glory of Islam and launch *Jihad* for it."
267 John Calvert, *Sayyid Qutb and the Origin of Radical Islam* (New York: Columbia University Press, 2010), 53: "Britain reserved for itself the right to secure the imperial lifeline of the Suez Canal, protect foreign interests and communities in Egypt, defend Egypt against foreign aggression, and maintain its controlling interests in Sudan, which the Anglo-Egyptian Condominium had governed since 1899."
268 Hazem Kandil, *Soldiers, Spies and Statesmen: Egypt's Road to Revolt* (London: Verso, 2012), 8.

al-Nahdah in Tunisia, and the Islamic Salvation Front in Algeria."[269] A different interpretation of al-Banna's thought and movement would alter interpretations of other groups and political movements associated with al-Banna's ideas.[270]

Consideration of the foundations for his theory easily identifies one element that is similar to al-Afghani's thought: Western domination and socio-economic injustices. Although European colonial power in the Middle Eastern region was ending during al-Banna's lifetime, Western influences had not disappeared. Al-Banna associates Western influences with moral decay:

> This libertine investigation to vice, this beguiling pleasure, this frivolous self-indulgence, in the streets, in meeting-places, in summer resorts, in the country all contradict what Islam counsels us to follow in the way of chastity, decency, renunciation, and dedication to serious work and abstinence from frivolous activities.[271]

He particularly objects to the freedom that Western and Westernizes women enjoy in social life and the work place. The notion of the "half-naked woman" is found in a number of his writings.[272] His critique of Western materialism, however, is far more naïve and anti-intellectual than al-Afghani's. Charles Wendell describes al-Banna as "quite as simplistic and rigid in his views as many an amateur Western critic of Muslim morality and customs."[273] Al-Banna concludes that the "civilization of the West [...] is now bankrupt and in decline. Its foundations are crumbling, and its institutions and guiding principles are falling

---

[269] Ahmad S. Moussalli, "Ḥasan al-Bannā's Islamist Discourse on Constitutional Rule and Islamic State," *Journal of Islamic Studies* 4, no. 2 (1993): 162. Although this is a definitional flaw, not a logical flaw in the strict sense, Moussalli's association of al-Banna as less radical and therefore mainstream is not entirely convincing, despite the fact that his analysis of al-Banna is generally sound.

[270] Cf. Christine Sixta Rinehart, "Volatile Breeding Grounds: The Radicalization of the Egyptian Muslim Brotherhood," *Studies in Conflict & Terrorism* 32 (2009): 953–988, who apparently associates all anti-state violence as terrorism and aims to portray al-Banna and the Muslim Brotherhood as a terrorist organization from its founding.

[271] Ḥasan al-Banna, "To What Do We Summon Mankind," in Ḥasan al-Banna, *Five Tracts of Ḥasan al-Bannā' (1906–1949): A Selection from the* Majmūʿat Rasāʾil al-Imām al-Shahīd Ḥasan al-Bannāʾ, trans. and annotated Charles Wendell (Berkeley: University of California Press, 1978), 90.

[272] Charles Wendell, "Introduction," in *Five Tracts of Ḥasan al-Bannā'*, 7. Although this is not the main topic discussed here, his negative image of women and his traditional view of their role in society and particularly in the family is ironically still reflected, more than half a century later, in the Muslim Brotherhood statement issued in rejection of the UN Declaration of Women's Rights. See, "Muslim Brotherhood Statement Denouncing UN Women Declaration for Violating Sharia Principles" (http://www.ikhwanweb.com/article.php?id=30731) 15.03.2013.

[273] Wendell, "Introduction," 4.

apart."²⁷⁴ Given that al-Banna was most active between the 1920s and 1940s, this image of the West as "crumbling" unsurprisingly agrees with the existential experience of crisis experienced by Western intellectuals after the devastating experience of the First World War. A not insignificant number of intellectuals searched for a new religiosity outside the traditional institutionalized Churches that had morally failed and displayed an alienation from society.²⁷⁵ Hermann Hesse's *Steppenwolf* and *Glasperlenspiel* are among the literal expressions of this mood. None of these Western critiques of civilization, however, supports the idea of massive re-Christianization. Al-Banna, however, argued that Christianity as a whole has lost its spiritual bases. He considers Christianity to be "a tool to subjugate the ignorant and justify the conquest of the rest of the world."²⁷⁶

An evaluation of al-Banna views on the legitimacy of violence cannot avoid the ambiguity and contradictions in his writings. Yet, al-Banna's actions are far less ambiguous. Johannes Jansen writes that "[i]t is with Ḥasan al-Bannā that professional violence became part and parcel of the movement we now call Islamic fundamentalism. He and his followers not only committed professional violence but they also suffered from it."²⁷⁷ The implementation of a militia, the "Special Apparatus" (*al-Niẓām al-Khāṣṣ*), in 1940 implies his approval for violent actions to reach the Muslim Brotherhood's main objectives: the "liberation of the entire Muslim world from all sorts of foreign domination" and the "establishment of an Islamic state in the Muslim world which should implement the laws of Islam and its social system, and propagate its message to mankind."²⁷⁸ Both his focus on the implementation of shariʻa and his belief that Islam's and the Brotherhood's mission is "universal and all encompassing"²⁷⁹ implies that his scope far surpasses al-Afghani's concern for traditional Muslim lands, not

---

274 Al-Banna, "Towards the Light," in *Five Tracts of Ḥasan al-Bannāʾ*, 106.
275 For instance, see Bettina Koch, "Ein Dadaist auf der Suche nach dem *neuen* Menschen: Hugo Ball zwischen Wissenschafts- und Gesellschaftskritik und katholischen Mystizismus," in *Einsprüche: Politik und Sozialstaat im 20. Jahrhundert. Festschrift für Gerhard Kraiker*, ed. Antonia Grunenberg (Kovač, Hamburg, 2005), 115–127.
276 Ana Belén Soage, "Ḥasan al-Bannā or the Politicisation of Islam," *Totalitarian Movements and Political Religions* 9, no. 1 (2008): 31.
277 Jansen, *The Dual Nature of Islamic Fundamentalism*, 40.
278 A. Z. al-Abdin, "The Political Thought of Ḥasan al-Bannā," *Islamic Studies* 28, no. 3 (1989): 222, 230. Tariq Ramadan, *Au sources du renouvenau musulman: D'al-Afghānī à Ḥassan al-Bannā un siècle de réformisme islamique* (Paris: Bayard Éditions/Centurion, 1998), 170–1, argues that al-Banna opposes violent action, although this interpretation must be seen in context of al-Banna's vague and unspecific rejection of revolution.
279 Ḥasan al-Bannā, "Our Mission," in *Five Tracts of Ḥasan al-Bannāʾ*, 47.

mankind as a whole. Yet, other aspects of his teaching significantly differ from al-Afghani. Al-Afghani had great admiration for rationality and sciences; because scientific truth cannot contradict religious truth, religious interpretation needs to be adjusted to scientific revelation. Al-Afghani admits, however, that "[as] long as humanity exists, the struggle will not cease between dogma and free investigation, between religion and philosophy."[280] Hasan al-Banna sides clearly with dogma when he states, the "Qurʾān does not distinguish between secular and religious science, but advocates both, summing up the natural sciences in one verse, expostulating on the behalf and making knowledge of them a means of reverencing Him and a path to knowing Him."[281] Indeed, the imposition of human law and philosophy leads mankind to the realm of *jahiliyya*.[282] Furthermore, he discards the traditional Islamic practice that "recognizes a de facto separation between the religious and temporal realms of human activity, including distinct sources of jurisdiction in the Muslim polity."[283]

Furthermore, al-Banna is not willing to acknowledge the existence of a political realm because he considers Islam to be an all-embracing religion that provides laws and regulations for all aspects of life for entities ranging from an individual man or woman to a nation. Consequently, Islam absorbs the political in its entirety.[284] Given traditionally interpretations of Islam, al-Banna's all-embracing concept of Islam is technically an innovation that invokes the suspicion of heresy in a traditional understanding, which is not different from medieval Christian views. To avoid accusations of heresy or even apostasy, this novelty is displayed as a rediscovery of the true and essential Islam that was lost for centuries and was only truly fulfilled in Muhammad's original community. In contrast, al-Banna and his followers consider the distinction between the spiritual and the political realm to be a foreign innovation that foreigners brought to Islam.[285] In keeping with al-Ghazali, "al-Banna considers the government as only an appendix to *Sharīʿa,* and not its legislator;" any law or government

---

280 Al-Afghānī, "Answer of Jamāl ad-Dīn to Renan," 187.
281 Al-Banna, "Towards the Light," 115–6. See also Ana Belén Soage, "Hasan al-Banna and Sayyid Qutb: Continuity or Rupture?" *The Muslim World* 99, no. 2 (2009): 300.
282 Moussalli, "Ḥasan al-Bannā's Islamist Discourse on Constitutional Rule and Islamic State," 166.
283 Abdulaziz Sachedina, *The Islamic Roots of Democratic Pluralism* (Oxford: Oxford University Press, 2001), 5.
284 Al-Banna, "To What Do We Summon Mankind," 74, 87.
285 Soage, "Ḥasan al-Bannā or the Politicisation of Islam," 26–7.

that contradict shari'a is deemed unnatural and "puts man on a collision course with the state."[286]

This all-embracing concept of Islam severely impacts state legitimacy. As outlined in the introduction, a conflict between political necessity and religion's moral standards is unavoidable because any governmental action that follows the law of political necessity potentially conflicts with religious law and jeopardizes the government's legitimacy in the eyes of the faithful, such as al-Banna. Notably, al-Banna's ambiguity persists even when he reintroduces *jihad* as a means to achieve his concept of an Islamic state. Ana Belén Soage notes that

> al-Bannā insisted on Islam's 'benevolent' attitude towards minorities and maintained that peaceful relations with non-Muslim states were possible [...]. However, elsewhere he asserted that Muslims must fight *jihad* until all people proclaim that 'there is no God but God and Muḥammad is the messenger of God'.[287]

As previously highlighted, the pre-modern perception of *jihad* is that it is the only means of guaranteeing Muslims' security and freedom. Following this logic, al-Banna claims that "[t]oday the Muslims [...] are compelled to humble themselves before non-Muslims and are ruled by unbelievers. Their lands have been trampled over, and their honor besmirched."[288] In other words, al-Banna believes that the entire Muslim world is under siege by non-Muslims and in a permanent state of warfare. Even so, he considers *jihad* to be a tool for peace, not oppression. This interpretation does not mean that he promotes what is generally called the *greater jihad*, which refers to the believer's inner struggle compared to the actual fighting associated with the term *lesser jihad*. On the contrary, al-Banna dismisses the distinction as an invention "to divert people from the importance of fighting, preparing for combat, and resolving to undertake it and embark on God's way,"[289] a view that aligns with modern scholarship. As outlined earlier, David Cook convincingly demonstrated that the concept of the *greater jihad* is an apologetic invention with no foundation in Islam's history.[290] While al-Banna's concept of *jihad* as actual fighting aligns with its original meaning, he is not confined by the traditional understanding of the concept. Whereas *jihad* is commonly considered to be a collective duty, Ana Belén Soage regards

---

286 Moussalli, "Ḥasan al-Bannā's Islamist Discourse on Constitutional Rule and Islamic State," 168, 170.
287 Soage, "Hasan al-Banna and Sayyid Qutb," 304.
288 Ḥasan al-Banna, "On Jihād," in Ḥasan al-Banna, *Five Tracts of Ḥasan al-Bannāʾ*, 150.
289 Ibid., 155.
290 Cook, *Understanding Jihad*, 32–48.

Hasan al-Banna as the first author to describe *jihad* as an individual duty to be added to the pillars of Islam, though the idea of *jihad* as an individual duty has been attributed to Ibn Taymiyya.[291]

As discussed in an earlier chapter, traditional participation in *jihad* is usually restricted to a particular group of people. Children can only take part with their parents' consent, slaves cannot participate without their masters' consent, and debtors cannot participate without their creditors' consent. Al-Banna argues that *jihad* is an individual obligation, and accordingly, he rejects these previous restrictions. He declares that "the woman and slave shall go forth without the permission of husband or master. In the same way the child shall go forth without the permission of his parents, and the debtor without the permission of his creditor."[292] His internal logic supporting his argument and rejecting permission stems from his argument that evading and abstaining from *jihad* is "one of the seven mortal sins that guarantee annihilation."[293] Following the logic of his argument, the prohibition of *jihad* by superiors must be omitted to prevent eternal death.

Traditionally, the People of the Book (Christians and Jews) are neither subjected to Islamic conversion efforts nor targeted in jihadist enterprises. However, al-Banna bases his theory on a hadith that allows fighting the People of the Book. This hadith promises that "God doubles the rewards of those who fight them" because *jihad* "is not against polytheists alone, but against all who do not embrace Islam."[294] This notion follows the inner logic of al-Banna's theory because he perceives Christianity to be a religion in name only, bereft of spirituality. This argument labels Christians as unbelievers rather than People of the Book, as the latter believe essentially in the same God as Muslims. Moreover, his understanding of the universality and all-encompassing nature of Islam makes the extension of *jihad* to the People of the Book a natural consequence. The combined theses of *jihad* as an individual obligation and the avoidance of *jihad* as a mortal sin potentially renders all Muslims who do not follow these demands as sinners, if not unbelievers, against whom violent actions would be justifiable.

Yet, al-Banna introduces two additional aspects that impact later thinkers and activists. First, he reemphasizes the concept of the martyr.[295] Silvia Horsch-Al Saad's study showed that the idea of martyrdom is not technically

---

291 Soage, "Hasan al-Banna and Sayyid Qutb," 305.
292 Al-Banna, "On Jihād," 147–8.
293 Ibid., 133.
294 Ibid., 142.
295 Ibid., 133, 141.

of qur'anic origin. The contemporary meaning of the term *shahīd,* now understood to be martyr, has been adopted as the result of a discourse between different religious cultures. For a considerable period of time, this term's meaning oscillated somewhere between traitor and suicide, both of which have well-known consequences for one's status in paradise.²⁹⁶ The perspective of modern Islamic studies argues that the idea of the martyr, which is central in contemporary militant discourses, is a later invention. The second aspect, which is not fully explored by al-Banna, became rather virulent among later activists focusing on the Tatars (Mongols) and the Crusades.²⁹⁷ The reference to the Mongols subliminally references Ibn Taymiyya's famous fatwa on the Mongols, which was previously discussed and will be explained in more detail in the context of Sayyid Qutb's and 'Abd al-Salam Faraj's thought. Although the rhetoric of the Crusades is completely absent in al-Afghani's writings, al-Banna's comparison of the current struggle with the Crusades is remarkable, though not surprising, given that an Arabic term for Crusaders (*al-ḥurūb al-ṣalīyya*) did not appear until the nineteenth century among Syrian Christians. The study of the Crusades became more popular among Arab historians in the twentieth century, and the contemporary interpretation of the history of the Crusades reads as "imperialism ahead of its time."²⁹⁸

Although Hasan al-Banna responds to the same underlying problem that al-Afghani addresses, al-Banna's answer addresses Islam rather than socio-economic injustices and the aftermath of colonial rule. This tactic is a result of al-Banna's belief that his version of Islam responds to and solves the challenges of modernity. The most interesting questions are typically difficult to answer. In this case, perhaps the most interesting question is whether al-Banna would have turned to Islam in the absence of other problems. Sayyid Qutb, however, takes some of al-Banna's ideas even further.

Sayyid Qutb: Jihad against Jahiliyya

Similar to Hasan al-Banna, Sayyid Qutb argues that lacking and corrupt religiosity partially contributes to existing socio-economic and political problems in the Muslim world. Following popular opinion of the time, he links the Crusades to imperialism and Zionism, a connection that has become popular among Arab

---

296 Horsch-Al Saad, *Tod im Kamp:*, 77, 297, 237.
297 Ḥasan al-Banna, "Between Yesterday and Today," in Ḥasan al-Banna, *Five Tracts of Ḥasan al-Bannā'*, 20 – 21.
298 Sivan, *Modern Arab Historiography of the Crusades*, 9, 11, 15.

historians.²⁹⁹ Indeed, Qutb goes further than most historians who analyze the contemporary situation through the Crusades, claiming that the West has a hatred of Islam that was "born of the Crusading spirit, which is latent in the European mind" and reminding the reader to not "forget the role of international Zionism in plotting against Islam and the polling against it in the forces of the Crusade imperialists and the communist materialists alike."³⁰⁰ He argues that internal problems in the Muslim world, particularly in Egypt, are caused by corruptive Western influences on Islamic civilization. His conceptualization of the West includes philosophy and philosophic rationality. He dismisses the Islamic philosophy of Ibn Sina and Ibn Rushed, although al-Afghani heavily admired these authors, as "reflections of Greek philosophy, which has no connection whatsoever with the overall concept and philosophy of Islam."³⁰¹ Qutb canonizes the certain Qur'anic "modes of reasoning that are uncongenial to, for instance, Western reasoning, such as on the question of the relation of politics and religion" in contrast to what he perceives to be Western reasoning.³⁰² Instead of reason, both al-Banna and Qutb favor God's guidance "for a direct, personal and intuitive understanding of the Revelation."³⁰³

While Sayyid Qutb agrees with many of al-Banna's arguments, other ideas are more dependent on Mawdudi. Both Qutb and Mawdudi "share a common perspective [that] concerns the method for bringing about an Islamic Revolution." Although al-Banna was more charismatic, Qutb's legacy "has become far more important in Egypt, though in a controversial, to some extent inconsistent, and often misunderstood" manner.³⁰⁴ The three dominant concepts in Sayyid Qutb's thought are *hakimiyya*, *jahiliyya*, and *jihad*. *Hakimiyya*, usually rendered as "governance" or "sovereignty," is a term that is difficult to translate in Western languages; thus, to borrow once again from Hayden White, the translation is religiously contaminated. The term does not refer to governance or sovereignty in general, but to God's rule because God is the absolute sovereign. Neither human governance, particularly secular human governance, nor any divine governance outside Islam qualifies as *hakimiyya* because "[e]ven the West real-

---

299 Ibid., 24.
300 Sayyid Qutb, *Social Justice in Islam*, trans. John B. Hardi, rev. trans. and intro. Hamid Algar (Oneonta: Islamic Publications International, 2000), 270, 275.
301 Qutb, *Social Justice in Islam*, 291.
302 Sadiki, The Search for Arab Democracy, 97.
303 Ana Belén Soage, "Islamism and Modernity: The Political Thought of Sayyid Qutb," *Totalitarian Movements and Political Religions* 10, no. 2 (2009): 192.
304 Leonard Binder, *Islamic Liberalism: A Critique of Development Ideologies* (Chicago: University of Chicago Press, 1988), 183, 175.

ises that Western civilization is unable to present any healthy values for the guidance of mankind."[305]

Of these three concepts, *hakimiyya* is the goal, *jahiliyya* is the antithesis, and *jihad* is the method to overcome *jahiliyya* and to reach *hakimiyya*. As Sayed Khatab notes, Qutb jointly develops his theory of *jahiliyya* and *hakimiyya* and reminds us of the controversial argument that "*jahiliyya* does not refer to a particular period or place, nor does it refer to a particular race. Rather, it is the opposite condition of Islam, state and law."[306] Qutb reinterprets *jahiliyya*. Originally, the term referred to pre-Islamic times, that is, a period prior to the Islamic Revelation and a period that is understood to be a time of ignorance when Islam was unknown. Qutb argues that true knowledge has been lost and that unconverted people or Muslims in name only fail to fully embrace Islam and live in the state of *jahiliyya*. This argument partially results from the corruption and oppressiveness of the current age. Qutb further contends that if people were completely free of constraints and sufficiently knowledgeable of Islam, everyone would freely embrace Islam.[307]

Another problem is Qutb's belief that one must live in a truly Muslim community or state to live a Muslim life without err. This community existed during Muhammad's time. As long as this community is not realized, Muslims are forced to comply with authorities and acknowledge ideas that contradict the revealed truth. This system needs to be abolished, by force, if necessary:

> Since this movement comes into conflict with the *Jahiliyya* which prevails over ideas and beliefs, and which has a practical system of life and a political and material authority behind it, the Islamic movement had to produce parallel resources to confront this *Jahiliyya*. This movement uses the method of preaching for reforming ideas and beliefs; and it uses physical power and *Jihad* for abolishing the organizations and authorities of the *Jahili* system which prevented people from reforming their ideas and beliefs but forces them to obey their erroneous ways and makes them serve human lords instead of the Almighty Lord.[308]

Qutb's core ideology relies not only on Mawdudi and al-Banna but also on Ibn Taymiyya's fourteenth-century treatment of the Mongols. As discussed at length in an earlier chapter, Ibn Taymiyya accused the Mongols of failing to truly convert to Islam. Thus, he doubts their conversion and considers them to be unbelievers who are Muslims in name, not in reality. Ibn Taymiyya argues that *jihad*

---

305 Sayyid Qutb, *Milestones*, (Damascus: Dar Al-Ilm, n.d.), 7.
306 Sayed Khatab, *The Political Thought of Sayyid Qutb: The Theory of jahiliyyah* (London: Routledge, 2006), 10, 59.
307 Zaman, *Modern Islamic Thought in a Radical Age*, 200–1.
308 Qutb, *Milestones*, 55.

against the Mongols is not only justifiable but that it is a religious obligation. This argument helped modern Sunni Islamists to establish the right to rebel against political authorities. In this context, Ibn Taymiyya classifies the Mongol violation of fundamental Islamic principles as "polytheism of the jahiliyya [pre-Islamic]."[309] Ibn Taymiyya borrows the concept of *jahiliyya* from the pre-Islamic period, that is, the period before the revelation and prior to the introduction of Islam. During this period, Islamist writers translated the theorem that Islam generally "has reverted to a state of jahiliyya, true Muslims find themselves in a state of war against the apostates and that jihad is but a defensive response to the 'war of annihilation' the apostates conduct against Islam."[310] Sayyid Qutb, who influenced generations of Islamist thinkers, is deeply indebted "to Ibn Taymiyya's fourteenth-century formulation of the right to revolt against rulers who violate the terms of Islamic law."[311] Influenced by the Ibn Taymiyya-based theory, Qutb provides the theoretical foundation for his "most influential disciple," Muhammad ʿAbd al-Salam Faraj, to justify Anwar al-Sadat's assassination.[312] With reference to Ibn Taymiyya, Sayyid Qutb could legitimize revolt against authorities within the framework of traditional Sunni thought. The theme from Sayyid Qutb's "creative reinterpretation" argues that (Sunni) Islamic law justifies the use of violence and revolt against authorities. Qutb's reasoning overcomes any ambiguity in al-Banna's argument about the legitimacy of revolution. Furthermore, fellow Muslims who are no longer perceived to be Muslims could be targeted by *jihad*.[313] However, scholars do not agree on the militancy of Sayyid Qutb's ideas because most of his work was written while imprisoned and had to pass the prison's censors. Consequently, crucial aspects of his writings allow for a wide range of interpretations that range from his portrayal as the godfather of al-Qaeda and the September 11th attacks to a truly democratic thinker.[314] The truth is expected to lie somewhere in the middle. It is certain, however,

---

309 Sivan, *Radical Islam*, 98–9.
310 Ibid., 85.
311 Roxanne L. Euben, Muhammad Qasim Zaman, "Sayyid Qutb, 1906–1966," in *Princeton Readings in Islamist Thought: Texts and Contexts from al-Banna to Bin Laden*, ed. Roxanne L. Euben and Muhammad Qasim Zaman (Princeton: Princeton University Press, 2009), 135.
312 Albert J. Bergesen, "Sayyid Qutb in Historical Context," in *The Sayyid Qutb Reader: Selected Writings on Politics, Religion, and Society*, ed. Albert J. Bergesen (New York: Routledge, 2008), 5–6.
313 Sivan, *Radical Islam*, 94, 103.
314 John C. Zimmerman, "Sayyid Qutb's Influence on the 11 September Attacks," *Terrorism & Political Violence* 16 (2004): 222–252. Sayed Khatab, "The Voice of Democratism in Sayyid Qutb's Response to Violence and Terrorism," *Islam and Christian-Muslim Relations* 20 (2009): 315–332.

that the imprisonment and torture experienced by Qutb and other Muslim Brothers triggered a more radical position and moved them from their original intent of societal reformation to a more radical stand.[315]

Without Qutb's execution in 1966 under Nasser's Egypt, "there would have been a fair possibility that Qutb would have clarified many of the controversial terms he had posited in his writings." Moreover, his internationally protested execution was not justified, and it unnecessarily created another martyr whose works were translated into numerous languages almost immediately after his execution. As Adnan Musallam notes, Khomeini translated Qutb's works into Farsi, and a later President of Afghanistan, Burhanuddin Rabbani, provided a translation into Dari.[316]

Although the traditional reading of Qutb usually emphasizes a strong indication for a violent call for action, Labri Sadiki reminds us that Qutb's thoughts provide an alternative because

> many Islamists, especially various Muslim Brotherhoods and off-shoot movements from within them such as in Sudan and Jordan have, since the 1980s and 1990s, shunned Sayyid Qutb's radicalism, replacing it with a Qur'ānic language that is moderate and conciliatory in its tone, at the same time, appropriated the language of a democratic, civil society. In a sense, this is akin to how liberalism sprang from within conservatism.[317]

Egyptian 'Abd al-Salam Faraj, perhaps one of the most radical followers or re-interpreters of Ibn Taymiyya's and Sayyid Qutb's ideas, did not follow this moderate path.[318]

'Abd al-Salam Faraj: Theory put into Action

Faraj, the founder of *Jama'at al-Jihad*, reaches the peak of his influence in the 1980s. Faraj is considered to be the "Jihad mentor" for Sadat's assassination.

---

[315] Michael Youssef, *Revolt Against Modernity: Muslim Zealots and the West* (Leiden: Brill, 1985), 75.
[316] Adnan A. Musallam, *From Secularism to Jihad: Sayyid Qutb and the Foundation of Radical Islam* (Westport: Praeger, 2005), 171–2.
[317] Sadiki, *The Search for Arab Democracy*, 120–1.
[318] For more moderate voices see the very usefull collection in John J. Donohue and John L. Esposito (ed.), *Islam in Transition: Muslim Perspective* (Oxford: Oxford University Press, 2007), esp. 143–202.

His most famous work, *The Absent Precept* or *The Forgotten Duty*,[319] which was influenced by both Ibn Taymiyya and Sayyid Qutb, was ironically also influenced by Khomeini's *The Islamic Government*, despite Ibn Taymiyya's hostility towards Shiʻa "heresies."[320] He mentions neither Sayyid Qutb nor Khomeini, but he frequently references Ibn Taymiyya's fatwa against the Mongols. A number of paragraphs in his treatise begin with the words "Ibn Taymiyya says...." Faraj's use of Ibn Taymiyya, however, has been harshly criticized by moderate Muslims in Egypt.[321]

The short treatise does not lack originality.[322] It is a program to achieve an Islamic state, which Faraj considers to be "the duty of all Muslims."[323] In his comparison of contemporary rulers with the Mongols, he accuses them (the contemporary rulers) of *ridda* (apostasy) and indicates that they must be killed.

> They prayed and fasted, but they refused to give up usury. Thus, they were described as fighting God and his Apostle. If fighting them was necessary, how much more important is it to fight those who omit so many elements of the *shariʾa* like the Tatars [Mongols]. All Muslim *ulama* have agreed that any group of people who refuses to perform any of the obvious Islamic duties must be fought [he lists the five pillars and the prescripts of the sunna] until all religion is God's.[324]

In essence, Faraj states that an apostate is any Muslim who does not always follow all Islamic precepts, and he argues that Muslims are thus justified to fight them. Faraj believes that Sadat's simple act of publicly raising a glass of wine with infidels (Western leaders) is sufficient reason for his assassination. Such public behavior, however, did not make Sadat an apostate only for Faraj and his circle, as moderate Muslims also doubted Sadat's Islamic faith. Moreover, Sadat's government included non-believers (Copts), who were frequently photographed in the daily news, and Faraj perceived their presence to be a permanent offense. Faraj and members of *Jamaʻat al-Jihad* claimed that non-Muslims must

---

319 A complete English translation of *The Forgotten Duty* can be found in Michael Youssef, *Revolt Against Modernity*, 146–177. For excerpts of the text, see Muhammad ʻAbd al-Salam Faraj, "The Neglected Duty," in *Princeton Readings in Islamist Thought: Texts and Contexts from al-Banna to Bin Laden*, ed. Roxanne L. Euben and Muhammad Qasim Zaman (Princeton: Princeton University Press, 2009), 327–343.
320 Sivan, "Sunni Radicalism in the Middle East and the Iranian Revolution," 26.
321 Johannes J. G. Jansen, "The Creed of Sadat's Assassins: The Contents of 'The Forgotten Duty' Analysed," *Die Welt des Islams* NS 25 (1985): 4–5.
322 Gilles Kepel, *Muslim Extremism in Egypt: The Prophet and Pharaoh* (Berkeley: University of California Press, 1985), 194.
323 Faraj, *The Forgotten Duty*, in Youssef, *Revolt Against Modernity*, 149.
324 Ibid, 154.

follow Islamic precepts and that denouncement indicates an incomplete belief in Islam and denies the truth of Islam.[325]

These radical thoughts, however, are partially grounded in a radical reading of the Qur'an. Q 5:44 plays a central role in legitimizing radical anti-governmental thoughts and actions. This section is usually read as "He who does not judge by what God has revealed is an unbeliever," but Faraj, as well as 'Umar 'Abd al-Rahman and Usama bin Laden, read the section as "those who do not *govern* by what God has revealed are unbelievers." This second interpretation provides a qur'anic justification for rebellion against the state.[326] As implied by the treatise's title, the central issue for Faraj is the consideration of *jihad* as the forgotten duty or precept. Similar to Hassan al-Banna and Sayyid Qutb before him, Faraj renders this issue to be the individual duty of all true Muslims.

Giles Kepel summarizes the situation in Egypt at the time of Sadat's assassination by stating that "at the moment of [Sadat's] death, Sadat's unpopularity had reached new depths. He had filled Egypt's prisons to bursting with people of every political stripe, including the most moderate, and Sadat himself had lapsed into an isolation bordering to paranoia."[327]

Qutb's and Faraj, as al-Banna before them, emphasize that the state's legitimacy must rest on Islam. Although this demand is a political goal in itself, this language turns political problems into religious ones and conceals an oppressive regime and other issues that are political in the common sense, namely, that of an oppressive regime. In addition, Qutb expresses great disappointment in the outcome of the Egyptian Revolution of 1952, which did not fulfill the promises that motivated the Muslim Brotherhood's support.[328] Sadat's aim to modernize Egypt also fueled conflicts with Islamist groups. After releasing Islamists imprisoned by Nasser for their opposition to the regime, Sadat "encouraged the formation of Islamic groups at Egypt's colleges and universities, hoping they would form a counterweight to the Nasserite purists." This move actively contributed to the Islamization of Egypt's society. At the same time, Sadat relied heavily on al-Azhar's *ulama* to legitimize policy that was not necessarily "Islamic." Al-Azhar's support in the 1977 food riots, which were declared to be un-Islamic,

---

325 Youssef, *Revolt Against Modernity*, 87, 89.
326 In Roxanne L. Euben and Muhammad Qasim Zaman, "Muhammad 'Abd al-Salam Faraj, 1954–1982," in *Princeton Readings in Islamist Thought: Texts and Contexts from al-Banna to Bin Laden*, ed. Roxanne L. Euben and Muhammad Qasim Zaman (Princeton: Princeton University Press, 2009), 325.
327 Gilles Kepel, *Jihad: The Trail of Political Islam* (Cambridge, MA: Belkap Press, 2002), 87.
328 See Joel Gordon, "The Myth of the Savior: Egypt's 'Just Tyrants' on the Eve of Revolution, January-July 1952," *Journal of the American Research Center in Egypt* 26 (1989): 223–237.

was motivated by constitutional change. In return, Sadat agreed to introduce sharia as the foundation of the Egyptian constitution and mandate religious education. He even relied on al-Azhar's *ulama* for a fatwa declaring that alcohol consumption is Islamic. This ongoing bargaining with an *ulama* willing to sanction policies, including the peace treaty with Israel, to further Islamize the state increased the expectations of Islamist groups that he had empowered for other political goals, while the regime became increasingly less willing and able to meet these expectations.[329] Superficially, Sadat's strategy worked sufficiently well for quite some time. Although no Egyptian revolution comparable to the Iranian Revolution occurred during his regime, his actions nourished frustrations that turned into violence against the state. The conflict in Egypt and other Sunni dominated lands was almost entirely fought through religious language, and it is rather questionable whether a similar radicalization emphasizing a religious goal would have occurred under less oppressive circumstances.

3.2.2 Shi'i Theory and the Iranian Revolution

In Zayar's Marxist interpretation of the Iranian Revolution he suggests that because the Iranian Revolution was seized from the working class, it must be read in all but religious terms. Zayar claims that the Islamic fundamentalists "systematically distorted the real facts of the Iranian revolution. In this way, they did their best to conceal and deny the role of the working class in the revolution. This lie has been repeated by the imperialists who have their own reasons for misrepresenting the nature of the Iranian revolution, particularly to confuse and disillusion the workers of the West."[330] It goes without saying that Zayar's Marxist interpretation that the Islamists "did their best to conceal and deny the role of the working class in the revolution"[331] is biased. Nonetheless, his claim that the Iranian Revolution was seized by "Islamic fundamentalists" is a valid point. If not already at the dawn of the Iranian Revolution, soon thereafter the battle over the revolution's legacy was in full progress. In this sense, the Iranian Revolution clearly serves as a prime example of Kippenberg's notion that a religious interpretation of a conflict alters the conflict's nature. Indeed, a religious interpretation does not only alter a conflict's nature, but it can also alter the nature of an entire revolution.

---

329 Masoud, "The Arabs and Islam," 138.
330 Yazar, *Iran... Revolution in Resilience* (Lahore: The Struggle Publications, 2000), 73.
331 Ibid., 73.

We owe a contrary interpretation of the Iranian Revolution that is as biased as Zayar's to Murtuza Mutahhari. Although Mutahhari's importance is contested, he is usually considered the chief ideologist of the Iranian Revolution and "the ayatollah who had been groomed to succeed Khomeini."[332] However, his assassination soon after the Iranian Revolution rendered that impossible. Hamid Dabashi describes Mutahhari as the "chief ideologue of the Iranian Republic"[333] who, nonetheless, "began to worry about its theocratic consequences" soon after the revolution's success.[334] Mutahhari, however, does not leave any doubt that Khomeini had the support of the entire Iranian population and that "he was completely in harmony with the thinking and feeling of the people of Iran and their needs."[335] For Mutahhari,

> [t]he secret of the success of the leader lay in the fact that he advanced the struggle within the mold of Islamic concepts. [...] Imam Khomeini fought against oppression, injustice, colonialism and exploitation by means of the belief that a Muslim should not crouch beneath the burden of oppression, that a Muslim should not allow himself to become servile, that a believer should not be under the heel of the unbeliever.[336]

Furthermore, by denying other opposition groups credit for the revolution's success, Mutahhari refuses to admit any Marxist or Socialist impact on either Khomeini or the Iranian Revolution.[337] It is unclear how Khomeini was inspired by Marxist/Communists ideas in the later 1960s or whether he was even influenced by 'Ali Shari'ati because in his writings, he usually does not give much credit, particularly not to foreign sources.[338]

If one evaluates scholarly discourses on the origins of the Iranian Revolution, the picture that emerges is, to say the least, complex. For instance, Robert E. Looney, who criticizes primarily the Shah's planning modules and techniques, argues that "the Shah's demise can be traced almost exclusively to a set of eco-

---

332 Ervand Abrahamian, *A History of Modern Iran* (Cambridge: Cambridge University Press, 2008), 191.
333 Hamid Dabashi, *Theology of Discontent: The Ideological Foundations of the Islamic Revolution in Iran* (New York: New York University Press, 1993), 147.
334 Dabashi, *Islamic Liberation Theology*, 159.
335 Morteza Motahari, "The Nature of the Islamic Revolution," in *Iran, a Revolution in Turmoil*, ed. Afshar Haleh (Albany: State University of New York Press, 1985), 208.
336 Motahari, "The Nature of the Islamic Revolution," 208.
337 Ibid., 218.
338 Ervand Abrahamian, "Khomeini: Fundamentalist or Populist?," *New Left Review* 186 (1991): 110.

nomically related factors."³³⁹ In contrast, Misagh Parsa emphasizes social factors, some of which, such as unequal pay and a failure to improve workers' conditions, are similar to Looney's economic factors and fit well into Henry Shue's basic rights discourse. Parsa sees the revolutionary struggle as "largely carried out by a coalition of classes and political groups, each mobilized by separate interests and conflicts."³⁴⁰ In a rather different vein, Ervand Abrahamian argues that the real roots for the Iranian Revolution can be found in in the 1953 coup that ousted Mossadeq and reinstated Muhammad Reza Shah, Reza Shah's son. As implied earlier, dependency on foreign powers, at least in tendency, undermines a regime's domestic legitimacy. For Iran, following the coup, this is clearly the case because the Shah's power was associated "with the British, the Anglo-Iranian Oil Company, and the imperial powers. It also identified the military with the same imperial powers – especially the CIA and MI6." By destroying the base for the more secular-oriented political parties, primarily *Tudeh* (The People's Party of Iran) and the *National Front*, although unintended, it strengthened the "Islamic 'fundamentalist' movements."³⁴¹ In part, this is due to the Shah's anti-clerical politics that destroyed the clerics' influence on the educational and legal systems and undermined their role as prime interpreters of high culture, which generated opposition from the traditional clergy.³⁴² Abrahamian also emphasizes that most activists did not belong to the economically deprived but instead came from a prosperous middle class.³⁴³

Nonetheless, these non-clerical movements did not completely disappear.³⁴⁴ To present a more complete picture of the different groups that formed a broad oppositional front, it is worth examining the guerilla movements that emerged in the early 1970s and played a significant role in the revolution of 1979. Among numerous Marxist and Islamic groups, three groups in particular are noteworthy:

---

339 Robert E. Looney, *Economic Origins of the Iranian Revolution* (New York: Pergamon Press, 1982), 3, 265.
340 Misagh Parsa, *Social Origins of the Iranian Revolution* (New Brunswick: Rutgers University Press, 1989), 1, 141, 145.
341 Abrahamian, *A History of Modern Iran*, 122. Abrahamian, "Khomeini," 103–105, rightfully demands caution when using the term "fundamentalist" because it is at least misleading, if not wrong, to apply a term that usually refers to Protestants in the twentieth century U.S. for members of Islamic movements in the Middle East.
342 Zhand Shakibi, "Pahlavīsm: The Ideologization of Monarchy in Iran," *Politics, Religion & Ideology* 14, no. 1 (2013): 122–4.
343 Ervand Abrahamian, "The Guerrilla Movement in Iran, 1963–77," in *Iran, a Revolution in Turmoil*, ed. Afshar Haleh (Albany: State University of New York Press, 1985), 150.
344 For a detailed analysis of the opposition movements and groups, see Ervand Abrahamian, *Iran Between Two Revolutions* (Princeton: Princeton University Press, 1982), 450–495.

The *Marxist Feda'i*, the *Islamic Mujahedin*, and the *Marxist Mujahedin*. The members of the guerrilla groups are from the young intelligentsia. The *Marxist Feda'i* group is essentially an offspring of the *Tudeh* and the *National Front*'s Marxist wing. Most members of this group have a secular modern middle class background. The group attracts students from the arts and liberal arts and is inspired by the guerrilla movements in Latin America. In contrast, the more conservative *Islamic* and the *Marxist Mujahedin* groups recruit students from the physical sciences (the so-called STEM disciplines) and people with more traditional backgrounds such as merchants, clergy, and the traditional middle class. These two groups evolved predominantly from the *National Front*'s religious wing and the *Liberation Movement*. Among the latter's leading figures were Mahmud Taliqani, Mehdi Bazagan, and 'Ali Shari'ati. Despite the—at first glance—different outlooks of the *Feda'i* and the *Mujahedin*, their revolutionary interpretations of Islam show striking similarities. Both Taliqani and Bazagan had secret ties with Khomeini. For instance, a few days prior to the revolution, Bazagan secretly negotiated with the SAVAK, the Shah's secret police force.[345] Although the guerrilla movements did not receive much credit for their role in the Iranian Revolution, these organizations "delivered the regime its coup de grâce."[346]

'Ali Shari'ati's Legacy

With Shari'ati's death in 1977, his role in the 1979 revolution was largely limited to his legacy. Yet, this does not render his influence insignificant. Protesters in the streets at the dawn of the revolution were carrying images of Shari'ati alongside Khomeini's image. Nonetheless, Shari'ati's popularity does not negate the fact that the tensions between Khomeini and Mutahhari, on one side, and Shari'ati, on the other side, were crucial. To a certain degree and in terms of the patterns of their thinking, the differences between Mutahhari/Khomeini and Shari'ati are similar to those between al-Banna and al-Afghani. One can observe a similar shift from religious-cultural identity that is perceived primarily as a tool in the struggle against oppression and injustice to a theocratic conception of religion that reduces all socio-economic and political problems and injustices to the absence of a particular manifestation of religion and faith. Moreover, Shari'ati and Khomeini appeal to different audiences and recruit their followers from

---
345 Abrahamian, "The Guerrilla Movement in Iran, 1963–77," 150–160. Abrahamian, *Iran Between Two Revolutions*, 481–489.
346 Abrahamian, *Iran Between Two Revolutions*, 495.

different social groups. As John Foran notes, "[w]here Khomeini appealed to the young seminarians and traditional bazaar merchants [...], Shari'ati struck a responsive chord among high school and university students."[347] This difference in audience is also emphasized by the fact that, at least in tendency, the majority of the revolutionary clergy came from rather traditional rural or small town environments with a lower middle and working class or peasant background. Thus, their involvement in the revolution propelled their status and prestige. The more senior clerics, who refrained from political involvement, originated from families of "prestigious ulama or influential politicians and merchants."[348]

Contrary to Shari'ati, Khomeini and Mutahhari (as well as the clergy that supported them) were suspicious of any Marxist influences. It is certainly not wrong to assume similar motives as those that made the clerical establishment in 1925 and 1953 supportive of the monarchy's restoration, that is, the fear that an alternative ideology (chiefly socialism) could rise to supremacy and undermine the clerics' position.[349] Indeed, Mutahhari committed himself to studying secular trends, particularly Marxism, to refute them because he "deemed it necessary to confront the secular ideas spreading fast in Iran." Mutahhari even utilized Islamic philosophical issues as a weapon against secular ideologies. Hamid Dabashi describes the relationship between Mutahhari and Shari'ati as "outright hostility."[350] For Khomeini, Marxist and other secular organizations were at least suspicious, and thus, he denounces them as "apparently Islamic but in truth hostile to it," which echoes Nizam al-Mulk's attempts of bringing non-Sunni sects in disrepute. For Khomeini, "[i]t is quite possible that groups engaged in anti-Islamic and anti-religious activities in Iran, under various names and with different methods, are political organizations created by foreigners in order to weaken Islam, the sacred Shi'i religion, and the exalted position of the clerics."[351]

However, to a certain degree, Khomeini and Shari'ati can be regarded as the yin and yang of the Iranian Revolution. They are contrarily interdependent, in terms of both their thinking and the audiences that they reach. Their interdependence in appealing to different social groups, however, does not necessarily mean a mutual intellectual interdependence, although some similarities be-

---

347 John Foran, "A Theory of Third World Social Revolutions: Iran, Nicaragua, and El Salvador Compared," *Critical Sociology* 19, no. 3 (1992): 13.
348 Eric Hooglund, "Social Origins of the Revolutionary Clergy," in *The Iranian Revolution & the Iranian Republic*, ed. Nikki R. Keddie and Eric Hooglund (Syracuse: Syracuse University Press, 1986), 74–83, quote 83.
349 Dabashi, *Islamic Liberation Theology*, 91.
350 Dabashi, *Theology of Discontent*, 148, 151, 157.
351 Khomeini, quoted in Dabashi, *Theology of Discontent*, 474.

tween Shari'ati's language and Khomeini's imply that the latter has borrowed at least some concepts from Shari'ati. Nonetheless, Shari'ati's exceptional popularity among large sections of the young intelligentsia contributed to his controversiality and to the clerical establishment's opposition to him. He, similar to al-Afghani, views the clerical establishment as an institution that legitimizes social oppression.[352] Similar to al-Afghani, Shari'ati has been portrayed as a devout believer, a secularist, and an atheist and has been perceived as both an Islamic Marxist and the "Muslim answer to Marx."[353] While Abrahamian confirms Shari'ati's "love-hate relationship with Marx" and Fatollah Marjani contends that Shari'ati was "quite critical of the Marxist ideology," Dabashi emphasizes that there is "no doubt that his chief frame of reference, his conception of history, society, class, state apparatus, economy, culture, his program of political action, his strategy of revolutionary propaganda are all in the classical Marxist tradition."[354]

This confusion about Shari'ati does not exist without reason. Shari'ati opposes blind imitation, whether it is blind imitation of Western culture or blind imitation of a (Western) ideology. While Marx is a great inspiration for him and while he adopts Marxists analytical tools, he favors solutions that are rooted in "existing cultural, historical, and social resources."[355] Shari'ati's rationale for opposing any one-to-one adaptation of Marx is found in his analysis of Third World societies. Compared to Western societies, he suggests that Asian and African nations are living not in the nineteenth or twentieth centuries, but rather in the thirteenth century. Thus, nineteenth-century solutions (such as Marx's) are of limited imitational use. Alternatively, he suggests exploring fourteenth-century ideas to learn how the West transitioned from medieval to modern society.[356]

Yet, this does not mean that Shari'ati was not inspired and influenced by other nineteenth- and twentieth-century thinkers. Shari'ati translated numerous works, including those of Sartre, Che Guevara, and Fanon, into Persian. In short, Shari'ati borrowed ideas whenever they deemed useful and applicable, inde-

---

[352] Behrooz Ghamari-Tabrizi, "Contentious Public Religion: Two Conceptions of Islam in Revolutionary Iran: Ali Shari'ati and Abdolkarim Soroush," *International Sociology* 19, no. 4 (2004): 511.
[353] Abrahamian, *Iran Between Two Revolutions*, 467.
[354] Abrahamian, *Iran Between Two Revolutions*, 467. Fatollah Marjani, "Introduction," in Ali Shariati, *Man and Islam*, trans. Fatollah Marjani (Houston: Filinc, 1981), xix. Dabashi, *Theology of Discontent*, 137.
[355] Ali Shariati, *Man and Islam*, trans. Fatollah Marjani (Houston: Filinc, 1981), 119.
[356] Ibid., 103–4.

pendent of their Islamic or Western origins.³⁵⁷ Indeed, Yadullah Shahibzadeh speaks of "the trio of Marxism, existentialism and Islam [that] plays significant roles in his project of the Islamist ideology."³⁵⁸ Thus, Shari'ati's attitude toward the West, contrary to Khomeini's and Mutahhari's, is neither simplistic nor particularly hostile. Instead, he advocates a critical appreciation of Western achievements to understand and to undermine Western dominance. He suggests that

> [w]hat I am saying is that, let's imitate; that is, lets first find out from which route, through what type of thinking, growth, moral, action, anxiety, outlook, world vision, and past, this [Western] man became the boss, so that we can study and know the causes and conditions in order to imitate him.³⁵⁹

Although he is deeply impressed by Frantz Fanon, he differs fundamentally with him on one point. Fanon insists on the abolition of religion and tradition to fight the oppressors, while Shari'ati maintains that a successful struggle is conditional upon regaining one's cultural identity. Cultural identity, for Shari'ati, equates to religious identity.³⁶⁰ This religious identity, however, has to be the proper identity because, for Shari'ati, the two opposing and "hostile poles" of freedom and servitude "have always been armed with a mental and reflective weapon—religion."³⁶¹ As for all other religions, Shari'ati assumes for Islam the existence of two religions, two islams, one "that commits crime, creates reactionaries, concocts opiates, murders freedom, and protects the status quo", and the other Islam, "the true one, that has always fought with its criminal counterpart and in the process it has been victimized."³⁶²

Using both Islamic terminology and popular philosophical concepts (Marxism and existentialism), Shari'ati creates an Islamic ideology that appeals to the traditional audience (the bazaaris and the traditional religious people) and the more secular oriented intelligentsia, which means that he manages to "bridge the social divide between the more traditional and modern segments of Iran's

---

357 Kingshuk Chatterjee, *'Ali Shari'ati and the Shaping of Political Islam in Iran* (New York: Palgrave Macmillan, 2001), 198.
358 Yadullah Shahibzadeh, *From Totalism to Perspectivism: An Intellectual History of Iranian Islamism from Shariati to the Advent of Khatami* (Oslo: University of Oslo, 2008), 109.
359 Shariati, *Man and Islam*, 65.
360 Abrahamian, *Iran Between Two Revolutions*, 465. Elizabeth F. Thompson, *Justice Interrupted: The Struggle for Constitutional Government in the Middle East* (Cambridge: Harvard University Press, 2013), 290.
361 Shariati, *Man and Islam*, 17.
362 Ibid., 86.

youth."³⁶³ His favored method, which has some similarities with al-Afghani's (whom Shari'ati studied), certainly contributed to his political opponents' attempts to discredit Shari'ati and his ideas. Shari'ati has clearly internalized the need to appeal to people of different social groups in a different manner, a lesson al-Afghani adopted from Ibn Sina:

> I must observe what the mullah does and how he deals with people. Why are people listening to him? Is it his talk that has attracted people or some other kind of tradition and heritage? If we find our answer not only can we talk to villagers more effectively and sincerely, but consequently, we can occupy the mullah's position and find a base for the free-thinker in society. Otherwise, we are going to get nowhere by sitting and philosophizing.³⁶⁴

This approach, if successfully applied, makes Shari'ati (and his followers) a threat to the traditional clergy because it potentially undermines their power and authority. Furthermore, contrary to most of the contemporary advocates of political Islam, whether they are Sunni or Shi'i, his focus is not on the establishment of Islamic government and the enforcement of Islamic law.³⁶⁵ For him, Islam, in its true form, equals a revolutionary movement that has "nothing in common with the conservative doctrine preached by the traditional 'ulama."³⁶⁶ In short, Shari'ati's contributions to violent revolutionary struggle are twofold. First, he was able to create an Islamic ideology that appeals to the traditional and the progressive youth. Second, he created a new language that allows for the expression of revolutionary struggle in traditional Islamic terms. For instance, he transforms *jihad* into "revolutionary struggle;" the *mujahid* becomes a "revolutionary fighter;" the unbeliever (*kafir*) is a "passive observer;" the worshiping of idols (*shirk*) is interpreted as "political submission;" and the meek (*mustazatan*) become "the oppressed masses."³⁶⁷

For Ali Shari'ati, these reinterpretations of religious language are meant to attract the more religious segment of Iran's youth to the revolutionary cause against the oppressive regime, not to legitimize *jihad* against members of other creeds just because they are members of other creeds.

---

363 Chatterjee, *'Ali Shari'ati and the Shaping of Political Islam in Iran*, 117.
364 Shariati, *Man and Islam*, 107–8.
365 Chatterjee, *'Ali Shari'ati and the Shaping of Political Islam in Iran*, 94.
366 Abrahamian, *Iran Between Two Revolutions*, 472–3.
367 Abrahamian, *A History of Modern Iran*, 145.

Mutahhari's Jihad

Murtaza Mutahhari, despite his hostility towards Shari'ati, adopts some of his revolutionary language. However, in Mutahhari's writings, religion or religious language is not simply a tool to reach a political end. Instead, revolution is a means to oppose and to end oppression and oppressive regimes. For Mutahhari, religion is not a means to an end, the means is the end. This is particularly apparent in his essay "Jihad in the Quran." While he maintains for *mustaḍʿafīn* the traditional reading of "the meek," he further provides the reader with an additional reading similar to Shari'ati's, "the oppressed."[368] A similar language is also present in Khomeini's post-1970 writings.[369] Daryoush Ashouri suggests that Khomeini and his circle had to replace the obscure language of the *madrassa* with a more accessible language, and for this purpose, he borrowed freely from his ideological rivals.[370] In a similar vein, Mutahhari redefines *jihad*'s qualification as defensive, which corresponds with his qur'anic understanding of *jihad*. To Mutahhari, *jihad* does not mean "a war of aggression, of superiority, or of domination." He states that aggression that makes resistance (*jihad*) mandatory does not necessarily mean "one party invading the territory of another." For him, aggression can also occur in one's own territory by "subjecting to torture and tyranny a group from within its own people, a group that is weak and powerless." Furthermore, he concludes that in such a situation "Muslims cannot remain indifferently aloof. Muslims have the mandate to free such afflicted people." He continues, stating that "[i]n all these conditions *jihad* is an urgent necessity; and such a *jihad* is defensive, in resistance to transgression, injustice, and oppression."[371]

In accordance with al-Banna and Sayyid Qutb, he also discusses the meaning of the People of the Book against whom fighting *jihad* is considered illegitimate. Mutahhari claims that those who qualify as People of the Book are members of these creeds not only in name. Fighting against all "who do not believe in God or in the last day" and "who are not religious in accordance with any true religion" is permitted.[372] This interpretation corresponds with Sayyid Qutb's and

---

368 Murtaḍa Muṭahhari, "Jihad in the Qur'an," in *Jihad and Shahadat: Struggle and Martyrdom in Islam*, ed. Mehdi Abedi and Gary Legenhausen (North Haledon: Islamic Publications International, 1986), 92.
369 Abrahamian, "Khomeini," 112–3.
370 Daryoush Ashouri, "Creeping Secularism," *Comparative Studies of South Asia, Africa and the Middle East* 31, no. 1 (2011): 50.
371 Muṭahhari, "Jihad in the Qur'an," 92.
372 Ibid., 83.

Maududi's, both see *jihad* as justified when one of the following three conditions is met:

1. Defense
2. Revolution against tyranny
3. Establishment of the shari'ah.[373]

Yet, Mutahhari does not go as far as Muhammad Hanidullah, who sees the conditions for a defensive *jihad* fulfilled when one fights a "(a) punitive war against the enemies of Islam," "(b) sympathetic war in support of oppressed Muslims in foreign lands," "(c) punitive war against rebels within an Islamic state," or "(d) idealistic war fought in order to command the good and prevent the commission of evil."[374] These three conditions are sufficiently broad to justify the fighting of others in almost all circumstances. The central issue in both cases rests not as much on tyranny and oppression because it redefines tyranny as the absence of sharia. Moreover, the focus moves to the power over definition: who qualifies and who does not qualify as a Muslim. The power to define is also one of the central issues in pre-modern discourses because it prevents the problem of socio-economic and political justice and injustice from being noticed as a political problem. The political problem becomes disguised as a religious problem over (orthodox, in whatever definition) faithfulness. This technique of disguise goes so far as to spread different messages to different audiences. Khomeini is a paradigmatic example of this strategy. To seminarists, he emphasized the necessity of guardianship of the jurists, while "he scrupulously avoided the subject in public pronouncements. Instead, he hammered the regime on a host of political, social, and economic shortcomings."[375] Indeed, in the year prior to the Iranian Revolution, he did not mention his theocratic idea of Islamic government even once outside his inner circle.[376] This method, however, also follows the approach al-Afghani adopted from Ibn Sina.

However, this shift in perspective has crucial consequences for the legitimacy of authority. For Mutahhari, the concept of justice is central to the legitimate state and the legitimate ruler. Mutahhari contends that full legitimacy is only achievable if the state and the ruler rest on religion, which challenges not

---

[373] Mahmoud Ayoub and Gary Legenhausen, "Introduction," in *Jihad and Shahadat: Struggle and Martyrdom in Islam*, ed. Mehdi Abedi and Gary Legenhausen (North Haledon: Islamic Publications International, 1986), 15.
[374] Ayoub and Legenhausen, "Introduction," 15
[375] Abrahamian, *A History of Modern Iran*, 147. See also Abrahamian, "Khomeini," 113.
[376] Keppel, *Jihad*, 111.

only the monarchical system under the Shah but also "any political judicial and political system [that rests] on liberal-democratic or radical-revolutionary (both secular) grounds."[377] In other words, any version of secularity is instantly associated with illegitimacy and injustice. Mutahhari, however, does not go as far as Khomeini, who equates just government with the guardianship of the jurists. Indeed, he raises some (unheard) concerns about the Islamic genie in the revolutionary's bottle of theocratic consequences.[378]

Khomeini: The Jurists' Guardianship

With Khomeini, the question of justice is again the key issue. As Hamid Dabashi posits,

> 'justice' was Khomeini's principle political concern. The Iranians had been wronged. Their just due had to be given to them. This 'given to them' necessitated both leading them through a revolution and remaining in power to secure their this- and otherworldly salvation.[379]

If one bears in mind, however, that Khomeini had a less religious message for the general public or that he at least turned his message into a secular language of social, political, and economic injustice, the general public has reasons not to consider guardianship of the jurist the *only* legitimate and just version of government. Indeed, not even the religious foundation of government would be a necessity for political legitimacy. Yet, for Khomeini, any government that is not Islamic lacks *per se* any legitimacy. Similarly, it applies to any ruler who does not possess the appropriate faith and who deserves at best "total non-cooperation." Khomeini's emphasis on the need for religious rule is valid. When he became politicized in the 1940s, he thought the "westernized elites of the Muslim world were ultimately aiding the cause of the western imperialists and only Islam could prevent their success."[380]

Thus, as Kingshuk Chatterjee rightfully notes, the "equation of Khomeini with political Islam was mostly an illusion that caught on quickly as much in the Islamic world as in the west. The Shah was dislodged by a resistance move-

---

377 Dabashi, *Theology of Discontent*, 212.
378 Dabashi, *Islamic Liberation Theology*, 212.
379 Dabashi, *Theology of Discontent*, 413.
380 Chatterjee, 'Ali Shari'ati and the Shaping of Political Islam in Iran, 65, 69.

ment, which was supposed to be the same as the Islamic movement that came into power. That was not the case."[381]

Khomeini has become the face of the Iranian Revolution, and although flawed, the perception of Khomeini has shaped his legacy and influence in the Muslim world,[382] which invites one too easily to overlook that the Iranian Revolution was an enterprise of various opposition movements and groups. The *People's Fedayi* instantly raised concerns and issued a warning that Khomeini's appeal to Islam might be just another means for oppression. In an open letter to Khomeini, these concerns were expressed beyond doubt.

> But if, on the contrary, the purpose of appealing to Islam and its teachings is the repressing of every opposing thought, form and opinion, the chaining of thought and revival of an inquisition and instruments of repression, the revival of the slogan of "only one party" and the muffling of every freedom-seeking voice under the pretext of defending the Koran and the Shari'a, we are certain every liberationist patriot will condemn it and we believe that the people also will rise to expose and destroy it because they see it as a ploy in the hands of imperialism and reaction.[383]

Tudeh, on the contrary, does not adhere to the *People's Fedayi*'s strategy of instant confrontation. Rather, they aim to demonstrate that their goals and convictions are in total agreement with Islam.[384] Whether it was strategy or naivety, in an interview, Iraj Eskandari, the Secretary General of the *Tudeh* party, admits some disagreements with the religious leaders. For him, these disagreements would be only an issue "if the matter concerned the creation of a theocratic state. But as far as we know, the Iranian religious leaders have not called at all for anything of the sort."[385]

Soon after the revolution, it became obvious how mistaken Iraj Eskandari's assessment was. Indeed, in Khomeini's *Final Discourse*, he accuses the *Fedayi* and *Tudeh* of plotting against the Islamic Republic and calls it "necessary [to]

---

381 Ibid., 5.
382 For the image of Khomeini in Western media before and after the revolution, see Rob Leurs, "Ayatollah Khomeini: The Changing Face of Islam," *Estudos em Comunicação* 12 (2012): 25–45.
383 "People's Fedayi Open Letter to Khomeini," trans. Behzad Touhidi, *MERIP Reports* 75/76 (1979): 31a-31b.
384 Ehsan Tabari, "Tudeh: 'Socialism and Islam'," trans. Masood Moin, *MERIP Reports* 75/76 (1979): 29–30.
385 Iraj Eskandari, "Tudeh Leader on the Religious Movement: From an Interview with Iraj Eskandari, Secretary General of the Tudeh Party," *MERIP Reports* 75/76 (1979): 30b.

vigilantly neutralize such forms of plots."³⁸⁶ Whether one calls it theocracy or something else, Khomeini aimed for a regime that resembles remarkably well some notions of Hobbes's sovereign. He places the Shi'i clergy, the interpreters of religious law, outside and above the state. In other words, the state and government are above religious law. Thus, it is not surprising that Khomeini's innovative concept of the state and the rule by jurisprudence finds opposition from some grand Ayatollahs.³⁸⁷

For Khomeini, however, the need for Islamic government follows the inner logic of his thoughts. Similar to al-Banna or Qutb, he sees the absence of true Islamic faith the single reason for injustice and (imperialist) oppression. As he outlines in *Islamic Government*, "the solution of social problems and the relief of human misery require foundations in faith and morals; merely acquiring material power and wealth, conquering nature and space have no effect in this regard."³⁸⁸ In other words, he portrays the sociopolitical problem of injustice as a religious problem, a perspective that is evidenced in *Kashf al-Asrar* of 1943, which is usually considered Khomeini's first distinctively political statement. In this discourse, he describes an oppressive government as one that does not perform its duties. By contrast, a non-oppressive government "is cherished and honored by God."³⁸⁹ From his perspective, none of the existing governments are "based on justice or a correct foundation that is acceptable to reason." Although he first equates justice with the respect for property and defines injustice as a transgression "against the property and rights of others," he emphasizes that justice and legitimate government cannot exist outside God's realm. "[G]overnment must run in accordance with god's law."³⁹⁰ Later, he calls tyrannical governments (he has primarily the Shah's regime in mind but also the "West" more broadly) "fundamentally opposed to Islam itself and the existence of the reli-

---

386 Ruhollah Khomeini, *Imam's Final Discourse: The Text of the Political and Religious Testament of the Leader of the Islamic Revolution and the Founder of the Islamic Republic of Iran, Imam Khomeini* (Tehran: Ministry of Guidance and Islamic Culture, 1989), 39–40, 52.
387 Maziar Behrooz, "Factionalism in Iran under Khomeini," *Middle Eastern Studies* 27, no. 4 (1991): 599, 604. Nikki R. Keddie, "Is Shi'ism Revolutionary?," in *The Iranian Revolution & the Iranian Republic*, ed. Nikki R. Keddie and Eric Hooglund (Syracuse: Syracuse University Press, 1986), 122.
388 Ruhollah Khomeini, "Islamic Government," in Ruhollah Khomeini, *Islam and Revolution*, trans. Algar Hamid (London: Kegan Paul, 2002), 36.
389 Ruhollah Khomeini, "A Warning to the Nation (1943)," in Ruhollah Khomeini, *Islam and Revolution*, trans. Algar Hamid (London: Kegan Paul, 2002), 169.
390 Ibid., 169–70.

gious class."³⁹¹ It is the West, usually referred to as "imperialists," that insists on a separation between religion and politics. To Khomeini, the rhetoric of separation is aimed at discrediting religious scholars and Islam alike. It is "designed to misrepresent us and make the ʿulama and their institutions appear to be the opium for the people."³⁹² Far from being opium for the people, Khomeini considers the *ulama* to be the "'national consciousness [that] stood firm as the 'fortress of independence' against imperialism, secularism, and other 'isms' imported from the West."³⁹³

In many respects, Khomeini's anti-Western rhetoric is far more aggressive than the rhetoric of the thinkers previously discussed. Similar to Nizam al-Mulk's fanciful genealogy that draws the Ismaʿili threat of his age back to pre-Islamic Mazdak, Khomeini paints a genealogy of Jewish resentment against Islam that goes back to the early years of Islam, and he contends that the beginning of the irreligious imperialist threat is founded in the medieval Crusades.

> From the beginning, the historical movement of Islam has had to content with the Jews, for it was they who first established anti-Islamic propaganda and engaged in various stratagems and as you can see, this activity continues down to the present. Later they were joined by other groups, who were in certain respects more satanic than they. These new groups began their imperialist penetration of the Muslim countries about three hundred years ago, and they regarded it as necessary to work for the extirpation of Islam in order to attain their ultimate goals. It was not their aim to alienate the people from Islam in order to promote Christianity among them, for the imperialists really have no religious belief, Christian or Islamic. Rather, throughout this long historical period, and going back to the Crusades, they felt that the major obstacle in the path of their materialistic ambition and the chief threat to their political power was nothing but Islam and its ordinances, and the belief of the people in Islam. They therefore plotted and campaigned against Islam by various means.³⁹⁴

Apparently, Khomeini is following the fashion among Arab historians of his time who consider the Crusades to be "imperialism ahead of its time" and interpret the Crusades in the context of the foundation of the state of Israel.³⁹⁵ However, compared to Sayyid Qutb, Khomeini is by no means excessive in his use of ref-

---

391 Ruhollah Khomeini, "The Afternoon of ʿAshura (June 3, 1963)," in Ruhollah Khomeini, *Islam and Revolution,* trans. Algar Hamid (London: Kegan Paul, 2002), 177.
392 Ruhollah Khomeini, "In Commemoration of the First Martyrs of the Revolution (Feb. 19, 1978)," in Ruhollah Khomeini, *Islam and Revolution,* trans. Algar Hamid (London: Kegan Paul, 2002), 219. Khomeini, "Islamic Government," 38.
393 Abrahamian, "Khomeini," 112.
394 Khomeini, "Islamic Government," 27–8.
395 Sivan, *Modern Arab Historiography of the Crusades,* 9.

erences to the Crusades. While he is not that explicit in his references to the Crusades, he nonetheless emphasizes the premise that the current problem is a problem of old. Contrary to the general assumption that Islam in early times focuses more on obedience than on revolution and that one should not engage in violent struggle unless there are realistic chances of succeeding, Khomeini stresses that "[t]he leader of the Muslims taught us that if a tyrant rules despotically over the Muslims in any age, we must rise up against him and denounce him, however unequal our forces may be, and that if we see the very existence of Islam in danger, we must sacrifice ourselves and be prepared to shed our blood."[396]

In this sense, Khomeini's reasoning resembles that of al-Ghazali, who suggests that in an inferior position, it is preferable to seek martyrdom. At the same time, Khomeini contradicts the position of the North Indian 'ulama, who argues that the Muslims are under Christian protection and fighting *jihad* can only be justified when a victory is likely.[397] He compares the "imperialists" of his own time and their predecessors to satanic forces and corruption. This dualistic perspective places righteousness and justice with Islam. Everything that is not Islamic (for instance, he considers Wahhabi Islam as anti-Quar'anic)[398] is described as *kafir* (unbelief) and *ṭāghūt* (idol, but also used as *ṭāghin*, meaning tyrant, oppressor). To Khomeini, "all non-Islamic systems of government are the systems of *kufr*, since the ruler is an instance of *taghut*, and it is our duty to remove from the life of Muslim society all traces of *kufr* and destroy them."[399]

The underlying thought that he also shares with most modern Islamists, as discussed in the context of Hassan al-Banna and Sayyid Qutb earlier, is the idea that a Muslim cannot live a righteous life in accordance with Islam outside the Muslim society. If transferred into a simple equation, for Khomeini, Islam equals justice. Anything extra, anything beyond Islam, equals corrupt, criminal, and oppressive regimes. Thus, he argues that there is "no choice but to destroy those systems of government that are corrupt in themselves and also entail the corruption of others and to overthrow all treacherous, corrupt, oppressive, and criminal regimes." Fighting those corrupt and un-Islamic regimes is the duty of all Muslims.[400] The goal is the formation of a universal movement to "es-

---

396 Ruhollah Khomeini, "Muharram: The Triumph of Blood over the Sword (Nov. 23, 1978)," in Ruhollah Khomeini, *Islam and Revolution*, trans. Algar Hamid (London: Kegan Paul, 2002), 242 (242–245).
397 Ourghi, *Muslimische Positionen zur Berechtigung von Gewalt*, 19, 23.
398 Khomeini, *Imam's Final Discourse*, 8.
399 Khomeini, "Islamic Government," 48.
400 Ibid., 48.

tablish Islamic government in places of tyrannical regimes."⁴⁰¹ Thus, Khomeini's claim falls into Bassam Tibi's observation of a new de-secularization (*De-Säkularisierung*) and de-Westification (*Entwestlichung*) movement that gained impetus in the 1970s with the emerging concept of "neo-*jihad*," the aim of which is to fight for the de-Westification of the world.⁴⁰² While Khomeini's primary focus is Iran, he considers the Iranian Revolution to be just the beginning of a movement for the liberation of all oppressed nations.

As previously discussed, in classic *jihad* theory, engagement in armed *jihad* is dependent on various means, and reasons to be exempt from such a *jihad* are numerous. However, Khomeini does not leave any doubt that there are no exemptions. Beyond *repetitio mater historiae*, repetition is the mother of Khomeini's revolutionary teaching. In his *Islamic Government*, the message that engaging in armed *jihad* to force "the norms of government to conform to the principles and ordinances of Islam" is the duty of all Muslims is repeated over and over again. For those who cannot engage in an armed struggle, he delivers the following message: "But at least do not stay silent. If they strike you on the head, cry out in protest! Do not submit to oppression; such submission is worse than oppression itself."⁴⁰³

When suggesting non-violent means of opposition, Khomeini is more in keeping with the classic legal Shiʻi position: "It is the duty of everyone to oppose it, to refrain from aiding it in any way to refuse to pay taxes or render any assistance to this oppressive regime of transgressors." In addition, he suggests that all workers and officials in the oil industry do whatever is in their power to prevent oil exports to oppressive (meaning non-Islamic) regimes.⁴⁰⁴ However, Khomeini does not except any excuses for non-engagement in the struggle against the regime. To Khomeini, staying silent and not acting is not only suicide, but it also aids, at least tacitly, the existing regime. He further denounces those who do not engage in (active) resistance against the regime, claiming that they are guilty of treason both against Islam and the Iranian nation. All of those who support the Shah's "tyrannical regime" and conspire against the Islamic movement are "traitors."⁴⁰⁵ At the end of *Islamic Government*, he summarizes the action that must be taken, including a violent overthrow that topples the regime in power: "Let us overthrow tyrannical government by: (1) severing all relations with governmental

---

401 Khomeini, "Islamic Government," 108.
402 Tibi Bassam, *Kreuzzug und Djihad: Der Islam und die christliche Welt* (München: Bertelsmann, 1999), 238–9, 254.
403 Khomeini, "Islamic Government," 115.
404 Khomeini, "Muharram," 243.
405 Ibid., 245.

institutions; (2) refusing to cooperate with them; (3) refraining from any action that might be construed as aiding them; and (4) creating new judicial, financial, economic, cultural, and political institutions."[406]

Khomeini, however, has to face one problem that relates to the Islamic tradition of exempting the People of the Book from being targeted through *jihad*. His strategy here is again similar to Nizam al-Mulk's and Ibn Taymiyya's, although Nikki Keddie suggests that Khomeini is rather following the example of the Nizari Isma'ilis "who similarly had violence-prone leaders convinced they possessed the absolute truth."[407] In his earlier suggestion to infiltrate the army, however, one may see some parallels to the Nizari Isma'ilis' strategy.[408]

The key issue is how to justify fighting those under the concept of *jihad* who are traditionally not considered justifiable targets. The answer Khomeini provides redefines who belongs to Islam and who belongs to any of the creeds that traditionally constitute the People of the Book. Similar to Mutahhari, who considers it justified to fight all who are religious only in name but not in belief, Khomeini targets not just non-Muslims but also all of those whom he suspects of being Muslims only in name, particularly those who abuse Islam and the Qur'an for political gain. For Khomeini, "[s]elfish people and oppressors exploited the Holy Qur'an as a tool at the service of governments who opposed the Holy Qur'an, under various pretexts and with premeditated plots."[409] The idea behind his argument echoes the precepts of Ali Shari'ati's regarding two islams, a false Islam that supports oppression and a true Islam that seeks liberation. While Khomeini, however, goes beyond Shari'ati's concept of two islams, similar to Shari'ati, he accuses parts of the religious establishment of providing tyrannical regimes with religious legitimacy.[410] More than that, these segments of the religious establishment abuse the Qur'an by legitimizing corruption and injustice.[411] Khomeini deems some of the traditionalists as simply incompetent because they "have not attained the level of *ijtihad* and who mere transmit *hadith* know nothing about all this; hence they are incapable of discerning the true practice of the Messenger of God."[412] One needs to add, however, that Husain's martyrdom, which is central in Khomeini's revolutionary interpretation of Islam,

---

406 Khomeini, "Islamic Government," 146,
407 Keddie, "Is Shi'ism Revolutionary?," 122.
408 Ruhollah Khomeini, "In Commemoration of the Martyrs at Qum (April 3, 1963)," in Ruhollah Khomeini, *Islam and Revolution*, trans. Algar Hamid (London: Kegan Paul, 2002), 176.
409 Khomeini, *Imam's Final Discourse*, 7.
410 Khomeini. "Islamic Government," 144.
411 Khomeini, *Imam's Final Discourse*, 7.
412 Khomeini, "Islamic Government," 70.

though it was invented by Muhammad Baqir as-Sadr and further developed by Ali Shari'ati, is not accepted among all Shi'i scholars and does not have any relevance in the Sunni tradition.[413]

Khomeini, however, does not only accuse the Iranian *ulama* of such misdeeds and incompetence. He also targets other Muslim governments, Saudi Arabia in particular, because in Wahhabism, Khomeini sees a "superstitious cult" whose intent is to abuse Islam and the Qur'an. In addition to the question whether Sunni or Shi'i Islam is the only true Islamic creed, attacking Saudi Arabia means attacking the one country in the region that "cultivates its identity as the heartland of Islam." It is also the country in the region with the tightest alliance between the political and the religious part of the regime. As such, the Saudi pan-Islamism and their support for the Palestine resistance movement can be considered a direct challenge of Khomeini's ambitions.[414]

Khomeini's rhetoric is one of an assumed universal conspiracy against true Islam.[415] Assuming there is only one true (interpretation of) Islam, all other interpretations must be false, is in the context of absolute divine truth logically sound and mistaken at the same time; it is still humans who are responsible for the interpretation. However, following the logic of knowing the only truth, all other readings of Islam, whether they are Sunni or Shi'i, are either heretical innovations (heretics add things) or atheist corruptions (atheists take things away).[416]

For Khomeini, whether they are innovators, atheists, or mistaken supporters of the regime, they are all hypocrites who follow the logic of old. While he does not refer to any of the medieval Sunni theologians, in substance, he argues that these same hypocrites cannot be considered Muslims, and therefore, fighting *jihad* against them is mandatory. The same applies to the People of the Book. Because "the imperialists really have no religious belief, Christian or Islamic." It is not simply that he considers Christians or Jews to be unbelieving materialists. Rather, he associates all Christians and Jews and all Westernized Muslims with imperialism, and thus, they are either hypocrites or unbelievers against whom fighting *jihad* is justified.[417]

Khomeini's rhetoric of mandatory revolution and resistance abruptly stops when governance of the Imam is addressed. While his revolutionary interpreta-

---

413 Ourghi, *Islamische Positionen zur Berechtigung von* Gewalt, 39–40.
414 Thomas Hegghammer, *Jihad in Saudi Arabia: Violence and Pan-Islamism since 1979* (Cambridge: Cambridge University Press, 2010), 2 (quote), 17, 20.
415 Khomeini, *Imam's Final Discourse*, 8.
416 Khomeini, "Islamic Government," 53.
417 Ibid., 27.

tion of (Shi'i) Islam diverges from traditional interpretations in significant aspects, his understanding of the Imam's governance follows the fictional (in the sense that it refers to an undetermined future) tradition after the concept of the invisible Imam was born. Although Khomeini never referred to him as the returned Mahdi, his expectations for obedience are similar. To Khomeini, "[t]he governance of the Imams differs, of course, from that of all others; according to the Shi'i school, all the commands and instructions of the Imam must be obeyed, both during their lifetime and after their death."[418]

Soon after the Iranian Revolution, the full meaning of this concept became visible. As previously explained, *Tudeh*, who, among other groups, supported Khomeini, was mistaken in their assumption that Khomeini was not interested in the establishment of an Islamic theocracy. The rhetoric against all opposition to the Islamic movement was instantly translated into political practice.

> Marxist-Leninists, Islamic-Marxists, liberals, and nationalists who had joined the anti-Shah uprising eventually became the revolution's victims. The Communist Tudeh party's top leadership was either executed or jailed. The people's Mojadeddin and other left-leaning smaller groups were literally annihilated. One estimate is that nearly 20,000 of the young revolutionaries who had taken up arms against the ruling *Akhonds* were later executed.[419]

The same reasoning that Khomeini applies to justify the revolution, indeed, to mandate the revolution and the violent overthrow, has been applied in response to opposition groups that are not in agreement with the outcome of the revolution, namely, that the Iranian Revolution turned into an Islamic Revolution that replaced the oppression of the Shah's regime with a theocratic regime that was not any less oppressive. Indeed, the new regime's response to formerly supportive opposition proves that Hamid Dabashi is right when he suggests that "[s]o far as Shi'ism in on the side of the oppressed it is in its full revolutionary blossoming. The instant that it becomes fully institutionalized into an apparatus of power it *ipso facto* mutates into a most brutal theocratic tyranny."[420]

Of course, this is not the only outcome of the Iranian Revolution, as the revolution significantly changed the political landscape of the entire Middle Eastern region. Karen A. Feste posits that one of the most lasting results of the Iranian Revolution is that "Islamist movements have become a central force on the political landscape of the Arab world." Furthermore, she emphasizes that "[c]on-

---

[418] Ibid., 97.
[419] Manouchehr Ganji, *Defying the Iranian Revolution: From a Minister to the Shah to a Leader of Resistance* (Westport: Praeger, 2002), 109.
[420] Dabashi, *Islamic Liberation Theology*, 69.

servative and anti-Western sentiments in the Middle East were strengthened significantly by the Iranian revolution."[421]

3.3 Summary and Comparison

All previously discussed thinkers and movements revolve around the question of a true understanding of a particular religion that reflects on socio-economic and political conditions. The only exception to this rule seems to be Alfonso López Trujillo and Roger Vekemans, who aimed at a truly theological discourse that, as Daniel Levine notes, "resists 'politics' as such, but politics lies clearly in the core of all these disputes."[422] López Trujillo and Vekemans are unwilling to acknowledge that their supposedly apolitical approach is political in itself. Although they concede the existence of severe problems in the socio-economic and in the political sphere, their politics of non-engagement implicitly favors the existing order. Their support for the existing order is twofold: first, it concerns the hierarchy of the Church (and its power over exegesis) and second, the order of the political realm. Moreover, they are the only authors discussed in the previous sections who fully recognize the autonomy of the political sphere. In this sense, they are reluctantly political and, with respect to the political sphere, accidentally hegemonic. However, they are hegemonic as far as the hierarchy of the Catholic Church is concerned.

For all other authors and movements discussed in the previous sections, the distinction between the political and the religious sphere is blurred. Whereas most authors and movements that have been included in the narrative are clearly anti-hegemonic, Corrêa de Oliveira (TFP) and a post-revolutionary Khomeini fall out of this pattern. For Hasan al-Banna and Sayyid Qutb, we can assume that their ultimate goal was to create a new hegemony, a hegemony that is based on religious law and its coercive enforcement. The common theme uniting these authors and movements is the assumption that their respective opponents lack soundness of faith and a true understanding of the tenets of Christianity or Islam. The authors are divided by the consequences they associate with their analysis. The key issue here is whether religious disagreement in itself justifies violence against the other. Additionally, the authors disagree whether otherness

---

421 Karen A. Feste, *The Iranian Revolution and Political Change in the Arab World* (The Emirates Occasional Papers 4; Abu Dhabi: The Emirates Center for Strategic Studies and Research, 1996), 33.
422 Levine, *Religion and Politics in Latin America*, 53.

primarily includes people associated with a different creed or if it remains a conflict within one religious creed that is broadly defined.

To address these questions, it is worth emphasizing that the Latin American discourse is a discourse over Catholicism (with the exception of TFP and Corrêa de Oliveira), whereas the Middle Eastern discourses focus on Islam and the (religious) other that is perceived as extra-religious and usually associated with a vague notion of the "West." Despite fundamental differences between the Latin American and the Middle Eastern discourses, some parallels and similarities are significant. These parallels one finds primarily a) in liberation theology (especially Comblin and Ellacuría) and al-Afghani and Shari'ati and b) between Corrêa de Oliveira and al-Banna and Qutb as well as Khomeini.

To concentrate first on al-Afghani and Shari'ati in relation to Comblin and Ellacuría, we are confronted with four thinkers who move from an analysis of socio-economic conditions to potentials that lie in religion and that allow for a response to the socio-economic and political problems by targeting the underlying structures of power. All share in the belief that the existing religious establishment is, at least partly, responsible for and contributes to the existing problems. To explore the parallels of this reasoning, it is worth referring back to 'Ali Shari'ati. In *What Is to Be Done* he notes,

> [a]n enlightened person should be aware that the deviant and reactionary elements—which have always been against the masses and have always played with their destiny and exploited them—misuses religion as an effective weapon to divert the feelings and the attention of the masses from their present affairs and make them think about past problems only. They divert people's attention from the present as well as the actual and material problems while, in the name of religion keeping people preoccupied with the afterlife as well as abstract and subjective issues, so that Muslims are prevented from striving for a comfortable, affluent, and free life.[423]

Shari'ati identifies the religious establishment as one of the key issues that hinders structural change. The religious establishment distracts the people (the masses) from pressing political and socio-economic problems. By emphasizing the world to come, it disguises the political problems of the time. Here, religion appears as a means to maintain order for the benefit of an elite. In doing so, Shari'ati draws on a conflict between the elite and the masses, or the ordinary people. His answer to the problem is not, as Fanon suggests, abolishing religion, but reforming religion. He places religion in the service of unifying the people

---

[423] 'Ali Shari'ati, *What Is to Be Done: The Enlightenment Thinkers and an Islamic Renaissance*, ed. Farhang Rajaee, Foreword John L. Esposito (North Haledom: Islamic Publications International, 1986), 20.

culturally. Thus, religion has to be reinterpreted in a way that it incorporates the pressing socio-economic and political need of the time. For this purpose, he creates a narrative of two religions, a false one of oppression and a true one of liberation. A similar approach is visible in al-Afghani, who identifies tyranny and the "misuse and misinterpretation of religion with the intention of legitimizing the existing religious and social order."[424] In short, true religion is associated with justice and freedom, whereas false religion is equated with injustice and oppression. Religion, in this context, becomes part of the problem and of the solution. As Daniel Brumberg implies, the underlying "consensus building approach" is of limited success "unless all groups check their religion at the door."[425]

A similar logic is fundamental to liberation theologians. This is particularly visible in José Comblin's discussion of true and false religion that matches ʿAli Shariʿati's narrative fairly well—except that liberation theologians' politicization of religion is far more limited. Although they aim for a Latin American identity that is distinct from "Western" identity, this identity is not exclusively based on religion, even though popular religiosity contributes to it. Nevertheless, their logic and their legitimation of revolution and revolutionary violence is based on a similar distinction between true and false religion, a false religion of oppression that sanctions structural violence and a true religion of liberation. Here, religious liberation (salvation) goes hand in hand with socio-economic and political liberation—despite their attempt to argue within a theological rather than a Marxist framework. Moreover, Shariʿati's critique of the religious establishment's focus on the world to come instead of the problems in this world applies to the Latin American context as well. This critique relates particularly to the conflict between liberation theologians and the official responses of the Vatican and conservative bishops in league with the Roman Curia as exemplified above with López Trujillo and Vekemans. It needs to be noted, however, that neither of these authors is explicitly or implicitly anti-modern. Neither of them explicitly aims for a religious state that is ordered and governed in accordance with divine law.

In contrasting the claims of liberation theologians with those of Shariʿati and al-Afghani, the language used to support their claims is worth noting. Liberation theologians borrowed from other disciplines such as biology and psychology (Ellacuría) or sociology (Torres) to create a language and concepts

---

424 Jansen, *The Dual Nature of Islamic Fundamentalism*, 27.
425 Daniel Brumberg, "Islam is not the Solution (or the Problem)," *The Washington Quarterly*, 29, no. 1 (2005–06): 98–9.

that seem appropriate to their task. Only in a second step did they relate their concepts to religion (sin, redemption). In contrast, al-Afghani and Shari'ati, although they were versed in the latest discourses in the social and natural sciences, had to rely on religious language and concepts. Although they are partly influenced by similar discourses in other disciplines, they had to adjust religious concepts to their needs by avoiding a *new* or *newly* sounding terminology. In other words, they had to redefine standard religious language to make it applicable to their particular purposes. This approach includes the notion that their language had to be appropriate to their audiences. In their discourses, however, the socio-economic and political problems they were responding to remained at the forefront.

Perhaps with the exception of TFP and Corrêa de Oliveira, one finds neither in liberation theology, nor in their theological counterparts the idea of a religious state that needs to be fulfilled or rather restored. By contrast, some Islamist discourses are prominently dominated by the idea of a religious state that has to be fulfilled to overcome injustice. We will return to TFP's approach and goals shortly. Whereas Mutahhari, Khomeini, Qutb, and al-Banna engage in redefining religious terminology to adjust it to their purpose (in the cases of Mutahhari and Khomeini, one can see significant parallels to Shari'ati), they also represent a shift from visible socio-economic problems and goals to religious ends. With Qutb, to a lesser degree in Khomeini, the Crusades become rhetorically more prominent, emphasizing that the current problems are the outcome of a long history of Western domination. In their approach, religion is perceived as the solution to all other problems they identify. Whereas liberation theologians operate within the concept of social justice that is influenced by Catholic social teaching and is essentially social ethics and thus combines ethics and Catholic morality, the aforementioned Muslim thinkers place all morality within the concept of religious law. It is, to speak with Qutb, *jahiliyya*, pre- and un-Islamic conditions that have to be overcome to restore a just (Islamic) order.

To frame this issue in the thinking of Hasan al-Banna, national independence depends on "moral reform and strict adherence to Islam."[426] The socio-political conditions that must be overcome are perceived as rooted entirely in moral decay. Al-Banna and Qutb associate moral decay with all that does not comply with their (Islamic) standard of morality. To "restore" the anticipated order, any means, even the use of professional violence, the "Special Apparatus," might be mandatory. Despite the explicit anti-modern rhetoric employed by al-Banna and Qutb, their approach to Islam and its tenets shows some features of modernity.

---

426 Kandil, *Soldiers, Spies, and Statesmen*, 8.

Contrary to traditional approaches, their interpretation of Islam depends on their own engagement with the Qur'an. Both al-Banna and Qutb rely on "a direct, personal and intuitive understanding of the Revelation."⁴²⁷ The problem inherent with this individualistic approach, however, is obvious. Their intuitive reading is set as absolute and true, whereas another reader of the same sacred texts may come up with an entirely different understanding of Revelation and attach to his or her reading a similar truth claim.

José Comblin and Pope John Paul II can be used to contrast al-Banna's and Qutb's approach. For Comblin, the opponent is not the non-Christian, even the atheist is rather the "fool" than the "enemy." Even though John Paul II sees liberation theology's alternative reading of Christianity as "an act of aggression against orthodoxy and ecclesiastical unity" and labels liberation theologians as "internal enemies" of the Church, he does not conclude that the enemy has to be fought violently or even be killed.⁴²⁸ Ironically, whereas pre-revolutionary Khomeini and Mutahhari, despite their explicit anti-Marxist outlook, apply Torres's approach to the collaboration with other, including Marxist, groups, their post-revolutionary approach resembles that of the Church as expressed in López Trujillo and Vekemans. In essence, post-revolutionary Khomeini's anti-Marxist outlook even resembles that of Corrêa de Oliveira's.

To a certain degree, although both Comblin and John Paul II are theologians, they also reflect a traditional and a modern approach to religious doctrines and exegesis. John Paul II's main concern is the authority of the institution in questions of faith, whereas José Comblin and his fellow liberation theologians represent a modern, mere individualistic approach. However, neither of the liberation theologians goes as far as al-Banna and Qutb in their individualistic slant that is absolute in its demands. The outcome of their individualistic reading of Islam and its tenets is not simply opening the gate for numerous competing interpretations that allow for the labeling of the other as non-Muslim who can be violently fought. Moreover, the identification of socio-economic and political problems with Islam disguises the nature of a conflict and turns socio-economic and political issues entirely into a problem of true fulfillment of a particular interpretation of Islam. A similar pattern is also visible in Mutahhari's and Khomeini's approach, although their narrative gains additional complexity through their rhetoric that disguises, to the vast majority of Iranians of their time, their true intentions.

---

427 Belén Soage, "Islamism and Modernity," 192.
428 Melendez, "The Catholic Church in Central America," 556.

The outcome of the Iranian Revolution is a political-religious system that is understood as theocratic. The leaders of the Iranian revolution, particularly Khomeini, were successful in denying all other groups that contributed to its success any credit. Given the *Marxist Feda'i* group's inspiration through Latin American guerrilla strategies and liberation theology, one could clearly see more parallels between pre-revolutionary Iran and Latin American discourses. However, their post-revolutionary impact has been minimized as nonexistent. To a certain degree, Mutahhari and Khomeini represent a hybrid case. The hybridity is owed to their rhetoric that delivered one message to the general people and another message to the seminarists. The goal is seen in a state that is completely ordered according to one interpretation of Islam, represented by the guardians, in which Islam is not simply the means to a particular end, but as the means itself. The rhetoric used towards the people is essentially secular by emphasizing socio-economic injustice and political oppression without particular references to Islam being the only answer. This ambiguity is already visible in one of Khomeini's earliest political writings in which he first relates injustice to the transgression of property rights (socio-economic). Later, he associates just and legitimate government with God's rule. Nonetheless, Khomeini exhaustively uses political terms such as tyranny and oppression, which implies a political problem that ordinarily asks for political answers. Compared with the rhetoric of other Muslim thinkers of his time, his rhetoric becomes significantly more anti-Western. He employs a rhetoric that is particularly directed against "imperialism, secularism, and other 'isms' imported from the West."[429] Like al-Banna and Qutb, Mutahhari and Khomeini redefine who may and who may not be targeted through *jihad*. The redefinition of legitimate targets of *jihad* follows his anti-rhetoric and includes other Muslim regimes, particularly Saudi Arabia, he accuses of having betrayed Islam by abusing Islam for mundane purposes.

Similar to Qutb and al-Banna, political legitimacy is no longer separate from religious legitimacy. Full or complete legitimacy has to rest exclusively on religion, which renders all other foundations of legitimacy illegitimate, unjust, and oppressive. This rhetoric and underlying concept of legitimacy does not recognize any foundation but God. It corresponds in a rather peculiar way with Corrêa de Oliveira and his TFP movement, although, compared with Khomeini, Corrêa de Oliveira's elitism is only reflected in the elitist status of the guardians. Yet, if one replaces "Christendom" with "Islam" and Corrêa de Oliveira's understanding of the fulfillment of Christendom in the Middle Ages with the concept of the ideal Islamic community under Muhammad, Corrêa de Oliveira has much in

---

429 Abrahamian, "Khomeini," 112.

common with some of the Muslim thinkers discussed above. In addition, he shares in their view that whoever does not agree with a particular concept and interpretation of religion qualifies instantly as the enemy. Contrary to liberation theologians and even the traditional Church, the enemy is not simply somebody who shares the same religion only in name and not in practice does not follow Corrêa de Oliveira's interpretation of Catholicism, but the enemy also includes members of other religions, particularly Islam. To phrase it in Islamic terminology, the enemy includes the People of the Book and all who are only Christians in name. With Khomeini and Mutahhari, he also shares in the explicit anti-Marxist, anti-communist, and anti-liberal approach. Corrêa de Oliveira's emphasis of inequality, however, violates one of the fundamentals of Islam that emphasizes equality—similar to early Christendom.

4 Insights and Implications: Duties, Rights, and Legitimizing Violence

To conclude as we began, this chapter reassesses the key concepts outlined in the introduction (rights, justice, and legitimacy; religion and legitimacy). Thereafter, it aims at identifying patterns legitimizing political violence in transcultural perspective. Because this book is also a contribution to *Comparative Political Theory* (CPT), a discipline that predominantly focusses on *The West* and *The Other*, it is worth exploring how the West is reflected in the texts we have discussed previously.

Given the scope of the book, none of the discourses analyzed is free of religious language or arguments. Yet, in some if not most discourses, although the discourses are framed in religious language, religion is not made into the cause of conflict; rather, religious morality is invoked to denounce the deprivation of moral rights as well as socio-economic and political injustices. Thus, it is worth bearing in mind, as Kippenberg notes, that "a link between religion and violence is neither impossible nor necessary." Nonetheless, a conflict's nature may alter through the conflict's religious interpretation.[1]

While this observation is already true for cases in which the non-religious origin of a conflict is evident and the non-religious problems are only religiously framed, it is certainly true for conflicts that are fully interpreted as a conflict over religious truths. From a scriptural interpretation that is claimed to be the only true interpretation, political claims may derive. Even in this scenario, religion is not necessarily the original cause of conflict. Yet, the second scenario causes additional challenges. These challenges do not simply concern political legitimacy itself; they also concern possibilities for conflict resolution. Common sense suggests that conflicts over socio-economic and political injustice can be solved by removing the injustices. Conflicts that are fought over competing truth claims provide a far more difficult task for conflict resolution because they undermine the basic principles of politics.

4.1 The West

The idea of the West is perhaps among the most contested concepts in the history of ideas as well as in modern and contemporary political discourse. As an

---

1 Kippenberg, *Violence as Worship*, 199–200.

analytical tool, the category of the West or of Western civilization (often used interchangeably with Western modernity) seems to be of limited value. *The West* is frequently employed polemically, although some features associated with the West appear more frequently. One of the recurrent features is the notion of secularity, despite the fact that the so-called secularization theorem has not remained unchallenged.[2] For our purpose, we employ Enrique Dussel, who reasons about *The West* and *The Other* in terms of periphery and center. With respect to the regions and time-periods addressed, Dussel considers medieval Christian Europe detached from the regional centers of the time, whereas the Muslim Middle East is one of the regional centers. For the twentieth and twenty-first centuries, Dussel relates neither the modern Middle East nor Latin America to the center. Dussel, however, includes regional elites, independently of their geographical location, in the Western center but excludes the deprived minorities in the geographical "center."[3] If we accept Dussel's model, we may locate a *The West* versus *The Other* conflict within the authors and movements previously addressed. Instead of introducing another definition of the *West*, the images of the *West* as expressed in some of the texts discussed deserve further exploration.

Except for Corrêa de Oliveira and the bishops writing in defense of the Vatican's position without explicitly engaging in a discourse about the West and the other, almost all of the contemporary authors have a critical perspective of the West or Western civilization. Al-Afghani and Shariʻati apply a critical yet appreciative approach to the West. For the liberation theologians, the critique on the West is best expressed by José Comblin. He associates Western civilization with "science, democracy, and Christianity" and relates it to the *National Security State*. Thus, he links the West to the (military) elites in Latin America and the United States and Europe more broadly.[4] Comblin criticizes this concept of the West on three grounds. First, true democracy only exists for the elites; the vast majority of the people remains excluded from the "Western value" democracy. With democracy truly fulfilled, his objection against the West diminishes. Second, in order to enforce these Western values, the military juntas use violent force to subject the people. The second critique refers back to the first one: "democracy" exists only for the elite and reflects rather on an oligarchic system. Third, he criticizes the abuse of Christianity for hegemonic aims. For Comblin, Christianity is reduced to a tool that aims at the creation of a national identity

---

2 Hans Blumenberg, *Die Legitimität der Neuzeit*, erneuerte Ausgabe (Frankfurt/M.: Suhrkamp, 1996), 73–98. It is usually assumed that without Christianity, Western modernity, whatever is meant by it, would have been unthinkable, ibid., 39.
3 Dussel, *Ethics of Liberation*, 24–5, 405–6.
4 Comblin, *The Church and the National Security State*, 77.

and hegemonic domination. Moreover, this Christianity is empty. It is a conglomerate of dead symbols. The institutionalized Church supports this emptied Christianity in order to maintain the status quo. These dead symbols he regards as disconnected from his notion of "true" Christianity. In response to this empty Christianity, he aims at a different concept of Christianity that serves as a foundation for a non-Western Latin American identity. Ignacio Ellacuría shares Comblin's basic critique. Ellacuría argues for an authentic Latin American Christianity that is distinct from the versions of Christianity that exist in Europe or Northern America.[5] If one bear in mind that Enrique Dussel is intellectually linked to the liberation theology movement, it comes of no surprise that his distinction between periphery and center matches Comblin's and Ellacuría's critique of the West fairly well. Hélder Câmara supports this perspective when he speaks of "internal colonialism" that is based on "a handful of privileged citizens." Câmara explicitly included "the big wealthy church" in the privileged.[6]

Western domination is the core of al-Afghani's and Shari'ati's critique. For them, socio-economic injustices are direct consequences of Western domination. Yet, both appreciate science and other achievements they associate with Western civilization. Instead of rejecting Western civilization as a whole, their objective includes learning from the positive aspects, while rejecting all elements they associate with Western domination's and hegemony's negative consequences. Particularly Shari'ati emphasizes critical imitation.[7] Neither al-Banna and Qutb nor Khomeini share this appreciative-critical approach. Both al-Banna and Qutb regard the West as equipollent to moral decay. Similar to Comblin and other liberation theologians, they consider the religion of the West (Christianity) as empty religiosity. Religion exists only in name as symbols and rhetoric. Although this view is close to liberation theologians' critique, their rhetoric of moral decay has a different quality. None of the liberation theologians draws on the distinction between "beguiling pleasures" and "frivolous self-indulgence," related to the West, and "chastity, decency, renunciation, and dedication to serious work," al-Banna regards as essentials of Islam.[8]

Qutb, however, goes even a step further. In addition to associating the West with moral decay that influences Islamic culture negatively, he ascribes to the West a hatred of Islam that originates in the Crusades. Moreover, for Qutb the West embodies "international Zionism […] plotting against Islam," "Crusade im-

---

5 Ellacuría, "The Christian Challenge of Liberation Theology," 132–5.
6 Câmara, "Violence in the Modern World," 48.
7 Shariati, *Man and Islam*, 65.
8 Al-Banna, "To What Do We Summon Mankind," 90.

perialists," and "communist materialists."[9] Both al-Banna and Qutb reject philosophical rationality, including Islamic philosophy, as Western.[10] In essence, they associate all influences outside their narrow understanding of Islam with the West and, thus, consider them damnable. Their rhetoric, with the exception of the explicit rejection of all philosophical traditions, is echoed by Khomeini for whom all Christians, Jews, and "Westernized" Muslims qualify as "imperialists," hypocrites, and unbelievers.[11] Here, again, the underlying distinction between *The West* and *The Other* resembles Dussel's distinction between periphery and center. This is particularly true if we consider al-Afghani's and Shari'ati's critique of the local elites, although neither of them attaches the Western label to them. Thus, superficially, Dussel's conception applies to the modern Islamist context as well. Yet, Dussel's ethical-philosophical approach is free from any references to an *Other* that aims for an identity that is distinctly different and morally superior.

Ironically, many of the features the Muslim thinkers reject as "Western," Corrêa de Oliveira criticizes as explicitly non-Western and alien to Western civilization: "pagan" philosophy, secularism, democracy, socialism and communism, and a Christianity that has betrayed its principles. For Corrêa de Oliveira, Christianity has been penetrated by the "smoke of Satan."[12] Similar to the Muslim thinkers he aims at a political realm that is ordered in accordance with and subjected to divine law. In essence, Corrêa de Oliveira associates most of the elements, with the exception of capitalism and imperialism, with anti-Western influences he rejects. If one would replace "Christendom" in Corrêa de Oliveira's polemics with "Islam," most of the Muslim thinkers referred to above would be in striking agreement with his ultraconservative Christian critique.

In short, these polemical approaches treat *The West* as an empty vessel that can be filled, for various, although inconsistent, reasons, with whatever is rejected, or, in the case of Corrêa de Oliveira, appreciated. As implied in the introduction, academic works are not always free from such polemics. Thus, *The West* as an analytical tool is of limited use. Unless the polemics itself is the focus of the analysis, at the very least, caution is mandatory.

---

9 Qutb, *Social Justice in Islam*, 270, 275.
10 Sadiki, *The Search for Arab Democracy*, 97.
11 Khomeini, "Islamic Government," 27.
12 Corrêa de Oliveira, *Revolution and Counter-Revolution*, 145.

4.2 Legitimacy, Rights, and Justice

For good reasons, one could discuss the three concepts legitimacy, rights, and justice separately. If one follows Max Weber, who is not interested in the distinction between a state's legitimate and illegitimate use of force against its citizens, one could indeed discuss legitimacy without any references to discourses on rights or justice.[13] Yet, our concern is not legitimacy itself, but legitimacy crisis and the transformation of a perceived legitimacy to a perceived illegitimacy. In an ideal situation, this transformative process results in a new foundation of legitimacy. In less ideal situations, old and new legitimacies may clash violently. For the perception of legitimacy, concepts of justice and injustice, and, to a certain degree, rights are essential, even though these concepts are not always theoretically reflected or internalized.

As illustrated with reference to Ronald Dworkin, in the context of the liberal constitutional state that is based on constitutionally protected rights, the relationship between rights and legitimacy is obvious. Yet, even in the democratic constitutional state the right to (violent) resistance remains in place for exceptional cases in which legal means of defense fail.[14] For the Islamic context, however, Abdolkarim Soroush suggests that the discourse is predominantly duty bound because the "language of religion (especially that of Islam as exemplified by the Qur'an and the Tradition) is the language of duties, not of rights."[15] By contrast, al-Afghani relates (illegitimate) despotic government to the deprivation of the subjects' rights.[16] Thus, although in the Islamic context rights discourses are less prominent, the concept of rights is certainly not absent. The fact that the relationship between rights and duties is less explored does not undermine the philosophical connection between rights and duties. Although these discourses may subordinate a rights language to other values, the idea that basic rights have been violated is definitely present, even though the rights idea is not prominent.

If one reassesses the language of duties briefly, one can identify an element that connects Faraj, Qutb, and Khomeini with John of Salisbury and William of Ockham, although in a rather odd way. Both John of Salisbury and William of Ockham emphasize the duty to resist. For Ockham, having the power but not resisting a heretic pope means failing in one's duties, indeed, in one's religious duties. Yet, in John of Salisbury, the duty to resist and if necessary even to kill a

---

13 Weber, *Wirtschaft und Gesellschaft*, 822.
14 Grimm, "Das staatliche Gewaltmonopol," 25–6.
15 Soroush, "The Sense and Essence of Secularism," 62,
16 Al-Afghani, "Despotic Government," 22a. Although expressed without invoking any explicit rights-language, his argument corresponds with the Zaydi jurist Ibn al-Murtada.

tyrannical ruler is both a religious duty (towards God) and a political duty (towards the Republic). Corresponding to Ockham's duty of fighting a heretic pope, Khomeini stresses the "duty to remove from the life of Muslim society all traces of *kufr* and [to] destroy them."[17] For Faraj, establishing an Islamic state is "the duty of all Muslims."[18] Although the medieval Christian and the twentieth century Muslim thinkers significantly differ in their judgments what qualifies as *kufr* or heresy (John of Salisbury speaks about injustice), they draw from the ruler's neglected duties the conclusion of an individual duty to resist and to remove the existing government.

In this context, it is worth recalling Henry Shue's intervention that people "can certainly have rights that they do not know they have."[19] This observation is also true for all premodern discourses. At least in the Christian contexts, even if "rights" are not explicitly stressed, over time, a rights-language becomes more prominent. In other words, even if rights or rather the reflection on rights is not at the forefront of a conflict's language, it does not mean that they do not exist. Contrary to the juridified discourses of the liberal constitutional state, in premodern or authoritarian states, rights and the violation of basic rights are rather judged according to a moral law and moral doubts that reflect on situations or actions that are perceived as unjust.[20] These moral doubts reflect a disagreement between the positive law and the perception of justice. Moral doubts may be based on (secular) ethics or on religiously informed morality through which norms of justice are expressed. The transition from perceived legitimacy to perceived illegitimacy, thus, corresponds to the moral collapse of the old legitimacy.[21] The substance of moral doubts, whether articulated as such or not, is the existence of basic rights. Following Henry Shue, these basic rights include the right to subsistence. Shue's position corresponds to Enrique Dussel's. Dussel relates a legitimacy crisis to a "life reproduction crisis" for the "victim" because "[i]n the victim, dominated or excluded by the system, the living, empirical, concrete human subjectivity is revealed, it appears as 'interpellation' in the latest instance: it is the subject who can no longer live and cries out in pain," but also involve security and liberty, including "the liberty of participation."[22]

Although the principal narrative of the liberal constitutional state aims at the exclusion of religious reasoning, the implementation of religious values is

---

17 Khomeini, "Islamic Government," 48.
18 Faraj, *The Forgotten Duty*, in Youssef, *Revolt Against Modernity*, 149.
19 Shue, *Basic Rights*, 72.
20 Hennis, "Legitimacy," 84.
21 Dussel, *Ethics of Liberation*, 403.
22 Shue, *Basic Rights*, 9, 71. Dussel, *Ethics of Liberations*, 384, 405.

not uncommon in democratic settings. In critique of the dominant public reason argument Bryan T. McGraw notes, "while religion's political engagement can pose problems, the public reason argument is overly apprehensive and neglects the way in which religion and religious political parties in particular can help secure political legitimacy, not undermine it."[23] This view is also in agreement with the later Rawls.[24] If one bears these reservations in mind, although they apparently contradict the secularity postulate, except for the absence of legal channels that protect (moral) rights and allow for non-violent means of conflict resolution, the first scenario is not too different from the reasoning in the context of the liberal constitutional state.

If one abstracts from the fact that in the premodern context legitimacy is tied to God because, ultimately, all power comes from God, one can identify cases in which religiously framed morality (without explicit claims for religious rule or an alternation of divine rule) represents primarily the standard of justice as expressed in the concept of divine justice. The more explicit interaction between religion and legitimacy are addressed in the next section. Some of the previously discussed authors or movements are of a hybrid character, i.e. either one finds initially elements in their reasoning that fit into both schemes or their reasoning has changed over time, usually by moving towards a stronger emphasis of religious goals. Another outcome of transformative processes involves the possibility that the new legitimacy may turn into a new hegemony. To phrase it with Enrique Dussel, "the victims who were once homeless end up installing beautiful fences to protect their newly acquired comfort from others who are the new poor,"[25] the new excluded, or the new heterodoxy.

To emphasize cases in which a legitimacy crisis is based on the deprivation of rights or other versions of oppression, the most obvious cases in the premodern context are William of Pagula, Ibn Khaldun, John of Salisbury, and, to some degree, William of Ockham, the Nizari Isma'ilis, and the early Kharijites in league with 'Ali but also the early Muslim community. Ironically, although we have focused with Nizam al-Mulk on the conflict between the Seljuqs and the Nizari Isma'ilis, Nizam al-Mulk also invokes the Arabic saying, "A kingdom may last while there is irreligion, but it will not endure when there is oppres-

---

[23] Bryan T. McGraw, "Religious Parties and the Problem of Democratic Political Legitimacy," *Critical Review of International Social and Political Philosophy* 17, no. 3 (2014): 290.
[24] John Rawls, "The Idea of Public Reason Revisited," *The University of Chicago Law Review* 64, no. 3 (1996): 765–807. Also published as the final chapter in John Rawls, *Political Liberalism*, expanded edition (New York: Columbia University Press, 2005), 373–385.
[25] Dussel, *Ethics of Liberation*, 427.

sion."²⁶ Thus, although he frames the conflict with the Nizari Isma'ilis as a conflict over orthodoxy (even though it is primarily a conflict over power), he admits that oppression and particularly the deprivation of property rights is more harmful to the stability of the political realm than irreligion. Among the modern thinkers and movements one finds similar elements in the liberation theologians, al-Afghani, Shari'ati, and in some of the groups that were in league with Khomeini without sharing in his goal of a theocratic state that is ordered in accordance with his interpretation of divine law as the only expression of justice and just order.

For William of Pagula, the key issue is the people's deprivation of their right to subsistence, which included their right to property but also their right to free movement. The latter is violated through the king's ability to demand forced labor. What William describes here the priests at the Medellín Conference call "the violence of hunger."²⁷ Similar to the Latin American priests, William cannot do much more than appealing to the king's good will. Religious language is used both as an expression of justice and as a means to make the king see sense—by threatening him with negative consequences in this and in the afterlife.²⁸ William of Pagula represents also an early case of a conflict between legality and legitimacy. Parliament has granted the king rights William perceives as unjust and harmful. His critique of the violence committed against the people resembles Ignacio Ellacuría's notion of "legalized violence," which he regards as "the worst violence of all."²⁹ Ibn Khaldun, without an explicit reference to a conflict between legality and legitimacy, emphasizes a similar conflict as represented by William of Pagula: the injustice committed by the denial of rights, particularly property rights and forced labor, which is essentially a deprivation of one's freedom and one's right to subsistence. For Ibn Khaldun, depriving the people of their rights necessarily results in rebellion. Without making it explicit, the people take the basic rights, Henry Shue has identified, for granted—with the exception of the right to participate, which glimpses through in William of Pagula's notion that the people have the right to take a new king. Yet, as soon as a more just order is restored, the people's right to participate dissolves. For the premodern

---

26 Nizam al Mulk, *The Book of Government*, 1.2.1.
27 Peruvian Bishops' Commission for Social Action, "Latin America," 81.
28 This is basically the same strategy as applied by Pope Francis to threaten the mafia. Pope Francis, however, stopped at threatening with hell, whereas William suggests that the people are in their moral rights if they rebel. Lizzy Davies, "Pope Francis to Mafia: Repent or 'End up in Hell'" (http://www.theguardian.com/world/2014/mar/22/pope-francis-warns-mafiosi-to-repent-or-end-up-in-hell) 21.03.2014.
29 Ellacuría, *Freedom Made Flesh*, 198. See also Câmara, "Violence in the Modern World," 51.

context, however, the lack of consciousness for the right to participate is not surprising. This right or rather the disregard of the right to participate, in addition to the right to life and subsistence, has been emphasized by all liberation theologians discussed. Camilo Torres, for instance, considers a governmental authority that is only legitimized by twenty percent (the elite) of the people both "illegitimate and tyrannical."[30] From a different angle, José Comblin reemphasizes the right to participate by the normative claim that society must be "based on liberty and free agreement."[31]

Whereas the right to participate is not prominent in the premodern and modern examples of Islamic thinking narrated above, a similar emphasis on the right to property and freedom exists. Similar to Ibn Khaldun, although phrases in a different language, al-Afghani associates the people's deprivation of their property rights and freedom, including forced labor, with versions of despotic government, whether domestically or foreign (colonial). He compares a despotic government to a highway robber: The despot as the highway robber "holds up travelers and steals their money, their provisions, their clothes which protect them from the heat and cold, and the other necessities of life, leaving them in the wilderness or desert bare-foot, naked and hungry, with all resources cut off."[32] For al-Afghani the response to despotic government has to be resistance and eventually the overthrow of such rule.

The violation of property rights and other socio-economic rights is also in the center of the conflict between ʿUthman and the early Kharijites and Shiʿites. They revolt because justice is frequently obstructed. Although framed in religious language, the early Kharijites see ʿUthman's legitimacy jeopardized because under his rule, the Muslim community has become a corrupt and oppressive regime. Soon thereafter, the conflict is no longer about socio-economic issues, but has transformed into a conflict over religious truth. Thus, Salim Ibn Dhakwan accuses the radicalized Kharijites precisely of having turned socio-economic issues into a problem over religious truth.[33]

John of Salisbury offers a broader perspective that is based on the explicit assumption that security is essential to a just and well-ordered realm.[34] In the corrupt and tyrannical realm, the people's security and their subsistence are disturbed. John's corrupt system shows features of structural violence as emphasized by liberation theologians. For John, corruption and tyranny also resemble

---

30 Torres, "Message to the Christian," 368.
31 Comblin, *The Church and the National Security State*, 120.
32 Al-Afghani, "Despotic Government," 22a.
33 Sālim Ibn Dhakwān, *Sīrat Sālim*, 3.133.
34 John of Salisbury, *Policraticus*, 3.1.

a violation of the overarching principle of divine justice. John's theory suggests, although his religiously infused language emphasizes duties, fundamental rights that belong to the people. John, however, is also a hybrid case because he regards corruption and tyranny hindrances to salvation. Moreover, he emphasizes both the responsibility towards the earthly republic and the responsibility towards God. John also invokes the idea of tyranny as a divine means to punish and to correct a sinful people.

Although for different reasons, William of Ockham is another hybrid case. The main reason for his hybridity, however, lies less in his general argument, but rather in his target, the pope. Whereas he frequently refers to rights the people/believers have been deprived off, he sees the outcome as a result of the papacy's corruption that has turned sound faith into heresy and heresy into an expression of sound faith.[35] Nonetheless, Ockham's main concern is political: oppression, seizure of property and rights, disturbance of peace, tyranny, and so on. Yet, compared to "secular" tyranny, papal tyranny is worse because it abuses faith for the oppression of the people. In this sense, Ockham's underlying argument relates to Shari'ati's and Comblin's. Both accuse the religious establishment of having invented a religion of oppression. Although neither of them leaves the political sphere, they are forced to respond with a religious-theological argument, not with a political argument.

4.3 Legitimacy and Religion

Ockham's main concern, the abuse of religion, in a "heretical" interpretation, as a means of oppression, leads us to more concrete relationships between legitimacy and religion. If pushed to the extreme, a legitimacy that bases itself primarily on a religious truth claim undermines the two chief principles of politics: necessity and compromise. Logically, it is impossible to compromise on a claimed absolute truth, even if it is only *my* truth and not the truth of *others*. If I have the power to enforce *my* truth, it turns hegemonic and oppressive; if I do not have the power to enforce *my* truth, I get nothing and may become a target of coercion and persecution. In the political sphere, the ability to compromise means, although one does not necessarily get all one wants, most likely one gets more than one would get without being willing to compromise.[36] This fundamental truth about politics is not limited to democratic settings, although it is

---

35 Ockham, *The Power of Emperors and Popes*, chap. 7.
36 Robert E. Goodin, *On Settling* (Princeton: Princeton University Press, 2012), 52.

more obvious there, but applies to politics in general. Even in the premodern context, rulers had to take the needs and moral rights of their subjects into account. If a ruler neglects and violates the subjects' moral rights, his rule turns into tyranny, which marks the end of politics. This is also the fundamental message behind John of Salisbury's "whom it is permitted to flatter, it is permitted to slay."[37] If one cannot speak truth to power anymore, the minimal room for public debate that exists in the premodern context has been taking away. The ruler does now longer take into account that he is as dependent of his people as the people depend on him. A similar thought has been expressed in numerous Muslim mirrors for princes. The general narrative suggests, if justice is not restored, the ruler's realm is jeopardized. For instance, *The Sea of Precious Virtues*, a twelfth century anonymous Persian mirror for princes, illustrates the correlation between justice and stability with the story of King Bahran who "used to commit tyranny, oppression, and injustice, and would not heed counsel." Eventually, he has to learn his lesson: "Know therefore that kingship depends upon the populace."[38]

Superficially, mundane tyranny has not much in common with the absolute religious truth claims introduced at the beginning of this section. Yet, both fundamentally undermine the core principles of the political. In a sense, if one particular truth claim is enforced, the (violent) oppression of those who do not share into the very interpretation, whether they follow a different creed or a different understanding of the same creed, is likely. In this context, religious belief is also a means for inclusion and exclusion. Inclusion and exclusion based on a religion also undermines the freedom of religion and, as Brian J. Grim and Roger Finke have shown, usually results in an increase in violent conflicts. Even if a formal separation of state and religion exists, states may be tempted to secure an alliance with the dominant religion because "such alliances secure additional support for the state and reduce the risk of the dominant religion serving as an organizational vehicle for challenging the state."[39] Simultaneously, the state may foster expectations it cannot fulfill, whether it is the implementation of religious doctrine or socio-economic expectations the state has nourished.[40]

Such a scenario does not only allow a state in league with a religious creed to coerce all those who disagree; it also allows members of the hegemonic creed

---

37 John of Salisbury, *Policraticus*, 3.15.
38 *The Sea of Precious Virtues (Baḥr al-Favāʾid): A Medieval Islamic Mirror for Princes*, trans. from the Persian, ed. Julie Scott Meisami (Salt Lake City: University of Utah Press, 1991), 7.2.119. The story of Bahran is a rather common example in Persian mirrors for princes. See, for instance, Nizam al-Mulk, *The Book of Government*, 1.4.5–24.
39 Brian and Finke, *The Price of Freedom Denied*, 10, 51 (quotation), 71.
40 Akbarzadeh and Saeed, "Islam and Politics," 5.

to persecute and to discriminate again fellow citizens or subjects who do not share or are suspected of not sharing their belief. In tendency, this scenario is well illustrated by the Latin American situation narrated previously. The core example may be seen in the TFP movement that fosters an alliance with the military juntas to enforce their interpretation of Christianity. TFP, however, exemplifies a paradox case because their ultimate goal is the restoration of a utopian version of medieval Christendom that gives the Roman papacy the same power over the temporal sphere as popes like Boniface VIII or John XXII claimed to possess. As in the Middles Ages, their ultimate goal is not in the interest of those in political power, whether it is a military junta or an authoritarian regime more generally. From a political perspective, even if an alliance between the state and dominant religious organizations is wanted and is seen as a means to generate support and stability, such an alliance suffers under potential conflicts between political necessity and religious law or faith; eventually, the state is endangered of losing its legitimacy in the eye of the faithful. Although taken to the extreme, ʿAbd al-Salam Faraj illustrates such a case.

As apparent in the Christian medieval conflicts between ecclesiastical and temporal power, the alliance between organizations of faith and political authority may also turn against the temporal authority itself, namely when the spiritual authority gains influence and power over the political sphere. Whereas temporal and ecclesiastical power join forces against an internal threat (exemplified through the Cathars) or against an assumed external threat (the Crusades), the ecclesiastical power can also turn against the temporal power, demanding superiority over the spiritual *and* temporal sphere. This claim finds its sharpened expression in Boniface VIII's promulgation "that it is altogether necessary to salvation for every human creature to be subjected to the Roman Pontiff."[41] Giles of Rome underscores the claim by arguing that there is no justice outside the Church. This understanding is also visible in James of Viterbo, who equates temporal power that does not accept ecclesiastical supremacy with tyranny. Ironically, Qutb, al-Banna, and Khomeini echo almost exactly Boniface's, Giles's, and James's language and claim. Here, justice and legitimate political order is explicitly tied to the enforcement of a particular interpretation of divine law. In their eyes, without all aspects of divine law enforced, legitimacy cannot exist. Thus, room for negotiation and compromise does not exist either.

In most instances, the absolute claim cannot be properly enforced and because compromise is impossible, the result is violent conflict. In the conflict between temporal and ecclesiastical power, the violent results have been illustrat-

---

[41] *Unam Sanctam*, in Tierney, *The Crisis of Church & State*, 189.

ed with William of Ockham, who uses similar arguments as have been brought forth by the papal party in the reverse. The tyranny of the temporal power is now the tyranny of the papacy. Yet, using the same religion in a similar context for opposite claims renders the supposed teachings of the religion meaningless; indeed, it undermines faith and religion itself.

A problem that fundamentally relates to religion as the only or at least the main foundation of legitimacy is the problem of inclusion and exclusion. The strategy of denouncing the other as heretic, apostate, or non-believer is and (unfortunately) remains a very successful tool in order to secure support. To some extent, this method has been employed by almost all premodern and modern authors and movements narrated throughout the book. In this context, however, it is worth noting that this approach goes hand in hand with redefining orthodoxy (inclusion) and heterodoxy (exclusion). While this approach is already visible in Nizam al-Mulk, Ibn Taymiyya adds a new dimension to it. A person who qualifies under normal circumstances just as a sinner turns under the conditions of the Mongol threat into an unbeliever or, worse, an apostate. A similar method is visible in the Christian context. The Cathars or other opponents are marked as heretics, unbelievers, or enemies of the faith. As Herbert Grundmann notes, the stereotyped accusations of heresy created heresies that were never reality.[42]

Yet, it is worth noting that in the twentieth century Latin American context discussed, although it is still applied, this method loses most of its power, whereas it seems to gain speed in the Islamic setting. It appears almost as an irony of history that the language used during the Crusades that dehumanizes the enemy and portrays him or her as pagan, idolater, or infidel has become a common feature among contemporary Islamists' *jihad* theories, whereas in the Christian context, after a few centuries, the crusading idea has become a blunt sword—despite the occasionally applied "crusades against communism" language that has been used only by defenders of the status quo.[43]

If one looks at the problem of legitimacy based on religion in a more general way, the first question one needs to ask is who has authority over defining ortho-

---

42 Grundmann, "Der Typus des Ketzers," 325.
43 Although this volume does not cover modern European discourses, it is worth noting that Crusading rhetoric had a short revival following the French Revolution. See Adam Knobler, "Holy Wars, Empires, and the Portability of the Past: The Modern Uses of Medieval Crusades," *Comparative Studies in Society and History* 48, no. 2 (2006): 293–325. It needs to be noted, although it is outside the book's scope, that the crusading rhetoric had a short revival under the Bush administration shortly after the September 11 attacks in New York and Washington, D.C. See, for instance, Jonathan Lusthaus, "Religion and State Violence: Legitimation in Israel, the USA and Iran," *Contemporary Politics* 17, no. 1 (2011): 6–8.

doxy and the power to enforce it? Moreover, what are the consequences of an attempt to enforce the hegemonic interpretation coercively? While the problem of defining is a lesser problem in premodern context, simply because the authorities who possess defining power have a better power base, in the modern and contemporary context, it is a serious problem. As soon as it is assumed that the religious authorities that is responsible for a certain ruling or interpretation is in league with or has been bought by the political authority the problem becomes more severe. The likelihood that the "authoritative" interpretation is consider unsound and is answered by a counter-interpretation should not be underrated. Qutb and al-Banna add another dimension to the problem: the religious truth they set absolute is based on their subjective reading of the Qur'an and the Hadith. A similar approach is not uncommon among evangelical Christians. Yet, "the attribution of ultimate sovereignty to God is of no practical significance until some agency is identified that can authoritatively decide what God's decrees are."[44] Without such an accepted authority, the legitimacy of as state lives under the permanent threat of subjective counter-interpretations that potentially undermine political legitimacy. Of course, it is rather a different question whether legitimacy based on one religious faith is desirable at all because it potentially undermines religious freedom and gives room for violent conflict. Another question, however, is whether the radicalization of thinkers like al-Banna or Qutb could have been prevented by a state that were more responsive to their (valid) socio-economic concerns.

4.4 Patterns Legitimizing Political Violence

Corresponding to the previous discussion on legitimacy, the patterns legitimizing political violence follow in general two designs: either they respond to conflicts predominantly fought over socio-economic and political injustices or they are articulated as conflicts over orthodoxy. If the conflict over socio-economic or political injustices escalates, it may turn into a conflict that is expressed as a conflict over orthodoxy. Conflicts over injustice are anti-hegemonic conflicts, whereas conflicts expressed as conflicts over orthodoxy may be hegemonic as well as anti-hegemonic. This section unfolds the main variants of the two main patterns.

1. Conflicts over Injustice: While almost all anti-hegemonic discourses discussed throughout the book emphasize other issues than religion itself as the cause of

---

44 Ka Ka Khel, "Legitimacy of Authority in Islam," 178.

conflict, the discourses, nonetheless, had to be framed in religious language. Particularly in the premodern context, religion represented the only available standard of social justice that was available in a particular cultural-religious context.

A. *Restoration of Justice:* At least for the discourses we have discussed most of the anti-hegemonic discourses aim at the restoration of justice. Thus, they aim at ending (unbearable forms of) oppression. As soon as the main cause of conflict is resolved, the legitimacy crisis is over; legitimacy is restored. We have illustrated this fundamental lesson through numerous examples. To stress this pattern with one particular example, Ibn Jamaʿa advises the ruler in case of revolts caused by injustice to remove the injustice and only to fight the rebels in case the rebels continue to rebel after justice has been restored.[45] The frequency of this advice, however, indicates that rulers did not necessarily follow this advice; eventually the conflict escalated violently. In the premodern context, however, radicalization is likely to take a religious coloring, whereas in the modern context, the radicalization may not necessarily mean religious radicalization. It may take the form of a violent struggle for regime change in the fullest political sense. Instead of just replacing the ruler, the violent struggle aims at the establishment of a different form of government. Aiming at a religious state may be one but by no means the *only* possible solution to the conflict (in case of a successful establishment of a religious state, the outcome may be religious hegemony and eventually oppression as illustrated through post-revolutionary Iran).

B. *Regime Change:* Particularly the examples taken from liberation theology imply that religious radicalization is not a necessary consequence. Yet, the conflicts may radicalize politically: demands for structural reform may turn into demands for structural revolution, i.e. regime change. Camilo Torres illustrates such a case of political radicalization. For him, the two subcultures, the elites and the masses, speak and exist in different subcultural realms and are incapable of any form of meaningful dialogue or non-violent conflict resolution.[46]

C. *Transition to a Conflict over Orthodoxy:* If injustice still persists and has not been removed, the conflict is endangered of radicalizing into a conflict that is eventually fought and expressed as a conflict over religious doctrine and its enforcement, although this is not a necessary consequence. Thus, the conflict changes its nature by its articulation as a conflict over religious interpretation. The early Kharijites may serve as one example. The transformation of a conflict that is eventually expressed in questions of orthodoxy versus heterodoxy

---

45 Ibn Jamaʿa, *Taḥrīr al-aḥkām* 16.1.
46 Torres, "Two Subcultures," 258–9.

marks also the transition towards the second pattern, conflicts articulated as conflicts over orthodoxy.

Although only the second radicalization explicitly transforms a political conflict into a religious conflict, both radicalizations potentially leave the realm of politics or rather turn the conflict into the right of the stronger, as expressed through Thrasymachus in Plato's *Republic*.[47] Depending on the outcome, the previously anti-hegemonic movement may turn into the new hegemony. This transformation refers back to Dussel's dilemma: the former victims create, in defense of their newly acquired privileges, new versions of exclusion.

2. Conflicts over Orthodoxy: Conflicts over orthodoxy or rather conflicts articulated as conflicts over orthodoxy may appear as hegemonic or anti-hegemonic conflicts. In the latter case, although the conflict may start out as an anti-hegemonic conflict, the conflict is likely to show signs of hegemonic aspirations.

A. *Defense or Expansion of Power:* In this category fall almost all premodern hegemonic conflicts over power. The emphasis lies on power or domination, not on religion *per se*. Whether it is the Seljuq Empire or the Church, both claim for themselves the power to define what qualifies as orthodoxy and heterodoxy. In cases of conflict, the real or imagined threat is portrayed as heterodoxy. In this context it is worth noting that in the premodern Muslim context, after Islam has itself established, at least in the Sunni context, *jihad* is less an instrument of conversion, but rather a tool in order to extend the territory (resources) and to demand submission to power. Conversion is not at the forefront. Other expressions of submission (paying taxes) are sufficient. If a legitimacy crisis already exists, whether caused by an internal or an external threat, the stress on and the enforcement of orthodoxy becomes more prominent. This is true for threats to power in the premodern Islamic world as it is true for the conflicts between the temporal and ecclesiastical powers in the Christian context. Ironically, the main reasoning of the medieval Church for absolute power over the temporal and the spiritual sphere shows some striking parallels to both al-Banna and Qutb but also and even more so to Khomeini. Whereas post-revolutionary Khomeini falls into the first category of defense and expansion of power, al-Banna, Qutb, and post-revolutionary Khomeini exemplify conflicts phrased as conflicts over orthodoxy corresponding to the category of hegemonic aspirations.

B. *Hegemonic Aspirations:* Hegemonic aspiration relates to religious movements that start out as anti-hegemonic movements but do not simply aim at

---

[47] George F. Hourani, "Thrasymachus' Definition of Justice in Plato's 'Republic'," *Phronesis* 7, no. 2 (1962): 110–120.

the removal of socio-economic and political injustice. Hegemony is the end. With respect to their aspirations, they appear to be more prone to violent means than other movements discussed previously. For al-Banna and Qutb, who exemplify unfulfilled hegemonic aspirations, it is worth noting that both started out as reformists, but radicalized over time. To a certain degree, although without the explicit end of a religious state, they moved through a similar radicalization as Camilo Torres. Hegemonic aspiration also implies the creation of an identity that is based almost entirely of a religious belief-system that is considered superior and the only true one. The opponent is portrayed as the enemy of the faith and can be fought out of the suspicion that he or she does not follow the same spiritual conviction. Thus, compromising is not an option. Moreover, this perception goes hand in hand with the belief that a truly religious life is only possible in a state that enforces religious law. Otherwise, the believers have "to obey [the system's] erroneous ways." The irreligious system forces the believer to "serve human lords instead of the Almighty Lord."[48] Thought through, an aspirational hegemonic movement aims at the replacement of a regime that is perceived as oppressive. Even if political oppression has been removed, it remains oppressive because it is irreligious. The new regime is likely to oppress, coerce, or persecute the new religious nonconformists.

Some of these features are also present in the rhetoric of the Crusades, particularly in the later stages in which the "enemy" becomes more and more dehumanized and portrayed as the Antichrist. Another feature that shows some parallels to contemporary Islamist movements can be seen in the Church's aspiration for establishing and manifesting her power basis at home as well as the aspiration for expanding territorially to the Holy Lands. These aspirations go hand in hand with a transformation of religious principles from an emphasis on *caritas* to *potestas*.

4.5 Implications for Conflict Prevention and Resolution

In terms of conflict resolution or conflict prevention, it is necessary to understand the real causes behind a conflict. Even if a conflict already underwent the transformative process from a conflict over socio-economic and political injustice to a conflict over religious doctrine, the original causes of conflict are nonetheless important. The original causes of a conflict can be resolved. The best conflict prevention, however, is the lesson of old, namely the removal of in-

---

[48] Qutb, *Milestones*, 55.

justice as soon as a conflict emerges. Yet, the easiest solution is often the most difficult and unlikely to achieve. Generating support through religious means in order to access and to maintain power may be too tempting, despite the most likely long term negative effects as outlines by Grim's and Finke's study because, as quoted at the beginning of this book, "[r]eligions, by whatever names they are called, all resemble each other. No agreement and no reconciliation are possible between these religions and philosophy. Religion imposes on man its faith and its belief, whereas philosophy frees him in totally or in part."[49]

This book focused on two religious cultures. Both religious cultures are monotheist religions, or, as Jan Assmann calls them, "counter-religious" or "secondary religious."[50] Consequently, this book does not shed any light on the question whether monotheist religions are more prone to violence than non-monotheist religions, as suggested by Assmann. In addition, this book does not contribute to the questions whether other means of identity and of exclusion and inclusion (skin-color, race, or ethnicity) are similar conflict-loaded as conflicts that are expressed in religious language and transformed into conflicts over religious doctrine.[51] Yet, what this book illustrates is the significance of socioeconomic and political reasons for violent conflict often portrayed as religious conflicts. Independently whether the conflict is framed in religious or secular language and independently whether a conflict is eventually perceived as a conflict over religious truth, Ronald Dworkin normative claims quoted at the beginning of this book still hold true if adjusted to the particular contexts discussed.[52] Applied to the discourses discussed throughout the book, if a government or ruler does not treat the people with equal concern and respect or treats one group nobler than another, a situation of inclusion and exclusion exists. While in premodern or traditional societies a certain degree of inequality and exclusion is generally accepted, there are limits to acceptable inequality and exclusion. The essential limits are usually expressed in a violation of the rights Henry Shue identifies as rights of subsistence. In this context Enrique Dussel's discussion of the "new emerging social subjects" that discover new rights is of similar relevance.[53] Even though in both premodern contexts the newly discovered rights

---

49 Al-Afghānī, "Answer of Jamāl ad-Dīn to Renan," 187.
50 Assmann, *Moses the Egyptian*, 170.
51 Anthony Oberschall's analysis of ethnic conflicts, *Conflict and Peace Building in Divided Societies: Responses to Ethnic Violence* (London: Routledge, 2007), 1–40, however, suggests strong similarities between conflicts that are framed in a language of ethnicity and conflicts that are expressed in religious language.
52 Dworkin, *Taking Rights Seriously*, 272–3.
53 Dussel, *Ethics of Liberation*, 407.

have initially no permanence and violent response only lasts as long as the unbearable crisis lasts (the subjects do not identify as victims of structural violence), in the modern context unbearable oppression may act, although unintentionally, as a long-lasting game-changer. Removing the existing socioeconomic and political injustices will most like end a true legitimacy crisis as described by Wilhelm Hennis. Unless a conflict turns into a conflict over orthodoxy, the conflict, independently of the language in which it is framed, remains entirely a political problem that asks for political solutions. Although Kippenberg's suggestions that a religious interpretation alters the nature of a conflict is valid, the lesson for the political scientist or political analyst is not to take the language in which a conflict is expressed as the cause of the conflict itself. Thus, current public and academic discourses that that emphasize Islam or any other religion as cause of a conflict, most like miss a conflict's core and any conflict resolution strategy that derives from such an interpretation seems to be of limited success.

The initial idea for this book was born out an increasing uneasiness over the prevalent language of "Islamic terrorism," which resembles an interpretation of a political conflict in religious terms. Akhar Ahmed's recent study implies that the current conflicts phrased in the language of religious terrorism are everything but conflicts based on religion. Rather, Ahmed suggests that the conflicts he analyzes are primarily conflicts between the center and the periphery, in which "[c]entral governments cynically and ruthlessly exploited the war on terror to pursue their own agenda against the periphery."[54] Although without being expressed in the language of terrorism, this interpretation also holds true for most of the modern cases discussed in the book but also at least partly for the premodern cases explored. Yet, a comparison of premodern and modern cases also demonstrates that the use of religion for political means shows striking similarities not only across the ages, but also across religious cultures. Thus, looking into the past sheds a different light on contemporary conflicts. Although students of history learn that history does not repeat itself, looking into the past may nonetheless prove insightful for understanding the present and present conflicts particularly.

---

54 Akbar Ahmed, *The Thistle and the Drone: How America's War on Terror Became a Global War on Tribal Islam* (Washington, D.C.: Brookings Institution Press, 2013), 9.

Bibliography

Abalos, David. "The Medellin Conference." *Cross Currents* 19 (1969): 113–132.
'Abd al-Salām Faraj, Muhammad. *The Forgotten Duty.* In Michael Youssef. *Revolt Against Modernity: Muslim Zealots and the West*, 146–177. Leiden: Brill, 1985.
Abdin, A. Z. al-. "The Political Thought of Ḥasan al-Bannā." *Islamic Studies* 28, no. 3 (1989): 219–234.
Abdullah, M. Amin. "Introductory Elaboration on the Roots of Religious Violence: The Complexity of Islamic Radicalism." In *Innerer Friede und die Überwindung der Gewalt: Religiöse Traditionen auf dem Prüfstand. V. Internationales Rudolf-Otto Symposion, Marburg*, edited by Hans-Martin Barth and Christoph Elsas, 150–158. Hamburg: EB-Verlag, 2007.
Abgral, Jean-Marie. *Soul Snatchers: The Mechanics of Cults.* New York: Algora, 1996.
Abrahamian, Ervand. "Khomeini: Fundamentalist or Populist?" *New Left Review* 186 (1991): 102–119.
Abrahamian, Ervand. "The Guerrilla Movement in Iran, 1963–77." In *Iran, a Revolution in Turmoil*, edited by Afshar Haleh, 149–174. Albany: State University of New York Press, 1985.
Abrahamian, Ervand. *A History of Modern Iran.* Cambridge: Cambridge University Press, 2008.
Abrahamian, Ervand. *Iran Between Two Revolutions.* Princeton: Princeton University Press, 1982.
Abou El Fadl, Khaled. *Rebellion and Violence in Islamic Law.* Cambridge: Cambridge University Press, 2001.
Afghānī, Sayyid Jamāl ad-Dīn al-. "Answer of Jamāl ad-Dīn to Renan." In Nikki Keddie, *An Islamic Response to Imperialism: Political and Religious Writings of Sayyid Jamāl ad-Dīn "al-Afghānī,"* 181–189, 2nd ed. Berkeley: University of California Press, 1983.
Afghānī, Sayyid Jamāl ad-Dīn al-. "Despotic Government." In L. M. Kenny, "Al-Afghānī on Types of Despotic Government." *Journal of the American Oriental Society* 86, no. 1 (1966): 19–27.
Afghānī, Sayyid Jamāl ad-Dīn al-. "Lecture on Teaching and Learning." In Nikki Keddie, *An Islamic Response to Imperialism: Political and Religious Writings of Sayyid Jamāl ad-Dīn "al-Afghānī,"* 101–108, 2nd ed. Berkeley: University of California Press, 1983.
Afghānī, Sayyid Jamāl ad-Dīn al-. *Réfutation des Matérialistes*, treduction sur la 3e édition Arabe avec introduction et notes par A.-M. Goichon. Paris: Paul Geuthner, 1942.
Afghānī, Sayyid Jamāl ad-Dīn al-. "The Reign of Terror in Persia." *The Contemporary Review* 61 (1892): 238–248.
Afghānī, Sayyid Jamāl ad-Dīn al-. "The Truth about the Neicheiri Sect and an Explanation of the Neicherie" [Refutation of the Materialists]. In Nikki Keddie. *An Islamic Response to Imperialism: Political and Religious Writings of Sayyid Jamāl ad-Dīn "al-Afghānī,"* 130–180, 2nd ed. Berkeley: University of California Press, 1983.
Aguilar, Mario I. "Cardinal Raúl Silva Henríquez, the Catholic Church, and the Pinochet Regime, 1973–1980: Public Responses to a National Security State." *The Catholic Historical Review* 89, no. 4 (2003): 712–731.
Ahmed, Akbar. *The Thistle and the Drone: How America's War on Terror Became a Global War on Tribal Islam.* Washington, D.C.: Brookings Institution Press, 2013.

Ahmed, Safdar. *Reform and Modernity in Islam: The Philosophical, Cultural and Political Discourses among Muslim Reformers.* London: I. B. Tauris, 2013.
Akbarzadeh, Shahram and Abdullah Saeed. "Islam and Politics." In *Islam and Political Legitimacy*, edited by Shahram Akbarzadeh and Abdullah Saeed, 1–13. London: Routledge Curzon, 2003.
Alatas, Syed Farid. "Rejecting Islamism and the Need for Concepts Within the Islamic Tradition." In *Islamism: Contested Perspectives on Political Islam*, edited by Richard C. Martin and Abbas Barzegar, 87–92. Stanford: Stanford University Press, 2010.
Amitai-Preiss, Reuven. "Ghazan, Islam and Mongol Tradition: A View from the Mamlūk Sultanate." *Bulletin of the School of Oriental and African Studies* 59 (1996): 1–10.
Angenendt, Arnold. "Die Kreuzzüge: Aufruf zum 'gerechten' oder zum 'heiligen' Krieg?" In *Krieg und Christentum: Religiöse Gewalttheorien in der Kriegserfahrung des Westens*, edited by Andreas Holzem, 341–367. Paderborn: Schöningh, 2009.
Angenendt, Arnold. *Toleranz und Gewalt: Das Christentum zwischen Bibel und Schwert.* Münster: Aschendorff, 2009.
Ansari, Ali M. "*L'état, c'est moi:* The Paradox of Sultanism and the Question of 'Regime Change' in Modern Iran." *International Affairs* 89, no. 2 (2013): 283–298.
Armour, Rollin. *Islam, Christianity, and the West: A Troubled History.* Maryknoll: Orbis, 2002.
Ashouri, Daryoush. "Creeping Secularism." *Comparative Studies of South Asia, Africa and the Middle East* 31, no. 1 (2011): 46–52.
Assmann, Jan. *Moses the Egyptian: The Memory of Egypt in Western Monotheism.* Cambridge: Harvard University Press, 1997.
Assmann, Jan. *The Price of Monotheism.* Stanford: Stanford University Press, 2010.
Avalos, Hector. *Fighting Words: The Origins of Religious Violence.* Amherst: Prometheus Books, 2005.
Averroes [Ibn Rushd]. "The Chapter on Jihad from Averroes's Legal Handbook *Al-Bidāyah.*" In *Jihad in Medieval and Modern Islam: The Chapters on Jihad from Averroes' Legal Handbook 'Bidayat al-Mudjtahid and The Treatise 'Koran and Fighting' by the Late Shaykh al-Azar, Mahmud Shaltut*, edited by Rudolph Peters, 9–25. Leiden: Brill, 1977.
Ayoub, Mahmoud and Gary Legenhausen. "Introduction." In *Jihad and Shahadat: Struggle and Martyrdom in Islam*, ed. Mehdi Abedi and Gary Legenhausen, 1–46. North Haledon: Islamic Publications International, 1986.
Azmeh, Aziz al-. *Ibn Khaldun in Modern Scholarship: A Study in Orientalism.* London: Third World Centre for Research and Publishing, 1981.
Azmeh, Aziz al-. *Muslim Kingship: Power and the Sacred in Muslim, Christian, and Pagan Politics.* London: I.B. Tauris, 1997.
Babayan, Kathryn. *Mystics, Monarchs, and Messiahs: Cultural Landscapes of Early Modern Iran.* Cambridge: Harvard University Press, 2002.
Backer, Larry Catá. "Theocratic Constitutionalism: An Introduction to a New Global Ordering." *Indiana Journal of Global Legal Studies* 16 (2009): 85–172.
Badawi, Zaki. *The Reformers of Egypt – A Critique of Al-Afghani, 'Abduh and Ridha.* Slough Berks: The Muslim Institute/The Poen Press, 1396/1976.
Bailey, Norman A. "*La Violencia* in Colombia," *Journal of Inter-American Studies* 9, no. 4 (1967): 561–575.
Bannā', Ḥasan al-. *Memoirs of Hasan al Banna Shaheed*, translated by M.N. Shaikh. Karachi: International Islamic Publishers, 1981.

Bannā', Ḥasan al-. "To What Do We Summon Mankind," in Ḥasan al-Banna', *Five Tracts of Ḥasan al-Bannā' (1906–1949): A Selection from the* Majmū'at Rasā'il al-Imām al-Shahīd Ḥasan Al-Bannā', translated and annotated by Charles Wendell, 69–102. Berkley: University of California Press, 1978.

Bannā', Ḥasan al-. "Towards the Light," in Ḥasan al-Banna, *Five Tracts of Ḥasan al-Bannā' (1906–1949): A Selection from the* Majmū'at Rasā'il al-Imām al-Shahīd Ḥasan Al-Bannā', translated and annotated by Charles Wendell, 103–132. Berkley: University of California Press, 1978.

Bannā', Ḥasan al-. "Our Mission." In Ḥasan al-Banna, *Five Tracts of Ḥasan al-Bannā' (1906–1949): A Selection from the* Majmū'at Rasā'il al-Imām al-Shahīd Ḥasan Al-Bannā', translated and annotated by Charles Wendell, 40–68. Berkley: University of California Press, 1978.

Bannā', Ḥasan al-. "On Jihād." In Ḥasan al-Banna', *Five Tracts of Ḥasan al-Bannā' (1906–1949): A Selection from the* Majmū'at Rasā'il al-Imām al-Shahīd Ḥasan Al-Bannā', translated and annotated by Charles Wendell, 133–161. Berkley: University of California Press, 1978.

Bannā', Ḥasan al-. "Between Yesterday and Today." In Ḥasan al-Banna', *Five Tracts of Ḥasan al-Bannā' (1906–1949): A Selection from the* Majmū'at Rasā'il al-Imām al-Shahīd Ḥasan Al-Bannā', trans. and annotated Charles Wendell, 13–39. Berkeley: University of California Press, 1978.

Bartolo da Sassoferrato. *De tyranno*. In Diego Quaglioni. *Politica e diritto nel Trecento Italiano: Il "De Tyranno" di Bartolo da Sassoferrato (1314–1357), con L'edizione crittica dei trattati "De Guelphis et Gebellinis," "De regimine civitatis" e "De tyranno,"* 175–213. Firenze: Olschki, 1983.

Barfield, Thomas. *Afghanistan: A Cultural and Political History.* Princeton: Princeton University Press, 2010.

Bartlett, W.B. *The Assassins: The Story of Medieval Islam's Secret Sect.* Stroud: Sutton, 2001.

Bashir, Hassan. *Europe and the Eastern Other: Comparative Perspectives on Politics, Religion, and Culture before the Enlightenment.* Lanham: Lexington, 2013.

Beasley-Murray, Jon. *Posthegemony: Political Theory and Latin America.* Minneapolis: University of Minnesota Press, 2010.

Berryman, Phillip. "El Salvador: From Evangelization to Insurrection." In *Religion and Political Conflict in Latin America*, edited by Daniel H. Levine, 58–78. Chapel Hill: The University of North Carolina Press, 1986.

Berryman, Phillip. *Subborn Hope: Religion, Politics, and Revolution in Central America.* Maryknoll: Orbis Books, 1994.

Behrooz, Maziar. "Factionalism in Iran under Khomeini." *Middle Eastern Studies* 27, no. 4 (1991): 597–614.

Bergesen, Albert J. "Sayyid Qutb in Historical Context." In *The Sayyid Qutb Reader: Selected Writings on Politics, Religion, and Society*, edited by Albert J. Bergesen, 3–13. New York: Routledge, 2008.

Bielefeldt, Heiner. "Von der päpstlichen Universalherrschaft zur autonomem Bürgerrepublik: Aegidius Romanus, Johannes Quidort von Paris, Dante Alighieri und Marsilius von Padua im Vergleich." *Zeitschrift für Rechtsgeschichte, Kan. Abt.* 72 (1987): 70–130.

Binder, Leonard. *Islamic Liberalism: A Critique of Development Ideologies.* Chicago: University of Chicago Press, 1988.

Blumenberg, Hans. *Die Legitimität der Neuzeit,* erneuerte Ausgabe. Frankfurt/M.: Suhrkamp, 1996.
Bonner, Michael David. *Jihad in Islamic History: Doctrines and Practices.* Princeton: Princeton University Press, 2006.
Bonine, Michael E., Abbas Amanat, and Michael Ezekiel Gasper, ed. *Is There a Middle East? The Evolution of a Geopolitical Concept.* Stanford: Stanford University Press, 2012.
Boyle, Leonard E. "The *Oculus Sacerdotis* and Some Other Works of William of Pagula." *Transactions of the Royal Historical Society*, 5th series, 5 (1955): 81–110.
Boyle, Leonard E. "William of Pagula and the *Speculum Regis Edwardi III.*" *Mediaeval Studies* 32 (1970): 329–36.
Bozarslan, Hamit. "Le Jihâd: Réceptions et usages d'une injonction Coranique d'hier à aujourd'hui." *Vingtième Siècle: Revue d'histoire* 82 (2004): 15–29.
Browers, Steven R. "Pinochet's Plebiscite and the Catholics: The Dual Role of the Chilean Church." *World Affairs* 155, no. 2 (1988): 51–58.
Brown, Warren. *Violence in Medieval Europe.* New York: Longman, 2010.
Brusco, Elisabeth E. "Colombia: Past Persecution, Present Tension." In *Religious Freedom and Evangelization in Latin America: The Challenge of Religious Pluralism*, edited by Paul E. Sigmund, 235–252. Maryknoll: Orbis, 1999.
Bulliet, Richard W. "Local Politics in Eastern Iran under the Ghaznavids and Seljuks" *Iranian Studies*, 11 (1978): 35–56.
Burke, Kevin F. and Robert Lassalle-Klein, ed. *Love that Produces Hope: The Thought of Ignacio Ellacuría.* Collegeville: Liturgical Press, 2006.
Braun, Manuel and Cornelia Herberichs, ed. *Gewalt im Mittelalter: Realitäten – Imaginationen.* München: Fink, 2005.
Busch, Briton Cooper. "Divine Intervention in the 'Muqaddimah' of Ibn Khaldun." *History of Religions* 3 (1968): 317–329.
Calvert, John. *Sayyid Qutb and the Origin of Radical Islam.* New York: Columbia University Press, 2010.
Câmara, Hélder. "Violence in the Modern World." In *Between Honesty and Hope: Documents from and About the Church in Latin America*, edited by Peruvian Bishops' Commission for Social Action, translated by John Drury, 47–54. Maryknoll Publications: Maryknoll, 1970.
Canning, Joseph. *Ideas of Power in the Late Middle Ages, 1296–1417.* Cambridge: Cambridge University Press, 2011.
Cardenal, Rodolfo. "The Martyrdom of the Salvadorean Church." In *Church and Politics in Latin America*, edited by Dermot Keogh, 225–246. Basingstoke: Macmillan, 1990.
Charfi, Mohamed. *Islam and Liberty: The Historical Misunderstanding.* London: Zed Books, 2005.
Charnay, Jean Paul. *Regards sur l'islam: Freud, Marx, Ibn Khaldun: Essais et philosophie.* Paris: L'Herne, 2003.
Chávez Hartley, Luis Alberto. "El perfil de un Batallador católico: Centenario de Plinio Correa de Oliveira." *La Razón Histórica: Revista hispanoamericana de Historia de las Ideas* 16 (2011): 86–88.
Claster, Jill N. *Sacred Violence: The European Crusades to the Middle East, 1095–1396.* Toronto: University of Toronto Press, 2009.
Clos, Ryne. "In the Name of the God Who Will Be: The Mobilization of Radical Christians in the Sandinista Revolution." *Journal for the Study of Radicalism* 6, no. 2 (2012): 1–52.

Comblin, José. *Called for Freedom: The Changing Context of Liberation Theology*, translated by Phillip Berryman. Maryknoll: Orbis, 1998.
Comblin, José. *The Church and the National Security State.* Mayknoll: Orbis, 1979.
Comblin, José. "The Holy Spirit." In *Mysterium Liberationis: Fundamental Concepts of Liberation Theology*, edited by Ignacio Ellacuría and Jon Sobrino, 462–482. Maryknoll: Orbis, 1993.
Cook, David. *Understanding Jihad.* Berkeley: University of California Press, 2005.
Cook, Michael. *Commanding Right and Forbidding Wrong in Islamic Thought.* Cambridge: Cambridge University Press, 2000.
Coppe Caldeira, Rodrigo. "Bispos conservadores brasileiros no Concílio Vaticano II (1962–1965): D. Geraldo de Proença Sigaud e D. Antônio de Castro Mayer." *Horizonte* 9, no. 24 (2011): 1010–1029.
Corrêa Oliveira, Plinio. *Nobility and the Analogous Traditional Elites in the Allocutions of Pius XII: A Theme Illustrating American Social History.* York: The American Society for the Defense of Tradition, Family and Property (TFP), 1993.
Corrêa Oliveira, Plinio. *Revolution and Counter-Revolution*, 3rd English ed. Spring Grove: The American Society for the Defense of Tradition, Family and Property, 1993.
Crone, Patricia. *God's Rule: Government and Islam.* New York: Columbia University Press, 2004.
Crone, Patricia. "Ninth-Century Muslim Anarchists." *Past & Present* 167 (2000): 3–28.
Crone, Patricia and Fritz Zimmermann. *The Epistle of Sālim Ibn Dhakwān.* Oxford: Oxford University Press, 2001.
Dabashi, Hamid. *Authority in Islam: From the Rise of Mohammad to the Establishment of the Umayyads.* Edison: Transaction Publishers, 1989.
Dabashi, Hamid. *Islamic Liberation Theology: Resisting the Empire.* London: Routledge, 2008.
Dabashi, Hamid. *Shi'ism: A Religion of Protest.* Cambridge: Belknap Press, 2011.
Dabashi, Hamid. *Theology of Discontent: The Ideological Foundations of the Islamic Revolution in Iran.* New York: New York University Press, 1993.
Daftary, Farhad. *The Assassin Legends: Myths of the Isma'ilis.* London: I. B. Tauris, 1995.
Daftary, Farhad. *The Ismā'īlīs: Their History and Doctrines.* Cambridge: Cambridge University Press, 1990.
Daftary, Farhad. "Ḥasan-i Ṣabbāḥ and the Origins of the Nizārī Isma'ili Movement." In *Medieval Isma'ili History and Thought*, edited by Farhad Daftary, 181–204. Cambridge: Cambridge University Press, 1996.
Dailey, Suzanne. "Religious Aspects of Colombia's *La Violencia:* Explanations and Implications." *Journal of Church and State* 15 (1973): 381–406.
Dallmayr, Fred. "Comparative Political Theory: What is it Good For?" In *Western Political Thought in Dialogue with Asia*, edited by Takashi Shogimen and Cary J. Nederman, 13–24. Lanham: Lexington, 2008.
Darling, Linda T. *History of Social Justice and Political Power in the Middle East: The Circle of Justice From Mesopotamia to Globalization.* Florence: Routledge, 2012.
Davenport, Anne A. "The Catholics, the Cathars, and the Concept of Infinity in the Thirteenth Century." *Isis*, 88, no. 2 (1997): 263–295.
Davies, Lizzy. "Pope Francis to Mafia: Repent or 'End up in Hell'." http://www.theguardian.com/world/2014/mar/22/pope-francis-warns-mafiosi-to-repent-or-end-up-in-hell.
De Kadt, Emanuel. "Paternalism and Populism: Catholicism in Latin America." *Journal of Contemporary History* 2, no. 5 (1967): 89–106.

Delong-Bas, Natana J. *Wahhabi Islam: From Revival and Reform to Global Jihad.* Oxford: Oxford University Press, 2004.
De Mattei, Roberto. *The Crusader of the 20th Century: Plinio Correâ de Oliveira.* Gracewing: Leominster, 1998.
Dien, Mawil Izzi. *Islamic Law: From Historical Foundations to Contemporary Practice.* Notre Dame: Notre Dame University Press, 2004.
Donohue, John J. and John L. Esposito, ed. *Islam in Transition: Muslim Perspectives.* Oxford: Oxford University Press, 2007.
Drake, Harold Allen. *Constantine and the Bishops: The Politics of Intolerance.* Baltimore: Johns Hopkins University Press, 2000.
Drobinski, Matthias. "Vorwürfe gegen Papst Franziskus: Die Wahrheit wird euch frei machen." *Süddeutsche Zeitung* 65 (March 18, 2013): 4.
Duby, Georges. "Preface." In *A History of Private Life, Vol. II: Revelations of the Medieval World*, ed. Georges Duby, translated by Arthur Goldhammer, ix-xii. Cambridge: Harvard University Press, 1988.
Dussel, Enrique. *Ethics of Liberation: In the Age of Globalization and Exclusion.* Durham: Duke University Press, 2013.
Dussel, Enrique. "¿Fundamentación de la ética? La vida humana: De Porfirio Miranda a Ignacio Ellacuría." *Andamios* 4 (2007): 157–205.
Dussel, Enrique. *A History of the Church in Latin America: Colonialism to Liberation (1492–1979)*, translated by Alan Neely. Grand Rapits: Eerdmans, 1981.
Dussel, Enrique. "La politique vaticane en Amérique Latine: Essai d'interprétation historico-sociologique." *Social Compass* 37, no. 2 (1990): 227–224.
Dussel, Enrique. "Theology of Liberation and Marxism." In *Mysterium Liberationis: Fundamental Concepts of Liberation Theology*, edited by Jon Sobrino and Ignacio Ellacuría, 85–102. Maryknoll: Orbis, 1993.
Dworkin, Ronald. *Taking Rights Seriously.* Cambridge, MA: Harvard University Press, 1977.
Elias, Norbert. *The Symbol Theory*, edited with an introduction by Richard Kilminster. London: Sage Publications, 1991.
Ellacuría, Ignacio. "The Christian Challenge of Liberation Theology." In *Essays on History, Liberation, and Salvation*, edited by Michael E. Lee, commentary by Kevin F. Burke, 123–135. Maryknoll: Orbis, 2013.
Ellacuría, Ignacio. *Freedom Made Flesh: The Mission of Christ and His Church.* Maryknoll: Orbis, 1976.
Ellacuría, Ignacio. "The Historicity of Christian Salvation." In *Essays on History, Liberation, and Salvation*, edited by Michael E. Lee, commentary by Kevin F. Burke, 137–168. Maryknoll: Orbis, 2013.
Ellacuría, Ignacio. "Latin American Quincentenary? Discovery or Cover-up?" In *Essays on History, Liberation, and Salvation*, edited by Michael E. Lee, commentary by Kevin F. Burke, 27–38. Maryknoll: Orbis, 2013.
Enayat, Hamit. *Modern Islamic Political Thought: The Response of the Shīʿī and Sunni Muslims to the Twentieth Century.* London: I.B. Tauris, 1988.
Engineer, Asghar Ali. "Islam and Secularism." In *Islam in Transition: Muslim Perspectives*, edited by John J. Donohue and John L. Esposito, 136–142, 2nd ed. Oxford: Oxford University Press, 2007.
Eskandari, Iraj. "Tudeh Leader on the Religious Movement: From an Interview with Iraj Eskandari, Secretary General of the Tudeh Party." *MERIP Reports* 75/76 (1979): 30.

Esposito, John L. *The Future of Islam*. Oxford: Oxford University Press, 2010.
Esposito, John L. *Islam and Politics*. Syracuse: Syracuse University Press, 1984.
Euben, Roxanne L. and Muhammad Qasim Zaman, *Princeton Readings in Islamist Thought: Texts and Contexts from al-Banna to Bin Laden*. Princeton: Princeton University Press, 2009.
Faggioli, Massimo. "Vatican II: The History and the Narratives." *Theological Studies* 73, no. 4 (2012): 749–767.
Faus, José Ignacio González. "Sin." In *Mysterium Liberationis: Fundamental Concepts of Liberation Theology*, edited by Jon Sobrino and Ignacio Ellacuría, 532–542. Maryknoll: Orbis, 1993.
Feste, Karen A. *The Iranian Revolution and Political Change in the Arab World* (The Emirates Occasional Papers 4). Abu Dhabi: The Emirates Center for Strategic Studies and Research, 1996.
Firestone, Reuven. *Jihad: The Origin of Holy War in Islam*. Oxford: Oxford University Press, 1999.
Fleischer, Cornell H. *Bureaucrat and Intellectual in the Ottoman Empire. The Historian Mustafa Âli (1541–1600)*. Princeton: Princeton University Press, 1986.
Fleischer, Cornell H. "Royal Authority: Dynastic Cyclism, and "Ibn Khaldûnism" in Sixteenth-Century Ottoman Letters." In *Ibn Khaldun and Islamic Ideology*, edited by Bruce B. Lawrence, 47–67. Leiden: Brill, 1984.
Flori, Jean. *Guerre sainte, jihad, croisade: Violence et religion dans le christianisme et l'islam*. Paris: Éditions du Seuil, 2002.
Flori, Jean. "Jihad et guerre sainte." *Cités* 14 (2003): 57–60.
Foran, John. "A Theory of Third World Social Revolutions: Iran, Nicaragua, and El Salvador Compared." *Critical Sociology* 19, no. 3 (1992): 3–27.
French, Jan Hoffman. "A Tale of Two Priests and Two Struggles: Liberation Theology from Dictatorship to Democracy in the Brazilian Northeast." *The Americas* 63 (2007): 409–443.
Friedman, Yohanan. "Jihād in Aḥmadī Thought." In *Studies in Islamic History and Civilization in Honour of Professor David Ayalon*, edited by Moshe Sharon, 221–235. Jerusalem: Cana, 1986.
Gadamer, Hans-Georg. *Wahrheit und Methode: Grundzüge einer philosophischen Hermeneutik*, 7th ed. Tübingen: Mohr Siebeck, 2010.
Galtung, Johan. "Violence, Peace, and Peace Research." *Journal of Peace Research* 6, no. 3 (1969): 167–191.
Ganji, Manouchehr. *Defying the Iranian Revolution: From a Minister to the Shah to a Leader of Resistance*. Westport: Praeger, 2002.
Gerassi, John. "Introduction: Camilo Torres and the Revolutionary Church." In *Camilo Torres, Revolutionary Priest: The Complete Writings & Messages of Camilo Torres*, edited by John Gerassi, 3–56. New York: Random House, 1971.
Giles of Rome [Aegidius Romanus]. *Giles of Rome on Ecclesiastical Power: The De ecclesiastica potestate of Aegidius Romanus*, transation with introduction by R.W. Dyson. Woodbridge: Boydell Press, 1986.
Ghamari-Tabrizi, Behrooz. "Contentious Public Religion: Two Conceptions of Islam in Revolutionary Iran: Ali Shariʻati and Abdolkarim Soroush." *International Sociology* 19, no. 4 (2004): 504–523.

Gismondi, Michael A. "Transformations in the Holy: Religious Resistance and Hegemonic Struggles in the Nicaraguan Revolution." *Latin American Perspectives* 13, no. 3 (1986): 13–36.

Godrej, Farah. *Cosmopolitan Political Thought: Method, Practice, Discipline.* Oxford: Oxford University Press, 2011.

Gómez, Carlos Mario. "Economía y violencia en Colombia." *Quórum: Revista de Pensamiento Iberoamericano* 2 (2001): 159–173.

Goodin, Robert E. "The Development-Rights Trade-off: Some Unwarranted Economic and Political Assumptions." *Universal Human Rights* 1, no. 2 (1979): 31–42.

Goodin, Robert E. *On Settling.* Princeton: Princeton University Press, 2012.

Goodin, Robert E. *What's Wrong with Terrorism?* Cambridge: Polity, 2006.

Gordon, Joel. "The Myth of the Savior: Egypt's 'Just Tyrants' on the Eve of Revolution, January-July 1952." *Journal of the American Research Center in Egypt* 26 (1989): 223–237.

Gray, John. *Al Qaeda and What it Means to Be Modern.* New York: The New Press, 2003.

Griffel, Frank. *Apostasie und Toleranz: Die Entwicklung zu al-Ghazâlîs Urteil gegen die Philosophie und die Reaktion der Philosophen* (Leiden: Brill, 2000).

Griffel, Frank. *Al-Ghazali's Philosophical Theology.* New York: Oxford University Press, 2009.

Griffel, Frank. "Toleration and Exclusion: Al-Shāfiʿī and al-Ghazālī on the Treatment of Apostates." *Bulletin of the School of Oriental and African Studies* 64, no. 3 (2001): 339–354.

Grim, Brian J. and Roger Finke. *The Price of Freedom Denied: Religious Persecution and Conflict in the Twenty-First Century.* Cambridge: Cambridge University Press, 2011.

Grimm, Dieter. "Das staatliche Gewaltmonopol." In *Herausforderungen des staatlichen Gewaltmonopols: Recht und politisch motivierte Gewalt am Ende des 20. Jahrhunderts*, edited by Freia Anders and Ingrid Gilcher-Holtey), 18–38. Frankfurt/M.: Campus, 2006.

Grundmann, Herbert. "Ketzerverhöre des Spätmittelalters als quellenkritisches Problem." *Deutsches Archiv für Erforschung des Mittelalters* 21 (1965): 519–575.

Grundmann, Herbert. *Religious Movements in the Middle Ages: The Historical Links between Heresy, the Mendicant Orders, and Women's Religious Movement in the Twelfth and Thirteenth Century, with the Historical Foundations of German Mysticism*, translated by Steven Rowan, introduction by Robert E. Lerner. Notre Dame: University of Notre Dame Press, 1995.

Grundmann, Herbert. "Der Typus des Ketzers in mittelalterlicher Anschauung." In *Ausgewählte Aufsätze, Vol. 1: Religiöse Bewegungen*, edited by Herbert Grundmann, 313–327. Stuttgart: Anton Hiersemann, 1976.

Gutas, Dimitri. *Greek Thought, Arabic Culture: The Graeco-Arabic Translation Movement in Baghdad and Early ʿAbbāsid Society (2nd-4th/8th-10th Centuries).* Abingdon: Routledge, 1998.

Gutas, Dimitri. "The Study of Arabic Philosophy in the Twentieth Century: An Essay on the Historiography of Arabic Philosophy." *British Journal of Middle Eastern Studies* 29 (2002): 5–25.

Guibert of Nogent [Guibertus de Novigento]. *Historia que dicitur Gesta Dei per Farnco.* In *The Crusades: Idea and Reality, 1095–1274*, ed. by Louise Riley-Smith and Jonathan Riley-Smith, 45–49. London: Edward Arnold, 1981.

Gutiérrez, Gustavo. *A Theology of Liberation: History, Politics and Salvation*, 15th anniversary ed. Maryknoll: Orbis, 1988.

Hāʾirī, Abdul-Hādī. "Afghānī on the Decline of Islam." *Die Welt des Islams* 13, no. 1/2 (1971): 121–125.
Haleem, Harfiyah Abdel Oliver Ramsbotham, Saba Risaluddin, and Brian Wicker, ed. *The Crescent and the Cross: Muslim and Christian Approaches to War and Peace*. Houndsmills: Macmillan, 1998.
Haleh, Afshar, ed. *Iran, a Revolution in Turmoil*. Albany: State University of New York Press, 1985.
Hallaq, Wael B. "On Dating Malik's *Muwatta*." *UCLA Journal of Islamic and Near East Law* 1 (2002): 47–65.
Hallaq, Wael B. *The Origins and Evolution of Islamic Law*. 5th printing with corrections. Cambridge: Cambridge University Press, 2008.
Hamami, Táhir. "Ibn Khaldun: Life and Political Activity or the ʿallama on Board." In *Ibn Khaldun: The Mediterranean in the 14th Century, Rise and Fall of Empires: Exhibition in the Real Alcázar of Seville, May-September 2006*, edited by Jesús Viguera Molins, 304–315. Seville: Fundatión El legado andalusí, 2006.
Hebblethwaite, Peter. "The Vatican's Latin America Policy." In *Church and Politics in Latin America*, edited by Dermot Keogh, 49–64. Basingstoke: Macmillan, 1990.
Hegghammer, Thomas. *Jihad in Saudi Arabia: Violence and Pan-Islamism since 1979*. Cambridge: Cambridge University Press, 2010.
Hehl, Ernst-Dieter. "Heiliger Krieg – eine Schimäre? Überlegungen zur Kanonik und Politik des 12. und 13. Jahrhunderts." In *Krieg und Christentum: Religiöse Gewalttheorien in der Kriegserfahrung des Westens*, edited by Andreas Holzem, 323–340. Paderborn: Schöningh, 2009.
Hepple, Leslie W. "Geopolitics, Generals and the State in Brazil." *Political Geography Quarterly* 5, no. 4 (1986): 580–590.
Hillenbrand, Carole. "The Power Struggle between the Seljuqs and the Ismaʿilis of Alamūt, 487–518/1094–1124: The Seljuq Perspective." In *Medieval Ismaʿili History and Thought*, edited by Farhad Daftary, 205–220. Cambridge: Cambridge University Press, 1996.
Henderson, John B. *The Construction of Orthodoxy and Heresy: Neo-Confucianism, Islamic, Jewish, and Early Christian Patterns*. Albany: State University of New York Press, 1998.
Hennis, Wilhelm. "Legitimacy: On a Category of Civil Society." In Wilhelm Hennis, *Politics as Practical Science*, 77–120. Basingstoke: Palgrave Macmillan, 2009.
Hennis, Wilhelm. "Legitimität: Zu einer Kategorie der bürgerlichen Gesellschaft." In Wilhelm Hennis, *Politikwissenschaft und politisches Denken: Politikwissenschaftliche Abhandlungen II*, 250–296. Tübingen: Mohr Siebeck, 2000.
Hinsch, Wilfried. "Legitimacy and Justice: A Conceptual and Functional Clarification." In *Political Legitimization without Morality?*, edited by Jörg Kühnelt, 39–52. Dordrecht: Springer, 2008
Homann, Eckhard. "*Posse absolutum versus iusticia:* Zur antinomischen Bestimmung der päpstichen Macht bei Aegidius Romanus." In *Gewalt und ihre Legitimation im Mittelalter*, edited by Günther Mensching, 237–247. Würzburg: Königshausen und Neumann, 2003.
Hooglund, Eric. "Social Origins of the Revolutionary Clergy." In *The Iranian Revolution & the Iranian Republic*, edited by Nikki R. Keddie and Eric Hooglund, 74–83. Syracuse: Syracuse University Press, 1986.
Hoover, Jon. *Ibn Taymiyya's Theodicy of Perpetual Optimism: Islamic Philosophy, Theology and Science: Texts and Studies*. Leiden: Brill 2007.

Hoover, Jon. "The Justice of God and the Best of All Possible Worlds: The Theodicy of Ibn Taymiyya." *Theological Review* 27 (2006): 58–63.
Hopkins, Keith. *A World Full of Gods: The Strange Triumph of Christianity.* New York: Free Press, 2000.
Hopkins, Nicholas S. "Engels and Ibn Khaldun." *Alif: Journal of Comparative Poetics* 10 (1990): 9–18.
Horsch-Al Saad, Silvia. *Tod im Kampf: Figurationen des Märtyrers in frühen sunnitischen Schriften.* Würzburg: Ergon, 2011.
Hourani, Albert. *Arabic Thought in the Liberal Age, 1798–1939.* Oxford: Oxford University Press, 1970.
Hourani, George F. "Thrasymachus' Definition of Justice in Plato's 'Republic'." *Phronesis* 7, no. 2 (1962). 110–120.
Housley, Norman. "The Crusades and Islam." *Medieval Encounters* 13 (2007): 189–208.
Humbert of Romans. *Opera Tripartium.* In *The Crusades: Idea and Reality, 1095–1274*, ed. by Louise Riley-Smith and Jonathan Riley-Smith, 103–117. London: Edward Arnold, 1981.
Ibn Khaldūn, 'Abd ar-Raḥmān Ibn Muhammad. *The Muqaddimah: An Introduction to History*, translated from the Arabic by Franz Rosenthal, 3 vols., 2nd. ed. New York: Bollinger Foundation, 1967.
Ibn Taymiyya, Ahmad Ibn 'Abd al-Halīm. *Against Exremisms*, edited by Yahya M. Michot, foreword by Bruce L. Lawrence. Beirut: Dar Albouraq, 2012.
Ibn Taymiyya, Ahmad Ibn 'Abd al-Halīm. *Ibn Taymiyyah Expounds on Islam: Selected Writings of Shaykh al-Islam Taqi ad-Din Ibn Taymiyya on Islamic Faith, Life, and Society*, compiled and translated by Muhammad 'Abdul-Haqq Ansari. Riyadh: General Administration of Culture and Publication, 2000.
Ibn Taymiyya, Ahmad Ibn 'Abd al-Halīm. *A Muslim Theologian's Response to Christianity: Ibn Taymiyya's Al-Jawab al Sahih*, edited and translated by Tomas F. Michel. Delmare: Caravan Books, 1984.
Irwin, Robert. "Toynbee and Ibn Khaldūn." *Middle Eastern Studies* 33 (1997): 461–480.
Ismail, Salwa. "Democracy in Contemporary Arab Discourse." In *Political Liberalization and Democratization in the Arab World: Vol. 1: Theoretical Perspectives*, edited by Rex Brynen, Bahgat Korany, and Paul Noble, 93–128. Boulder: Lynne Rienner, 1995.
Jackson, Sherman. "Jihad in the Modern World." In *Islam in Transition: Muslim Perspectives*, edited by John J. Donohue and John L. Esposito, 394–408. Oxford: Oxford University Press, 2007.
James of Viterbo [Jacobus de Viterbio]. *De regimine Christiano: A Critical Edition and Translation*, edited by R.W. Dyson. Leiden: Brill, 2009.
James of Vitry [Jacobus de Vitriaco]. "Sermones Vulgares." In *The Crusades: Idea and Reality, 1095–1274*, edited by Louise Riley-Smith and Jonathan Riley-Smith, 67–69. London: Edward Arnold, 1981.
Janin, Hunt. *The Pursuit of Learning in the Islamic World, 610–2003.* Jefferson, McFarland: 2005.
Jansen, Johannes J. G. *The Dual Nature of Islamic Fundamentalism.* Ithaca: Cornell University Press, 1997.
Jansen, Johannes J. G. "The Creed of Sadat's Assassins: The Contents of 'The Forgotten Duty' Analysed." *Die Welt des Islams* NS 25 (1985): 1–30.
Jefferis, Jennifer L., *Religion and Political Violence: Sacred Protest in the Modern World.* London: Routledge, 2010.

John of Salisbury [Joannis Saresberiensis]. *Policraticus: Of the Frivolities of Courtiers and the Footprints of Philosophers*, edited and translated by Cary J. Nederman. Cambridge: Cambridge University Press, 1990.
Judex. "Una alternativa a la révolution: La accion no violenta organizada de Hélder Câmara." *Estudios Centro Americanos* 24, no. 246 (1969): 87–94.
Kaelber, Lutz. "Weavers into Heretics? The Social Organization of Early-Thirteenth-Century Catharism in Comparative Perspective." *Social Science History* 21, no. 1 (1997): 111–137.
Kamrava, Mehran. *Iran's Intellectual Revolution*. Cambridge: Cambridge University Press, 2008.
Kandil, Hazem. *Soldiers, Spies and Statesmen: Egypt's Road to Revolt*. London: Verso, 2012.
Kantorowicz, Ernst Hartwig. *Friedrich der Zweite*, 15th ed. Stuttgart: Klett-Cotta, 1995.
Kaufmann, Matthias. "Wilhelm von Ockham und Marsilius von Padua: Papstkritiker am Hofe Ludwigs des Bayern." In *Musis et Litteris: Festschrift für Bernhard Rupprecht zum 65. Geburtstag*, edited by Silvia Glaser and Andrea M. Kluxen, 569–580. München: Fink, 1993.
Kaye, Sharon. "There's No Such Thing as Heresy (And It's a Good Thing, Too): William of Ockham of Freedom of Speech." *The Journal of Political Philosophy* 6, no. 1 (1998): 41–52.
Keddie, Nikki R. *An Islamic Response to Imperialism: Political and Religious Writings of Sayyid Jamāl ad-Dīn "al-Afghānī."* 2nd ed. Berkeley: University of California Press, 1983.
Keddie, Nikki R. "Is Shiʻism Revolutionary?" In *The Iranian Revolution & the Iranian Republic*, edited by Nikki R. Keddie and Eric Hooglund, 113–126. Syracuse: Syracuse University Press, 1986.
Keddie, Nikki R. *Sayyid Jamāl ad-Dīn "al-Afghānī": A Political Biography*. Berkeley: University of California Press, 1972.
Kedourie, Elie. *Afghani and ʿAbduh: An Essay on Religious Unbelief and Political Activism in Modern Islam*, reprint. London: Cass: 1966.
Kedourie, Elie. "'The Elusive Jamāl al-Dīn al-Afghānī': A Comment." *The Muslim World* 59 (1969): 312–314.
Keen, Maurice H. "The Political Thought of the Fourteenth-Century Civilians." In *Trends in Medieval Political Thought*, edited by Beryl Smalley, 105–126. Oxford: Blackwell, 1965.
Kenney, Jeffrey T. *Muslim Rebels: Kharijites and the Politics of Extremism in Egypt*. Oxford: Oxford University Press, 2006.
Kenny, L. M. "Al-Afghānī on Types of Despotic Government." *Journal of the American Oriental Society* 86, no. 1 (1966): 19–27.
Kepel, Gilles. *Jihad: The Trail of Political Islam*. Cambridge, MA: Belkap Press, 2002.
Kepel, Gilles. *Muslim Extremism in Egypt: The Prophet and Pharaoh*. Berkeley: University of California Press, 1985.
Khadduri, Majid. *War and Peace in the Law of Islam*. Baltimore: Johns Hopkins Press, 1955.
Khan, M. A. *Islamic Jihad: A Legacy of Forced Conversion, Imperialism, and Slavery*. Bloomington: iUniverse, 2009.
Khan, Qamaruddin. *The Political Thought of Ibn Taymīyah*. Islamabad: Islamic Research Institute, 1973.
Khanbaghi, Aptin. *The Fire, the Star and the Cross: Minority Religions in Medieval and Early Modern Iran*. London: I. B. Tauris, 2006.
Khatab, Sayed. *The Political Thought of Sayyid Qutb: The Theory of jahiliyyah*. London: Routledge, 2006.

Khatab, Sayed. "The Voice of Democratism in Sayyid Qutb's Response to Violence and Terrorism." *Islam and Christian-Muslim Relations* 20 (2009): 315–332.
Khomeini, Ruhollah Musawi. *Imam's Final Discourse: The Text of the Political and Religious Testament of the Leader of the Islamic Revolution and the Founder of the Islamic Republic of Iran, Imam Khomeini*. Tehran: Ministry of Guidance and Islamic Culture, 1989.
Khomeini, Ruhollah Musawi. *Islam and Revolution*, translated by Algar Hamid. London: Kegan Paul, 2002.
Khomeini, Ruhollah Musawi. "The Afternoon of ʿAshura (June 3, 1963)." In Ruhollah Khomeini, *Islam and Revolution*, 177–180. London: Kegan Paul, 2002.
Khomeini, Ruhollah Musawi. "In Commemoration of the First Martyrs of the Revolution (Feb. 19, 1978)," in Ruhollah Khomeini, *Islam and Revolution*, trans. Algar Hamid (London: Kegan Paul, 2002), 212–227.
Khomeini, Ruhollah Musawi. "In Commemoration of the Martyrs at Qum (April 3, 1963)," in Ruhollah Khomeini, *Islam and Revolution*, 174–176. London: Kegan Paul, 2002.
Khomeini, Ruhollah Musawi. "Islamic Government," in Ruhollah Khomeini, *Islam and Revolution*, 25–166. London: Kegan Paul, 2002.
Khomeini, Ruhollah Musawi. "Muharram: The Triumph of Blood over the Sword (Nov. 23, 1978)," in Ruhollah Khomeini, *Islam and Revolution*, trans. Algar Hamid (London: Kegan Paul, 2002), 242–245.
Khomeini, Ruhollah Musawi. "A Warning to the Nation (1943)." In Ruhollah Khomeini, *Islam and Revolution*, 169–173. London: Kegan Paul, 2002.
Kingshuk, Chatterjee. *ʿAli Shariʿati and the Shaping of Political Islam in Iran*. New York: Palgrave Macmillan, 2001.
Kippenberg, Hans G. *Violence as Worship: Religious Wars in the Age of Globalization*. Stanford: Stanford University Press, 2011.
Knobler, Adam. "Holy Wars, Empires, and the Portability of the Past: The Modern Uses of Medieval Crusades." *Comparative Studies in Society and History* 48, no. 2 (2006): 293–325.
Knysh, Alexander. "'Orthodoxy' and 'Heresy' in Medieval Islam: An Essay in Reassessment." *The Muslim World* 83 (1993): 48–67.
Koch, Bettina. "Aegidius Romanus." In *Handbuch Staatsdenker*, edited by Rüdiger Voigt and Ulrich Weiß, 13b-15b. Stuttgart: Franz Steiner, 2010.
Koch, Bettina. "Against Empire? John of Paris's Defence of Territorial Secular Power in the Context of Dante's and Marsilius of Padua's Political Theories." In *John of Paris: Beyond Royal & Papal Power*, edited by Chris Jones. Turnhout: Brepols, forthcoming.
Koch, Bettina. "Ein Dadaist auf der Suche nach dem *neuen* Menschen: Hugo Ball zwischen Wissenschafts- und Gesellschaftskritik und katholischen Mystizismus." In *Einsprüche: Politik und Sozialstaat im 20. Jahrhundert. Festschrift für Gerhard Kraiker*, edited by Antonia Grunenberg, 115–127. Kovač, Hamburg, 2005.
Koch, Bettina. "Johannes von Salisbury und die Nizari Ismailiten unter Terrorismusverdacht: Zur kritischen Bewertung eines Aspekts in der aktuellen Terrorismusdebatte." *Zeitschrift für Rechtsphilosophie* 11, no. 2 (2013): 18–38.
Koch, Bettina. "Marsilius of Padua on Church and State." In *A Companion to Marsilius of Padua*, edited by Gerson Moreno-Riaño and Cary J. Nederman, 139–179. Leiden: Brill, 2011.

Koch, Bettina. "A Medieval Muslim-Christian Lesson on Political and Economic Liberalization." *Journal of Chinese, Indian, and Islamic Cultural Relations* 1 (2008): 73–88.
Koch, Bettina. "Priestly Despotism: The Problem of Unruly Clerics in Marsilius of Padua's *Defensor Pacis*." *Journal of Religious History* 36 (2012): 165–183.
Koch, Bettina. "Religious Dissent in Premodern Islam: Political Usage of Heresy and Apostasy in Nizam al-Mulk and Ibn Taymiyya." In *Religion, Power and Resistance from the Eleventh to the Sixteenth Centuries: Playing the Heresy Card*, edited by Karen Bollermann, Thomas M Izbicki, and Cary J. Nederman, 215–236. Houndmills: Palgrave Macmillan, 2014.
Koch, Bettina. "Yesterday's Tyrannicide, Today's Terrorist? Historic Acts of 'Terror' in Islam and in the West in Light of the Contemporary Debates on Terrorism." In *International Relations, Culture and Global Finance*, ed. Akis Kalaitzidis, 111–126. Athens: ATINER, 2011.
Koch, Bettina. *Zur Dis-/Kontinuität mittelalterlichen politischen Denkens in der neuzeitlichen politischen Theorie: Marsilius von Padua, Johannes Althusius und Thomas Hobbes im Vergleich*. Berlin: Duncker & Humblot, 2005.
Kofler, Hans. "Handbuch des islamischen Staats- und Verwaltungsrechtes von Badr-ad-din ibn Ğamāʾah." *Islamica* 6 (1934): 349–441.
Kofler, Hans. "Handbuch des islamischen Staats- und Verwaltungsrechtes von Badr-ad-din ibn Ğamāʾah." *Islamica* 7 (1935): 1–65.
Kofler, Hans. "Handbuch des islamischen Staats- und Verwaltungsrechtes von Badr-ad-din ibn Ğamāʾah." *Abhandlungen für die Kunde des Morgenlandes*, 33, no. 6 (1938): 18–129.
Kohn, Margaret. "Afghānī on Empire, Islam, and Civilization." *Political Theory* 37, no. 3 (2009): 398–422.
Kumaraswamy, P. R. "Islam and Minorities: Need for a Liberal Framework." *Mediterranean Quarterly* 3 (2007): 94–109.
Kymlicka, Will. *Multicultural Citizenship: A Liberal Theory of Minority Rights*. Oxford: Clarendon Press, 1995.
Lambert, Malcolm. *The Cathars*. Malden: Blackwell, 1998.
Lambton, Ann K. S. *State and Government in Medieval Islam: An Introduction to the Study of Islamic Political Theory: The Jurists*. Oxford: Oxford University Press, 1981.
Lange, Christian. *Justice, Punishment, and the Medieval Muslim Imagination*. Cambridge: Cambridge University Press, 2008.
Lapidus, Ira M. *Islamic Societies to the Nineteenth Century: A Global History*. Cambridge: Cambridge University Press, 2012.
Laqueur, Walter, ed. *Voices of Terror: Manifestos, Writings and Manuals of Al Qaeda, Hamas, and Other Terrorists from Around the World and Throughout the Ages*. Naperville: Sourcebook, 2005.
Lassalle-Klein, Robert. "Ignacio Ellacuría's Debt to Xavier Zubiri: Critical Principles for a Latin American Philosophy and Theology of Liberation," In *Love that Produces Hope: The Thought of Ignacio Ellacuría*, edited by Kevin F. Burke and Robert Lassalle-Klein, 88–127. Collegeville: Liturgical Press, 2006.
Lassalle-Klein, Robert. "Jesus of Galilee and the Crucified People: The Contextual Christology of Jon Sobrino and Ignacio Ellacuría." *Theological Studies* 70 (1990): 347–376.

Lauzière, Henri. "The Religious Dimension of Islamism: Sufism, Salafism, and Politics in Morocco." In *Islamist Politics in the Middle East: Movements and Change*, edited by Samer Shehata, 88–106. Abingdon/New York: Routledge, 2012.

Lawrence, Bruce B. *Defenders of God: The Fundamentalist Revolt Against the Modern Age*. Columbia: University of South Carolina Press, 1995.

Lee, Michael E. *Bearing the Weight of Salvation: The Soterology of Ignacio Ellacuría*, Foreword by Gustavo Gutiérrez. New York: Crossroad, 2009.

Lee, Michael E. "Liberation Theology's Transcendent Moment: The Work of Xavier Zubiri and Ignacio Ellacuría as Nonconstructive Discourse." *Journal of Religion* 83 (2003): 226–243.

Lepora, Chiara and Robert E. Goodin. *On Complicity and Compromise*. Oxford: Oxford University Press, 2013.

Le Tallec, Cyril. *Les sectes politiques: 1965–1995*. Paris: L'Harmattan, 2006.

Leurs, Rob. "Ayatollah Khomeini: The Changing Face of Islam." *Estudos em Comunicação* 12 (2012): 25–45.

Levine, Daniel H. "Conflict and Renewal." In *Religion and Political Conflict in Latin America*, edited by Daniel H. Levine, 236–255. Chapel Hill: University of North Carolina Press, 1986.

Levine, Daniel H. "From Church and State to Religion and Politics and Back Again" *Social Compass* 37, no. 2 (1990): 331–351.

Levine, Daniel H. *Religion and Politics in Latin America: The Catholic Church in Venezuela and Columbia*. Princeton: Princeton University Press, 1981.

Lochhead, David. "Monotheistic Violence." *Buddhist-Christian Studies* 21 (2001): 3–12.

Löwy, Michaël. "Modernité et critique de la modernité dans la théologie de la liberation." *Archives de Sciences Sociales des Religions* (1990) 71: 7–23.

Looney, Robert E. *Economic Origins of the Iranian Revolution*. New York: Pergamon Press, 1982.

López Trujillo, Alfonso. *Liberation or Revolution? An Examination of the Priest's Role in the Socioeconomic Class Struggle in Latin America*. Huntington: Our Sunday Visitor, 1977.

Lusthaus, Jonathan. "Religion and State Violence: Legitimation in Israel, the USA and Iran." *Contemporary Politics* 17, no. 1 (2011): 1–17.

Lynch, Cecelia. "Acting on Belief: Christian Perspectives on Suffering and Violence." *Ethics & International Affair* 14 (2000): 83–97.

Machiavelli, Niccolò. *The Prince*, in *Machiavelli: The Chief Works and Others*, Vol. 1, translated by Allan Gilbert, 10–96. Durham: Duke University Press, 1958.

MacIntyre, Alastair. *After Virtue: A Study in Moral Theory*. 3rd ed. Notre Dame: University of Notre Dame Press, 2007.

Mäkinen, Virpi. "Rights and Duties in Late Scholastic Discussion on Extreme Necessity." In *Transformations in Medieval and Early-modern Rights Discourse*, edited by Virpi Mäkinen and Petter Korkman, 37–46. Dordrecht: Springer, 2006.

Maier, Martin. "Karl Rahner: The Teacher of Ignacio Ellacuría." In *Love that Produces Hope: The Thought of Ignacio Ellacuría*, edited by Kevin F. Burke and Robert Lassalle-Klein, 128–143. Collegeville: Liturgical Press, 2006.

Malik Ibn Anas. *Al-Muwatta of Imam Malik ibn Anas: The First Formulation of Islamic Law*, translated by Aisha Abdurrahman Bewley. London: Kegan Paul, 1989.

March, Andrew F. "What Is Comparative Political Theory?" *The Review of Politics* 71, no. 4 (2009): 531–565.

Marjani, Fatollah. "Introduction." In Ali Shariati. *Man and Islam*, translated by Fatollah Marjani, xix-xxi. Houston: Filinc, 1981.
Martin, Richard C. and Abbas Barzegar. "Introduction: The Debate About Islamism in the Public Sphere." In *Islamism: Contested Perspectives on Political Islam*, edited by Richard C. Martin and Abbas Barzegar, 1–13. Stanford: Stanford University Press, 2010.
Marvin, Laurence W. "War in the South: A First Look at Siege Warfare in the Albigensian Crusade, 1209–1218." *War in History* 8, no. 4 (2001): 373–395.
Masoud, Tarek E. "The Arabs and Islam: The Troubled Search for Legitimacy," *Daedalus* 128, no. 2 (1999): 127–145.
Mawardi, ʿAlī Ibn Muhammad al-. *The Ordinances of Government: al-aḥkām al-sulṭāniyya w'al-wilāyāt al-dīniyya*, translated by Wafaa H. Wahba. Reading: Garnet, 1996.
McCaffrey, Emily. "Memory and Collective Identity in Occitanie: The Cathars in History and Popular Culture." *History and Memory*, 13, no. 1 (2001): 114–138.
McGrade, Arthur Stephen. *The Political Thought of William of Ockham: Personal and Institutional Principles*. Cambridge: Cambridge University Press, 1974.
McGraw, Bryan T. "Religious Parties and the Problem of Democratic Political Legitimacy." *Critical Review of International Social and Political Philosophy* 17, no. 3 (2014): 289–313.
Melendez, Guillermo. "The Catholic Church in Central America: Into the 1990s." *Social Compass* 39, no. 4 (1992): 553–570.
Mensching, Günther, ed. *Gewalt und ihre Legitimation im Mittelalter*. Würzburg: Königshausen und Neumann, 2003.
Mieth, Dietmar. "Aggression durch den Glauben? Eine christliche Sicht zum Thema 'Religion und Gewalt' unter besonderer Berücksichtigung des Toleranzbegriffes." In *Im Zeichen der Religion: Gewalt und Friedfertigkeit in Islam und Christentum*, edited by Christine Abbt and Donata Schoeller, 118–141. Frankfurt: Campus, 2008.
Miethke, Jürgen. *De potestate papae: Die päpstliche Amtskompetenz im Widerstreit der politischen Theorie von Thomas von Aquin bis Wilhelm von Ockham*. Tübingen: Mohr Siebeck, 2000.
Milson, Menahem. "The Elusive Jamāl al-Dīn al-Afghānī." *The Muslim World* 58 (1968): 304–307.
Michot, Yahya M. "Introduction." in Ibn Taymiyya, *Against Exremisms*, edited by Yahya M. Michot, foreword by Bruce L. Lawrence, xx-xxxii. Beirut: Dar Albouraq, 2012.
Michot, Yahya M. *Muslims under Non-Muslim Rule: Ibn Taymiyya on Fleeing from Sin; Kinds of Emigration; the Status of Mardin: Domain of War and Peace; the Conditions of Challenging Power: Texts Translated, Annotated, and Presented in Relation to Six Modern Readings of the Mardin Fatwa*. Oxford: Interface Publications, 2006.
Moazzam, Anwar. *Jamāl al-Dīn al-Afghāni: A Muslim Intellectual*. New Delhi: Naurang Rai, 1984.
Moisant, Joseph, ed. *De speculo regis Edwardi III, seu tractatu quem de mala regni administratione conscripsit Simon Islip, cum utraque ejusdem recensione manuscripta nunc primum edita*. Paris: Alphonsum Picard, 1891.
Montada, Josep Puig. "Al-Afghânî, a Case of Religious Unbelief?" *Studia Islamica* 100/101 (2005): 203–220.
Morton, Nicholas. "The Defence of the Holy Land and the Memory of the Maccabee." *Journal of Medieval History* 26 (2010): 275–293.

Moussalli, Ahmad S. "Ḥasan al-Bannā's Islamist Discourse on Constitutional Rule and Islamic State." *Journal of Islamic Studies* 4, no. 2 (1993): 161–174.

Moussalli, Ahmad S. *Moderate and Radical Islamic Fundamentalism: The Quest for Modernity, Legitimacy, and the Islamic State.* Gainesville: University Press of Florida, 1999.

Mufti, Malik. "Jihad as Statecraft: Ibn Khaldun on the Conduct of War and Empire." *History of Political Thought*, 30, no. 3 (2009): 385–410.

Muldoon, James. "*Auctoritas, Potestas* and World Order." In *Plentitude of Power: The Doctrines and Exercise of Authority in the Middle Ages: Essays in Memory of Robert Louis Benson*, edited by Robert C. Figueira, 125–139. Aldershot: Ashgate, 2006.

Muṭahhari, Murtaḍa. "Jihad in the Qurʾan." In *Jihad and Shahadat: Struggle and Martyrdom in Islam*, edited by Mehdi Abedi and Gary Legenhausen, 81–124. North Haledon: Islamic Publications International, 1986.

Muṭahhari, Murtaḍa [Motahari, Morteza]. "The Nature of the Islamic Revolution." In *Iran, a Revolution in Turmoil*, edited by Afshar Haleh, 201–219. Albany: State University of New York Press, 1985.

Musallam, Adnan. *From Secularism to Jihad: Sayyid Qutb and the Foundations of Radical Islam.* Greenwood: Westport, 2005.

Muslim Brotherhood. "Muslim Brotherhood Statement Denouncing UN Women Declaration for Violating Sharia Principles." http://www.ikhwanweb.com/article.php?id=30731.

Nagel, Tilman. *Staat und Glaubensgemeinschaft im Islam: Geschichte der politischen Ordnungsvorstellungen der Muslime, Vol. 2: Vom Spätmittelalter bis zur Neuzeit.* Zürich: Artemis, 1981.

Nazeer Ka Ka Khel, Muhammad. "Legitimacy of Authority in Islam." *Islamic Studies* 19, no. 3 (1980): 167–182.

Nederman, Cary J. "A Duty to Kill: John of Salisbury's Theory of Tyrannicide." *The Review of Politics* 50 (1988): 365–389.

Nederman, Cary J. "Introduction to the *Mirror of King Edward III*." In *Political Thought in Early Fourteenth-Century England: Treatises by Walter of Milemete, William of Pagula, and William of Ockham*, edited by Cary J. Nederman, 63–72. Tempe: Arizona Center for Medieval and Renaissance Studies, 2002.

Nederman, Cary J. *John of Salisbury.* Tempe: Arizona Center for Medieval and Renaissance Studies, 2005.

Nederman, Cary J. *Lineages of European Political Thought: Explorations Along the Medieval/Modern Divide from John of Salisbury to Hegel.* Washington, D.C.: The Catholic University Press, 2009.

Nederman, Cary J. "The Monarch and the Market Place: Economic Policy and Royal Finance in William of Pagula's *Speculum Regis Edward III*." *History of Political Economy* 33 (2001): 51–69.

Nederman, Cary J. "Property and Protest: Political Theory and Subjective Rights in Fourteenth-Century England." *The Review of Politics* 58 (1996): 323–344.

Nederman, Cary J. and Cathrine Campbell. "Priests, Kings, and Tyrants: Spiritual and Temporal Power in John of Salisbury's *Policraticus*." *Speculum* 66 (1991): 572–590.

Neumann, Peter R. and M.L.R. Smith. *The Strategy of Terrorism: How it Works, and Why it Fails.* Oxon: Routledge, 2008.

Oberschall, Anthony. *Conflict and Peace Building in Divided Societies: Responses to Ethnic Violence.* London: Routledge, 2007.

Offler, Hilary Seton. "Empire and Papacy: The Last Struggle." *Transactions of the Royal Historical Society* 6 (1956): 21–47.
O'Grady, Joan. *Heresy: Heretical Truth or Orthodox Error? A Study of Early Christian Heresies*. Longmead: Element Books, 1985.
Oliveros, Roberto. "History of the Theology of Liberation." In *Mysterium Liberationis: Fundamental Concepts of Liberation Theology*, edited by Ignacio Ellacuría and Jon Sobrino, 3–32. Maryknoll: Orbis, 1993.
Ourghi, Mariella. *Muslimische Positionen zur Berechtigung von Gewalt: Einzelstimmen, Revisionen, Kontroversen*. Würzburg: Ergon, 2010.
Paden, William D. "Perspectives on the Albigensian Crusade." *Tenso* 10, no. 2 (1995): 90–98.
Parsa, Misagh. *Social Origins of the Iranian Revolution*. New Brunswick: Rutgers University Press, 1989.
Paul, Nicholas L. *To Follow in Their Footsteps: The Crusades and Family Memory in the High Middle Ages*. Ithaca: Cornell University Press, 2012.
Pegg, Mark Gregory. "On Cathars, Albigenses, and Good Men of Languedoc." *Journal of Medieval History* 27 (2001): 181–195.
Peña, Milogras. "The Sadalitium Vitae Movement in Peru: A Rewriting of Liberation Theology." In *Religion and Democracy in Latin America*, edited by William H. Swatos, 101–116. New Brunswick: Transaction Publishers, 1995.
People's Fedayi. "People's Fedayi Open Letter to Khomeini," translated by Behzad Touhidi, *MERIP Reports* 75/76 (1979): 31–32.
Peruvian Bishops' Commission for Social Action. "Latin America: A Continent of Violence." In *Between Honesty and Hope: Documents from and About the Church in Latin America*, edited by the Peruvian Bishops' Commission for Social Action, translated by John Drury, 81–84. Maryknoll Publications: Maryknoll, 1970.
Peters, Edward. "Introduction: Heresy and Authority." In *Heresy and Authority in Medieval Europe*, edited by Edward Peters, 1–11. University Park: University of Pennsylvania Press, 1980.
Peters, Rudolph. "Introduction." In *Jihad in Medieval and Modern Islam: The Chapters on Jihad from Averroes' Legal Handbook 'Bidayat al-Mudjtahid' and The Treatise 'Koran and Fighting' by the Late Shaykh al-Azar, Mahmud Shaltut*, edited by Rudolph Peters, 1–8. Leiden: Brill, 1977.
Peters, Rudolph. *Jihad in Classical and Modern Islam: Updated Edition with a Section on Jihad in the 21st Century*. Princeton: Wiener, 2005.
Peters, Rudolph and Gert J.J. De Vries. "Apostasy in Islam." *Die Welt des Islams* 17 (1976/77): 1–25.
Pion-Berlin, David. "Latin American National Security Doctrines: Hard and Softline Themes." *Armed Forces & Society* 15 (1989): 411–429.
Pion-Berlin, David. "The National Security Doctrine, Military Threat Perception, and the 'Dirty War' in Argentina." *Comparative Political Studies* 21 (1988): 384–5.
Pottenger, John R. *The Political Theory of Liberation Theology: Towards a Reconvergence of Social Values and Social Science*. Albany: State University of New York Press, 1989.
Ptolemy of Lucca [Ptolemaeus Lucensis]. *On the Government of Rulers De Regimine Principum: With Portions Attributed to Thomas Aquinas*, translated by James M. Blythe. Philadelphia: University of Pennsylvania Press, 1997.
Poulat, Emile. "The Path of Latin American Catholicism." In *Church and Politics in Latin America*, edited by Dermot Keogh, 3–24. Basingstoke: Macmillan, 1990.

Qutb, Sayyid. *Milestones*. Damascus: Dar Al-Ilm, n.d.
Qutb, Sayyid. *The Sayyid Qutb Reader: Selected Writings on Politics, Religion, and Society*, edited by Albert J. Bergensen. (New York: Routledge, 2008.
Qutb, Sayyid. *Social Justice in Islam*, translated by John B. Hardi, revided translation and introduction by Hamid Algar. Oneonta: Islamic Publications International, 2000.
Rabasa, Angel. "Ideology, Not Religion," in *Islamism: Contested Perspectives on Political Islam*, edited by Richard C. Martin and Abbas Barzegar, 110–115. Stanford: Stanford University Press, 2010.
Racaut, Luc. "The Polemical Use of the Albigensian Crusade During the French Wars of Religion." *French History* 13, no. 3 (1999): 261–279.
Ramadan, Tariq. *Au sources du renouvenau musulman: D'al-Afghānī à Ḥassan al-Bannā un siècle de réformisme islamique*. Paris: Bayard Éditions/Centurion, 1998.
Rapoport, Yossef and Shahab Ahmed. "Ibn Taymiyya and his Times." In *Ibn Taymiyya and His Times*, edited by Yossef Rapoport and Shahab Ahmed, 3–20. Oxford: Oxford University Press, 2010.
Rawls, John. "The Idea of Public Reason Revisited." *The University of Chicago Law Review* 64, no. 3 (1996): 765–807.
Rawls, John. *Political Liberalism*, expanded edition. New York: Columbia University Press, 2005.
Reichberg, Gregory M., "Aquinas' Moral Theology of Peace and War," *The Review of Metaphysics* 64 (2011): 467–487.
Richard, Pablo. "Theology in the Theology of the Liberation." In *Mysterium Liberationis: Fundamental Concepts of Liberation Theology*, edited by Ignacio Ellacuría and Jon Sobrino, 150–168. Maryknoll: Orbis, 1993.
Riley-Smith, Jonathan. *The Crusades, Christianity, and Islam*. New York: Columbia University Press, 2008.
Riley-Smith, Louise and Jonathan Riley-Smith. "Introduction." In *The Crusades: Idea and Reality, 1095–1274*, edited by Louise Riley-Smith and Jonathan Riley-Smith, 1–36. London: Edward Arnold, 1981.
Rinke, Stefan. *Revolutionen in Lateinamerika: Wege in die Unabhängigkeit 1760–1830*. München: Beck, 2010.
Rinehart, Christine Sixta. "Volatile Breeding Grounds: The Radicalization of the Egyptian Muslim Brotherhood." *Studies in Conflict & Terrorism* 32 (2009): 953–988.
Robert of Rheims [Roberttus Remensis]. *Historia Iherosolimitana*. In *The Crusades: Idea and Reality, 1095–1274*, ed. by Louise Riley-Smith and Jonathan Riley-Smith, 42–45. London: Edward Arnold, 1981.
Rosenthal, Erwin I. J. *Political Thought in Medieval Islam: An Introductory Outline*. Cambridge: Cambridge University Press, 1962.
Rubenberg, Cheryl A. "US Policy toward Nicaragua and Iran and the Iran-Contra Affair: Reflections on the Continuity of American Foreign Policy." *Third World Quarterly* 10, no. 4 (1988): 1467–1504.
Sachedina, Abdulaziz. *The Islamic Roots of Democratic Pluralism*. Oxford: Oxford University Press, 2001.
Sadiki, Larbi. *The Search for Arab Democracy: Discourses and Counter-Discourses*. New York: Columbia University Press, 2004.
Safi, Omid. *The Politics of Knowledge in Premodern Islam: Negotiating Ideology and Religious Inquiry*. Chapel Hill: The University of North Carolina Press, 2006.

Sālim Ibn Dhakwān. *Sīrat Sālim*. In Patricia Crone and Fritz Zimmermann. *The Epistle of Sālim Ibn Dhakwān*, 37–145. Oxford: Oxford University Press, 2001.
Sánchez Lopera, Alejandro. "Ciencia, revolución y creencia en Camilo Torres: ¿Una Colombia secular?" *Nómadas* 25 (2006): 241–258.
Schmidtke, Sabine. "Neuere Forschungen zur Muʿtazila unter besonderer Berücksichtigung der späteren Muʿtazila ab dem 4./10. Jahrhundert." *Arabica* 45 (1998): 379–408.
Schmitt, Carl. *Politische Theologie: Vier Kapitel zur Lehre von der Souveränität*, 9th ed. Berlin: Duncker & Humblot, 2009.
Scholz, Richard. *Die Publizistik zur Zeit Philipps des Schönen und Bonifaz' VIII: Ein Beitrag zur Geschichte der politischen Anschauungen des Mittelalters*. Stuttgart: Enke, 1903.
Scholz, Richard. *Wilhelm von Ockham als politischer Denker und sein Breviloquium de principatu tyrannico*. Stuttgart: Hirsemann, 1944.
Schreiner, Klaus, ed. *Heilige Kriege: Religiöse Begründungen militärischer Gewaltanwendung: Judentum, Christentum und Islam im Vergleich*. München: Oldenbourg 2008.
Schulze, Reinhard. "Islamischer Puritanismus und die religiöse Gewalt." In *Im Zeichen der Religion: Gewalt und Friedfertigkeit in Islam und Christentum*, edited by Christine Abbt and Donata Schoeller, 34–56. Frankfurt: Campus, 2008.
Shakibi, Zhand. "Pahlavīsm: The Ideologization of Monarchy in Iran." *Politics, Religion & Ideology* 14, no. 1 (2013): 114–135.
Shahibzadeh, Yadullah. *From Totalism to Perspectivism: An Intellectual History of Iranian Islamism from Shariati to the Advent of Khatami*. Oslo: University of Oslo, 2008.
Sharīʿatī, ʿAlī [Shariati, Ali]. *Man and Islam*, translated by Fatollah Marjani. Houston: Filinc, 1981.
Sharīʿatī, ʿAlī. *What Is to Be Done: The Enlightenment Thinkers and an Islamic Renaissance*, edited by Farhang Rajaee, foreword by John L. Esposito. North Haledom: Islamic Publications International, 1986.
Shogimen, Takashi. "Defending Christian Fellowship: William of Ockham and the Crisis of the Medieval Church." *History of Political Thought* 26, no. 4 (2005): 607–624.
Shogimen, Takashi. *Ockham and Political Discourse in the Late Middle Ages*. Cambridge: Cambridge University Press, 2007.
Shogimen, Takashi. "William of Ockham and Conceptions of Heresy, c. 1250-c.1350." In *Heresy in Transition: Transforming Ideas of Heresy in Medieval and Early Modern Europe*, edited by Ian Hunter, John Christian Laursen, and Cary J. Nederman, 59–70. Aldershot: Ashgate, 2005.
Shue, Henry. *Basic Rights: Subsistence, Affluence, and U.S. Foreign Policy*, 2nd ed. Princeton: Princeton University Press, 1996.
The Sea of Precious Virtues (Baḥr al-Favāʾid): A Medieval Islamic Mirror for Princes, translated from the Persian and edited by Julie Scott Meisami. Salt Lake City: University of Utah Press, 1991.
Serbin, Kenneth P. "Dom Hélder Câmara: The Father of the Church of the Poor." In *The Human Tradition in Modern Brazil*, edited by Peter M. Beattie, 249–266. Scholarly Resources: Wilmington, 2004.
Sigmund, Paul E. "Introduction." In *Religious Freedom and Evangelization in Latin America: The Challenge of Religious Pluralism*, edited by Paul E. Sigmund, 1–8. Maryknoll: Orbis, 1999.
Sigmund, Paul E. *Liberation Theology at the Crossroads: Democracy or Revolution?* New York: Oxford University Press, 1990.

Sigmund, Paul E. "Revolution, Counterrevolution, and the Catholic Church in Chile." *Annals of the American Academy of Political and Social Science* 483 (1986): 25–35.

Sinner, Rudolf von. "Brazil: From Liberation Theology to a Theology of Citizenship as Public Theology." *International Journal of Public Theology* 1 (2007): 338–363.

Sivan, Emmanuel. *Interpretations of Islam: Past and Present*. Princeton: The Darwin Press, 1985.

Sivan, Emmanuel. *Modern Arab Historiography of the Crusades*. Tel Aviv: Tel-Aviv University, Shiloah Center for Middle Eastern and African Studies, 1973.

Sivan, Emmanuel. *Radical Islam: Medieval Theology and Modern Politics*, enlarged ed. New Haven: Yale University Press, 1990.

Sivan, Emmanuel. "Sunni Radicalism in the Middle East and the Iranian Revolution." *International Journal of Middle East Studies* 21 (1989): 1–30.

Sizgorich, Thomas. *Violence and Belief in Late Antiquity: Militant Devotion in Christianity and Islam*. Philadelphia: University of Pennsylvania Press, 2009.

Smith, Christian. *The Emergence of Liberation Theology: Radical Religion and Social Movement Theory*. Chicago: University of Chicago Press, 1991.

Soage, Ana Belén. "Hasan al-Banna and Sayyid Qutb: Continuity or Rupture?" *The Muslim World* 99, no. 2 (2009): 295–311.

Soage, Ana Belén. "Ḥasan al-Bannā or the Politicisation of Islam." *Totalitarian Movements and Political Religions* 9, no. 1 (2008): 21–42.

Soage, Ana Belén. "Islamism and Modernity: The Political Thought of Sayyid Qutb." *Totalitarian Movements and Political Religions* 10, no. 2 (2009): 189–203.

Sobrino, Jon. "Ignacio Ellacuría, the Human Being and the Christian: 'Taking the Crucified People Down from the Cross'." In *Love that Produces Hope: The Thought of Ignacio Ellacuría*, edited by Kevin F. Burke and Robert Lassalle-Klein, 1–67. Collegeville: Liturgical Press, 2006.

Sols Lucia, José. *La teología histórica de Ignacio Ellacuría*. Madrid: Editorial Trotta, 1999.

Soroush, Abdolkarim. "The Sense and Essence of Secularism." In Abdolkarim Soroush, *Reason, Freedom, and Democracy in Islam: Essential Writings of Abdolkarim Soroush*, 54–68. Oxford: Oxford University Press, 2000.

Springer, Devin R., James L. Regens and David N. Edger. *Islamic Radicalism and Global Jihad*. Washington, D.C.: Georgetown University Press, 2009.

Srour, Hani. *Die Staats- und Gesellschaftstheorie bei Sayyid Ğamāladdīn "Al Afghānī" als Beitrag zur Reform der islamischen Gesellschaften in der zweiten Hälfte des 19. Jahrhunderts*. Freiburg: Klaus Schwarz, 1977.

Stein, Andrew J. "El Salvador." In *Religious Freedom and Evangelization in Latin America: The Challenges of Religious Pluralism*, edited by Paul E. Sigmund, 113–128. Maryknoll: Orbis, 1999.

Strindberg, Anders and Mats Wärn. *Islamism: Religion, Radicalization, and Resistance*. Cambridge: Polity Press, 2011.

Sussman, Cornelia and Irving Sussman. "The Case of Camilo Torres: The Problem of Obedience." *Catholic World* 204, no. 1224 (1969): 356–361.

Swartz, Nico Patrick. "Thomas Aquinas: On Law, Tyranny and Resistance." *Acta Theologica* 30, no. 1 (2010): 145–157.

Syed, Mairay. "Jihad in Classical Islam Legal and Moral Thought." In *Just War in Religion and Politics*, edited by Jacob Neusner, Bruce D. Chilton, and R.E. Tully, 135–162. Lanham: University Press of America, 2013.

Tabari, Ehsan. "Tudeh: 'Socialism and Islam'," translated by Masood Moin. *MERIP Reports* 75/76 (1979): 29–30.
Tamer, Georges. "The Curse of Philosophy: Ibn Taymiyya as Philosopher in Contemporary Islamic Thought." In *Islamic Theology and Law: Debating Ibn Taymiyya and Ibn Qayyim al-Jawyiyya*, edited by Birgit Krawietz and Georges Tamer, 328–374. Berlin: De Gruyter, 2013.
Thompson, Elizabeth F. *Justice Interrupted: The Struggle for Constitutional Government in the Middle East*. Cambridge: Harvard University Press, 2013.
Tierney, Brian. *The Crisis of Church & State, 1050–1300*. Englewood Cliffs: Prentice-Hall, 1964.
Tierney, Brian. *The Idea of Natural Rights: Studies on Natural Rights, Natural Law, 1150–1624*. Grand Rapids: Eerdmans, 2001.
Tibi, Bassam. *Kreuzzug und Djihad: Der Islam und die christliche Welt*. München: Bertelsmann, 1999.
Tomar, Cengiz. "Between Myth and Reality: Approaches to Ibn Khaldun in the Arab World." *Asian Journal of Social Science* 36, no. 3–4 (2008): 590–611.
Torres, Camilo. *Revolutionary Priest: The Complete Writings & Messages of Camilo Torres*, edited by John Gerassi. New York: Random House, 1971.
Torres, Camilo. "Crossroads of the Church in Latin America." In *Revolutionary Priest: The Complete Writings & Messages of Camilo Torres*, ed. John Gerassi, 327–334. New York: Random House, 1971.
Torres, Camilo. "How Pressure Groups Influence the Government." In *Revolutionary Priest: The Complete Writings & Messages of Camilo Torres*, edited by John Gerassi, 250–251. New York: Random House, 1971.
Torres, Camilo. "The Integrated Man." In *Revolutionary Priest: The Complete Writings & Messages of Camilo Torres*, edited by John Gerassi, 245–249. New York: Random House, 1971.
Torres, Camilo. "Is the Priest a Witch Doctor?" In *Revolutionary Priest: The Complete Writings & Messages of Camilo Torres*, edited by John Gerassi, 98–100. New York: Random House, 1971.
Torres, Camilo. "Message to the Christian." In *Revolutionary Priest: The Complete Writings & Messages of Camilo Torres*, edited by John Gerassi, 367–369. New York: Random House, 1971.
Torres, Camilo. "Message to the Colombians from the Mountains." In *Revolutionary Priest: The Complete Writings & Messages of Camilo Torres*, edited by John Gerassi, 425–427. New York: Random House, 1971.
Torres, Camilo. "Revolution: Christian Imperative." In *Revolutionary Priest: The Complete Writings & Messages of Camilo Torres*, edited by John Gerassi, 260–290. New York: Random House, 1971.
Torres, Camilo. "Social Change and Rural Violence in Colombia." In *Revolutionary Priest: The Complete Writings & Messages of Camilo Torres*, edited by John Gerassi, 188–250. New York: Random House, 1971.
Torres, Camilo. "Two Subculture," in *Revolutionary Priest: The Complete Writings & Messages of Camilo Torres*, edited by John Gerassi, 256–260. New York: Random House, 1971.
Tripp, Charles. *The Power and the People: Paths of Resistance in the Middle East*. Cambridge: Cambridge University Press, 2013.

Twomey, Gerald S. "Pope John Paul II and the 'Preferential Option for the Poor'." *Journal of Catholic Legal Studies* 45 (2006): 321–368.
Urban II, Pope [Urbanus II, Papa]. "Urban to His Partisans in Bologna, 19 September 1096." In *The Crusades: Idea and Reality, 1095–1274*, ed. by Louise Riley-Smith and Jonathan Riley-Smith, 38–39. London: Edward Arnold, 1981.
Urban II, Pope [Urbanus II, Papa]. "Urban to the Counts of Besalú, Empurias, Roussillon and Cerdaña and Their Knights, c. January 1096–29 July 1099." In *The Crusades: Idea and Reality, 1095–1274*, ed. by Louise Riley-Smith and Jonathan Riley-Smith, 40. London: Edward Arnold, 1981.
ʿUthaymīn, ʿAbd Allāh Ṣāliḥ al-. *Muḥammad ibn ʿAbd al-Wahhāb: The Man and His Works*. London: I.B. Tauris, 2009.
Valente, Claire. *The Theory and Practice of Revolt in Medieval England*. Aldershot: Ashgate, 2003.
Vekemans, Roger. *Caesar and God: The Priesthood and Politics*. Maryknoll: Orbis, 1972.
Völkl, Martin. *Muslime – Märtyrer – Militia Christi: Identität, Feindbild und Fremderfahrung während der ersten Kreuzzüge*. Stuttgart: Kohlhammer, 2011.
Waltz, James. "Muḥammad and the Muslims in St. Thomas Aquinas." *The Muslim World* 66 (1976): 81–95.
Watt, William Montgomery. *Islam and the Integration of Society*. London: Kegan Paul, 1961.
Weber, Max. *Wirtschaft und Gesellschaft: Grundriß der verstehenden Soziologie*, 5th rev. ed. Tübingen: Mohr Siebeck, 1980.
Weiß, Alexander. "Vier Laster einer vergleichenden politischen Theorie und das Projekt einer globalen Demokratietheorie." In *Nichtwestliches politisches Denken: Zwischen kultureller Differenz und Hybridisierung*, edited by Holger Zapf, 65–73. Wiesbaden: Springer, 2012.
Weiss, Dieter. "Arabische Wirtschaftspolitik im Lichte der Systemtheorie von Ibn Khaldūn." *Die Welt des Islams* 28 (1988): 585–606.
Wendell, Charles. "Introduction." In Ḥasan al-Banna, *Five Tracts of Ḥasan al-Bannā' (1906–1949): A Selection from the* Majmūʿat Rasāʾil al-Imām al-Shahīd Ḥasan Al-Bannā', translated and annotated by Charles Wendell, 1–10. Berkley: University of California Press, 1978.
White, Hayden. *Tropics of Discourse: Essays in Cultural Criticism*. Baltimore: Johns Hopkins University Press, 1978.
Whitfield, Teresa. *Paying the Price: Ignacio Ellacuría and the Murdered Jesuits of El Salvador*. Philadelphia: Temple University Press, 1994.
William of Ockham [Guilemus de Ockham]. I *Dialogus* 5.1–5, text and translation by John Scott. http://www.britac.ac.uk/pubs/dialogus/t1d51.html.
William of Ockham [Guilemus de Ockham]. I *Dialogus* 6.36–50, text and translation by George Knysh, August 2002, revised May 2004. http://www.britac.ac.uk/pubs/dialogus/t1d6c.html.
William of Ockham [Guilemus de Ockham]. I *Dialogus* 7.24–34, edited by George Knysh. http://www.britac.ac.uk/pubs/dialogus/RevRev1 %20Dial.%207.24–34.pdf.
William of Ockham [Guilemus de Ockham]. I *Dialogus* 7.42–51, edited by George Knysh. http://www.britac.ac.uk/pubs/dialogus/t1d742.html.
William of Ockham [Guilemus de Ockham]. I *Dialogus* 7.65–73, edited by George Knysh. http://www.britac.ac.uk/pubs/dialogus/t1d765.html.
William of Ockham [Guilemus de Ockham]. *The Power of Emperors and Popes*. translated and edited by Annabel S. Brett. Bristol: Thoemmes Press, 1998.

William of Ockham [Guilemus de Ockham]. *A Short Discourse of Tyrannical Government: Over Things Divine and Human, but Especially Over the Empire and Those Subject to the Empire, Usurped by Some Who Are Called Highest Pontiffs*, edited by Arthur Stephen McGrade, translated by John Kilcullen. Cambridge: Cambridge University Press, 1992.

William of Pagula [Guilemus de Pagula]. *Mirror of King Edward III*, in *Political Thought in Early Fourteenth-Century England: Treatises by Walter of Milimete, William of Pagula, and William of Ockham*, edited and translated by Cary J. Nederman, 73–139. Tempe: Arizona Studies for Medieval and Renaissance Studies, 2002.

Virani, Shafique N. *The Ismailis in the Middle Ages: A History of Survival, a Search for Salvation.* Oxford: Oxford University Press, 2007.

Yavari, Neguin "Mirrors for Princes or a Hall of Mirrors? Nizam al Mulk's *Siyar al-muluk* Reconsidered." *Al-Masāq: Islam and the Medieval Mediterranean*, 20 (2008): 47–69.

Yazar. *Iran... Revolution in Resilience.* Lahore: The Struggle Publications, 2000.

Youssef, Michael. *Revolt Against Modernity: Muslim Zealots and the West.* Leiden: Brill, 1985.

Zaidi, Manzar. "A Taxonomy of Jihad." *Arab Studies Quarterly* 31, no. 3 (2009): 21–34.

Zaman, Muhammad Qasim. *Modern Islamic Thought in a Radical Age: Religious Authority and Internal Criticism.* Cambridge: Cambridge University Press, 2012.

Zimmerman, John C. "Sayyid Qutb's Influence on the 11 September Attacks." *Terrorism & Political Violence* 16 (2004): 222–252.

Index

Abou el Fadl, Khaled, 20, 66, 67, 68, 103, 104, 105, 225
Abrahamian, Ervand, 181, 182, 183, 185, 186, 186, 187, 188, 189, 193, 204, 225
Affiliation, political, 23, religious, 14, 23, 91, 106
Afghānī, Sayyid Jamāl ad-Dīn al-, 1, 15, 21, 114, 158–170, 173, 174, 177, 183, 185, 187, 189, 200, 201, 202, 207, 208, 209, 210, 213, 214, 223, 226, 233, 235, 237, 239, 242, 244
Agression, 3, 28, 50, 59, 81, 86, 141, 144, 167, 188, 203, 239
Akbarzadeh, Shahram, 15, 16, 216, 226
Allende, Salvador Guillermo, 117
Angenendt, Arnold, 26, 28, 30, 32, 36, 79, 226
Apostasy, 14, 77, 78, 81, 82, 88, 92, 159, 170, 178, 232, 237, 241
Apostate, 26, 31, 47, 77, 78, 82, 86, 89, 111, 160, 176, 178, 218, 232
Aquinas, Thomas, see Thomas Aquinas
Argentina, 18, 115, 126, 241
Assassination, 91,92, 105, 106, 112, 121, 136, 163, 176, 177, 178, 179, 181
Assmann, Jan, 3, 7, 24, 30, 31, 223, 226
Atheism, 89, 128, 153, 154, 155
Averroes, see Ibn Rushd
Azhar, al-, 47, 179, 180
Azmeh, Aziz al-, 67, 96, 103, 226

Bannā', Ḥasan al-, 21, 160, 161, 166–176, 178, 179, 183, 188, 192, 194, 199, 200, 202, 203, 204, 209, 217, 219, 221, 222, 225, 226, 227, 231, 240, 242, 244, 246
Bartolo da Sassoferrato, 57, 227
Berryman, Phillip, 129, 135, 136, 138, 227, 229
Boff, Leonardo, 117
Boniface VIII, Pope, 43, 147, 154, 217
Bonner, Michael, 67, 70, 228
Brazil, 119, 120, 125, 126, 129, 130, 152, 153, 231, 233, 243, 244

Caliph, 62, 73, 75, 77, 92, 102, 109, 110, 111
Caliphate, 73, 79, 84, 92, 96
Câmara, Hélder, 119, 125, 126, 152, 208, 213, 228, 235, 243
Canning, Joseph, 42, 238
Caritas, 28, 29, 34, 40, 52, 108, 121, 222, see also Charity
Cathars, 28, 35–41, 90, 110, 133, 217, 218, 229, 235, 237, 239, 241
Charfi, Mohamed, 14, 17, 47, 228
Charity, 121, 123, 124, 127, 150, see also Caritas
Chile, 117, 125, 126, 145, 228, 244
Chinggis Khan, 87
Christendom, 3, 17, 19, 23, 26–30, 34, 39, 44, 153, 154,156, 157, 204, 205, 209, 217
Cold War, 114
Colombia, 18, 119, 120, 121, 124, 226, 228, 229, 232, 243, 245
Comblin, José, 21, 114, 118, 125–134, 137, 139, 142, 152, 156, 200, 201, 203, 207, 208, 214, 215, 229
Cook, David, 68, 69, 70, 71, 229
Cook, Michael, 20, 229
Corrêa de Oliveira, Plinio, 3, 21, 118, 126, 152–157, 199, 200, 202–205, 207, 209, 228, 229
Counter-violence, 2, 20, 21, 66, 80, 117, 118, 128, 140, 141, 156
Crone, Patricia, 67, 95, 99, 100, 101, 102, 103, 229, 253
Crusades, 19, 24, 25, 27–37, 41, 69, 73, 81, 90, 107–111, 121, 130, 157, 173, 174, 193, 194, 202, 208, 217, 218, 22, 230, 232, 234, 237, 239, 241, 242, 244, 259, Albigensian, 39, 110, 242

Dabashi, Hammid, 67, 99, 115, 181, 184, 185, 190, 198, 229
Daftary, Farhad, 89, 90, 91, 94, 95, 229, 233
Dallmayr, Fred, 5, 229
Defense, 10, 52, 62, 82, 129, 138, 157, 161, 189, 207, 210, 221

Democracy, 18, 117, 226, 129, 134, 145, 160, 163, 174, 177, 207, 209, 231, 241, 242, 243, 244
Dictatorship, 114, 126, 130, 132, 134, 231
Disobedience, 43, 50, 53, 78, 92, 94, 103, 104, 108, 150
Dissent, 14, 20, 23, 24, 26, 29, 35, 36, 39, 40, 76, 77, 80, 81, 82, 108, 110, 115, 143, 237
Domination, 57, 84, 93, 108, 117, 139, 168, 169, 188, 202, 208, 221
Drake, H. A., 1, 28, 230
Duby, Georges, 11, 15, 230
Dussel, Enrique, 13, 108, 109, 116, 117, 119, 132, 140–142, 144, 156, 207–109, 211, 212, 221, 223, 230
Duty, collective (jihad), 74, 75, 86, 88, 171 individual (jihad), 74, 75, 88, 172, 179,
Dworkin, Ronald, 8, 9, 10, 12, 64, 210, 223, 230

El Salvador, 135–138, 184, 227, 231, 244, 246
Elias, Norbert, 5, 7, 8, 230
Elite, 81, 89, 95, 99, 120, 122, 129, 131, 134, 135, 154, 162, 190, 200, 207, 209, 214, 220, 229
Engels, Friedrich, 6, 132, 234
Ellacuría, Ignacio, 21, 118, 121, 126, 129, 132, 134–142, 146, 156, 160, 200, 201, 208, 213, 228, 229, 230, 231, 237, 238, 241, 242, 244, 246
Enayat, Hamit, 16, 130
Equity, 57, 62, 97, 154
Esposito, John L., 16, 18, 160, 163, 177, 200, 230, 231, 234, 243
Establishment, 7, 15, 80, 99, 114, 128, 156, 157, 167, 169, 184, 185, 187, 189, 196, 198, 200, 201, 215, 220, 229

Faraj, ʿAbd al-Salam, 160, 173, 176–179, 210, 217, 225
Finke, Roger, 4, 216, 223, 232
Firestone, Reuven, 26, 69, 231
Fitna, 67, 199, 104, 107
Freedom, 10, 49, 62, 64, 83, 126, 129, 131, 133, 134, 141, 146, 147, 150, 159, 168, 171, 186, 191, 201, 213, 214, from oppression, 60, of speech 58, of the Church, 113, religious, 4, 121, 157. 166, 216, 219, 228, *see also* Liberty

Gadamer, Hans-Georg, 7, 231
Gaitán Ayala, Jorge Eliécer, 120, 121
Geopolitics, 2, 114, 115, 129, 228, 233
Ghazālī, Abū Ḥāmid Muḥammad ibn Muḥammad al-, 70, 82, 91, 92, 178, 194, 232
Giles of Rome, 19, 27, 43–48, 52, 113, 154, 217, 231
Goodin, Robert E., 1, 10, 143, 215, 232, 238
Griffel, Frank, 82, 91, 92, 232
Grim, Brian J., 4, 216, 223, 232
Grundmann, Herbert, 24, 37, 38, 40, 68. 218, 232
Guardianship of jurists (Khomeini), 189–190
Guerrilla, 119, 120, 147, 182, 183, 204, 225
Guibert of Nogent, 33, 232
Gutas, Dimitri, 5, 82, 232
Gutiérrez, Gustavo, 21, 117, 120, 127–128, 137, 232, 238

Ḥākimiyya, 167, 174–175
Habermas, Jürgen, 13
Hallaq, Wael B., 7, 37, 71, 233
Hegemony, 11, 23, 113, 115, 125, 206, 209, 217, 225
Hennis, Wilhelm, 8, 12, 13, 18, 224, 233
Heresy, 15, 24, 26–29, 31–32, 34–38, 40–42, 48–54, 58, 68, 82, 85–86, 90, 92–94, 112, 128, 130–131, 133, 141, 144, 147, 170, 178, 211, 215, 218, 232, 233, 235, 236, 237, 241, 243
Hesse, Hermann, 169
Hierarchy, 17, 44, 80, 127, 153, 154, 155, 156, 199
Holy Land, 29–30, 32–36, 39, 41, 110, 222, 239
Horsch-Al Saad, Silvia, 69, 71, 172, 173, 234
Hourani, Albert, 163, 221, 234
Humbert of Romans, 34, 41, 234

Ibadi jurists, 20, 100, 105–106, 112
Ibn Jamāʿa, 20, 73–77, 80, 98, 100, 220

Ibn Khaldūn, 'Abd ar-Raḥmān Ibn Muhammad, 6, 11, 20, 73, 78–80, 95–98,
   108, 113, 164, 212, 213, 214, 226, 228,
   231, 233, 234, 240, 245, 246
Ibn Rushd, 'Abū l-Walīd Muḥammad Ibn
   'Aḥmad, 20, 73–76, 226, 241
Ibn Taymiyya, Aḥmad Ibn 'Abd al-Halīm, 7, 14,
   20, 22, 68, 74, 81–90, 104–105, 110–
   111, 159, 161, 166, 172, 175–178, 218,
   233, 234, 237, 239, 242, 245
Ijtihād, 103, 196
Illegitimacy, 18, 115, 154, 156, 160, 190, 210,
   211 see also Legitimacy
Imami jurists, 103–106, 112
Injustice, 4, 49, 62–64, 66, 76, 85, 95–97,
   100, 102–106, 111–113, 119, 122, 128,
   139, 140–142, 144, 147, 160, 166–168,
   173, 181, 183, 188–190, 196, 201–202,
   204, 206, 208, 210–211, 213, 216, 219,
   220, 222, 224
Innocent III, Pope, 36, 39–41, 110
Innocent IV, Pope, 42
Iran-Contra Affair, 114, 242
Iranian Oil Company, 182
Islamic Mujahedin, 183

Jāhiliyya, 159, 160, 167, 170, 172–176, 202,
   235
James of Viterbo, 20, 43–48, 50, 56, 111, 112,
   113, 154, 217, 234
James of Vitry, 34, 234
John of Paris, 43, 112
John of Salisbury, 19, 27, 55–62, 65, 106, 112,
   113, 210, 211, 212, 214, 215, 216, 235,
   240
John Paul II, Pope, 143, 144, 203
John XXII, Pope, 43, 49, 51, 52, 217
Junta, 115, 116, 125, 126, 131, 144, 151, 156,
   207, 217

Keddie, Nikki R., 1, 158, 159, 161, 162, 163,
   165, 165, 184, 192, 196, 225, 233, 235
Kedourie, Ellie, 21, 159, 161, 162, 163, 165,
   235
Kepel, Gilles, 178, 179, 235
Kharijites, 20, 67, 70, 99–103, 105, 113, 212,
   214, 220, 235

Khomeini, Ruhollah Musawi, 21, 103, 160,
   166, 177, 178, 181, 183–199, 202–205,
   208–211, 213, 217, 221, 225, 227, 236,
   238, 241
Kippenberg, Hans G., 3, 113, 166, 180, 206,
   224, 236
Kofler, Hans, 73, 237
Kymlicka, Will, 14, 237

Lambton, Ann K. S., 20, 66, 99, 237
Legitimacy, political, 8, 10, 12–15, 23, 114,
   127, 190, 204, 206, 212, 219, religious,
   14, 156, 160, 196, 204, see also Illegitimacy
Levine, Daniel, 19, 21, 117, 136, 143, 145, 152,
   199, 227, 238
Liberty, 9, 10, 14, 17, 47, 50, 58, 64, 80, 112,
   126, 132, 133, 134, 140, 164, 211, 214,
   228, see also Freedom
Lopez Trujillo, Alfonso, 21, 117, 118, 144–152,
   199, 201, 2013, 238

Machiavelli, Niccolò, 151, 238
Malik Ibn Anas, 71, 72, 74, 78, 107, 108, 109,
   233, 238
Mamluk, 81, 84, 86, 87, 88, 226
Marsilius of Padua, 36, 43, 45, 49, 227, 235,
   236, 237
Martin, Richard C., 15, 226, 239, 242
Martyrdom, 33, 34, 40, 41, 54, 69, 72, 109,
   116, 134, 135, 136, 172, 188, 189, 194,
   196, 226, 228, 240
Marx, Karl, 6, 132, 147, 185, 228
Marxism, 124, 130, 132, 147, 148, 184, 186,
   230
Marxist, 6, 20, 115, 117, 132, 139, 140, 146,
   147, 148, 149, 152, 180, 181, 182, 184,
   185, 198, 201, 203, 205
Marxist Mujahedin, 183
Materialists, 158, 162, 165, 174, 193, 197, 209,
   225
Mawardi, 'Alī Ibn Muhammad al-, 20, 73, 75,
   77, 78, 89, 108, 239
Mawdudi, Sayyid Abul A'la 166, 174, 175
McGrade, Arthus Stephen, 49, 50, 51, 53,
   239, 247

Medellín, 117, 118, 119, 129, 136, 152, 213, 225
Michael of Cesena, 40
Michot, Yahya, 82, 83, 105, 234, 239
Minorities, 8, 13, 14, 83, 89, 92, 118, 221, 222, 123, 129, 158, 163, 171, 207, 235, 237
Mongols, 24, 81, 82, 83, 86, 87, 88, 89, 110, 111, 159, 173, 176, 178, 218, 226
Morality, 4, 9, 12, 14, 18, 67, 155, 158, 168, 202, 206, 211, 212, 233
Motahari, Morteza, *see* Muṭahhari, Murtaḍa
Muhammad, Prophet, 15, 17, 31, 32, 67, 74, 82, 87, 170, 171, 175, 204
Muqaddimah, 76, 79, 96–98, 228, 234
Muslim Brotherhood, 22, 99, 161, 166–169, 177, 179, 240, 242
Muṭahhari, Murtaḍa, 21, 160, 181, 184, 186, 188–190, 196, 202, 203, 204, 205, 240
Muʿtazilah, 85, 103, 159, 243

Najdiyya, 99, 102, 103
National Front, 182, 183
National security, *see* Security
National Security State, *see* Security
Nederman, Cary J., 5, 11, 14, 36, 50, 56, 57, 58, 59, 61, 229, 235, 236, 237, 240
Nicaragua, 114, 124, 127, 184, 231, 232, 242
Nizam al-Mulk, 14, 20, 68, 74, 81, 81, 83, 89–94, 97, 110, 111, 165, 184, 193, 229, 239, 241
Nizari Ismaʿilis, 20, 55, 60, 81, 89–95, 98, 99, 105, 106, 110, 111, 112, 165, 196, 212, 213, 229, 236
Nussbaum, Martha, 6

Obedience, 8, 9, 11, 12, 13, 49, 51, 59, 60, 66, 67, 76, 77, 79, 84, 98, 108, 124, 143, 163, 194, 198
Ockham, *see* William of Ockham
Oppression, 14, 26, 39, 41, 50, 60, 80, 87, 95, 103, 106, 111, 112, 118, 119, 131, 137, 139, 141, 142, 166, 167, 181, 183, 185, 188, 189, 191, 192, 195, 196, 198, 201, 204, 212, 213, 215, 216, 220, 222, 224
Orthodoxy, 20, 22, 23, 24, 28, 29, 32, 39, 52, 66, 67, 68, 81, 85, 86, 93, 110, 127, 144, 153, 161, 163, 203, 213, 218, 219, 220, 221, 224, 333, 236, 241
Ourghi, Mariella, 4, 70, 194, 197, 241

Paganism, 3, 24, 30, 31, 102, 155, 157, 167, 209, 218
Pan-Islamism, 15, 25, 161, 165, 197, 233
Papacy, 23, 29, 42, 43, 44, 46, 111, 112, 153, 156, 215, 217, 218, 241
People's Fedaʾi, 183, 191, 204, 241
Persecution, 4, 18, 28, 67, 82, 91, 108, 118, 119, 215, 228, 232
Peter the Venerable, 31
Peters, Rudolph, 73, 74, 82, 83, 87, 226, 241
Philip II, French King, 39, 40, 43, 44, 243
Pierre des Vaux de Cernay, 38, 39
Pinochet Ugarte, Augusto José Ramón, 116, 125, 126, 225, 228
Plenitudo potestatis, 36, 42, 43, 44, 45, 46, 49
Policraticus, 55–60, 65, 112, 214, 216, 235, 240
Potestas, 28, 29, 34, 40, 42, 108, 121, 122, 240
Propaganda, 28, 30, 31, 81, 93, 109, 185, 193
Property, 11, 47, 61, 62, 63, 64, 66, 75, 77, 78, 80, 88, 93, 95, 97, 100, 101, 102, 112, 113, 156, 164, 192, 2014, 213, 214, 213, 214, 215, 229, 240
Punishment, divine, 28, 55, 59, 60, 98, 113, 142, of sin 142, temporal, 35, 47, 57, 100

Qutb, Sayyid, 21, 99, 160, 161, 166, 167, 170–179, 188, 192, 193, 194, 199, 200, 202, 203, 204, 209, 210, 217, 219, 221, 222, 227, 228, 235, 240, 242, 244, 247

Rahner, Karl, 136, 137, 238
Rawls, John, 212, 242
Rebellion, 11, 20, 67, 91, 94, 98, 99, 103, 104, 105, 106, 113, 135, 148, 159, 179, 213, 225
Resistance, 4, 9, 14, 15, 19, 20, 27, 34, 50, 53, 54, 55, 65, 66, 84, 94, 104, 105, 112, 119, 125, 127, 140, 142, 150, 163, 166, 188, 190, 195, 197, 198, 210, 214, 231, 237, 244, 245

Revolt, 2, 20, 27, 30, 76, 83, 84, 87, 92, 93, 94, 99, 154, 155, 163, 167, 176. 177, 214, 220, 225, 235, 238, 246, 247
Revolution, counter, 21, 116, 118, 133, 143, 153–157, Cuban, 144, Egyptian, 179, 180, 181, French, 154, 218, Iranian, 103, 160, 180–187, 191, 195, 198, 199, 204, Persian 165
Robert of Rheims, 34, 242
Rosenthal, Erwin I.J., 20, 66, 234, 242

Scholz, Richard, 43, 44, 45, 46, 49, 55, 242, 243
Robert of Rheims, 33, 242
Romero, Óscar, 135, 138
Salehi-Isfahani, Djavad, 8
Sālim Ibn Dhakwān, 67, 100, 101, 102, 105, 113, 214, 229, 243
Saracens, 33, 34
Second Vatican Council, 152, 153, 55, 229, 231
Secularism, 16, 17, 153, 154, 155, 177, 188, 193, 204, 209, 210, 226. 230, 230, 240, 244
Security, 10, 57, 60, 64, 66, 134, 159, 164, 171, 211, 214 National security, 114, 125, 129, 132, 133, 152, 241, National Security State, 21, 114, 116, 118, 125, 126, 129, 130, 131, 132, 156, 207, 225, 229
Seljuqs, 89, 90, 93, 94, 95, 98, 105, 212, 228, 233, Seljuq Empire 78, 81, 88, 89, 91, 103, 110, 221
Shariʻa, 8, 16, 18, 86, 87, 88, 159, 160, 168, 169, 170, 171, 180, 189, 240
Shariʻati, ʻAli, 21, 160, 181, 183–187, 188, 190, 196, 197, 200, 201, 202, 207, 208, 209, 213, 215, 231, 236, 239, 243
Shogimen, Takashi, 5, 49, 50, 53, 229, 243
Shue, Henry, 8, 10, 13, 60, 64, 164, 182, 211, 213, 223, 243
Sigmund, Paul E., 18, 117, 126, 135, 228, 243, 244
Siyar al-Muluk, 81, 89, 90–94, 247
Societies for the Defense of Tradition, Family, and Property (TFP), 2, 3, 21, 118, 126, 131, 152–157, 199, 200, 202, 204, 217, 229

Solidarity, 69, 150, 163
Soroush, Abdolkarim, 18, 185, 210, 231, 244
Sovereign, 15, 192
Sovereignty, 89, 155, 160, 174, 219
Speculum regis, 56, 61, 63, 66, 81, 228, 240
State, religious, 23, 156, 160, 201, 202, 220, 222
Stein, Andrew, 135, 136, 244
Subsistence, 10, 11, 60, 61, 63, 64, 66, 164, 211, 213, 214, 223, 243

Tamer, Georges, 68, 81, 245
Terrorism, 1, 17, 106, 166, 170, 173, 230
TFP, see Society for the Defense of Tradition, Family, and Property
Thomas Aquinas, 27, 31, 35, 55, 109, 154, 241, 242, 244, 246
Torres, Camilo, 21, 116, 118, 119, 120–127, 132, 141, 145, 157, 201, 203, 214, 220, 222, 231, 243, 244, 245
Tudeh, 182, 183, 191, 198, 230, 245
Tyrannicide, 55–60, 112, 237, 240
Tyranny, 33, 47–51, 55–61, 84, 103, 111, 113, 123, 126, 161, 164. 165, 179, 188, 189, 192, 194–196, 198, 201, 243, 244, 247

Ulama, 15, 47, 178, 179, 180, 184, 187, 193, 194, 197
Urban II, Pope, 29, 2, 33, 34, 246
Urban IV, Pope, 41

Vatican II, see Second Vatican Council
Vekemans, Roger, 21, 117, 118, 145–151, 154, 199, 201, 203, 246
Victim, 13, 91, 105, 134, 136, 137, 146, 186, 198, 211, 212, 221, 224
Violencia, la, 121, 122, 226, 229, 232

War, holy, 25, 26, 79, 218, 231, 236, secular, 26
Weber, Max, 9, 13, 149, 210, 246
White, Hayden, 8, 174, 246
William of Ockham, 19, 27, 49–56, 61, 66, 97, 112, 210, 211, 212, 215, 218, 235, 239, 240, 243, 246, 247
William of Pagula, 11, 19, 27, 56, 61–66, 95, 97, 112, 113, 228, 240, 247

Zealots (Judea), 144, 181, 231, 252
Zaydi jurists, 20, 104, 105, 106, 112, 210

Zimmermann, Fritz, 67, 100, 101, 102, 229, 247

www.ingramcontent.com/pod-product-compliance
Lightning Source LLC
Chambersburg PA
CBHW051114230426
43667CB00014B/2569